Charming Small Hotel Guides

FRANCE

D0950613

CHARMING SMALL HOTEL GUIDES

FRANCE

EDITED BY

Fiona Duncan & Leonie Glass

Interlink Books

An imprint of Interlink Publishing Group, Inc.
Northampton, Massachusetts

12th edition

Published in 2005 by
Interlink Books
An imprint of Interlink Publishing Group, Inc
46 Crosby Street, Northampton, Massachusettes 01060
www.interlinkbooks.com

Editorial Director Andrew Duncan
Editors Fiona Duncan & Leonie Glass
Contributing editors Jane Anson, David Dallas, Jan Dodd, Luke Glass, Peter Henson, Diana Johnson, Sophie Page, George & Elfrida Pownall, Jenny Rees & Nicky Swallow
Production Editor Sophie Page
Maps Map Creation

This series is conceived, designed and produced by
Duncan Petersen Publishing Ltd.,
31 Ceylon Road, London W14 OPY

Library of Congress Cataloging-in-Publication Data available

ISBN 1-56656-563-4

DTP by Duncan Petersen Publishing Ltd
Printed by Polygraf, Slovakia

Contents

Don't leave for France without the perfect companion for this guide: *Charming Restaurant Guides, France* (UK title) or *Charming French Restaurants* (US title).

INTRODUCTION

IN THIS INTRODUCTORY SECTION

Welcome to this new expanded edition of *Charming Small Hotel Guides, France,* with dozens of new entries. We are pleased to report that the changes made recently – see below – have been well received. Readers have found it even more accessible, and more colourful than earlier editions.

• *Every hotel now has a colour photograph and full or half-page entry of its own. No more entries without a photograph.*

• *The layout has been changed in order to take you more quickly to essential booking information.*

• *The indexes have been improved.*

• *The maps have been upgraded.*

We hope that you will think these real improvements, rather than change for its own sake. In all other respects, the guide remains true to the values and qualities that make it unique (see opposite), and which have won it so many devoted readers. This is its 11th update since it was first published in 1988. It has sold hundreds of thousands of copies in the U.K., U.S.A. and in five European languages.

WHY ARE WE UNIQUE?

This is the only independently-inspected (no hotel pays for an entry) English-language accommodation guide that:

- has colour photographs for every entry;

-concentrates on places that have real charm and character, including the quirky kind;

- is highly selective;

- is particularly fussy about size. Most hotels have fewer than 20 bedrooms; if there are more, the hotel must have the feel of a much smaller place. We have found that a genuinely warm welcome is much more likely to be experienced in a small hotel;

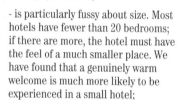

- gives proper emphasis to the description, and doesn't use irritating symbols;

- is produced by a small, non-bureaucratic company with a dedicated team of like-minded inspectors.

See also '*So what exactly do we look for?*', page 8.

SO WHAT EXACTLY DO WE LOOK FOR?
OUR SELECTION CRITERIA

• A peaceful, attractive setting. Obviously, if the entry is in an urban area, we make allowances, but even there we seek out the quiet places.

• A building that is handsome, interesting or historic; or at least with real character.

• Adequate space, but on a human scale. We don't go for places that rely too much on grandeur, or with pretensions that could be intimidating.

• Good taste and imagination in the interior decoration. We reject standardized, chain hotel fixtures, fittings and decorations.

• Bedrooms that look like real bedrooms, not hotel rooms, individually decorated.

• Furnishings and other facilities that are comfortable and well maintained. We like to see interesting antique furniture that is there to be used, not simply revered.

• Proprietors and staff who are dedicated and thoughtful, offering a personal welcome, but who aren't intrusive or overly effusive. *The guest needs to feel like an individual.*

• Interesting food. In France, it's still the norm for food to be above average, although this isn't always the case these days. There are, however, very few, if no, entries in this guide where the food is not of a high standard.

• A sympathetic atmosphere; an absence of loud people showing off their money; or the 'corporate' feel.

Degres de Notre-Dame, Paris

A FATTER GUIDE, BUT JUST AS SELECTIVE

In order to accommodate every entry with a whole-page description and colour photograph, we've had to print more pages. *But we have maintained our integrity by keeping the selection to around 330 entries.*

Over the years, the number of charming small hotels in France has increased steadily – not dramatically. We don't believe that there are presently many more than about 350 truly charming small hotels in France, and that, if we included more, we would undermine what we're trying to do: produce a guide which is all about places that are more than just a bed for the night. Every time we consider a new hotel, we ask ourselves whether it has that extra special something, regardless of category and facilities, that makes it worth seeking out.

TYPES OF ACCOMMODATION IN THIS GUIDE

Despite its title, the guide does not confine itself to places called hotels or places that behave like hotels. On the contrary, we actively look for places that offer a home-from-home (see page 10). We include small- and medium-sized hotels; plenty of traditional guesthouses (pensions) and village *auberges*, some offering just bed and breakfast, some offering food at other times of the day, too; restaurants-with-rooms, and some private houses with accommodation provided they offer something special. You will find extremely luxurious places to stay in this book, as well as very basic ones. The majority, however, fall into our second price category (see page 11), at between 90 and 140 Euros for a double room with breakfast, but there are many places which cost considerably less, and some which cost a great deal more.

NO FEAR OR FAVOUR

To us, taking a payment for appearing in a guide seems to defeat the object of producing a guide. If money has changed hands, you can't write the whole truth about a hotel, and the selection cannot be nearly so interesting. The self-evident truth seems to us to be proved at least in part by the fact that pay guides are so keen to present the illusion of independence: few admit on the cover that they take payments for an entry, only doing so in small print on the inside.

Not many people realize that on the shelves of bookshops there are many more hotel guides that accept payments for entries than there are independent guides. This guide is one of the few that do not accept any money for an entry.

Hotel d'Aubusson, Paris

HOME FROM HOME

Perhaps the most beguiling characteristic of the best places to stay in this guide is the feeling they give of being in a private home – but without the everyday cares and chores of running one. To get this formula right requires a special sort of professionalism: the proprietor has to strike the balance between being relaxed and giving attentive service. Those who experience this 'feel' often turn their backs on all other forms of accommodation – however luxurious.

THE FRENCH HOTEL SCENE

Our latest survey of French hotels for this new, expanded edition of the guide has left us in little doubt about just how much we like them, and how much we enjoy staying in them. Quite apart from the fact that many of them are in wonderful buildings and beautiful locations, their standards of welcome, ambience, cleanliness, attention to detail and food are – on the whole – above average. That's not to say, of course, that we don't have to dig deep to winkle out the gems: places where all the required ingredients come together. We came across delightful hotels with wonderfully retro decoration, but an atmosphere that was blighted by Gallic *froideur*; and other hotels that needed a good dollop of French *savoir faire* and chic to bring them alive. Sometimes, though, the chic is cloyingly overdone. We've seen quite enough, for example, of the studied Côte Sud style, where the rooms look like a photo shoot for a magazine and you feel the dead hand of the interior designer behind every artfully placed wicker basket or bowl of lavender.

We recently completed a major update of our *Charming Small Hotel Guide* to Italy and it's our gut feeling about Italian hotels that they are particularly admirable because so many of them are handed on from one generation to another, thereby maintaining standards, while at the same time keeping pace with the modern guest's requirements. This is unfortunately not the case in Britain (also recently updated), while France, we feel, falls somewhere between the two. It was sad visiting some of our favourite 'old time' hotels knowing that there was no one to continue in the same vein once the present elderly patron had let go. There's no doubt that the old-fashioned, family-run *auberge* will become harder and harder to find as the years roll on. New enterprises in France, however, while not the same, should give cause for optimism. You will find plenty of new entries in this edition where we found that the owners, who might never have run a hotel or guesthouse before, had an innate sense of what makes a memorable place in which to stay, and were often superb cooks too.

The food is of course a huge bonus of French hotels. With the rise of fast food and today's quick-fix urban mentality, it's possible these days to eat very badly in France, but equally you can still eat superbly if you know where to look, and most of the hotels in this guide are centres of excellence.

Quibbles aside, we are delighted with this selection of French hotels. After all, when we have finished an inspection trip, all we want to do is return.

CHECK THE PRICE FIRST

In this guide we have adopted the system of price bands, rather than giving actual prices as we did in previous editions. This is because prices were often subject to change, after we went to press. The price bands refer to a standard double room (high season rates) with breakfast for two people. They are as follows:

€	under 100 Euros
€€	100-170 Euros
€€€	170-250 Euros
€€€€	250-340 Euros
€€€€€	over 340 Euros

To avoid unpleasant surprises, always check what is included in the price (for example, tax and service, breakfast and afternoon tea) when making the booking. Many hotels have special off-peak rates, and some require a minimum stay of more than one night. Half-board may also be obligatory, but this is usually only the case in country guesthouses.

HOW TO FIND AN ENTRY

In this guide, the entries are arranged in geographical groups. First, the whole of France is divided into three major sections; the book starts with Northern France, then proceeds to Central France and lastly Southern France (including Corsica). Within these sections, the entries are grouped by regions.

Within each regional section the entries follow a set sequence. First comes an area introduction, an overview of the region and the accommodation scene within it. Next come the full entries, arranged alphabetically by city, town or nearest village. If several occur in or near one town, entries are arranged in alpha order by name of hotel. Full page entries come first, in alpha order, followed by half page entries, in their alpha order.

To find a hotel in a particular area, use the maps following this introduction to locate the appropriate pages.

To locate a specific hotel, whose name you know, or a hotel in a place you know, use the indexes at the back, which list entries both by hotel name, by nearest place name, and by the administrative *département* (Alpes-Maritimes, Var, Vaucluse etc) in which they fall.

HOW TO READ AN ENTRY

THE SOUTH-WEST

AGNAC

CH.PECHALBET
COUNTRY HOTEL

47800 Agnac (Lot-et-Garonne)
TEL and FAX 05 53 83 04 70
E-MAIL pechalbet@caramail.com WEBSITE www.eymet-en-perigord.com

WHEN HENRI PEYRE and his wife, Françoise, fled from the crowded shores of the Riviera in 1995 in search of somewhere quiet in the country, their initial idea was to provide *chambres d'hôte* with breakfast only. But they found that guests were most reluctant to tear themselves away from the huge rooms and peace of this beautiful 17thC château to go out to eat in restaurants at the end of the day and last year Mme Peyre gave in to pressure and now cooks dinner. 'It's very pleasant,' says her husband. 'We all gather on the terrace to watch the sunsets, then eat by candlelight and talk and talk. It's sometimes very difficult to get our guests to bed.' Prices are kept deliberately low to encourage people to come for several days, or even weeks, at a time. There is a huge amount of space – rooms, furnished with charming antiques, are enormous and all open on to the terrace. Sheep graze in the park, when autumn comes around logs crackle in the massive stone fireplace and there is mushrooming in the woods. For guests M. Peyre has his own list of what he claims are entirely secret places that he has discovered himself to be visited nearby. Reports please.

NEARBY Eymet (4 km); Bergerac (25 km).
LOCATION on 40-hectare country estate; signposted S of Eymet on D933 to Miramont; ample car and garage parking
PRICE ⓔ
FOOD breakfast
ROOMS 5 double and twin, all with bath or shower
FACILITIES 2 sitting rooms, billiard room, bar, dining room, terrace, gardens, swimming pool
CREDIT CARDS AE, SC
DISABLED no special facilities CHILDREN welcome
PETS accepted
CLOSED Dec
PROPRIETOR Henri Peyre

Name of hotel

Type of establishment

Description – never vetted by the hotel

Places of interest within reach of the hotel

This sets the hotel in its geographical context and should not be taken as precise instructions as to how to get there; always ask the hotel for directions.

Rooms described as having a bath usually also have a shower; rooms described as having a shower only have a shower.

Essential booking information.

Closed: when given in months e.g. Nov-Apr, this means from the beginning of the first month to the beginning of the second month. The closing days and months of restaurants are also given.

Some or all the public rooms and bedrooms in an increasing number of hotels are now non-smoking. Smokers should check the hotel's policy when booking.

This information is only an indication for wheelchair users and the infirm. Always check on suitability with the hotel.

City, town or village, and region, in which the hotel is located.

Telephoning France from abroad
To call France from the U.K. dial 00, then the international dialling code 33, then dial the number, excluding the initial 0. From the U.S., dial 001 33.

Postal address and telephone, fax, e-mail and website address, if available.

The price, or rather price band, quoted includes the cost of breakfast for two people. We have not quoted prices for lunch and dinner, but we have indicated where half-board is obligatory. Other meals, such as afternoon tea, may also be available, and sometimes included in the price of a room. 'Room service' refers to food and drink, usually full meals, which can be served in the room.

Some or all the public rooms and bedrooms in an increasing number of hotels are now non-smoking. Smokers should check the hotel's policy when booking.

Children are almost always accepted, usually welcomed, in French hotels. There are often special facilities, such as cots, high chairs, baby listening and early supper. Check first if they may join parents in the dining room. We use the word 'accepted' to indicate that children are allowed in a hotel, and 'welcome' where we perceived a positive bias towards them.

We list the following credit cards:
AE American Express
DC Diners Club
MC Mastercard
V Visa

Always let the hotel know in advance if you want to bring a pet. Even where pets are accepted, certain restrictions may apply, and a small charge may be levied.

In this guide, we have used price bands rather than quoting actual prices. They refer to a standard double room (high season rates, if applicable) with breakfast for two people. Other rates – for other room categories, times of the year, weekend breaks, long stays and so on – may well be available. In some hotels, usually out-of-the-way places or restaurants-with-rooms – half-board is obligatory. Always check when booking. The price bands are as follows:

€ under 100 Euros
€€ 100-170 Euros
€€€ 170-250 Euros
€€€€ 250-340 Euros
€€€€€ over 340 Euros

Tipping
In larger hotels, 1.50 Euros for a piece of luggage taken to your room by an employee is normal, as well as a small tip for the chambermaid. In restaurants, the words *service compris* on the bill indicate that tax and 15% service charge have been included. If pleased with the food and service, however, it is customary to leave an extra tip.

REPORTING TO THE GUIDE

Please write and tell us about your experiences of small hotels, guesthouses and inns, whether good or bad, whether listed in this edition or not. As well as hotels in France, we are interested in hotels in Italy, Spain, Austria, Germany, Switzerland, Greece and the U.S.A. We assume that reporters have no objections to our publishing their views unpaid.

Readers whose reports prove particularly helpful may be invited to join our Travellers' Panel. Members give us notice of their own travel plans; we suggest hotels that they might inspect, and help with the cost of accommodation.

The address to write to us is:

Editor, *Charming Small Hotel Guides*,
Duncan Petersen Publishing Limited,
31 Ceylon Road,
London W14 0PY.

Checklist
Please use a separate sheet of paper for each report; include your name, address and telephone number on each report.

Your reports will be received with particular pleasure if they are typed, and if they are organized under the following headings:

Name of establishment
Town or village it is in, or nearest
Full address, including postcode
Telephone number
Time and duration of visit
The building and setting
The public rooms
The bedrooms and bathrooms
Physical comfort (chairs, beds, heat, light, hot water)
Standards of maintenance and housekeeping
Atmosphere, welcome and service
Food
Value for money

We assume that in writing you have no objections to your views being published unpaid, either verbatim or in an edited version. Names of major outside contributors are acknowledged, at the editor's discretion, in the guide.

HOTEL LOCATION MAPS

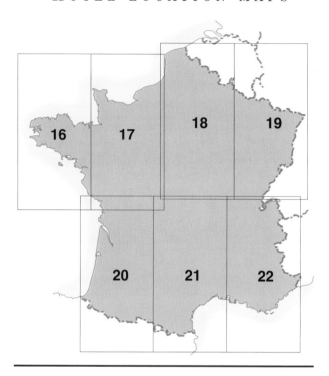

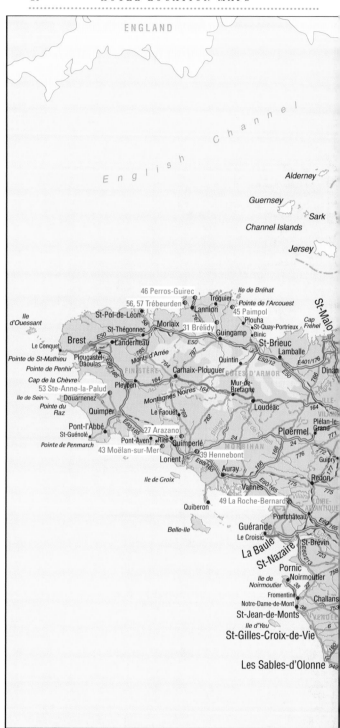

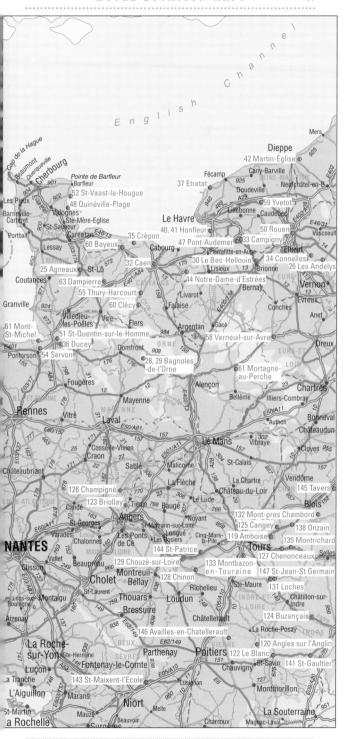

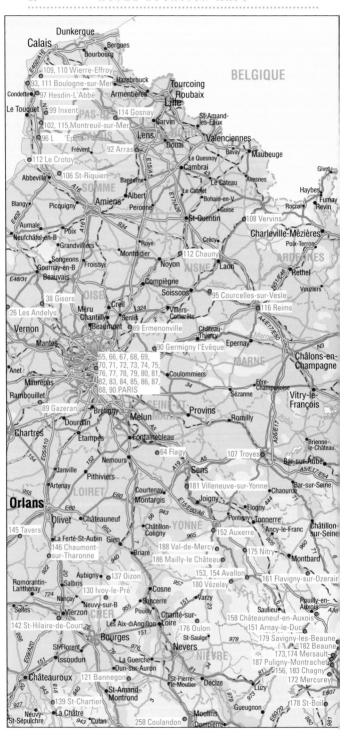

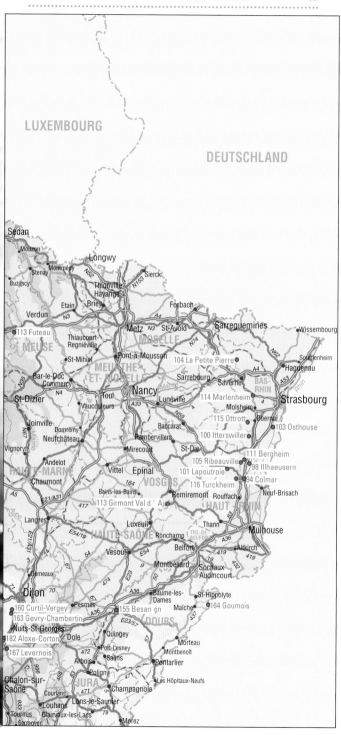

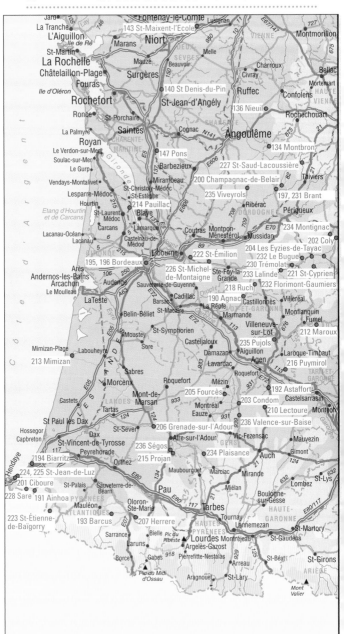

A. 335 Castillon-du-Gard
B. 265 Avignon
C. 334 Villeneuve-lèz-Avignon
D. 318, 319 St-Rémy de-Provence
E. 284 Fontvieille
F. 338 St Mathieu
G. 327 Tourrettes-sur-Loup
H. 312 Roquefort-les-Pins
I. 290 Haut-de-Cagnes
J. 315, 316, 339 St-Paul-de-Vence
K. 298, 299, 300 Nice

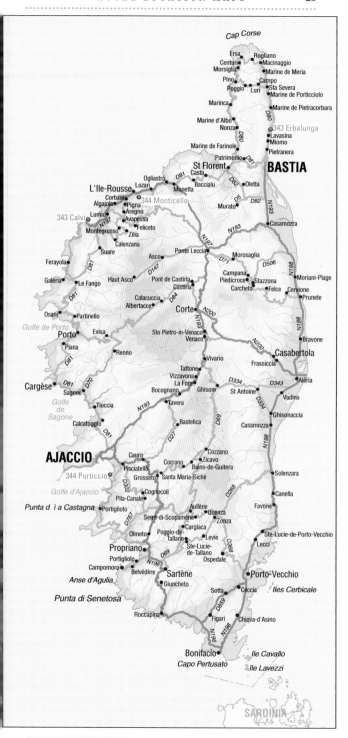

THE NORTH-WEST

HOTELS IN THE NORTH-WEST

THE NORTH-WEST IS familiar territory to many British visitors. Lush Normandy, full of apple orchards and contented cows, is close enough to be convenient for a weekend break, and many people who live in the west of Britain prefer to use the Normandy ports when aiming further south. Particularly well placed for the ports – and beaches – are the traditional **Auberge du Clos Normand** at Martin-Eglise near Dieppe (page 42), the more sophisticated **La Chaumière** and **Le Manoir du Butin**, both at Honfleur near Le Havre (pages 40 and 41), **Le Dauphin** in the centre of Caen (page 32), and, within striking distance of Cherbourg at St-Vaast-la-Hougue on the Cotentin peninsula, the **Hôtel de France et des Fuchsias** (page 52), an old favourite of the guide. Also useful for the ports are the **Hôtel Vent d'Ouest** at Le Havre (tel 02 35 42 50 69), **La Maison de Lucie** (tel 02 31 14 40 40) and **Hôtel des Loges** (tel 02 31 89 38 26), both at Honfleur, and **La Marine** (tel 02 33 53 83 31), a restaurant-with-rooms in Barneville-Carteret near Cherbourg.

Our recommendations for this new edition cover the breadth of the region, from the Côte d'Albâtre's chalk cliffs (**Domaine St Clair - Le Donjon** at Etretat, page 37) and the beautiful banks of the Seine (**La Chaîne d'Or** at Les Andelys, page 26, and **Le Moulin de Connelles**, page 34) to the lush landscape of Calvados country (**Ferme de la Rançonnière** at Crépon, page 35) and of the region known as *Suisse Normande* around the Orne valley (**Manoir du Lys** and **Bois Joli**, a first-time long entry, both at Bagnoles-de-l'Orne, pages 28 and 29, and new find, **Relais de la Poste** at Thury-Harcourt, page 55). We also have a discovery in the unspoiled Perche region, **Hôtel du Tribunal** in Mortagne (page 61). This is the first edition to feature a hotel in the Norman capital, Rouen, as a long entry: the modest but appealing **Hôtel des Carmes** (page 50). Two other useful hotels in the centre are **Hôtel de la Cathédrale** (tel 02 35 71 57 95) and **Le Vieux Carré** (tel 02 35 71 67 70), both with pretty courtyard gardens.

On the border with Brittany is the most popular tourist sight in France: Mont-St-Michel. One of our hotels, **Auberge St-Pierre** is on the Mont itself (page 61), but a couple of others (**Le Gué du Holme** at St-Quentin-sur-le-Homme, page 51, and **Auberge du Terroir** at Servon, page 54) provide accommodation within reach, but away from the crowds. If these are full, **Le Montgomery** is a comfortable traditional hotel also within striking distance at Pontorson (tel 02 33 60 00 09).

To the west, Brittany is bucket-and-spade country, and has much in common with Cornwall – a dramatic coastline, and a vigorous climate. If you are using the port of St-Malo, you could start or end your journey at the stylish **Le Valmarin** (tel 02 99 81 94 76). On the rugged north coast, between scores of oyster beds and sandy beaches, in the old fishing port of Paimpol, we have the down-to-earth **Repaire de Kerroc'h** (page 45) and, in the resort of Perros-Guirec, the upmarket **Manoir du Sphinx** (page 46). There are two more hotels around the headland in Trébeurden (pages 56 and 57) and inland, the **Château de Brélidy** (page 31). **Hôtel de la Plage** is a popular, if now pricey, family hotel at Ste-Anne-la-Palud (page 53) on the windswept west coast, and just inland at Plonevez-Porzay, **Manoir de Moëllien** (tel 02 98 92 50 40) is a typical Breton château. The scenery is tamer and the climate milder on the south coast, and here we recommend another château (**Château de Locguénolé** at Hennebont, page 39), a mill (**Les Moulins du Duc at Moëlan-sur-Mer**, page 43) and one of the region's finest restaurants (**Auberge Bretonne** in La Roche-Bernard, page 49).

THE NORTH-WEST

AGNEAUX

CHATEAU D'AGNEAUX

~ CHATEAU HOTEL ~

avenue Ste-Marie, 50180 Agneaux (Manche)
TEL 02 33 57 65 88 **FAX** 02 33 56 59 21
E-MAIL chateau.agneaux@wanadoo.fr **WEBSITE** www.chateau-agneaux.com

A S YOU TURN DOWN a rather suburban road, albeit tree-lined, on the out-skirts of St-Lô, you might ask yourself if you've really done the right thing. Don't worry: a delight awaits you. The Château d'Agneaux turns out to be small, perfectly formed (since the tail-end of the 13th century) and to occupy a fairy-tale position high on an almost sheer wooded bluff over-looking a narrow, pastoral section of the Vire valley. The previous owner knocked down the new 16thC wing when he made his home here. The only 21stC intrusion is the occasional sight (but not sound) of a busy little two-car diesel train on the far side of the valley. "TGV Normande!" quips M. Groult, the Château's present, lucky owner whose own sanctuary boasts a fireplace big enough to seat a brass band.

The bedrooms, some in a separate keep, are baronial enough for four-posters to be the rule rather than the exception. The standard of decora-tion, the quality of the furniture and the finely finished bathrooms should suit the fussiest of château-hoppers. If your budget will stretch to it, and you can cope with heights, go for No. 4 – the biggest of them all and with glorious views across and up the valley. The beamed and flagged dining room offers fine regional cuisine and a better than adequate wine list.

NEARBY Bayeux (38 km); Normandy beaches; golf.
LOCATION 1.5 km W of St-Lô, turn right in Agneaux signed to Château; car parking
FOOD breakfast, dinner
PRICE €€
ROOMS 12; 7 double, 3 twin, one suite, one family, all with bath; all rooms have phone, TV, minibar
FACILITIES sitting room, dining room, meeting room, terrace, garden, tennis
CREDIT CARDS AE, DC, MC, V **CHILDREN** accepted
DISABLED one ground floor room
PETS accepted
CLOSED never
PROPRIETOR M. Groult

THE NORTH-WEST

LES ANDELYS

LA CHAINE D'OR
～ RIVERSIDE HOTEL ～

25-27 rue Grande, Le Petit Andely, 27700 Les Andelys (Eure)
TEL 02 32 54 00 31 **FAX** 02 32 54 05 68
E-MAIL chaineor@wanadoo.fr **WEBSITE** www.lachainedor.com

UNDER AN HOUR from Paris, on a lazy curve in the Seine and overlooked by the pale remains of Richard the Lionheart's 12thC Château Gaillard, the cares of the world start to recede as soon as you pull into the peaceful gravelled courtyard of this 18thC inn. Despite being only a stone's throw from the centre of this little town, it could not be closer to the Seine without falling in. After more than 15 years, it changed hands in July 2003, but the new owners have retained the young, enthusiastic and professional staff, as well as its Michelin-starred chef, and travellers are as warmly welcomed as ever. Six of the ten attractively decorated bedrooms look out over the river, one into the courtyard and the remainder towards the town church. Though not an antiques gallery, the furniture is real enough to have collected a few scars over the last 100 years or so, and the bathrooms are a good deal newer.

The restaurant looks out over the river – raw beams, warm yellow rough-plastered walls, fresh flowers and a massive stone fireplace surround the tables that stand on the black-and-white tiled floor. Excellent food, with the quality lasting through the salad and into the cheese and puddings, and a full, but by no means ruinous, wine list should satisfy the pickiest of diners. If you are in the neighbourhood, look no further.

～

NEARBY Giverny (45 km); Lyons-la-Forêt (21 km); Rouen (38 km).
LOCATION in Le Petit Andely on river Seine; car parking
FOOD breakfast, lunch, dinner
PRICE €€€
ROOMS 10; 7 double, 3 twin, all with bath or shower; all rooms have phone, TV; 5 have hairdrier
FACILITIES sitting room, breakfast room, restaurant, meeting room, terrace, courtyard garden **CREDIT CARDS** AE, MC, V **CHILDREN** accepted
DISABLED access difficult **PETS** accepted
CLOSED Jan to early Feb; restaurant Sun dinner, Mon and Tue lunch in low season
PROPRIETORS Sylvia and Gérard Millet

THE NORTH-WEST

ARZANO

CHATEAU DE KERLAREC

~ CHATEAU HOTEL ~

29300 Arzano (Finistère)
TEL 02 98 71 75 06 **FAX** 02 98 71 74 55
E-MAIL chateau-de-kerlarec@wanadoo.fr **WEBSITE** www.chateaux-france.com/kerlarec

COMPLETED IN 1830 by the Dandilo family (descended from a long line of Venetian doges), Château de Kerlarec, already decrepit, was left empty in 1989. Six years later Monique and Michel Bellin arrived looking, I suspect, for somewhere to house her fascinating collection of silver, porcelain, glass, furniture, pictures and *objets*. It must have been touch and go for a while, but eventually they managed to get it all in. The result is rather like the interior of Ali Baba's cave, except her arrangements are artistic rather than haphazard and betray a deep sense of humour and even deeper sense of history. As well as being unmolested architecturally, much of the château's original interior decoration has survived – even the original wallpaper in the *salon* is more or less intact.

The Bellins have the resuscitation of the building well in hand, and have already created a cool white gallery and meeting space beneath the old *porte-cochère*. There are four wonderfully theatrical bedrooms on the second floor: each has an antechamber which doubles as a sitting room, and then a gentle limbo takes you past rafters into a tower bedroom. All are different, with one resembling the set for *The 1001 Nights* and another a confection in white and gold. Given notice, Mme Bellin will lay on *crêpes* or a vast seafood platter for dinner.

~

NEARBY Lorient (20 km); Quimper (40 km); Iles de Glénan; Pont Aven.
LOCATION 6 km E of Quimperlé on the D22; car parking
FOOD breakfast, supper by arrangement
PRICE €
ROOMS 6; one double, 5 suites, all with bath or shower
FACILITIES sitting room, dining room, meeting room, terrace, garden, swimming pool, tennis
CREDIT CARDS not accepted **CHILDREN** accepted
DISABLED access difficult **PETS** accepted
CLOSED never
PROPRIETORS Monique and Michel Bellin

THE NORTH-WEST

BAGNOLES-DE-L'ORNE

BOIS JOLI

~ SPA HOTEL ~

12 avenue Philippe-du-Rozier, 61140 Bagnoles-de-l'Orne (Orne)
TEL 02 33 37 92 77 **FAX** 02 33 37 07 56
E-MAIL boisjoli@wanadoo.fr **WEBSITE** www.hotelboisjoli.com

YOU MIGHT BE IN THE MIDDLE of the chic spa town of Bagnoles, but it's hard to believe it here, surrounded as you are by lush gardens of sequoia and oak trees leading right into the Andaines forest. The house is an Anglo-Norman villa, an upright late-19thC building, partly timbered and cheerful looking with window boxes of flowers. And there are no unpleasant surprises in store. Appropriately chosen antiques and period furniture complement the woodwork and traditional decoration. Overlooking the grounds, the bedrooms are pretty, airy and furnished with upholstered Empire-style pieces and *toile-de-jouy* or floral fabrics.

Yvette and Daniel Mariette are just as concerned for their guests' peace of mind as their comfort. The gardens, a haven for wildlife, are dotted with daybeds so you can relax in the sun or shade. Thermal baths and other sybaritic health treatments are also available. For the more energetic, there's horse riding, golf and mountain biking locally, and the Mariettes run mushroom hunting weekends between late September and late October (phone for details).

Dishes from the well-regarded kitchen, such as *cervelat* sausages of scorpion fish and sea bass with saffron, combine flavours of the region with exotic spices. After dinner you could try your luck at the casino.

NEARBY casino; Alençon (49 km); Suisse Normande; golf; riding.
LOCATION in centre of town; car parking
FOOD breakfast, lunch, dinner
PRICE €€
ROOMS 20 double and twin, all with bath or shower; all rooms have phone, TV
FACILITIES sitting room, dining room, health centre, lift, garden
CREDIT CARDS AE, DC, MC, V **CHILDREN** accepted
DISABLED no special facilities
PETS accepted
CLOSED mid-Feb to late Mar
PROPRIETORS Yvette and Daniel Mariette

THE NORTH-WEST

BAGNOLES-DE-L'ORNE

MANOIR DU LYS

~ COUNTRY HOTEL ~

La Croix Gauthier, route de Juvigny, 61140 Bagnoles-de-l'Orne (Orne)
TEL 02 33 37 80 69 **FAX** 02 33 30 05 80
E-MAIL manoirdulys@lemel.fr **WEBSITE** www.manoir-du-lys.fr

THIS DELIGHTFUL, typically Norman half-timbered hunting lodge, with geraniums at its foot and dripping from its balconies, has, among its many advantages, not one but two swimming pools, one indoors, the other outside. It was reopened as a hotel by the Quintons in 1985 after a long period of disuse, and many improvements have been introduced since, though the swish facilities have their down side, and it can get crowded. The new building is harmonious, and bedrooms, including seven new wooden pavilions in forest clearings (designed for families), are very attractive – all spacious and well equipped, with stylish furnishings. Most de luxe rooms are long and narrow with balconies overlooking the gardens.

Marie-France oversees the smart dining rooms (also overlooking the gardens, through floor-to-ceiling windows) where you can enjoy her son Franck's Michelin-starred cooking, which is rooted in local tradition but respects contemporary trends. In fine weather you can dine outside. There is also a polished little bar/sitting room with a huge open fire and a grand piano (played on Friday nights). The Quintons are warm hosts and organize popular educational 'mushroom' weekends, during which up to 120 varieties may be picked in the surrounding woods; English-language tuition can be laid on. A recent reader was unimpressed by the restaurant – both food and service – but found the reception 'warm and helpful'.

~

NEARBY Alençon (47 km); Suisse Normande; golf.
LOCATION in middle of countryside in forest of Andaines; car parking
FOOD breakfast, lunch, dinner
PRICE €€
ROOMS 32; 25 double, 23 with bath, 2 with shower; 7 suites with bath; all have phone, TV, minibar **FACILITIES** bar/sitting room, dining rooms, billiards, garden, indoor and outdoor swimming pools, tennis **CREDIT CARDS** AE, DC, MC, V
CHILDREN welcome **DISABLED** one specially adapted bedroom **PETS** accepted
CLOSED early Jan to mid-Feb; restaurant Sun dinner and Mon, Nov to Easter
PROPRIETORS Marie-France and Paul Quinton

THE NORTH-WEST

LE BEC-HELLOUIN

AUBERGE DE L'ABBAYE
~ VILLAGE INN ~

27800 Le Bec-Hellouin (Eure)
TEL 02 32 44 86 02 **FAX** 02 32 46 32 23
E-MAIL catherine-fabrice.c@wanadoo.fr **WEBSITE** www.auberge-abbaye-bec-hellouin.com

THIS GERANIUM-DECKED 18thC inn, squarely in the centre of a row of half-timbered houses, looks across the village green to the entrance of the abbey of Notre-Dame du Bec, from which it takes its name. Open to the public, the abbey's well-tended gardens are well worth the short walk needed to get to them. After 40 years, the Sergent family have sold up. It must have been a terrible wrench, but they can take heart from the fact that they have left the *auberge* in the very capable hands of Catherine and Fabrice Conroux, a congenial, go-ahead couple with realistic plans. They have already renewed all the essential services, and were poised to launch a programme of renovation and redecoration, including new carpets and bathrooms, as we went to press.

On our last visit (before the Sergents left), we were struck by the heart-warmingly traditional character of the place: polished tile floors and gleaming furniture. Everything was in apple-pie order. Well aware that it is its character that people love about this inn, the Conroux intend to preserve it. The beamed dining room has immaculate stone walls and the traditional red-and-white checked tablecloths; in summer tables are set under parasols in the central courtyard. Tables and benches for informal meals are ranged along the raised terrace at the front of the inn. The pretty low-ceilinged bedrooms are up quite a steep flight of stairs.

NEARBY Rouen (30 km); Château du Champ-de-Bataille; golf.
LOCATION in village 6 km N of Brionne; car parking
FOOD breakfast, lunch, dinner
PRICE €
ROOMS 10; 5 double, 5 twin, all with bath; all rooms have phone, TV
FACILITIES sitting area, bar/dining room, terrace, courtyard garden
CREDIT CARDS MC, V **CHILDREN** accepted
DISABLED access difficult **PETS** accepted
CLOSED 2 weeks Jan, last 2 weeks Nov; restaurant Tue and Wed Oct to Apr
PROPRIETORS Catherine and Fabrice Conroux

THE NORTH-WEST

BRÉLIDY

CHATEAU HOTEL DE BRELIDY

~ CHATEAU HOTEL ~

Brélidy, 22140 Bégard (Côtes d'Armor)
TEL 02 96 95 69 38 **FAX** 02 96 95 18 03
E-MAIL chateau.brelidy@worldonline.fr **WEBSITE** www.chateau-brelidy.com

BEHIND THE AUSTERE granite exterior of this fine 16thC Breton château, typical of the area's architecture, our reporter discovered a series of comfortable, homely rooms filled with antiques. The château was painstakingly and sympathetically restored over three decades by Pierre and Eliane Yoncourt-Pemezec, retaining the enormous fireplaces, original stone staircase and beamed ceilings. Even though the Yoncourt-Pemezecs moved on in 2002, handing over to the Langlets, the refreshingly natural atmosphere is unchanged. Nothing has been dressed up and there's not a trace of pretension. Even dinner feels like a family meal.

Beyond the peaceful 6-hectare garden of lawns and hydrangeas is some of the most glorious countryside you'll see in the region: gentle hills reach to the horizon, punctuated by copses and threaded by hedgerows dotted with wild flowers. Some of the best views are from the vast windows of one of the suites (these alone seem to justify the 22 euro premium over the cost of a superior double room). Appropriately the bedrooms are named after flowers, and four have their own terraces.

Keen fishermen have a choice of rivers and lakes in the grounds.

~

NEARBY Guingamp (15 km); Lannion (30 km).
LOCATION in countryside outside village, follow signs from the D15; car parking
FOOD breakfast, dinner
PRICE €€
ROOMS 14; 12 double and twin, 2 suites, all with bath or shower; all rooms have phone, TV, hairdrier
FACILITIES sitting room, dining room, billiards room, Jacuzzi, terrace, garden, fishing **CREDIT CARDS** AE, MC, V
CHILDREN accepted
DISABLED access possible
PETS accepted
CLOSED Jan to Apr
PROPRIETORS William and Carole Langlet

THE NORTH-WEST

LE DAUPHIN

～ TOWN RESTAURANT-WITH-ROOMS ～

29 rue Gémare, 14000 Caen (Calvados)
TEL 02 31 86 22 26 **FAX** 02 31 86 35 14
E-MAIL dauphin.caen@wanadoo.fr **WEBSITE** www.le-dauphin-normandie.com

ANY HOTEL THAT HAS private parking in the centre of Caen is a pearl almost beyond price, and parking is not the only quality that Le Dauphin, now a Best Western hotel, possesses. A scant three minutes' walk from William the Conqueror's castle, this former priory doesn't really reveal its age until you get inside. Exposed stone walls, beams and the stone staircase all show the kind of restoration that is more preoccupied with quality than with cost: the building is probably in better shape now than it was 200 years ago.

Sylvie and Stéphane Pugnat (he is the chef) make a lively team and give the place a very welcoming atmosphere. The excellent cuisine is Norman, and Stéphane scores extra points by leaving space in his menus for any fish that appealed to him at the market. Crisp white linen, high-backed red velvet chairs, fresh flowers and a thoughtful wine list will keep you company in the restaurant while you wait for your food. The Pugnats bought the building next door some years back, which has given them space for 15 tasteful new bedrooms; the remaining 22 are divided between the main building and an annexe. Most of the new rooms and bathrooms, and the ones in the original annexe, are larger than those in the main building, and priced accordingly. Without being an antique roadshow, all the rooms are well decorated, well furnished and thoroughly comfortable.

NEARBY quartier des Quatrans; château; church of St-Pierre.
LOCATION in town centre, 2 streets W of the château; car parking
FOOD breakfast, lunch, dinner; room service during day
PRICE €€
ROOMS 37; 32 double and twin, 5 suites, all with bath; all rooms have phone, TV, minibar, hairdrier
FACILITIES sitting room/bar, restaurant, lift
CREDIT CARDS AE, DC, MC, V **CHILDREN** accepted
DISABLED one specially adapted room **PETS** accepted
CLOSED one week Feb, 2 weeks late Oct to early Nov; restaurant Sat lunch, Sun
PROPRIETORS Sylvie and Stéphane Pugnat

THE NORTH-WEST

CAMPIGNY

LE PETIT COQ AUX CHAMPS
～ COUNTRY HOTEL ～

La Pommeraie-Sud, Campigny, 27500 Pont-Audemer (Eure)
TEL 02 32 41 04 19 **FAX** 02 32 56 06 25
E-MAIL le.petit.coq.aux.champs@wanadoo.fr **WEBSITE** www.lepetitcoqauxchamps.fr

A THATCHED HOUSE WITH its own heliport – it sounds unlikely, but convention counts for little at this smart, secluded retreat, in rolling meadows and sweeping forests in the Risle valley. Le Petit Coq offers an intriguing mix of the rustic, the sophisticated and the downright idiosyncratic – a cocktail that may be too heady for some, to judge by our empty postbag.

The building, mostly 19th century, has two main wings with a spacious, airy, modern extension in between. The style varies considerably – modern cane furniture in the large sitting room, while antiques predominate in the restaurant, which has a huge open fireplace at one end. An intimate piano bar has been squeezed into the new building. The bedrooms are all furnished and arranged in different ways, some brightly coloured, others more restrained; none is particularly large.

Jean-Marie Huard, who returned to his Norman roots after some years in highly reputed restaurants in Paris, pays serious attention to detail, presentation and local tradition in his cooking – with impressive results.

～

NEARBY Pont-Audemer (6 km); Honfleur (30 km); golf.
LOCATION in countryside, 6 km S of Pont-Audemer; car parking
FOOD breakfast, lunch, dinner
PRICE €€
ROOMS 12; 6 double, 4 twin, one family, one suite, all with bath; all rooms have phone, TV, hairdrier
FACILITIES sitting room, 4 dining rooms, bar, garden, swimming pool, heliport
CREDIT CARDS AE, DC, MC, V
CHILDREN welcome
DISABLED no special facilities
PETS welcome
CLOSED Jan, Sun eve and Mon Nov to Mar
PROPRIETORS Fabienne Desmonts and Jean-Marie Huard

THE NORTH-WEST

CONNELLES

LE MOULIN DE CONNELLES

∽ RIVERSIDE HOTEL ∽

route d'Amfreville-sous-les-Monts, 27430 Connelles (Eure)
TEL 02 32 59 53 33 **FAX** 02 32 59 21 83 **E-MAIL** moulindeconnelles@
moulindeconnelles.com **WEBSITE** www.moulindeconnelles.com

SCARCELY A QUARTER OF AN HOUR from Monet's garden at Giverny, Le Moulin de Connelles is a fairy-tale sort of a place, with turrets and gables, beams and arches. It even has its own private 2-hectare island with – if you can find them hidden in its gardens – a heated swimming pool and tennis courts. Unless you really mean it, be wary of wishing out loud for a boat because in the twinkling of an eye you will be issued with a rowing boat to go exploring in. And, as if the location wasn't enough, the Petiteaus have also made a deeply comfortable, beautifully presented hotel, with a 'very young and enthusiastic, efficient and friendly' staff, for whom 'nothing is too much trouble', according to one visitor.

Spanning the mill-stream as it does, the (excellent) restaurant seems to be hovering over the water. Steamed salmon parcels, baked sea bass, kidneys cooked in three kinds of mustard are sometimes part of the offering from a highly-regarded kitchen. Sitting under the terrace awning, looking down at the mill's reflection and the lily pads floating in the quiet water, it is difficult to imagine wanting to be anywhere else on a summer evening.

The bedrooms are quietly and impeccably furnished and have the kind of bathrooms that you want to wrap up and take home with you. If you're feeling rich, the view from the corner suite (No. 7) is difficult to beat.

∽

NEARBY Rouen (39 km); Evreux (30 km); golf; water sports.
LOCATION off D19 just N of Connelles beside river Seine; car parking
FOOD breakfast, lunch, dinner
PRICE €€€-€€€€
ROOMS 13; 7 double and twin, 6 suites, all with bath; all rooms have phone, TV, minibar, hairdrier, safe
FACILITIES sitting room, meeting room, bar, restaurant, terrace, garden, swimming pool, tennis, fishing **CREDIT CARDS** AE, DC, MC, V
CHILDREN accepted **DISABLED** access difficult **PETS** accepted **CLOSED** hotel and restaurant early Jan to early Feb, Oct to Apr Sun dinner, Mon, Tue lunch
PROPRIETORS Hubert and Luce Petiteau

THE NORTH-WEST

CREPON

FERME DE LA RANCONNIERE

~ COUNTRY HOTEL ~

route d'Arromanches, 14480 Crépon (Calvados)
TEL 02 31 22 21 73 **FAX** 02 31 22 98 39
E-MAIL hotel@ranconniere.com **WEBSITE** www.ranconniere.com

THIS FORTIFIED FARM, well placed for visiting the D-Day beaches, is no smallholding. The oldest building is 13th century and the final touches were added sometime in the 15th century. The buildings form three sides of an enormous courtyard, and the fourth side, on the road, is guarded by a crenellated wall – obviously a safe haven for the farmers and their stock in more troubled times. Even out of season when we visited, both restaurants (one beamed and one barrel-vaulted) were bursting with French families who had driven out into the country for Sunday lunch and to celebrate the results of recent mayoral elections. A straw poll of several families revealed that they were there because the food was (a) good, (b) plentiful and (c) good value.

The original 35 bedrooms, some in each of the three buildings, are mostly baronial in size and much of their furniture is appropriately massive. Rugs on the tiled floors and tapestries on many of the walls also help to keep the 21st century firmly at bay. Despite their thickness, the walls might not shield you entirely from the popularity of the dining rooms: there is now an annexe in separate farmhouses (600 m away), which might suit those for whom peace is an absolute priority. Breakfast, highly recommended, is a buffet.

~

NEARBY Arromanches (7 km); Bayeux (12 km); Caen (25 km); Normandy beaches.
LOCATION on the D65 on the edge of the village; car parking
FOOD breakfast, lunch, dinner
PRICE €€
ROOMS 48 double, twin and triple, all with bath or shower; all rooms have phone, TV, hairdrier **FACILITIES** sitting room, 2 restaurants, meeting room, lift, garden
CREDIT CARDS AE, DC, MC, V **CHILDREN** accepted
DISABLED one specially adapted room
PETS accepted
CLOSED never
PROPRIETORS Mme Vereecke and Mme Sileghem

THE NORTH-WEST

DUCEY

AUBERGE DE LA SELUNE
~ VILLAGE HOTEL ~

2 rue St-Germain, 50220 Ducey (Manche)
TEL 02 33 48 53 62 **FAX** 02 33 48 90 30
E-MAIL info@selune.com **WEBSITE** www.selune.com

WHEN WE LAST VISITED, we found that extensive renovations have changed the character of this redoubtable small hotel. It used to be old fashioned in a conventional sort of way. Now the downstairs, at least, is modern in a somewhat soulless way. The glass and metal lobby connecting the two old buildings might look better in an airport hotel, and the emerald green of the furnishings will not appeal to all our readers. Nonetheless, it's highly recommendable, and we continue to receive readers' letters saying just that. Of the two conventional dining rooms, one is less formal than the other and gives on to a terrace with tables and chairs, from which you can enjoy the garden with the river bubbling in the background.

Bedrooms are all different, with bright colour schemes and pleasant, but relatively simple furnishings. No. 36 has a fine view over the garden. Bathrooms are dull, but practical. We can't fault this as a stopover, prices being particularly honest – if not good value – and staff, on our visit, dutiful and friendly. The food is well above average, with *pie au crabe* still a *pièce de résistance*. Breakfast is better than the norm. Ask about the salmon fishing.

~

NEARBY Avranches (11 km); Le Mont-St-Michel (20 km).
LOCATION by the river in the village, on the N176, SE of Avranches; car parking
FOOD breakfast, lunch, dinner
PRICE €
ROOMS 21; 14 double, 5 twin, one single, one family, all with bath; all rooms have phone; 16 have TV
FACILITIES sitting room, 2 dining rooms, bar, conference room, terrace, garden, salmon fishing **CREDIT CARDS** DC, MC, V
CHILDREN accepted
DISABLED access difficult
PETS not accepted
CLOSED first 2 weeks Dec; restaurant Mon Oct to Apr
PROPRIETOR Jean-Pierre Girres

THE NORTH-WEST

ETRETAT

DOMAINE ST CLAIR - LE DONJON

~ SEASIDE HOTEL ~

chemin de Saint Clair, 76790 Etretat (Seine-Maritime)
TEL 02 35 27 08 23 **FAX** 02 35 29 92 24
E-MAIL info@hoteletretat.com **WEBSITE** www.hoteletretat.com

THE EXTRAORDINARY LITTLE HOTEL, set on a steep hill only half an hour from Le Havre, that used to be just Le Donjon and one of our favourite places for a short break, has expanded, both in name and physically. In its new incarnation as the Domaine St Clair, it incorporates the original 19thC ivy-clad château and a recently acquired Belle-Epoque seaside villa.

Le Donjon is a former hilltop castle, with venerable origins and a secret subterranean channel to the sea, now safely surrounded by the leafy suburbs of Etretat. Inside, all is bright and light, decorated with Parisian sophistication. The dining room, candlelit and mirrored, with a breathtaking view over Etretat's famous cliffs, is wonderfully atmospheric. All the bedrooms – split between the two buildings – are different and immensely stylish; some are named after the celebrity friends of Camille de St-Phale, former *grande dame* of the château. Bathrooms, some in the turrets, are spacious and elegant in pure white. There is also an impeccably kept small swimming pool surrounded by sunshades and loungers.

The menu offers rather more possibilities for *pensionnaires*, with the option of choosing dishes from the *carte*, as well as the four-course *menu Gastronome*. We have been unable to visit the villa, so would welcome further reports.

~

NEARBY Fécamp (17 km); Le Havre (28 km).
LOCATION on hill behind the resort; car parking
FOOD breakfast, lunch, dinner
PRICE €€€-€€€
ROOMS 21; 19 double, 2 suites, 19 with bath (Jacuzzi), 2 with shower; all rooms have phone, TV; 14 have CD
FACILITIES sitting room, dining room, library, bar, garden, swimming pool
CREDIT CARDS AE, MC, V **CHILDREN** accepted
PETS accepted
DISABLED access difficult **CLOSED** never
PROPRIETOR M. Omar Abo-Dib

THE NORTH-WEST

GISORS

CHATEAU DE LA RAPEE
~ CHATEAU HOTEL ~

Bazincourt-sur-Epte, 27140 Gisors (Eure)
TEL 02 32 55 11 61 **FAX** 02 32 55 95 65

'A COMFORTABLE STAY, although we found the decoration, with carpets for wallcoverings, rather idiosyncratic,' commented one reporter on this 19thC Gothic mansion. Well, yes: perhaps we should have warned about the carpet; but it is more or less confined (along with the antlers) to the reception area. The rest of this grandly conceived but small-scale period piece is less eccentric.

The château lies in a peaceful setting at the end of a long, rutted forest track from Bazincourt. Inside, original features have been carefully preserved and, although the public areas are rather dark in places, the house has been pleasantly furnished with antiques and reproductions. Some of the spacious, calm bedrooms are quite stately, with fine country views, plenty of antiques and creaky wooden floors; others verge on the eccentric (but are antler-free). Immediately next to the house is a small, pleasant flower-garden.

Pascal and Philippe Bergeron take their cooking seriously – classic dishes, with some regional influences and occasional original flourishes. Further reports would be welcome.

~

NEARBY Jouy-sous-Thelle (25 km); Beauvais (32 km); riding.
LOCATION in countryside 4 km NW of Gisors; car parking
FOOD breakfast, lunch, dinner
PRICE €€
ROOMS 13; 12 double and twin, one apartment, all with bath or shower; all rooms have phone, TV, safe
FACILITIES sitting room, 2 dining rooms, bar, banqueting room, sauna, garden, terrace, swimming pool
CREDIT CARDS AE, DC, MC, V **CHILDREN** accepted by arrangement
DISABLED no special facilities
PETS not accepted
CLOSED Feb, last 2 weeks Aug; restaurant Wed
PROPRIETORS M. and Mme Bergeron

THE NORTH-WEST

HENNEBONT

CHATEAU DE LOCGUENOLE

~ CHATEAU HOTEL ~

route de Port-Louis en Kerivignac, 56700 Hennebont (Morbihan)
TEL 02 97 76 76 76 **FAX** 02 97 76 82 35
E-MAIL info@chateau-de-locguenole.com **WEBSITE** www.chateau-de-locguenole.fr

OWNED AND RUN BY THE de la Sablière family (son Bruno is the director), this handsome 200-year old château stands in its own extensive wooded park at the head of an arm of the Blavet estuary. A private pontoon allows direct access to the water, and sea-fishing and sailing can be organized on the spot. Rhododendrons and azaleas dot the grounds, walled gardens provide sheltered suntraps to relax in and a heated outdoor pool offers an attractive alternative to the nearby sea.

By almost any measure this is a very grown-up establishment. It has been a hotel now for more than 30 years but has never lost the feel of a comfortable stately home. The antique furniture standing on the glowing parquet floors would cost a prince's ransom today, but you get the distinct feeling that these pieces have been here since they were new. The bedrooms on the first floor are the grandest, but those on the second floor are full of character; one is a 'double-decker' with additional beds in a light and airy loft space. There are seven more bedrooms in the old manor house next door to the château.

The restaurant, dominated by a magnificent tapestry, has a deservedly high reputation – and a wine list to match.

~

NEARBY Lorient (5 km); Ile de Groix; Belle-Ile; golf; sailing.
LOCATION to the right off the D781 from Hennebont to Port-Louis, before D194 junction, on the Blavet estuary; car parking
FOOD breakfast, lunch, dinner; room service
PRICE €€€
ROOMS 9; 8 double and twin, one suite, all with bath; all rooms have phone, TV, minibar, hairdrier
FACILITIES sitting rooms, restaurant, sauna, terrace, garden, swimming pool, tennis, fishing **CREDIT CARDS** AE, DC, MC, V **CHILDREN** accepted
DISABLED access difficult **PETS** tolerated
CLOSED early Jan to early Feb; restaurant closed lunch Mon to Wed and Fri
PROPRIETORS de la Sablière family

THE NORTH-WEST

HONFLEUR

LA CHAUMIERE
~ COUNTRY HOTEL ~

route du Littoral, Vasouy, 14600 Honfleur (Calvados)
TEL 02 31 81 63 20 **FAX** 02 31 89 59 23
E-MAIL accueil@hotel-chaumiere.fr **WEBSITE** www.hotel-chaumiere.fr

STRICTLY SPEAKING A *chaumière* is a thatched cottage, but the Normans seem to have put tiles on this very handsome half-timbered house tucked into its manicured seaside meadow on the Seine estuary, minutes west of Honfleur. Compared to the stratospherically upmarket Ferme Saint Siméon a mile away, also owned by the Boelen family, it is a smaller, more relaxed establishment with nothing else between it and the sea. Run by a manager, it is a little difficult to forget that this is a business and not a vocation. Standards are high and so are prices, but the position alone goes a long way towards justifying the cost.

There is a cosy beamed and tiled restaurant with a view out over the estuary and a consistently high-class output, strong on seafood and fresh local produce and with a wine list to remember. In summer, tables are set on a sheltered sunny terrace guarded by flower beds and fruit trees. The beamed bedrooms are all decorated in fresh colours, with matching fabrics and wallpapers and sound wooden furniture. One, rather eccentrically, is bathroom and bedroom rolled into one: best avoided by those with a preference for privacy. The Pont de Normandie has cut the journey time from Calais to Honfleur to a couple of hours, making this a very undemanding destination for travellers from England. Golfers will also relish the challenge of two courses within ten miles.

~

NEARBY Deauville (15 km); Pont-l'Evêque (19 km); golf.
LOCATION W of Honfleur on the D513 to Deauville; car parking
FOOD breakfast, lunch, dinner
PRICE €€€-€€€€
ROOMS 9; 8 double and twin, one suite, all with bath; all rooms have phone, TV, minibar, hairdrier **FACILITIES** sitting area, restaurant, terrace, garden
CREDIT CARDS AE, MC, V **CHILDREN** accepted
DISABLED access difficult **PETS** accepted
CLOSED 2 weeks Jan, 2 weeks early Dec; restaurant Tue, Wed lunch, Thu lunch
PROPRIETORS Boelen family

THE NORTH-WEST

HONFLEUR

LE MANOIR DU BUTIN
~ SEASIDE HOTEL ~

Phare du Butin, 14600 Honfleur (Calvados)
TEL 02 31 81 63 00 **FAX** 02 31 89 59 23
E-MAIL accueil@hotel-lemanoir.fr **WEBSITE** www.hotel-lemanoir.fr

YOU GET A FIRM IMPRESSION that time runs a little more slowly than usual at this 19thC half-timbered Norman manor tucked into a wooded hillside just outside Honfleur. As well as a view across the Seine estuary, you are offered peace and quiet, vigorous management and attention to detail, and a hushed, slightly reverential yet welcoming atmosphere. Veronique Heulot greets all the guests herself and settles them into one of the ten deeply comfortable bedrooms. All of these are individually decorated, each themed to a different colour, with Pierre Frey fabrics, silk lampshades and smart sheets on the firm comfy beds, and all have excellent bathrooms. Every room is revamped periodically as a matter of routine, not just when it starts to look shabby. The one ground floor bedroom has no view, but has been given a large sunken bath by way of compensation.

There is a sizeable drawing room for residents which, beneath its beams, has a baronial fireplace surmounted by a hunting fresco that chases from one end of the room to the other. On the opposite side of the hall is the light and attractive restaurant, decorated in pale yellow, that offers a regional cuisine on shortish, changing menus as well as a serious selection of old Calvados. Our latest inspector reported that dinner was 'fine', service, 'attentive and ultra-polite', and breakfast, 'one of the best hotel breakfasts I have ever eaten'. He concluded: 'No one would be disappointed by the Manoir du Butin.'

~

NEARBY Deauville (15 km); Pont-l'Evêque (19 km); golf.
LOCATION just W of Honfleur on the D513 to Deauville; car parking
FOOD breakfast, lunch, dinner
PRICE €€-€€€€€
ROOMS 10 double and twin with bath; all rooms have phone, TV, minibar, hairdrier
FACILITIES sitting room, restaurant, terrace, garden **CREDIT CARDS** AE, MC, V
CHILDREN accepted **DISABLED** access difficult **PETS** accepted
CLOSED 2 weeks Jan, 3 weeks Nov; restaurant Wed, Thurs lunch, Fri lunch
MANAGER Veronique Heulot

THE NORTH-WEST

AUBERGE DU CLOS NORMAND
~ VILLAGE INN ~

22 rue Henri IV, 76370 Martin-Eglise (Seine-Maritime)
TEL 02 35 04 40 34 **FAX** 02 35 04 48 49

THE OUTSKIRTS OF DIEPPE are only a few minutes' drive away from this charming country inn, but you would never know it. The only real imponderable about this place is whether the dining room is in the kitchen – or the other way round. Either way the result is cosy and cheerful. Scooting around the flagged floor on his chef's stool, M. Lucas is exercising his culinary skills in public for the first time: 'cuisine ouverte' is how his wife describes it. M. and Mme Lucas bought the *auberge* in 2003 and closed it for several months whilst essential works were carried out. Before them, the Hauchecornes had been in charge for 23 years and, although its traditional Old French character was the mainstay of its appeal, parts of the hotel – the bedrooms in particular – were starting to show their age. We hear they have emerged from their renovation looking fresh and pretty, whilst the essence of the place remains unchanged.

Outside, the River Eaulne flows between the large garden and the pasture beyond, and this is the view for all the bedrooms which are in a separate annexe – purpose-built 100 years ago. On the ground floor is a large sitting room, reserved for the occupants of the rooms.

In their first season, M. Lucas has maintained the *auberge*'s excellent reputation for regional food, and Mme Lucas has proved a delightful and lively hostess, who clearly revels in her new job. A sign on the road says 'Enter lightly', but it's unlikely you'll be able to leave in the same fashion.

~

NEARBY forest of Arques; Côte d'Albâtre; Rouen (50 km).
LOCATION in the village, 5 km SE of Dieppe; car parking
FOOD breakfast, lunch, dinner
PRICE €
ROOMS 9 double and twin with bath or shower; all rooms have phone, TV
FACILITIES sitting room, dining room, terrace, garden
CREDIT CARDS AE, MC, V **CHILDREN** accepted **DISABLED** access difficult **PETS** accepted
CLOSED mid-Dec to mid-Jan; restaurant Mon to Wed
PROPRIETORS M. and Mme Lucas

THE NORTH-WEST

MOËLAN-SUR-MER

LES MOULINS DU DUC

~ CONVERTED MILL ~

29350 Moëlan-sur-Mer (Finistère)
TEL 02 98 96 52 52 **FAX** 02 98 96 52 53
E-MAIL tqad29@aol.com **WEBSITE** www.hotel-moulins-du-duc.com

IN THE WOODED HILLS OF FINISTERE, just above the lowest tidal reaches of the Belon, Les Moulins du Duc is an old mill that is still in the food business but has rocketed upmarket since it became a restaurant, with Thierry Quilfen, who started off as head chef, now the owner as well. You arrive to find manicured gardens round a small lake and apparently no building big enough to house a restaurant, let alone a 24-room hotel. The mill is below the dam which traps the water that used to turn its grindstone and, from a small cottage-like entrance perched on top of the dam, it expands downwards and outwards in an almost extra-dimensional way.

Bare stone, beams and tiled and timbered floors lead you through the bar and down to the lowest level where, almost in the river (big sliding windows open in summer), you can dine very seriously indeed at the white linen-covered tables. Given its location near the coast, it's not surprising that M. Quilfen majors on seafood. If you need more than a stroll by the lake to work up an appetite, try the indoor pool. All the bedrooms are in two-storey cottages dotted around the grounds, quietly decorated and with better-than-adequate bathrooms.

~

NEARBY Lorient (23 km); Quimper (45 km).
LOCATION from Quimperlé take the D783 through Baye and follow signs 1.2 km on left; car parking
FOOD breakfast, lunch, dinner; room service
PRICE €
ROOMS 24 double, twin and family, all with bath or shower; all rooms have phone, TV; some have minibar
FACILITIES sitting room, dining room, breakfast room, meeting room, bar, indoor swimming pool, terrace, garden
CREDIT CARDS AE, DC, MC, V **CHILDREN** accepted
DISABLED 2 specially adapted rooms **PETS** not accepted
CLOSED Dec to Mar
PROPRIETOR Thierry Quilfen

THE NORTH-WEST

NOTRE-DAME-D'ESTREES

AU REPOS DES CHINEURS

∽ COUNTRY GUESTHOUSE ∽

D50, Chemin de l'Eglise, 14340 Notre-Dame-d'Estrées (Calvados)
TEL 02 31 63 72 51 **FAX** 02 31 63 62 38 **E-MAIL** hotel.aureposdeschineurs@libertysurf.fr
WEBSITE www.au-repos-des-chineurs.com

THERE IS A FORMAL *brocante*, which doubles as a tea room, in this 17th and 18thC post house set in deep countryside between Cambremer and Moult. Rugs, china, porcelain, silver, pictures, mirrors and furniture are piled around you. But you can't afford to relax when you leave the *brocante* and walk through to the long, wide flagged hall that runs virtually the length of the house, because everything else here is for sale as well (barring the five cats, the very large dog and the bed you sleep in). Mme Steffen, who owns Le Repos and all the saleable and non-saleable items in it, not only turns her hand to teas and breakfasts but will also whizz up a snack at any other time of the day. If you need weightier fare, there are several restaurants a few minutes' drive away, and telling Mme Steffen what you need is no problem – she learned her English while living in Dallas.

The bedrooms, all with bathrooms, are comfortable and unfussy; those upstairs have floors stained to match the rest of their furnishings and decoration, and those downstairs have tiled floors. Some look up towards a pretty 16thC church perched at the top of the hill. Residents have a small sitting room in which to relax.

∽

NEARBY Caen (26 km); Pont-l'Evêque (25 km); Normandy beaches.
LOCATION edge of the village on the D50; car parking on road
FOOD breakfast, light meals from noon to 7 pm
PRICE ⓔ-ⓔⓔ
ROOMS 10; 7 double, 3 twin, all with bath or shower; all rooms have phone
FACILITIES tea room, garden
CREDIT CARDS MC, V
CHILDREN accepted
DISABLED not suitable
PETS accepted
CLOSED Jan to Mar (open Sat and Sun by request)
PROPRIETOR Mme Claudine Steffen

THE NORTH-WEST

PAIMPOL

LE REPAIRE DE KERROC'H

~ QUAYSIDE HOTEL ~

29 quai Morand, 22500 Paimpol (Côtes d'Armor)
TEL 02 96 20 50 13 **FAX** 02 96 22 07 46
E-MAIL repaire2kerroch@wanadoo.fr

SET ON THE NORTH COAST of Brittany, famous for its pink granite shore-line, Paimpol is a prosperous port with a working fishing fleet in one harbour and a bustling yacht marina in the other. Le Repaire de Kerroc'h, built at the end of the 18th century by Corouge Kersau, a famous local corsair, looks out over the latter. The flagged ground floor of this attractive, practical hotel is mostly given up to eating and drink-ing. At one end there is a fine, cosy restaurant that spills out towards the harbour in summer. Oysters, lobster, *coquilles*, salmon, pork and veal all put in an appearance somewhere on the menu, deftly treated in Yann Trebaol's kitchen and well presented by friendly staff. The wine list is extensive but sensibly includes a fine selection of modestly priced wines (reds from Graves and the Loire amongst them). There is also a small bistro at the other end of the hotel that is open both for lunch and for dinner and offers excellent value on a short menu.

The bedrooms vary in size from just big enough to acceptably spacious. There is also a two-bedroomed, two-bathroomed suite that would be ideal for people travelling together. All the bathrooms are very well equipped. It changed hands in January 2004. The new owner, M. Gehan, is charming and though he speaks little English, his wife is pretty fluent.

~

NEARBY Guingamp (31 km); St Brieuc (47 km); golf.
LOCATION in town on quayside opposite yacht marina; car parking
FOOD breakfast, lunch, dinner
PRICE ©©
ROOMS 13; 11 double and twin, 2 suites, all with bath; all rooms have phone, TV, minibar
FACILITIES sitting area, bar, 2 restaurants, meeting room, lift, terrace
CREDIT CARDS MC, V **CHILDREN** accepted
DISABLED access possible **PETS** accepted
CLOSED never
PROPRIETOR Hubert Gehan

THE NORTH-WEST

LE MANOIR DU SPHINX
~ SEASIDE VILLA ~

chemin de la Messe, 22700 Perros-Guirec (Côtes d'Armor)
TEL 02 96 23 25 42 **FAX** 02 96 91 26 13
E-MAIL lemanoirdusphinx@wanadoo.fr **WEBSITE** www.perros-guirec.com

PERCHED ON THE SHOULDER of a steep headland that shelters it from the fleshpots of Perros-Guirec, Le Manoir du Sphinx is reached by a small seaside lane and looks out across the bay of Tristrignel to the chain of islets that guard it. All the rooms have their own view of the sea – bar and restaurant included. Its steep hydrangea-studded gardens run all the way down to the low cliffs at the high-water mark – or to the edge of the moon-scape of rocks revealed by low tide.

There is nothing 'olde-worlde' about the Sphinx. Furniture and fittings are modern, a lift whisks you up to your room, and everything works the first time you press the button. Every bedroom has a little table and a couple of chairs by the window for those who want to put their feet up and read. Fabric-covered walls match the chairs, and bathrooms are first-rate.

The deeply comfortable restaurant, dressed in pale blue linen when we visited, is the shop window for M. Le Verge's excellent (predominantly sea-based) cooking. The Le Verges (M. and Mme are now aided by their children) offer a well-polished, well-furnished, hospitable hotel with a firm emphasis on peace and quiet, and with a sandy beach a short walk away.

~

NEARBY Lannion (11 km); Guingamp (43 km); St Brieuc (75 km).
LOCATION overlooking the sea beyond the town centre on the D788; car parking
FOOD breakfast, lunch, dinner
PRICE €€
ROOMS 20; 14 double, 6 twin, all with bath or shower; all rooms have phone, TV, hairdrier, safe
FACILITIES sitting room, restaurant, lift, garden
CREDIT CARDS AE, MC, V
CHILDREN accepted
DISABLED ground floor rooms available **PETS** accepted
CLOSED early Jan to late Feb; restaurant Mon and Fri lunch, Sun dinner in low season
PROPRIETORS Le Verge family

THE NORTH-WEST

PONT-AUDEMER

BELLE ISLE SUR RISLE
~ CHATEAU HOTEL ~

112 route de Rouen, 27500 Pont-Audemer (Eure)
TEL 02 32 56 96 22 **FAX** 02 32 42 88 96
E-MAIL hotel@bellile.com **WEBSITE** www.bellile.com

IF YOUR HEART SINKS SLIGHTLY as you drive along the unpromising suburban road towards Belle Ile for the first time, don't worry: the charming owner, Madame Yazbeck, felt exactly the same. When you cross the little bridge to the romantic setting of a private wooded island, your spirits will lift, and they will positively soar as you step into the elegant interior. Rescued from dereliction, this mid-19thC mansion has become a thoroughly well-equipped hotel without losing the welcoming feel of a private house. Period furniture is mixed with little oriental touches and sofas chosen with comfort firmly in mind.

You can choose between three *salons* to relax in, or head for the conservatory bar that doubles as a sunny breakfast room. Bedrooms are all large and impeccably decorated, with bathrooms to match. Delicious food is served in a raised conservatory with a wonderful view of the river at sunset. The wine list is extensive, with rare vintages at appropriate prices and more modest wines at everyday levels. If you feel the need to punish yourself for dinner, there are two swimming pools (one indoors), a small gym, a sauna and a tennis court.

Finding it 'exceptional', a recent reporter gives it a rave review: 'they were friendly, obliging and extremely helpful when my husband was taken ill. The rooms were spacious and immaculate (they changed all the bedding every day). The food was very good', and she is writing as a chef.

~

NEARBY Honfleur (25 km); Rouen (47 km); Pont-l'Evêque (26 km).
LOCATION just E of town on an island in the river Risle; car parking
FOOD breakfast, lunch, dinner
PRICE €€€-€€€€; half-board only in high season and at weekends
ROOMS 20; 13 double, 7 twin, all with bath; all rooms have phone, TV, minibar; most have hairdrier **FACILITIES** sitting rooms, dining room, conservatory, bar, health centre, terrace, garden, indoor and outdoor swimming pools, tennis
CREDIT CARDS AE, DC, MC, V **CHILDREN** accepted
DISABLED access difficult **PETS** accepted **CLOSED** Jan to mid-Mar
PROPRIETOR Mme Marcelle Yazbeck

THE NORTH-WEST

QUINEVILLE-PLAGE

CHATEAU DE QUINEVILLE

~ CHATEAU HOTEL ~

50310 Quineville-Plage (Manche)
TEL 02 33 21 42 67 **FAX** 02 33 21 05 79
E-MAIL chateau.quineville@wanadoo.fr **WEBSITE** www.chateau-de-quineville.com

IN A DRAB SEASIDE RESORT at the northern end of Utah Beach, this place has all the ingredients of a smart Relais et Château establishment: a fine, classically proportioned 18thC building (once inhabited by James Stuart), set in 12 hectares, with a tower dating back to the middle ages, an ice-house and *pigeonnier* in the grounds; an enticing swimming pool; a moat with a Giverny-style bridge. But there's a difference: it has not been 'got at'.

Run by a simple family who speak no English, it's both sincere and endearing – if you appreciate the old style of French provincial hotel, warts and all: run-of-the-mill comfort, old-fashioned wallpaper, unstinting puce velveteen in the bedrooms.

The graceful dining rooms, straddling the width of the house, lit from tall windows on both sides, are airy and charming, with original panelling. Here you can savour traditional Normandy cuisine; try to ignore the murals and huge arrangements of artificial flowers.

Forgive the shortcomings in service and housekeeping and rejoice in the quaintness. A cockerel and geese roaming within metres of the house make for a bright and early start to the day.

Golf, riding, tennis and sailing are all a short distance away.

~

NEARBY Ile de Tatihou; Les Iles St-Marcouf; Barfleur (22 km); Normandy beaches.
LOCATION 1 km from sea, in village, near church and town hall; car parking
FOOD breakfast, lunch, dinner
PRICE ⓔⓔ
ROOMS 26; 24 double and twin, 19 with bath, 5 with shower; 2 suites with bath; all rooms have phone
FACILITIES 2 sitting rooms, dining rooms, bar, billiards, garden, swimming pool, fishing lake **CREDIT CARDS** AE, MC, V **CHILDREN** accepted
DISABLED one suitable bedroom **PETS** accepted
CLOSED early Jan to mid-Mar
MANAGER Mme Ledanois

THE NORTH-WEST

LA ROCHE-BERNARD

AUBERGE BRETONNE
∼ TOWN RESTAURANT-WITH-ROOMS ∼

2 place Duguesclin, 56130 La Roche-Bernard (Morbihan)
TEL 02 99 90 60 28 **FAX** 02 99 90 85 00
E-MAIL jacques.thorel@wanadoo.fr **WEBSITE** www.auberge-bretonne.com

IF YOU COME TO LA ROCHE-BERNARD from the west, you reach it by crossing a dizzyingly high bridge over the Brière estuary which takes you into this partly medieval town. Auberge Bretonne is in the middle, overlooking what might pass for a town square if it were two or three times bigger. It has been owned and run by Solange and Jacques Thorel since 1980, and their priorities are quite simple: offer the finest and rarest wines they can find, the best possible food to accompany them and then a really comfortable bed for the night. Hardly surprising, then, that the *auberge* has built up a wide and dedicated following.

The dining room, pale yellow sponged walls and cool tiled floor, stretches round a little vegetable garden with lettuce, cabbage and onions ready for the kitchen. Jacques Thorel's cooking is sublime (earning him two Michelin stars): red mullet with chorizo compote; a feather light beetroot mousse; *coquilles St-Jacques* sprinkled with chopped truffles until invisible and then covered with fresh cream of asparagus; sea bass virtually unadorned; *brochette* of guinea fowl, stuffed with *foie gras* and macaroni; strawberries and cream – except the cream turns out to be a weightless elderflower froth. The wine list is exceptional and although some of the prices look heavy, you are being offered vintages no longer available on the open market.

∼

NEARBY Redon (32 km); Château de Rochefort-en-Terre.
LOCATION in the centre of town; car parking
FOOD breakfast, lunch, dinner
PRICE €€€€
ROOMS 8 double and twin with bath; all rooms have phone, TV
FACILITIES sitting area, bar, restaurant, lift
CREDIT CARDS AE, DC, MC, V **CHILDREN** accepted
DISABLED one specially adapted room **PETS** accepted
CLOSED mid-Nov to mid-Jan; restaurant Thu and lunch Mon, Tue and Fri
PROPRIETORS Solange and Jacques Thorel

THE NORTH-WEST

ROUEN

HOTEL DES CARMES

~ CITY BED-AND-BREAKFAST ~

33 place des Carmes, 76000 Rouen (Seine-Maritime)
TEL 02 35 71 92 31 **FAX** 02 35 71 76 96
E-MAIL hcarm@mcom.fr **WEBSITE** www.hoteldescarmes.fr.st

TRY TO TIME YOUR VISIT to coincide with the blossoming of the cherry trees, which you can see from most of the bedrooms in this endearing little B&B in a handsome 19thC town house. It could hardly have a better location – off a calm square, yet a few minutes' walk from the main sights, restaurants and shops – and makes a useful, inexpensive base. The wife of the good-humoured owner is an artist whose paintings and sculptures fill the open-plan ground floor, which functions as reception, sitting and breakfast rooms combined. It has a gently bohemian atmosphere, its walls painted in bands of colour, orange cloths on the breakfast tables and wicker furniture draped in throws.

A sweeping staircase leads to the bedrooms, which are simply furnished but attractive, and newly decorated in brightly co-ordinating colours with ceiling frescoes by Marie. Beds are covered with American patchwork quilts and small desks or tables and chairs are a bonus. Try for one of the front-facing rooms with floor-to-ceiling windows and ornamental balconies overlooking the quiet street.

In reception, you'll find plenty of guides and leaflets about Rouen and the region, and the charming Hervé makes the best possible use of his limited English. The Carmes comes without frills, but offers visitors on a budget friendly accommodation in the city centre.

~

NEARBY Cathedral; Musée des Beaux Arts; place du Vieux Marché.
LOCATION in the historic city centre; car parking in square outside
FOOD breakfast
PRICE €
ROOMS 12; 5 double, 2 twin, 5 triple, 8 with bath, 4 with shower; all rooms have phone, TV **FACILITIES** reception/sitting/breakfast area **CREDIT CARDS** AE, DC, MC, V
CHILDREN welome
DISABLED not suitable **PETS** accepted
CLOSED never
PROPRIETORS Hervé and Marie Dorin

THE NORTH-WEST

ST-QUENTIN-SUR-LE-HOMME

LE GUE DU HOLME
~ VILLAGE RESTAURANT-WITH-ROOMS ~

14 rue des Estuaires, 50220 St-Quentin-sur-le-Homme (Manche)
TEL 02 33 60 63 76 **FAX** 02 33 60 06 77
E-MAIL gue.holme@wanadoo.fr **WEBSITE** www.le-gue-du-holme.com

IF YOU ARE IN SEARCH of somewhere spectacular, look elsewhere. But if you want a comfortable place to stay near Mont-St-Michel, to avoid the crowds, and to get a taste of what real Norman cooking is all about – then here is your spot. Michel and Annie Leroux (he is the chef) own and run this spic-and-span restaurant-with-rooms opposite the church in the little village of St-Quentin. She prides herself on always being the first to open the doors in the morning and the last to lock up at night; he prides himself (justifiably) on his devotion to local produce from field, river or, above all, the sea. On the menu you will find lobster, turbot, bass and most of their friends and relations, all treated with a light hand to make sure that they are not robbed of their flavour. The wine list makes just as good reading as the menu.

The restaurant itself greets you with soft, warm colours, gentle lighting, starched white linen and fresh flowers. Most of the bedrooms are in a newer wing, good-sized and furnished in an uncluttered modern style. These are away from the road and look over a pretty, quiet garden filled with roses where breakfast is served in summer.

~

NEARBY Mont-St-Michel (22 km); Avranches (5 km).
LOCATION in the village; car parking
FOOD breakfast, lunch, dinner
PRICE €-€€€
ROOMS 10; 6 double, 3 twin, all with bath, one triple with shower; all rooms have phone, TV, hairdrier
FACILITIES sitting room, bar, restaurant, garden
CREDIT CARDS AE, DC, MC, V
CHILDREN accepted
DISABLED one specially adapted room
PETS accepted
CLOSED Sun Oct to mid-Apr; restaurant Sat lunch, Mon
PROPRIETORS Annie and Michel Leroux

THE NORTH-WEST

ST-VAAST-LA-HOUGUE

HOTEL DE FRANCE ET DES FUCHSIAS

~ SEASIDE TOWN HOTEL ~

20 rue Marechal Foch, 50550 St-Vaast-la-Hougue (Manche)
TEL 02 33 54 42 26 **FAX** 02 33 43 46 79
E-MAIL france-fuchsias@wanadoo.fr **WEBSITE** www.france-fuchsias.com

'THE GARDEN IS STILL in good order, as are the fuchsias, and the conservatory where we ate memorable, beautifully presented food is very enticing; friendly and efficient staff.' So says a reporter, confirming that the essential attractions of this perennially popular halt for Cherbourg ferry passengers (French and British alike) are unchanged.

The emphasis is on the restaurant; and the expressions of delight at the superb seafood platters, or the wonderfully presented produce from the Brix family farm, prove that the customers are happy, although one ultra critical and well-travelled couple recently found the food good but unexceptional. The wine list offers plenty of half bottles and good-value options, the service is friendly and efficient, the atmosphere warm – whether in the cosy dining room or in the conservatory, decorated by a local *décorateur anglais*.

At the far end of the delightful English-style garden, where free chamber music concerts are held on the last ten days of August, is the hotel's annexe. Here bedrooms are more spacious and more stylishly decorated than the fairly simple ones in the main part of the hotel. A suite sleeping two or three people and a ground floor bedroom have been created.

~

NEARBY Normandy beaches; Barfleur (12 km); Cherbourg (29 km).
LOCATION in quiet street near fishing port and marina; private car park
FOOD breakfast, lunch, dinner
PRICE €-€€
ROOMS 33; 32 double, one suite, all with bath or shower; all rooms have phone, TV
FACILITIES sitting room, restaurant, garden
CREDIT CARDS AE, DC, MC, V
CHILDREN welcome
DISABLED access possible
PETS tolerated
CLOSED early Jan to late Feb, Mon, Tue mid-Apr to Oct, Tue eve Nov, Dec and Mar
PROPRIETOR Mme Brix

THE NORTH-WEST

STE-ANNE-LA-PALUD

HOTEL DE LA PLAGE
~ SEASIDE HOTEL ~

boulevard Ste-Barbe, Ste-Anne-la-Palud, 29127 Plonévez-Porzay (Finistère)
TEL 02 98 92 50 12 **FAX** 02 98 92 56 54
E-MAIL info@plage.com **WEBSITE** www.plage.com

A SEASIDE HOTEL INDEED – metres from the shore, with a vast strand of pale sand just next door. But this is far from being a bucket-and-spade holiday hotel. Although prices might not be quite so high as those of many fellow Relais et Châteaux members, they are way beyond the range of most people's summer-fortnight-with-the-kids budget. And although children are welcome, as usual in France, there are no special facilities here for them.

It's as a place for relaxing, pampering breaks with an outdoors element that the Plage wins an entry here. The hotel combines its splendid, peaceful seaside setting – plus attractive pool and tennis court – with one of the best kitchens in Brittany (specializing, of course, in seafood), which earns a star from Michelin. Within the manicured grounds is a bar in a separate thatched cottage. Mme Le Coz and her staff generate a welcoming atmosphere; service is sometimes a little slow but always friendly, and details are not overlooked. Bedrooms are comfortable, even if they do tend towards traditional French styles of decoration, and some have stunning views (worth booking ahead).

~

NEARBY Locronan (10 km); Quimper (25 km).
LOCATION in countryside 4 km W of Plonévez; car parking
FOOD breakfast, lunch, dinner
PRICE €€€-€€€€
ROOMS 26; 10 double, 10 twin, 2 single, 4 family, all with bath; all rooms have TV, phone, minibar
FACILITIES sitting room, dining room, bar, conference room, lift, sauna, garden, swimming pool, tennis
CREDIT CARDS AE, DC, MC, V
CHILDREN welcome **DISABLED** access possible
PETS accepted
CLOSED mid-Nov to Apr; restaurant Tue lunch Sep to Jun
PROPRIETOR M. Le Coz

THE NORTH-WEST

SERVON

AUBERGE DU TERROIR

~ VILLAGE INN ~

Le Bourg, 50170 Servon (Manche)
TEL 02 33 60 17 92 **FAX** 02 33 60 35 26
E-MAIL aubergeduterroir@wanadoo.fr

IF YOU NEED TO STAY somewhere quiet and simple near Mont-St-Michel, and want to avoid the ugly rash of modern-box hotels that have sprung up within sight of the causeway, then leave the N175 to the east of Pontorson and go into Servon. Here you will find Auberge du Terroir, recommended to us by Annie Leroux who runs Le Gué du Holme (see page 51), and you'll be greeted warmly either by Annie or Thierry Lefort.

In Servon the front of each house faces into the village and their back gardens look out over open countryside. The *auberge* occupies two distinct houses: one is the old school house which contains three very satisfactory bedrooms (the one on the ground floor being properly equipped for handicapped guests), and a reading room advertised with total honesty 'for those Norman days' (i.e. when the rain is coming down in torrents); the other house has a rather un-Gallic Presbyterian history, and now contains a charming restaurant and three more bedrooms. Imaginative dishes from Périgord fill the menus.

The garden, with tennis court, is large enough for the most energetic children. Another bonus is the drive from here to Mont-St-Michel, on back roads virtually all the way.

~

NEARBY Mont-St-Michel (8 km); Avranches (15 km).
LOCATION in village 1 km N of N175 between Pontorson and Précey; car parking
FOOD breakfast, lunch, dinner
PRICE €
ROOMS 6; 5 double, one twin, all with bath or shower; all rooms have TV, phone
FACILITIES sitting room, restaurant, terrace, garden, tennis
CREDIT CARDS MC, V
CHILDREN accepted
DISABLED one specially adapted room
PETS accepted
CLOSED Feb, late Nov to early Dec; restaurant Wed, Sat lunch
PROPRIETORS Thierry and Annie Lefort

THE NORTH-WEST

THURY-HARCOURT

RELAIS DE LA POST

~ VILLAGE RESTAURANT-WITH-ROOMS ~

2 rue de Caen, 14220 Thury-Harcourt (Calvados)
TEL 02 31 79 72 12 **FAX** 02 31 39 53 55
E-MAIL lerelais@nol.fr

AT THE HEART OF THE glorious hilly and wooded region known as La Suisse Normande, Thury-Harcourt makes an appealing backdrop to this homely old ivy-clad coaching inn. Its 12 comfortable bedrooms, decorated in the style of Louis XV and XVI by the previous owner Nathalie Frémond, are restful and pleasing, but it's the restaurant, overseen by Jean-Marc Harau since April 2004, that makes this a really special place to stay. An elegant long room, with a remarkable pitched timber roof and a huge picture window which looks out to the garden at one end. It has a formal air, upholstered chairs and beautifully laid tables, covered in floor-length pink and white cloths. Jean-Marc aims to maintain the high standard of gastronomy set by his predecessor, Nathalie's husband Jean-François. The menu features traditional Norman fare: pigeon, duckling and seafood, including lobster and crayfish – all carefully prepared and cooked with delicacy – and afterwards it is almost *de rigeur* to sample the delectable hot apple tart, served with thick Normandy cream. In summer tables and chairs are set outside beneath parasols in the attractive courtyard.

Don't miss a stroll in the lovely grounds of the nearby ruined château (destroyed in 1944), with their herbaceous bordered lawns, tumbling banks of geraniums, and wooded trails leading down to the river Orne.

~

NEARBY Caen (28 km); D-Day beaches; Falaise (28 km).
LOCATION in centre of village; car parking
FOOD breakfast, lunch, dinner
PRICES €
ROOMS 12 double and twin, all with bath or shower; all rooms have phone, TV
FACILITIES bar, dining room, meeting room, sauna, courtyard
CREDIT CARDS AE, MC, V
CHILDREN accepted
DISABLED no special facilities **PETS** accepted
CLOSED never; restaurant Sun dinner and Mon Oct to Apr
PROPRIETORS Jean-Marc and Françoise Harau

THE NORTH-WEST

TRÉBEURDEN

MANOIR DE LAN KERELLEC

~ MANOR HOUSE HOTEL ~

22560 Trébeurden (Côtes d'Armor)
TEL 02 96 15 47 47 **FAX** 02 96 23 66 88
E-MAIL lankerellec@relaischateaux.fr **WEBSITE** www.lankerellec.com

L AN KERELLEC IS A GEM. Quietly situated on a wooded promontory to the west of Lannion, it is sheltered from the open sea by its own archipelago of shoals, rocks and islets that curves round it on all three sides. Not content with this stunning position, which guarantees each and every room a view of the sea, it has style as well. Gilles and Luce Daubé started the hotel in 1981 with seven rooms. Since then it has been gradually and sympathetically extended, and the quality of the decoration and furnishings raised. Oriental rugs vie with one another for floor space in the public rooms, even in the conservatory where little groups of immaculately upholstered chairs wait in convivial groups. The timbered roof of the restaurant looks like an upturned boat: come here in winter and you can dine by an open fire and drink your coffee in the *salon* by another one. Winter or summer, you will have been superbly fed and almost certainly have found plenty to tempt you on the wine list. (Pets are not allowed in the restaurant.)

The fashionably decorated bedrooms all have their fair allocation of fine antiques. They start at a reasonable size and get bigger as they become more expensive. If you are thinking of upgrading a bathroom at home, bring a camera and a notebook: the bathrooms here are superb. One even has the bath positioned so you can enjoy the view.

NEARBY Perros-Guirec (15 km); Tréguier (30 km).
LOCATION on promontory just S of resort, overlooking sea; car parking
FOOD breakfast, lunch, dinner
PRICE €€€-€€€€
ROOMS 19; 8 double, 11 twin, all with bath; all rooms have phone, TV, minibar, safe; some have cd player **FACILITIES** sitting rooms, conservatory, dining room, bar, room, terrace, garden **CREDIT CARDS** AE, DC, MC, V **CHILDREN** welcome
DISABLED some suitable rooms **PETS** accepted
CLOSED mid-Nov to mid-Mar
PROPRIETORS Gilles and Luce Daubé

THE NORTH-WEST

TREBEURDEN

TI AL-LANNEC
~ SEASIDE HOTEL ~

allée de Mezo-Guen, BP 3, 22560 Trébeurden (Côtes d'Armor)
TEL 02 96 15 01 01 **FAX** 02 96 23 62 14
E-MAIL resa@tiallannec.com **WEBSITE** www.tiallannec.com

HAPPY REPORTS ABOUT this handsome house on the 'pink granite' coast of Brittany suggest that the hotel manages to pamper while at the same time coping with the families who are drawn to this seaside holiday area.

The house stands high above the sea with a path down to the beach; its south-facing terrace has a splendid view over the bay of Lannion. It is a supremely comfortable hotel, with that elusive private-house feel. Bedrooms are thoughtfully decorated, light and airy but cosy, with fresh flowers and books, small tables and table lamps liberally used. Some have terraces or verandas. The dining room has the sea view, and is crisp and fresh with rich drapes and old stone walls. Antique and modern furnishings mix well in the comfortable sitting room, dotted with pot plants.

The house was completely renovated and opened as a hotel in 1978 by Gérard and Danielle Jouanny, and is run by them with a convincing blend of charm, taste and efficiency. Danielle's food is 'consistently delicious', the service 'five-star' and the welcome for children genuine – witness the swing and seesaw on the lawn.

~

NEARBY Perros-Guirec (15 km); Tréguier (30 km).
LOCATION in wooded grounds above resort, 10 km NW of Lannion; car parking
FOOD breakfast, lunch, dinner
PRICE €€€
ROOMS 33; 22 double and twin, 8 apartments, all with bath; all rooms have phone, TV, minibar, hairdrier, safe
FACILITIES 4 sitting rooms, dining room, bar, billiards/play room, beauty and fitness centre, lift, garden
CREDIT CARDS DC, MC, V
CHILDREN welcome
DISABLED 2 specially adapted rooms
PETS accepted
CLOSED mid-Nov to Mar
PROPRIETORS Gérard and Danielle Jouanny

THE NORTH-WEST

VERNEUIL-SUR-AVRE

LE CLOS

~ MANOR HOUSE HOTEL ~

98 rue de la Ferté-Vidame, 27130 Verneuil-sur-Avre (Eure)
TEL 02 32 32 21 81 **FAX** 02 32 32 21 36
E-MAIL leclos@relaischateaux.fr **WEBSITE** www.relaischateaux.fr/leclos

L E CLOS REMAINS one of our favourite upmarket French hotels – partly because it remains just affordable by ordinary mortals, but also because it avoids the pretension and vulgarity that afflict so many château-style places. Our latest report supports this view.

The hotel is on the edge of the pleasant little country town of Verneuil, in a quiet back street – though with a busy bypass visible (and just audible) in the background. It is a rather comical turn-of-the-century building of highly patterned brickwork, with a mock-medieval tower, set in well-kept leafy grounds with lawns and creeping willows that are overlooked by a large terrace. Inside, everything is of the highest quality: smart, antique-style cane chairs, heavy linen tablecloths and huge bunches of flowers in the dining room, neat reproduction armchairs in the *salon*, chintzy drapes in the bedrooms, deep pile carpets everywhere – even in the luxurious bathrooms. The bedrooms are light and airy, and furnished in individual style. The kitchen wins no awards, but produces a range of classical dishes with absolute professionalism and finesse.

~

NEARBY Château de Pin au Haras; Evreux (39 km); Chartres (56 km).
LOCATION on southern edge of town; car parking
FOOD breakfast, lunch, dinner
PRICE €€€
ROOMS 10; 4 double, 5 suites, one apartment, all with bath; all rooms have phone, TV
FACILITIES sitting room, 2 dining rooms, bar, garden, tennis
CREDIT CARDS AE, DC, MC, V
CHILDREN welcome
DISABLED no special facilities
PETS accepted
CLOSED mid-Dec to mid-Jan; restaurant Mon, Tue lunch
PROPRIETORS Patrick and Colette Simon

The North-West

Yvetot

Auberge du Val au Cesne

~ Country inn ~

Le Val au Cesne, 76190 Yvetot (Seine-Maritime)
Tel 02 35 56 63 06 **Fax** 02 35 56 92 78
E-MAIL valaucesne@hotmail.com **WEBSITE** www.valaucesne.fr

IN A QUIET WOODED VALLEY this half-timbered inn springs out at you from an otherwise unremarkable roadside, looking slightly as if the Norman builder had suddenly developed Swiss leanings. It started life as a restaurant, but as its popularity grew Jérôme Carel eventually created five boldly, almost alarmingly, decorated bedrooms. The maid who showed them off to us was particularly delighted by the way the bathroom furniture varied in colour to match the scheme of each bedroom. All in a separate building from the restaurant, three bedrooms are on the ground floor, a kind thought for those for whom stairs might become a challenge after dinner. The largest, which has its own outside staircase to the first floor, has more natural light than the others.

Cats, dogs, ducks, parakeets and prize poultry compare lengthy pedigrees with one another in the flower-filled garden, while inside are beams, log fires in winter, acres of family photos and a cuisine which is both regional and seasonal. A modestly priced *Logis de France* menu is always available too. The original snug dining room flows round a stone chimney breast into another room, and recently space on the first floor has been brought into play to extend the seating capacity of the restaurant.

~

NEARBY Rouen (30 km); Honfleur (67 km); Côte d'Albâtre.
LOCATION 3 km SE of Yvetot on the D5 to Fréville; car parking
FOOD breakfast, lunch, dinner
PRICE €
ROOMS 5 twin with bath; all rooms have phone, TV, hairdrier
FACILITIES bar, restaurant, terrace, garden
CREDIT CARDS AE, MC, V
CHILDREN accepted
DISABLED one specially adapted room
PETS accepted
CLOSED mid-Jan to Feb, late Aug to early Sep; restaurant Mon, Tue
PROPRIETOR Jérôme Carel

THE NORTH-WEST

HOTEL D'ARGOUGES

TOWN MANSION

21 rue St-Patrice, 14400 Bayeux (Calvados)
TEL 02 31 92 88 86
FAX 02 31 92 69 16
E-MAIL dargouges@aol.com
FOOD breakfast **PRICE** €
ROOMS 28
CLOSED never

T HE ARGOUGES IS A classically proportioned town house removed from the street – and the hurly-burly of tapestry watchers – in its own courtyard, but within a walking distance of all the main sights. Former home of the aristocratic d'Argouges family, it is now an efficiently run bed-and-breakfast. Rooms vary in size but are all decorated in quiet good taste and, for the most part, have larger than average bathrooms. Some are in an annexe across the courtyard. Guests can use a smart, light drawing room and the small but welcome garden at the back. This is a real oasis in which to relax after a hard day's touring or to lay plans for the day over breakfast. Last but not least, if you arrive by car you will appreciate the value of the hotel's off-street parking.

HOSTELLERIE DU MOULIN DU VEY

CONVERTED MILL

Le Vey, 14570 Clécy (Calvados)
TEL 02 31 69 71 08 **FAX** 02 31 69 14 14
E-MAIL www.reservations@ moulindu-vey.com **WEBSITE** www.moulinduvey.com **FOOD** breakfast, lunch, dinner
PRICE €-€€ **ROOMS** 25

CLOSED Dec to Feb; restaurant Sun dinner winter

W E ARE SAD TO REPORT that this once charming hotel is badly in need of investment. Nothing can detract from its lovely situation beside the broad river Orne, the unusual, attractive mill building smothered in creeper, and the wonderful peace and quiet, broken only by the restful sound of water falling over the weir. But inside, the furniture and decorations now look tawdry rather than pleasantly faded. The long steep stairway up to the bedrooms is dark and dingy. Our inspector complained of a 'worn-out bed that sagged towards the middle' and 'no bedside reading light', a 'stained' bath and 'mould' growing on the tile grouting. He did, however, enjoy dinner, which was 'expertly served and well cooked'.

THE NORTH-WEST

LE MONT-ST-MICHEL

AUBERGE SAINT-PIERRE

TOWN HOTEL

BP16, Grande Rue, 50116 Le Mont-St-Michel (Manche)
TEL 02 33 60 14 03
FAX 02 33 48 59 82
E-MAIL aubergesaintpierre@ wanadoo.fr **FOOD** breakfast, lunch, dinner **PRICE** €€ **ROOMS** 21
CLOSED never

MONT-ST-MICHEL'S CROWDS are thinner in the morning and evening, so it makes some sense to stay on the Mont itself, and the 15thC Auberge St-Pierre is one of a handful of hotels at its foot. It is close to the causeway, which is useful since all cars have to be left outside the walls and bags carried in. There is a large and busy restaurant at street level, where breakfast is served; but once on the first floor a pleasantly rustic calm takes over. Bear in mind, if you take a room in the annexe, that you will have many more stairs to climb than in the main building.

MORTAGNE-AU-PERCHE

HOTEL DU TRIBUNAL

TOWN HOTEL

4 place du Palais, 61400 Mortagne-au-Perche (Orne)
TEL 02 33 25 04 77
FAX 02 33 83 60 83 **E-MAIL** hotel.du. tribunal@wanadoo.fr
FOOD breakfast, lunch, dinner
PRICE €€ **ROOMS** 16
CLOSED never

ON A QUIET SQUARE in this otherwise busy market town and former regional capital, the Tribunal is an agreeable traditional hotel in a fine old timbered building. Although there is no entrance hall – the front door leads straight into the sitting room, with the reception desk tucked into a corner – it still manages to be cosy in a winningly old-fashioned way. The focal point is the fireplace, where an open fire roars in winter, and around which tables and comfy chairs are grouped. For dinner look no further than the Tribunal's own dining room, where the food from a well-stocked *menu du terroir* excels. Try the local speciality, black pudding, if you dare. In contrast to the rest of the hotel, the bedrooms – some in an annexe – are modern, comfortable, though otherwise unremarkable.

ILE-DE-FRANCE

HOTELS IN THE ILE-DE-FRANCE

IN THIS SECTION we combine Paris and the surrounding *départements* of Ile-de-France because, for many visitors, they are both parts of the same picture. If you're passing through the area and need a stopover, your instinct will probably be to stay outside the city; but if you're bent on a sightseeing holiday or a romantic break you will probably want to be in the heart of things. However, this is not always true: an overnight stop in Paris can work perfectly well, and a rural base for city sightseeing can be very restful.

Paris is a compact city – much more so than London, for example – and for many visitors choice of location is not critical (from the convenience point of view) unless you intend to spend a great deal of time in one place (the Louvre, say).

From the point of view of atmosphere and charm, location can make a great difference. It pays to know something about the districts (*arrondissements*) that make up the city. The one-digit or two-digit number at the end of Paris postcodes is the number of the *arrondissement*. Thus 75006 is the 6th, for example.

The *arrondissements* are numbered in a clockwise spiral starting in the centre on the Right Bank of the Seine (the northern bank). You will mainly be interested in the first turn of the spiral.

The 1st is an upmarket area extending from the place de la Concorde past the Louvre to Les Halles; we have one entry here (the appealing little **Relais du Louvre**, page 83). We have none in the 2nd and only one in the 3rd to the east (the luxurious and very expensive **Pavillon de la Reine** on page 82). But the spiral then turns back towards the Seine, and we have a number of entries in the 4th – in the revitalized Marais, east of the Pompidou Centre, including the original and excellent value **Hôtel de Nice** (page 81), as well as the pretty, feminine **Caron de Beaumarchais** (page 68), new to this edition – and on the alluring little Ile Saint-Louis, where the glossy **Hôtel du Jeu de Paume** (page 75) is one of a sprinkling of hotels along the main street.

Across the river, the 5th, 6th and 7th make up the Left Bank, with the Boulevard St-Germain its main axis. Between the Jardin des Plantes in the east and the Eiffel Tower in the west, there are more charming small hotels than anywhere else. In the 5th, the **Degrés de Notre-Dame** is a useful, traditional restaurant (page 70) with attractive rooms. In the 6th and the 7th, our entries range from the chic and pricey **Duc de St-Simon** (page 71) and newly revamped **L'Hôtel** (page 74) to the down-to-earth and reasonably priced **St-Paul** (page 86) and **Thoumieux** (page 88). The spiral then crosses the river again to bring you to the 8th, the Champs Elysées area and the gorgeous **Lancaster** (page 76).

Outside this first central spiral, our other entries are to the north, in the 9th (the **Chopin**, page 69 – a real find, and the **Langlois**, the old **Hôtel des Croisés** in a new guise, page 77); the 17th (the charming **Hôtel de Banville**, page 67); and the 18th (Montmartre), where the **Ermitage** (page 72) is a delightful, if different, choice. For even wider coverage, see *Charming Small Hotel Guide* Paris.

Outside Paris, we have two new Ile-de-France recommendations: one in in Ermenonville to the north-east (page 89) and the other in Gazeran in the heart of the Rambouillet forest to the south-west (page 89). Our other hotels are in Dampierre to the west, in Flagy to the south, and in Germigny-L'Evêque to the east; all within an hour's drive of the capital.

ILE-DE-FRANCE

DAMPIERRE

AUBERGE DU CHATEAU

~ VILLAGE INN ~

1 Grande Rue, 78720 Dampierre (Yvelines)
TEL 01 30 47 56 56 **FAX** 01 30 52 56 95

A TRADITIONAL INN with a calm, prosperous atmosphere which stands in the centre of a stone-built country village. The building dates back to 1650 and has always been a hostelry, probably putting up visitors to the Duc de Luynes, an influential figure in the time of Louis XIII, whose elegant château and surrounding park lie across the road. His descendants still live there.

The layout of the *auberge* bears witness to its age: floors rise and fall at will, there are low-slung beams at every turn, and rickety wooden staircases lead to the bedrooms. These are spacious and decorated in matching floral wallpapers and curtains; the ones at the front have a view of the château and its park; those at the rear overlook the hotel's small garden. Some have stone floors and marble-clad bathrooms. Part of the beamed dining room reaches out to a conservatory-style extension which runs along the front of the building, opening on to a roadside terrace.

Dampierre lies in the heart of the Parc Naturel de la Haute Vallée de Chevreuse, a lovely rural area which seems very far from Paris but is, in fact, only half an hour away by car. Also nearby are châteaux worth visiting, as well as walking and pony trekking.

~

NEARBY Versailles; Montfort l'Amaury.
LOCATION opposite the Château de Dampierre, 36 km SW of Paris, 16 km NE of Rambouillet; car parking
FOOD breakfast, lunch, dinner
PRICE €
ROOMS 20 double and twin, all with bath; all rooms have phone, TV
FACILITIES sitting room, dining room, terrace, garden
CREDIT CARDS AE, MC, V **CHILDREN** accepted
DISABLED not suitable
PETS accepted
CLOSED hotel never; restaurant Sun dinner, Mon
MANAGER M. Blot

ILE-DE-FRANCE

HOSTELLERIE DU MOULIN
~ CONVERTED MILL ~

2 rue du Moulin, 77940 Flagy (Seine-et-Marne)
TEL 01 60 96 67 89 **FAX** 01 60 96 69 51
E-MAIL aumoulin@wanadoo.fr **WEBSITE** www.aumoulin.fr

OVER THE YEARS, since its inclusion in our first edition, we have received a steady flow of readers' reports approving of this imaginatively converted flour mill an hour from Paris.

The setting, with tables in the grassy garden beside the stream that still gently turns the mill wheel, is idyllic, and creates a blissfully soporific effect. Beyond the neat gardens you look out on to cultivated fields which, until the 1950s, supplied the grain that was milled here. The heavy beams, wheels and pulleys of the mill dominate the cosy sitting room, and the bedrooms, named after cereals, are as quirkily captivating as you would hope in a building of this character; space is at a premium, and low beams lead some guests to move about with a permanent stoop.

The chef specializes mainly in traditional dishes, and the menu and *carte* have English translations, underlying the Moulin's popularity with British travellers. After running the hotel for more than 20 years, Claude Scheidecker recently retired. We haven't visited under the new regime, but are relieved to hear that M. Navarro is following his predecessor's example and keeping his prices admirably low. More reports please.

~

NEARBY Fontainebleau (23 km); Sens cathedral (40 km).
LOCATION in village, 23 km SE of Fontainebleau, 10 km W of Montereau; car parking
FOOD breakfast, lunch, dinner
PRICE €
ROOMS 10 double, twin and family, all with bath; all rooms have phone
FACILITIES sitting room, dining room, bar, garden, fishing
CREDIT CARDS AE, DC, MC, V
CHILDREN accepted
DISABLED access difficult
PETS accepted
CLOSED never; restaurant Sun dinner, Mon (except Easter and Whitsun: Mon dinner, Tue)
PROPRIETOR Dario Navarro

ILE-DE-FRANCE

HOTEL DE L'ABBAYE
~ TOWN HOTEL ~

10 rue Cassette, 75006 Paris
TEL 01 45 44 38 11 **FAX** 01 45 48 07 86
E-MAIL hotel.abbaye@wanadoo.fr **WEBSITE** www.hotel-abbaye.com

IF WE GAVE AWARDS, this gorgeous hotel would be a very strong contender.
Indeed, we find it hard to fault, with the single caveat that the standard
bedrooms are fairly small (and feel even smaller compared to the spa-
ciousness of the public rooms); you would do well to upgrade to a larger
room if you can afford it. One room on the ground floor has its own terrace, as do the four duplex apartments. There are also three new '*suite
salons*', in a different, more masculine style and equipped with an arsenal
of high-tech gadgets.

The moment one walks into this skilfully converted former abbey, one
feels calmed and cosseted. The hotel has a reputation for attentive yet
unobtrusive service which it justly deserves: the courteous staff seem genuinely eager to help. The public rooms are inviting yet chic, filled with
fresh flowers, and have several sitting areas furnished with attractively
upholstered sofas and armchairs and warmly lit by huge table lamps; in
cool weather there's an open fire. The conservatory-style breakfast
room/bar must be one of the most alluring in Paris, with walls covered in
trellis and French doors which overlook a large courtyard garden complete with fountain. Here you can have breakfast or a drink in warm
weather. Worth every penny.

~

NEARBY Jardin du Luxembourg; St-Sulpice.
LOCATION close to junction with rue de Meziers
FOOD breakfast
PRICE €€€€
ROOMS 44; 37 single, double and twin, 3 suites, 4 duplex apartments, all with bath;
all rooms have phone, TV, air conditioning, hairdrier
FACILITIES 2 sitting rooms, breakfast room/bar, internet booth, courtyard garden
CREDIT CARDS AE, MC, V **CHILDREN** accepted
DISABLED 2 rooms on ground floor **PETS** not accepted
CLOSED never
PROPRIETORS M. and Mme Lafortune

ILE-DE-FRANCE

HOTEL D'AUBUSSON

~ TOWN HOTEL ~

33 rue Dauphine, 75006 Paris
TEL 01 43 29 43 43 **Fax** 01 43 29 12 62
E-MAIL reservationmichael@hoteldaubusson.com **WEBSITE** www.hoteldaubusson.com

IF YOU PREFER your base in Paris to be a straightforward hotel, veering a little towards the anonymous, but with personal touches, rather than one with a distinct, enveloping personality, then the Aubusson is a good choice. On chilly days, a log fire crackles in the grate in the elegant sitting room; staff are welcoming and friendly; there is live jazz Thursday to Saturday nights; and prices remain reasonable for the four-star comfort offered.

The hotel – ten years old or so – occupies a 17thC honey-stone town house arranged around a large courtyard. A huge pair of double doors, formerly a coach entrance, lead from the street into the airy lobby. To the right, Café Laurent – in various incarnations – has attracted the literati and glitterati since 1690. The sitting room manages to be cosy despite its grand proportions with a high beamed ceiling, Versailles parquet floor and pretty furniture, lamps and mirrors. Appropriately, two Aubusson tapestries hang in the breakfast room next door.

The bedrooms cocoon their inhabitants behind heavy doors in silence and restrained, if fairly unimaginative, luxury. The most expensive are massive and beamed, but even the smallest are large by local standards.

~

NEARBY boulevard St-Germain; Ile de la Cité; Latin Quarter.
LOCATION corner of rue Christine; car parking
FOOD breakfast, light meals; 24 hr room service
PRICE €€€€
ROOMS 49 double and twin, all with bath; all rooms have phone, TV, air conditioning, minibar, hairdrier, safe
FACILITIES sitting room, breakfast room, café/bar, internet booth, lift, courtyard garden **CREDIT CARDS** AE, DC, MC, V
CHILDREN accepted
DISABLED 2 specially adapted rooms
PETS accepted
CLOSED never
MANAGER Pascal Gimel

ILE-DE-FRANCE

PARIS

HOTEL DE BANVILLE
~ TOWN HOTEL ~

166 blvd Berthier, 75017 Paris
TEL 01 42 67 70 16 **FAX** 01 44 40 42 77
E-MAIL hotelbanville@wanadoo.fr **WEBSITE** www.hotelbanville.fr

THIS 1930s TOWN HOUSE hotel offers an attractive combination of style, comfort and middle-of-the-road prices. Convenient, too, for motorists: finding your way from the Périphérique to boulevard Berthier is easy, and parking is not impossible.

The airy art deco building – the work of a celebrated architect, we're told – looks promising, and does not disappoint. Inside, all is tastefully decorated and comfortable, bordering on the luxurious . The public rooms have been totally refurbished in stylish soft creams and beiges, enlivened with the occasional dash of colour in a red sofa and chairs. The focal point of the elegantly furnished sitting area/bar is a grand piano, encircled by a ring of spot lights ingeniously set into the floor. A pianist plays here occasionally in the evening. The neutral colour scheme continues into the new look breakfast room, a soothing place to start the day, and a further reception room, which can be closed off for meetings.

The bedrooms are attractively decorated in individual styles, with thoughtfully chosen fabrics and antiques dotted throughout. Fresh flowers add a reassuring personal touch, as do such small services as having your bed turned down – a rare thing in the city nowadays. Staff are extremely friendly, and we suspect that this hotel would be far more expensive if it were on the Left Bank.

NEARBY Arc de Triomphe; Champs-Elysées; Palais des Congrès.
LOCATION on service road off blvd Berthier, between rue A. Samain and rue de Courcelles
FOOD breakfast
PRICE ⓔⓔⓔ **ROOMS** 42; 39 double and twin, 2 triple, 1 family room, all with bath or shower; all rooms have phone, TV, air conditioning, hairdrier, safe
FACILITIES sitting area/bar, sitting room, breakfast room, lift
CREDIT CARDS AE, MC, V **CHILDREN** accepted **DISABLED** no special facilities
PETS accepted **CLOSED** never
PROPRIETOR Mme Moreau

ILE-DE-FRANCE

PARIS

CARON DE BEAUMARCHAIS
~ TOWN HOTEL ~

12 rue Vieille-du-Temple, 75004 Paris
TEL 01 42 72 34 12 **FAX** 01 42 72 34 63
E-MAIL hotel@carondebeaumarchais.com **WEBSITE** www.carondebeaumarchais.com

THE FRONTAGE CONSISTS of huge plate glass windows surrounded by electric blue paintwork (the colour is known as 'Louis XV'), with the hotel's name emblazoned across the top. A glance inside reveals a square reception *salon* decorated in pretty pink and blue wallpaper with dainty antique furniture, soft lighting and a huge flower arrangement. The decoration might be a touch too chi-chi for our taste, but once inside, it is impossible not to be caught up in the warmth of this hotel and the staff who run it. Messieurs Bigeard *père et fils* genuinely want their guests to be contented and go to great lengths to ensure that they are.

The hotel's theme is the 18th century – colour schemes are based on the period and fabrics, taken from original designs – but more particularly Beaumarchais (he lived further down the street); there are framed pages from antique editions of the author's most famous work, *Marriage of Figaro*, in each of the small but pretty bedrooms. These have upholstered chairs, chandeliers and some pretty antiques, bought recently by the owners, which complement the 18thC style; some have walk-out balconies. Hand-painted tiles enliven the neat white bathrooms.

~

NEARBY Musée Carnavalet; place des Vosges; Notre-Dame.
LOCATION close to the rue de Rivoli
FOOD breakfast, brunch
PRICE €€
ROOMS 19 double and twin, 17 with bath, 2 with shower; all rooms have phone, modem point, TV, air conditioning, minibar, hairdrier
FACILITIES sitting area, breakfast room **CREDIT CARDS** AE, DC, MC, V
CHILDREN accepted
DISABLED access difficult, lift/elevator
PETS accepted
CLOSED never
PROPRIETORS Etienne and Alain Bigeard

ILE-DE-FRANCE

PARIS

CHOPIN
~ TOWN HOTEL ~

10 boulevard Montmartre (46 passage Jouffroy), 75009 Paris
TEL 01 47 70 58 10 **FAX** 01 42 47 00 70

DEFINITELY ONE of our top two-star hotels, with perhaps the most charming façade of all. It stands at the end of passage Jouffroy, one of the 19thC glass-and-steel roofed arcades which thread this no-frills shopping and theatre neighbourhood, and as you approach you may worry that it will be a tourist trap. Not at all. We found a warm and friendly welcome from the receptionist ("I like this job; I'm paid to smile"), and the caring hands of owner Philippe Bidal is immediately in evidence in the pretty little breakfast room, landings dressed up with a couple of chairs and a flower arrangement, and corridors clad in warm colours and lit by lights over the many pictures. Our room, No. 412, was one of the best, with coral-coloured walls and a third bed as well as simple furniture which included a desk and chairs, and a bright white bathroom. Tucked under the eaves and approached along a narrow, creaky corridor, it had the feel of an artist's garret. Set well back from the main roads, all the rooms are quiet. The continental breakfast is a cut above the average, yet reasonably priced, with hot milk for the coffee, as well as orange juice and yoghurt, while downstairs a buffet is served. Double room and breakfast for well under 100 euros.

~

NEARBY Musée Grévin; Grands Boulevards; Opéra Garnier.
LOCATION end of passage Jouffroy, which leads off boulevard Montmartre next to Musée Grévin
FOOD breakfast
PRICE €
ROOMS 36; 32 double, twin and triple, 12 with bath, 20 with shower; 4 single, one with bath, 3 with shower; all rooms have phone, TV
FACILITIES sitting area, breakfast room, lift **CREDIT CARDS** AE, DC, MC, V
CHILDREN accepted **DISABLED** access difficult **PETS** accepted
CLOSED never
PROPRIETOR Philippe Bidal

ILE-DE-FRANCE

PARIS

DEGRES DE NOTRE-DAME
~ TOWN HOTEL AND RESTAURANT ~

10 rue des Grands Degrés, 75005 Paris
TEL 01 55 42 88 88 **FAX** 01 40 46 95 34

ALMOST ALL THE SMALL HOTELS of Paris are without a dining room. Here, however, is an exception – the kind of family-run establishment well known in the French countryside, but rarely found in the city: a restaurant with rooms. The building is charmingly sited on a little tree-filled square, and the restaurant has the feel of a simple *auberge*, serving correspondingly rustic food: nothing special, but honest. This is where guests also have breakfast (served at any time) which, assures the cheerful *patron*, includes the freshest of bread, orange juice squeezed on the spot, and properly made coffee.

A steep wooden staircase (staff carry your bags), decorated with charming murals, leads to the bedrooms, which are good value, well equipped and distinctively decorated, with beamed ceilings, smart wooden furnishings and walls crammed with paintings, reflecting M. Tahir's passion for art. Some rooms have views over Notre-Dame; a few are tiny (it's worth paying 15-euros extra for a slightly bigger room); the ones at the front are the largest, most with triple windows on to the street; No. 24 is handsome, with an expansive desk in the centre; and the huge attic room (No. 501) has been totally revamped, and has an enormous bathroom. Staff are helpful and kind, and reporters appreciate the 'relaxed', 'homely' atmosphere.

~

NEARBY Notre-Dame; Musée de Cluny; Ile St-Louis.
LOCATION on tiny square at junction with rue Fréderic-Sauton, close to quai de Montebello
FOOD breakfast, lunch, dinner
PRICE ⓔⓔ
ROOMS 10 double, all with bath; all rooms have phone, TV, hairdrier; some rooms have minibar
FACILITIES restaurant, bar **CREDIT CARDS** MC, V
CHILDREN accepted **DISABLED** not suitable **PETS** accepted
CLOSED never
PROPRIETOR M. Tahir

ILE-DE-FRANCE

PARIS

DUC DE SAINT-SIMON

~ TOWN HOTEL ~

14 rue de St-Simon, 75007 Paris
TEL 01 44 39 20 20 **Fax** 01 45 48 68 25
E-MAIL duc.de.saint.simon@wanadoo.fr **WEBSITE** www.hotelducdessaintsimon.com

A RECENT STAY confirmed our belief that this is one of the most alluring, and consistently pleasing, small hotels in Paris, the perfect place for a special occasion such as an anniversary. First glimpsed through two pairs of French windows beyond a pretty courtyard, the interior looks wonderfully inviting; and so it is – there is a warm, beautifully furnished *salon* with the distinctly private-house feel that the Swedish proprietor seeks to maintain, and elegant yet cosy bedrooms, all individually decorated with not a jarring note. The twin bedrooms are more spacious than doubles. Everywhere you look are rich fabrics, gloriously overstuffed pieces of furniture and cleverly conceived paint effects. The kilim-lined lift is a particularly original idea.

The white-painted 19thC house backs on to an 18thC building behind, also part of the hotel, with a tiny secret garden wedged in between. Breakfasts can be had in the courtyard or in the intimate cellar bar; service is courteous, and Gun Karin Lalisse, the manager, runs the hotel with great charm and efficiency. Though prices are high, they are not unreasonable for what is offered.

NEARBY Invalides; Musée d'Orsay; Musée Rodin.
LOCATION between rue P. L. Courier and rue de Grenelle
FOOD breakfast, light meals
PRICE €€€€
ROOMS 34; 29 double and twin, 28 with bath, one with shower, 5 suites with bath; all rooms have phone, hairdrier, safe, TV on request; some rooms have air conditioning
FACILITIES 2 sitting rooms, bar, lift
CREDIT CARDS AE, DC, MC, V
CHILDREN accepted
DISABLED no special facilities **PETS** not accepted
CLOSED never
PROPRIETOR M. Lindqvist

ILE-DE-FRANCE

ERMITAGE

～ TOWN HOTEL ～

24 rue Lamarck, 75018 Paris
TEL 01 42 64 79 22 **FAX** 01 42 64 10 33

WE WERE ENTRANCED when we found the Ermitage, tucked away behind Sacré-Coeur. Only a sober wall plaque announces that this is a hotel, the door opening on to a smart little gold and cream lobby, followed by a dark-blue hall with deep-red carpet strewn with rugs. From the reception you can see a charming kitchen with its *faience* stove from Lorraine (breakfast is prepared here and served in your room) and a little terrace beyond. Also on the ground floor: an old-fashioned parlour, decorated in green, and filled with antiques, photographs and ornaments. Par for the course so far, you may think, yet the Ermitage has a decorative surprise which starts in the hall and continues all the way up the stairs, on walls, doors, glass panels, skirtings. These are the charming, shadowy paint effects and murals of the artist Du Buc; the sketchy scenes of Montmartre were done in 1986 when he was an old man.

Eclectic and friendly, with an atmosphere of calm familiarity, the Ermitage was the creation of Sophie Canipel's parents, who fell in love with the house some 30 years ago. Sophie took over when they retired and, in her friendly, dedicated care, the spirit of the hotel remains exactly the same. Bedrooms are by and large light and spacious, freshly decorated with floral wallpapers, lace curtains and large *armoires*. Bathrooms are tiny.

～

NEARBY Sacré-Coeur; Place du Tertre.
LOCATION at E end of rue Lamarck, close to Sacré-Coeur
FOOD breakfast
PRICE €
ROOMS 12; 11 double and twin, one family room, 11 rooms have bath or mini bath; all rooms have phone, hairdrier
FACILITIES sitting room
CREDIT CARDS not accepted **CHILDREN** accepted
DISABLED 2 rooms on ground floor **PETS** accepted
CLOSED never
PROPRIETOR Sophie Canipel

ILE-DE-FRANCE

PARIS

HOTEL DE FLEURIE

∽ TOWN HOTEL ∽

32 rue Grégoire-de-Tours, 75006 Paris
TEL 01 53 73 70 00 **FAX** 01 53 73 70 20
E-MAIL bonjour@hotel-de-fleurie.tm.fr **WEBSITE** www.hotel-de-fleurie.tm.fr

A MODEL HOTEL, rightly very popular, where charm, efficiency and up-to-date comforts go hand in hand. Renovated in the 1980s by the Marolleau family, who used to own the well-known Latin Quarter brasserie, Balzar, it combines an immaculate appearance (not least the pretty façade, elegantly lit at night, complete with statues in the niches) with a cosy, intimate feel. The hands-on owners – parents and two sons – are determined to keep it so, and the place always feels fresh, clean and well cared for.

Instantly eye-catching in the terracotta-tiled reception is a delightful *faience* stove picked up by Mme Marolleau in the flea market; the adjoining sitting room, with its exposed beams and section of ancient wall, has a discreet bar and little tables covered in Provençal cloths. The basement *cave*, where a generous breakfast is served, is equally cosy, cleverly lit by uplighters.

The spotless bedrooms do not disappoint. You will find pretty billowing curtains, walls of panelled wood and grasspaper, period style furniture, inviting beds and – a rare touch – fresh flowers. Bathrooms, all in pink-hued marble, are well equipped with thick towels on heated rails and towelling bathrobes.

∽

NEARBY boulevard St-Germain; St-Sulpice; Jardin du Luxembourg.
LOCATION between boulevard St-Germain and rue des Quatres-Vents
FOOD breakfast
PRICE €€€€
ROOMS 29; 19 double and twin, 17 with bath, 2 with shower, 10 single, 5 with bath, 5 with shower; all rooms have phone, TV, air conditioning, minibar, hairdrier, safe
FACILITIES sitting room, bar, breakfast room, lift **CREDIT CARDS** AE, DC, MC, V
DISABLED no special facilities **PETS** not accepted
CLOSED never
PROPRIETORS Marolleau family

ILE-DE-FRANCE

PARIS

L'HOTEL

~ TOWN HOTEL ~

13 rue des Beaux-Arts, 75006 Paris
TEL 01 44 41 99 00 **FAX** 01 43 25 64 81
E-MAIL reservation@l-hotel.com **WEBSITE** www.l-hotel.com

IF YOU HANKER after the opulence of a Jacques Garcia interior, but prefer a more low-key atmosphere than at the famous designer's other Paris hotel, Costes – darling of the fashion and film crowd – then head for L'Hôtel. Famous for its astonishing six-storey circular atrium, its connection with Oscar Wilde and its reign – in the 1970s and '80s – as the most louche and celebrity-studded hotel in town, L'Hôtel re-emerged two years ago from a period of tawdry decline. Garcia's opulent recreation of the hotel in its heyday conjures a mood of luxurious decadence, and in each of the 30 bedrooms he has created a different fantasy. Amongst the suites, lovers will adore Ottoman-inspired 'Pierre Loti' and 'Cardinal', with its pretty rooftop terrace. Those who can bear the *tristesse* can sleep in 'Oscar Wilde', the (now enlarged) room where the playwright expired beyond his means when the building was a crummy boarding house. Another amazing *chambre de luxe* contains the original mirrored *art deco* bedroom furniture of Mistinguett. The least expensive rooms are compact but dramatic, like sleeping in a velvet-lined jewel box. Best of all is the softly-lit stone-walled plunge pool, which guests can book exclusively for an hour at a time. Accompanied by champagne, candlelight and nothing more than a couple of bathrobes, it's impossibly romantic.

~

NEARBY boulevard Saint-Germain; Musée d'Orsay, Ile de la Cité.
LOCATION between rue Bonaparte and rue de Seine
FOOD breakfast, lunch, dinner; room service
PRICE €€€€€
ROOMS 30 double, twin and suites, all with bath; all rooms have phone, TV, air conditioning, minibar, safe, hairdrier
FACILITIES sitting room, bar, restaurant, courtyard, internet booth, plunge pool, beauty treatment room, lift **CREDIT CARDS** AE, DC, MC, V
CHILDREN accepted **DISABLED** no special facilities
PETS not accepted **CLOSED** never
MANAGER Béatrice Ruggieri

ILE-DE-FRANCE

PARIS

HOTEL DU JEU DE PAUME
~ TOWN HOTEL ~

54 rue St-Louis-en-l'Île, 75004 Paris
TEL 01 43 26 14 18 **FAX** 01 40 46 02 76
E-MAIL info@jeudepaumehotel.com **WEBSITE** www.hoteldujeudepaume.com

OF ALL THE HOTELS in the delightful rue St-Louis-en-l'Ile, this is the most original. Whereas the others are homely, the Jeu de Paume packs a stylish punch.

As its name implies, the building was the site of a 17thC *jeu de paume* court, built in the days when the 'palm game', forerunner to tennis, was all the rage; when the proprietors acquired it in the 1980s, however, it was a run-down warehouse. M Prache is an architect and he wrought something of a miracle on the building, opening out the heart of it right up to the roof, exposing all the old timber construction and slinging mezzanine floors around a central well. The impression of light and transparency is reinforced by a glass-walled lift and glass balustrades around the upper floors. Stone walls and all those beams add a reasuringly rustic feel. The sitting area has the appearance of a sophisticated private apartment, with leather sofas, subtle lighting and handsome stone fireplace. Nearby, at the reception desk, the chic, laid-back staff coolly deal with the guests while a modish golden retriever called Scoop pads around.

Bedrooms are smallish, perfectly pleasant, but nothing like as exciting as the rest of the hotel.

~

NEARBY Marais; Notre-Dame; Latin Quarter.
LOCATION halfway along the island's main street, near the junction with rue des Deux Ponts
FOOD breakfast
PRICE €€€€
ROOMS 32, including suites and duplexes, all with bath and shower; all rooms have phone, TV, minibar, hairdrier **FACILITIES** breakfast room, sitting room, bar, 2 conference rooms, internet booth, sauna, lift, courtyard garden
CREDIT CARDS AE, DC, MC, V **CHILDREN** accepted
DISABLED access difficult **PETS** accepted
CLOSED never
PROPRIETORS M and Mme Prache

ILE-DE-FRANCE

LANCASTER

~ TOWN HOTEL ~

7 rue de Berri, 75008 Paris
TEL 01 40 76 40 76 **FAX** 01 40 76 40 00
E-MAIL reservations@hotel-lancaster.fr **WEBSITE** www.hotel-lancaster.fr

IT'S HARD TO FAULT the Lancaster. Even the hotel's imperfect location seems to work to its advantage, as you step from the brash world of the Champs Elysées into a private house atmosphere of civilized calm and understated luxury. It's a hotel with a history: a grand *ancien régime*-style townhouse, purchased in 1930 by legendary hotelier Emile Wolf, who filled it with antiques and *objets d'art* and a starry array of guests including Noel Coward and Marlene Dietrich. Its present owner, Grace Leo-Andrieu has deftly brought the Lancaster up to date while preserving its atmosphere of unflashy glamour and carefully adding to Wolf's eclectic collection of furniture and art, much of which was acquired during the war when guests used barter to pay their bills; a system that resulted in some splendid Boris Pastoukhoff paintings.

Don't miss tea in the enchanting, pale green Salon Berri and a ride in the original red leather lift. Most stunning of all the stunning bedrooms is the suite dedicated to Marlene Dietrich, decorated in her favourite shades of lilac. As you would expect, prices are high, but exceptionally kind, courteous staff provide impeccable and unobtrusive service. Top chef Michel Troisgros took charge of the intimate restaurant in spring 2003.

NEARBY Arc de Triomphe; Champs Elysées.
LOCATION just N of Champs-Elysées
FOOD breakfast, lunch, dinner; room service
PRICE €€€€€
ROOMS 50 single, double and twin, 10 suites, all with bath; all rooms have phone, TV, air conditioning, minibar, hairdrier, safe
FACILITIES 2 sitting rooms, restaurant, meeting room, café/bar, garden, gym
CREDIT CARDS AE, DC, MC, V
CHILDREN accepted **DISABLED** lift/elevator
PETS not accepted **CLOSED** never
MANAGER Denys Courtier

ILE-DE-FRANCE

PARIS

LANGLOIS
~ TOWN HOTEL ~

63 rue Saint-Lazare, 75009 Paris
TEL 01 48 74 78 24 **FAX** 01 49 95 04 43
E-MAIL info@hotel-langlois.com **WEBSITE** www.hotel-langlois.com

WHEN WE FIRST VISITED the remarkable Hôtel des Croisés (now Langlois) a few years ago, it had been run by the same family for decades, during which time – and the key to its charm – it had remained largely unchanged. Then it was taken over. Improvements were made, thankfully, sympathetically. And then, in 2001, it starred in a Hollywood remake of Charade. In the film it was called the Langlois and, in honour of the movie, the owner kept the name. Though the clientele has become a bit more hip of late, the Langlois itself remains matronly, quiet and solid, with the air of a provincial town hotel.

The stone-fronted mansion is entered through double doors. The hall is baronial, with carved stone walls and an ornate wooden archway. To the right is a pretty breakfast room with faded pink Lloyd loom chairs. The original lift, with curtained windows, takes you up to the huge bedrooms, some with extraordinary ceramic fireplaces, plaster busts, big beds, leather armchairs and – the only changes – minibars and brand-new bathrooms. Under the eaves is an apartment which offers amongst the best value in Paris, with two twin bedrooms, a bathroom and kitchenette, and views of Montmartre. The hotel is handy for the Gare Saint-Lazare but is otherwise in a nondescript part of town.

~

NEARBY Gare Saint-Lazare; boulevard Haussman; Opéra Garnier.
LOCATION in stretch of street between square de la Trinité and rue de la Rochefoucauld
FOOD breakfast
PRICE €€
ROOMS 27; 26 with bath, one with shower; all rooms have phone, TV, minibar
FACILITIES breakfast room **CREDIT CARDS** AE, MC, V **CHILDREN** accepted
DISABLED access difficult, lift/elevator **PETS** accepted **CLOSED** never
PROPRIETOR Ahmet Abut

ILE-DE-FRANCE

PARIS

LATOUR MAUBOURG
~ TOWN HOTEL ~

150 rue de Grenelle, 75007 Paris
TEL 01 47 05 16 14 **FAX** 01 47 05 16 14
E-MAIL info@latourmaubourg.com **WEBSITE** www.latourmaubourg.com

IN A HANDY LOCATION by a quiet metro entrance and a taxi rank, this gracious hotel has the feel of a private house. To maintain it, Victor and Maria Orsenne, who live in an apartment on the premises with their children and their friendly dogs, Faust and Othello, have recently decided to accept only couples and families and decline groups of friends. Before the Orsennes took over in 1994, the building had been in the same family for 150 years. They have wisely left well alone, upgrading where necessary, but leaving the hotel's original proportions intact. A lovely wooden staircase, with elegant balustrades, sweeps up to the bedrooms. The best of these are entered by double doors, and have marble fireplaces, French windows and period paintings; some, including the suite, are huge. They are simply decorated, with creamy walls mixed with warmer colours for curtains and bedcovers. (You can choose between duvet or sheets and blankets; just let them know in advance.) We have had many plaudits from people who appreciate Maria's calm, friendly presence and the *pension*-style ambience (at night you keep your key and are given a code for the front door), although others have mentioned the need to spruce up some rooms and bathrooms.

~

NEARBY Invalides; Eiffel Tower; Musée d'Orsay; Musée Rodin.
LOCATION by La Tour-Maubourg metro, on the corner of boulevard de La Tour Maubourg
FOOD breakfast
PRICE €€
ROOMS 10; 7 double and twin, 6 with bath, one with shower; 2 single, one with bath, one with shower; one suite/family room; all rooms have phone, TV, minibar, hairdrier
FACILITIES sitting/breakfast room, internet booth
CREDIT CARDS MC, V **CHILDREN** accepted
DISABLED access difficult **PETS** not accepted **CLOSED** never
PROPRIETORS Victor and Maria Orsenne

ILE-DE-FRANCE

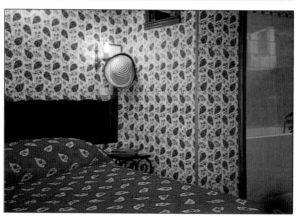

HOTEL DU LYS
~ TOWN HOTEL ~

23 rue Serpente, 75006 Paris
TEL 01 43 26 97 57 **FAX** 01 44 07 34 90
E-MAIL hoteldulys@wanadoo.fr **WEBSITE** www.hoteldulys.com

FOR MORE THAN 50 years the Hôtel du Lys, ideally situated in a very quiet street parallel to the lively boulevard Saint-Germain, has been a family-run hotel operated along *pension* lines. Nowadays it is in the hands of Marie-Helène Decharne, daughter of the original owners, and her husband. "We think of it more as a house than a hotel," she says. "Our guests are individuals; we give them a room and breakfast; after that they look after themselves, but when they are here, this is their home. Some of our clients have been returning regularly for 40 years."

In the 17th century the building was the *hôtel particulier* of loyal followers of the king, who proudly displayed the royal fleur de lys. Little has changed over the years. A venerable wooden staircase winds through the half-timbered stairwell to the bedrooms, all of which are individually decorated in pretty country-style fabrics. There are old wooden cupboard doors, beams, stone walls, a mixture of furniture and simple bathrooms. One room is tiny and pink, with a huge mirror behind the bed; another, next door, is just as sweet, with a jumble of beams in the ceiling. "We treat each room as if it were our own," says Mme Decharne.

~

NEARBY boulevard Saint-Germain; boulevard Saint-Michel, Musée de Cluny.
LOCATION parallel to boulevard Saint-Germain between rue Mignon and rue Hautefeuille
FOOD breakfast
PRICE €€
ROOMS 22 single, double and triple, 6 with bath, 16 with shower; all rooms have phone, TV
FACILITIES sitting room/breakfast room
CREDIT CARDS MC, V **CHILDREN** accepted
DISABLED not suitable **PETS** accepted **CLOSED** never
PROPRIETOR Mme Decharne

ILE-DE-FRANCE

HOTEL DE NESLE
~ TOWN HOTEL ~

7 rue de Nesle, 75006 Paris
TEL 01 43 54 62 41
E-MAIL contact@hoteldenesle.com **WEBSITE** www.hoteldenesle.com

Back in the 1960s, the Nesle, tucked away down a side street, was a happening place for a generation of drop-outs who dropped in and often stayed. In those days, no advance bookings were taken by Mme Busillet, its impressively proportioned proprietor. But times have changed, and it is with great regret that she now accepts, only by phone, advance bookings ("I'm so often let down"). Her clients have changed too, as likely professionals as backpackers these days; and she no longer serves breakfast, instead directing you to Chez Paul round the corner where you can breakfast well for a few euros. But the charm of this unique hotel, amusingly decorated by her son David, remains unchanged.

The reception room, and former breakfast room, is now transformed into a country cottage fantasy, the ceiling dripping with bunches of dried flowers (and a multitude of coloured glass balls at Christmas time). The next delight is the secret garden, entered from the first floor, complete with lawn, pond and palm. As for the bedrooms, you can see many of them on the hotel's excellent website. You might choose Molière, done up like a little theatre, or Sahara, with its own miniature *hammam*, or Victorian dolls house Mélanie. But remember, this is basic stuff. There are *no* extras, precious little storage space, and only one WC per four rooms.

~

NEARBY Musée d'Orsay, Ile de la Cité; boulevard Saint-Germain.
LOCATION in a little street off rue Dauphine
FOOD none
PRICE €
ROOMS 20; 12 double, 5 with shower, 7 with washbasin, none with WC; 8 single, 7 with shower, one with washbasin, none with WC; 4 communal WCs.
FACILITIES reception room **CREDIT CARDS** not accepted **CHILDREN** accepted
DISABLED not suitable **PETS** accepted
CLOSED never
PROPRIETOR Mme Renée Busillet

ILE-DE-FRANCE

PARIS

HOTEL DE NICE
~ TOWN HOTEL ~

42 bis rue de Rivoli, 75004 Paris
TEL 01 42 78 55 29 **FAX** 01 42 78 36 07
E-MAIL contact@hoteldenice.com **WEBSITE** www.hoteldenice.com

HERE IS A WONDERFULLY WACKY two star, every bit as comfortable and twice as enjoyable as many a more expensive three star. We thought it a terrific find, intrigued and not disappointed by what lay behind the vivid turquoise door and up the winding stairs.

The Nice is the enchanting creation of a previously high-flying professional couple who love both collecting and entertaining, although they have now passed on the running of the hotel to their daughter. The fruits of their hobby are everywhere – masses of period engravings and prints – particularly of Paris – mirrors, old doors, postcards, even a splendid portrait of Lady Diana Cooper. The effect is charming and highly individual – the panelled *salon*, for example, is a harmony of unco-ordinated colours, fabrics and furniture: antique, painted, modern, garden. The use of wallpaper copied from French 18thC designs makes the compact bedrooms feel fresh and pretty, with the off-beat addition of Indian cotton bedspreads, and doors and skirtings boldly painted in turquoise, orange or pillar-box red. Two attic rooms are particularly charming, with their own little balconies. Others look out on to a pretty square. You'll find only basic amenities here but plenty of character and youthful appeal.

~

NEARBY Musée Carnavalet; place des Vosges; Notre-Dame.
LOCATION near rue Vieille du Temple, on corner of rue de Rivoli and rue du Bourg Tibourg
FOOD breakfast
PRICE €€
ROOMS 23; 17 double and twin, one family room, all with bath or shower; all rooms have phone, TV, hairdrier
FACILITIES sitting/breakfast room, lift
CREDIT CARDS MC, V **CHILDREN** accepted
DISABLED no special facilities **PETS** accepted
CLOSED never
PROPRIETORS M. and Mme Vaudoux

ILE-DE-FRANCE

PARIS

PAVILLON DE LA REINE
~ TOWN HOTEL ~

28 place des Vosges, 75003 Paris
TEL 01 40 29 19 19 **FAX** 01 40 29 19 20
E-MAIL contact@pavillon-de-la-reine.com **WEBSITE** www.pavillon-de-la-reine.com

SET BACK FROM THE gloriously harmonious place des Vosges, approached through a calming courtyard garden, the Pavillon de la Reine has our vote for the most perfect location in Paris. It is run with calm professionalism by a dedicated and friendly team, although perhaps it lacks the intimacy of a true charming small hotel.

The fine 17thC mansion was once the residence of Anne of Austria, wife of Louis XIII. Rescued from near ruin, it now feels more like a baronial country house, with an impressive entrance hall and handsome, deep red sitting room with furniture upholstered in smart stripes, an honesty bar and a huge stone fireplace complete with roaring log fire. There are two flowery courtyards and a stone-vaulted breakfast room, where a delicious, healthy buffet, including exotic fruits and freshly squeezed juice, is served each morning.

Upstairs, via a wood-panelled lift, the smart, suitably luxurious bedrooms are all different, ranging from feminine *toile de jouy* to designer-decorated duplex suites in a Baroque riot of purple velvet and mauve silk. Whatever their outlook, they are all blissfully quiet.

~

NEARBY Musée Carnavalet; Musée Picasso; Ile St-Louis.
LOCATION entrance from N side of place des Vosges; car parking
FOOD breakfast; room service
PRICE €€€€€
ROOMS 56 double and twin, including standard, de luxe, duplex, junior suites and suites, all with bath; all rooms have phone, TV, air conditioning, minibar, hairdrier
FACILITIES sitting room, breakfast room, internet booth, lift, 2 courtyard gardens
CREDIT CARDS AE, DC, MC, V
CHILDREN accepted
DISABLED ground floor bedrooms
PETS accepted
CLOSED never
MANAGER Yves Monnin

ILE-DE-FRANCE

PARIS

LE RELAIS DU LOUVRE
~ TOWN HOTEL ~

19 rue des Prêtres-St-Germain-l'Auxerrois, 75001 Paris
TEL 01 40 41 96 42 **FAX** 01 40 41 96 44
E-MAIL contact@relaisdulouvre.com **WEBSITE** www.relaisdulouvre.com

IN A QUIET side street hard by the Louvre and the river, this sophisticated, flexible little hotel proves that, in the right hands, even the most featureless of bedrooms can be made to feel charming and welcoming. Most are standard box-shape, no more than adequate in size, although some have the benefit of beamed ceilings and floor-length windows. Ours had a terrific view on to the gables and gargoyles of St-Germain-l'Auxerrois opposite and, though small, felt extremely welcoming and comforting, with its pink hydrangea curtains and matching bedspread, elegant desk and bedside tables, each with a decent-sized lamp. On the walls were pretty 19thC fashion plates, and the television could be popped away in the upholstered box on which it sat. Breakfast is served in your bedroom.

Rooms are cleverly arranged so that a pair can be taken together, closed off behind a communal front door; two rooms on the ground floor have access to a little patio. There is also a fabulous penthouse suite with fully equipped kitchen. The manageress, Sophie Aulnette, and her close-knit staff pride themselves on trying to accommodate clients in the best way and to help with budgets wherever possible.

~

NEARBY Louvre; Ile de la Cité; Samaritaine store (roof-top view).
LOCATION in quiet side street parallel to Quai du Louvre, car parking opposite
METRO Pont-Neuf, Louvre-Rivoli
FOOD breakfast
PRICE €€
ROOMS 21; 10 double and twin with bath; 8 single, 3 with bath, 5 with shower; 2 junior suites; one penthouse suite; all rooms have phone, TV, minibar, hairdrier, safe
FACILITIES sitting area, internet booth, lift
CREDIT CARDS AE, DC, MC, V **CHILDREN** welcome
DISABLED 2 ground floor bedrooms **PETS** accepted
CLOSED never
MANAGER Sophie Aulnette

ILE-DE-FRANCE

LE SAINT-GREGOIRE

~ TOWN HOTEL ~

43 rue de l'Abbé-Grégoire, 75006 Paris
TEL 01 45 48 23 23 **FAX** 01 45 48 33 95
E-MAIL hotel@saintgregoire.com **WEBSITE** www.hotelsaintgregoire.com

A CHIC LITTLE HOTEL in a tall 18thC town house, run with affable charm by manager François de Bené. Le St-Grégoire was designed by Christian Badin of David Hicks – dusty pink walls, maroon carpets, floral peachy curtains, and crisp white linen bedspreads and chair covers – and a warm intimate atmosphere prevails. On wintry afternoons, an open fire blazes in the *salon,* a room dotted with antiques and knick-knacks, picked up by Mme Bouvier, the owner's wife, in flea markets and antique shops. Trellis on the walls and large French windows leading on to a tiny enclosed garden, full of flowers and ferns, make the back part of the sitting room feel more like a conservatory.

The colour scheme leads from the ground floor upstairs to equally attractive bedrooms, with beautiful antique chests of drawers, tables and mirrors; two bedrooms have private terraces. Bathrooms are mostly tiled in white; they tend to be small, but are well designed. The ubiquitous cellar breakfast room is a particularly pretty one, with woven floor, rush chairs and baskets decorating one wall.

~

NEARBY Musée Bourdelle; Jardin du Luxembourg; blvd St-Germain.
LOCATION between rue du Cherche Midi and rue de Vaugirard
FOOD breakfast
PRICE €€€
ROOMS 20 double and twin, all with bath; all rooms have phone, TV, air conditioning, hairdrier
FACILITIES sitting room, breakfast room, lift
CREDIT CARDS AE, DC, MC, V
CHILDREN welcome
DISABLED no special facilities
PETS accepted
CLOSED never
PROPRIETOR M. Bouvier

ILE-DE-FRANCE

PARIS

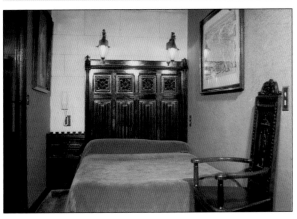

SAINT-MERRY
~ TOWN HOTEL ~

78 rue de la Verrerie, 75004 Paris
TEL 01 42 78 14 15 **FAX** 01 40 29 06 82
E-MAIL hotelstmerry@wanadoo.fr **WEBSITE** www.hotelmarais.com

RECENTLY WE HAVE received conflicting reports of this distinctive small hotel. Some readers love its church-like, medieval atmosphere: its heavily beamed ceilings, pale stone walls, wrought-iron fittings and splendid carved wood neo-Gothic furnishings, and will not contemplate staying anywhere else. Others have complained of claustrophobically small bedrooms and low standards of housekeeping. There are no public rooms to speak of, and breakfast, which is brought to your room, is prepared in a tiny galley behind the reception; a spiralling staircase is the only means by which you can reach your room. The hotel was sold recently, and we would welcome more reports of it under the new management.

This former presbytery of the adjacent church of St-Merri became a private residence after the 1789 revolution, and served for a time as a brothel before it was rescued from decay by its previous owner in the 1960s. He decided on its memorable – if sombre – style after acquiring some neo-Gothic furnishings which were languishing in the basement of the church. The hotel is famous for No. 9, where flying buttresses form a low canopy over the bed, whilst Nos 12 and 17 have remarkable bedheads. There is also a charming suite under the eaves.

~

NEARBY Pompidou Centre; Hôtel de Ville; Marais; Notre-Dame.
LOCATION in pedestrianized zone, on the corner of rue de la Verrerie and rue St-Martin
FOOD breakfast
PRICE €€€
ROOMS 12; 11 double and twin, one suite, all with bath or shower; all rooms have phone, hairdrier
FACILITIES small sitting area
CREDIT CARDS MC, V **CHILDREN** accepted
DISABLED not suitable **PETS** accepted
CLOSED never
PROPRIETOR Pierre Juin

ILE-DE-FRANCE

PARIS

SAINT-PAUL

~ TOWN HOTEL ~

43 rue Monsieur Le Prince, 75006 Paris
TEL 01 43 26 98 64 **FAX** 01 46 34 58 60
E-MAIL hotel.saint.paul@wanadoo.fr **WEBSITE** www.hotelsaintpaulparis.com

W E CONTINUE TO BE very fond of the Saint-Paul, a 17thC building that was renovated in the 1980s (and has just emerged from a further 18-month long refurbishment) and of its charming owner, Marianne Oberlin, who took over its management, along with the hotel cat, Sputnik, and labrador, Hugo, from her parents. The public rooms are stylish in an unfussy way with beamed ceilings, a mixture of stone and colour-washed walls, Indian rugs, *haute époque* and good country antiques, yellow and blue blinds and attractive yellow and blue striped armchairs. Facing the entrance, a courtyard garden is set behind a glass wall, carefully tended and full of colour year-round. The cellar breakfast room is a particularly elegant variation on the theme, with high-backed tapestry chairs and round wooden tables. If the reception rooms have a rural feel, so do the bedrooms, all of which are freshly decorated in different colours with co-ordinating fabrics and carefully lit bathrooms clad in ginger or reddish marble. Our room under the eaves felt cosy, with views over the rooftops; others have four-posters, wooden or antique brass bedsteads. All in all easy-going and well run: a pleasure to stay in.

~

NEARBY Latin Quarter; Musée de Cluny; Jardin du Luxembourg.
LOCATION about halfway along the street, between rue Racine and rue de Vaugirard
FOOD breakfast
PRICE €€€
ROOMS 31; 26 double and twin, including suites, duplex and family rooms, all with bath, 5 single, 2 with bath, 3 with shower; all rooms have phone, TV, minibar, hairdrier, safe; 8 rooms have air conditioning
FACILITIES sitting room, breakfast room, lift
CREDIT CARDS AE, DC, MC, V
CHILDREN accepted
DISABLED one room on ground floor **PETS** accepted
CLOSED never
PROPRIETORS Marianne Oberli

ILE-DE-FRANCE

PARIS

LE SAINTE-BEUVE
~ TOWN HOTEL ~

9 rue Ste-Beuve, 75006 Paris
TEL 01 45 48 20 07 **FAX** 01 45 48 67 52
E-MAIL saintebeuve@wanadoo.fr **WEBSITE** www.paris-hotel-charming.com

ALL IS DISCRETION AND understatement at this essentially simple little hotel with luxurious touches: plain cream walls, restrained patterns in the rich fabrics; beds draped in white, simple furniture mixing modern designs with country antiques, attractive pictures, fresh flowers strategically placed. A log fire burns in the classically-styled *salon*, where there is also a bar (and you can breakfast here too, if you wish).

The Sainte-Beuve always had an innate sense of style which rescued it from the rut and set it apart, along with some pampering extra services. Happily, this remains the case, despite its characterful founder, Bobette Compagnon, having sold the hotel to Jean-Pierre Egurreguy, who previously owned Brasserie Balzar. The *salon* has been redecorated but remains just as alluring, and the excellent breakfast – with bread from the master baker Mulot and newspapers, including the Herald Tribune – still arrives on a carefully laid tray and can still be ordered at any time of day until 10 pm. A selection of light dishes prepared in a neighbouring *bistrot* are also available, so that you need never leave your room. From the top floor, the winding, newly-carpeted wooden staircase makes a dizzying sight.

~

NEARBY boulevard du Montparnasse; Jardin du Luxembourg.
LOCATION off blvd Raspail, between places Lafou and Picasso
FOOD breakfast; room service for light meals and drinks
PRICE €€€
ROOMS 23 double and twin, including standard, de luxe, junior suites and 2 bedroom apartments, all with bath; all rooms have phone, TV, air conditioning, minibar, hairdrier, safe
FACILITIES sitting room, breakfast room, bar, internet booth, lift
CREDIT CARDS AE, MC, V **CHILDREN** accepted
DISABLED access difficult
PETS accepted
CLOSED never
PROPRIETOR Jean-Pierre Egurreguy

ILE-DE-FRANCE

PARIS

THOUMIEUX
～ TOWN RESTAURANT-WITH-ROOMS ～

79 rue Saint-Dominique, 75007 Paris
TEL 01 47 05 49 75 **FAX** 01 47 05 36 96
E-MAIL bthoumieux@aol.com **WEBSITE** www.thoumieux.fr

IN THE SHADOW of the Eiffel Tower, this friendly place, once a convent, revolves around a bustling brasserie, which has belonged to the Thoumieux family since the 1930s, and is now run by Françoise Thoumieux and her husband, Jean Bassalert, with the charming Franco-American, Michael at reception. Except for the addition of mirrored walls and modern prints, the cavernous restaurant, with its black fascia, dark red velvet curtains and banquettes, seems to have changed little since its opening. It specializes in the regional cuisine of the Southwest – *foie gras, cassoulet* and the like – and honest, drinkable house wines. On Sundays, it is full to bursting with families who have been going there forever.

The hotel entrance is to the right of the restaurant, and its stylish reception can be found on the first floor. The ten bedrooms are almost all surprisingly spacious, though, despite tasteful modern furniture, they remain slightly soulless. But the welcome is so warm and friendly, and the service so personal, that 80% of clients are repeat visitors, and a large proportion of them use Thoumieux as their Paris base. Breakfast is excellent, as you'd expect, and if you want a place that feels more like the sort found outside Paris, a friendly restaurant-with-rooms, then Thoumieux makes an excellent choice. The airy breakfast room can be hired for functions.

～

NEARBY Invalides; Musée Rodin; boulevard Saint-Germain; Eiffel Tower.
LOCATION between boulevard La Tour-Maubourg and rue Amélie
FOOD breakfast, lunch, dinner
PRICE €€€
ROOMS 10 double and twin, all with bath; all rooms have phone, TV
FACILITIES restaurant, breakfast room
CREDIT CARDS AE, MC, V
CHILDREN accepted **DISABLED** not suitable **PETS** accepted
CLOSED never
PROPRIETORS Françoise Thoumieux and Jean Bassalert

ILE-DE-FRANCE

ERMENONVILLE

LE PRIEURE
VILLAGE GUESTHOUSE

6 place de l'Eglise, 60440
Ermenonville (Oise)
TEL 03 44 63 66 70
FAX 03 44 63 95 01
E-MAIL le.prieure@club-internet.fr
WEBSITE hotel-leprieure.com
FOOD breakfast
PRICE €€
ROOMS 8
CLOSED Feb

O NE OF OUR FAVOURITE discoveries, Le Prieuré is more a private house than a hotel. An 18thC *gentilhommerie* standing right beside the church, which shadows the attractive garden, it is owned and run by Philippe and Christine Poulin, a committed young couple, who fell in love with it and have worked hard to restore and refurbish it. The bedrooms are fresh and pretty, with painted walls, fabric draped over some of the beds and a scattering of antiques. There are more antiques in the attractive beamed public rooms, including the elegant parlour, where breakfast is served. The garden is English in style, with roses and fruit trees, and a little terrace; try for one of the rooms that give on to it.

GAZERAN

VILLA MARINETTE
VILLAGE HOTEL

20 avenue du Général de Gaulle,
78125 Gazeran (Yvelines)
TEL 01 34 83 19 01 **FAX** 01 30 88
83 65 **E-MAIL** villamarinette
@wanadoo.fr **FOOD** breakfast,
lunch, dinner **PRICE** €€
ROOMS 5
CLOSED Sun eve to Tue eve

T HERE ARE A NUMBER OF REASONS for choosing to stay at Villa Marinette: first and foremost is the burgeoning reputation of its young owner-chef Sébastien Bourgeois, who served his apprenticeship at the famous Parisian restaurant, Carré des Feuillants. Secondly, it has a unique location, facing the village but with a splendid garden that gives directly on to the Rambouillet Forest, much prized by ramblers and mushroom-hunters. Finally, it has a wonderfully cosy, welcoming atmosphere, generated by the warm personalities of Sébastien and his wife Myriam, who have restored the old ivy-covered building with great taste and charm.

ILE-DE-FRANCE

GERMIGNY-L'EVEQUE

HOSTELLERIE LE GONFALON

VILLAGE HOTEL

2 rue de l'Eglise, 77910 Germigny-L'Evêque (Seine-et-Marne)
TEL 01 64 33 16 05**FAX** 01 64 33 25 59 **E-MAIL** le-gonfalon@wanadoo.fr
FOOD breakfast, lunch, dinner
PRICE € **ROOMS** 10
CLOSED mid-Feb to mid-Mar

T HE HOSTELLERIE, which our inspector happened upon as he passed by one day, is set in a lovely wooded position on a bend of the River Marne, overlooked by a tree-shaded terrace, where a menu based on fish and seafood dishes is served in summer – or in the beamed dining room in cooler weather. Germigny-L'Evêque is a quiet residential village, but only 20 minutes from Euro-Disney, making it a perfect spot to escape to after a demanding day in the land of make-believe. Bedrooms are smartly decorated and comfortable; the best have their own private covered terrace. Mme Collubi, who was in charge for some 30 years, recently retired, handing over to enthusiastic restaurateur Jean-Pierre Renaud. Reports please.

PARIS

LOUIS II

TOWN HOTEL

2 rue Saint-Sulpice, 75006 Paris
TEL 01 46 33 13 80
FAX 01 46 33 17 29
E-MAIL louis2@club-internet.fr
WEBSITE www.hotel-louis2.com
FOOD breakfast
PRICE €€
ROOMS 22
CLOSED never

T HIS IS A QUAINT old-fashioned establishment with a cared-for feeling, *mignon* bedrooms and '70s-style bathrooms, which might be too fusty for some people's tastes, but appeal to the nostalgic in others. The bedrooms have recently been redecorated. Each one is different, with pretty fabrics on the walls and elegant light fittings. The crochet bedspreads are specially made in Le Puy in the Auvergne, and mattresses – also handmade – are carefully maintained. Though expensive, breakfast is a real feast, with bread from Mulot, 17 types of jam, nine types of tea, two of coffee, superb hot chocolate, fruit salad, fresh orange juice, cheese and so on.

THE NORTH-EAST

HOTELS IN THE NORTH-EAST

We've made a special effort for this edition to discover some new addresses in our North-East region, as we felt we had neglected it a little of late. Although it does of course contain some popular holiday destinations, it is more often a part of France which is driven through rather than lingered in, and our readers are mostly looking for pleasant overnight stops, or bases for short breaks. There are still several *départments* in which we have no recommendations at all, but the region does embrace four areas worth singling out for their touristic interest and the quality of their hotels.

The hinterland of the main Channel ferry ports includes some pleasant rolling countryside, and of course proximity to those ports makes the area – particularly the *département* of Pas-de-Calais, containing Calais and Boulogne – prime territory for a quick weekend away. We have found several excellent new hotels here – including two in Boulogne and two in the Boulonnais countryside.

The *départments* of Oise and Seine-et-Marne, respectively to the north and east of the Île de France, contain some tourist highlights (Compiègne, Chantilly, Vaux-le-Vicomte). More or less due east of Paris, where the motorway from Paris to Strasbourg meets that coming down from Calais, is Champagne. Wherever there is wine there is a satisfyingly cultivated landscape, and here there is also the architectural spectacle of Reims, at the heart of the Champagne business as well as the region, of which the cathedral is only one part. Two new entries here, in the *départements* of Meuse and Marne respectively.

And then there are the forested hills of the Vosges, and beyond, Alsace, at the far eastern end of this region, against the German border. This is another wine region – a hilly one, with some wonderful scenery and the quaintest of prettily painted, half-timbered villages strung out along the so-called Route de Vin. Here, in particular, we have found some delightful new entries, full of local character, where you should sleep soundly and eat well on such German-influenced Alsatian delicacies as *choucroute* and *presskopf*, sausages, black puddings, *foie gras* and *tartes flambées*, washed down by the region's excellent white wines.

THE NORTH-EAST

ARRAS

L'UNIVERS

~ VILLAGE RESTAURANT-WITH-ROOMS ~

3-5 place de la Croix Rouge, 62000 Arras (Pas-de-Calais)
TEL 03 21 71 34 01 **FAX** 03 21 71 41 42
E-MAIL hotelunivers.arras@nageti.com **WEBSITE** www.hotelunivers.com

DON'T MISS OUT ON ARRAS. The famous squares (*places*) in the town centre are amazing, with their beautiful old gabled buildings. They are a good reason to choose the town as a stopping place (Channel Tunnel, less than an hour by car). Another is the Hôtel L'Univers, awkward to find in the backstreets behind the Hôtel de Ville, but as provincial town hotels in Northern France go, more worth the effort than most. Behind an arch off a pretty little square, the handsome hotel buildings form a peaceful rectangle of their own, pleasantly apart from the bustle. Inside, exposed brickwork contrasts with white Picardy stone giving the pleasant striped effect which is traditional hereabouts. The bedrooms we saw were in reasonable taste, uncluttered (clinical, perhaps), one all beiges and grey, the other powder blue. Bathrooms are smart, modern, acceptable, nothing special. Given the shortage of our type of hotel within reach of the Channel, the Univers is just about recommendable, despite the five conference rooms, housed separately. We counted off-road parking for 16 cars in the courtyard – on the face of it a bonus, but they can fill up quickly, which, we suspect, drives some guests mad – you may not reserve a space.

~

NEARBY Arras *places*.
LOCATION behind Hôtel de Ville, in own square; ask for directions;
car parking
FOOD breakfast, lunch, dinner
PRICE €€
ROOMS 38 double and twin, all with bath, or shower; all rooms have
phone, TV
FACILITIES sitting areas, dining room, bar, lift
CREDIT CARDS AE, MC, V
CHILDREN accepted
DISABLED 2 rooms suitable
PETS accepted **CLOSED** restaurant only, Sun dinner
MANAGER M. Lard

THE NORTH-EAST

BOULOGNE-SUR-MER

ENCLOS DE L'EVECHE

~ TOWN GUESTHOUSE ~

6 rue de Pressy, 62200 Boulogne-sur-Mer (Pas-de-Calais)
Tel 03 91 90 05 90 **Fax** 03 91 90 05 94
E-MAIL contact@enclosdeleveche.com **WEBSITE** www.enclosdeleveche.com

IT'S BEEN A LONG TIME since we were able to recommend somewhere pleasant to stay in Boulogne, a town that has much to offer, with its absorbing Nausicaa marine life centre, it's attractive and recently spruced-up old walled down, its excellent restaurants, pretty surrounding countryside and, for British visitors at least, its proximity to England. Now we have two: the smart Matelote (see page 111) and the *chambres d'hôtes* in this fine, recently renovated mansion located in the old walled town, privately owned and run with great care and attention by Pascaline and Thierry Humez, with Pascaline's father, in whose family the house has been for generations, sometimes good-humourdly taking control in their absence.

Pascaline Humez is responsible for the new decoration of Enclos de l'Evêché, which, as its name suggests, is close to the cathedral (some rooms have fine views of its dome). She has style and taste and it shows in each of the seven different – and differently priced – bedrooms, from seaside simple to Egyptian exotic. There's nothing standard about this place; it's plainly been done with affection and it shows. No dinner, but that couldn't matter less in Boulogne.

~

Nearby Nausicaa marine life centre, cathedral.
Location in centre of the old town close to cathedral; free public parking at the rear of the building
Food breakfast
Price €
Rooms 7 double and twin, all with bath; all rooms have phone, TV, hairdrier
Facilities sitting rooms, breakfast room
Credit cards MC, V
Children welcome
Disabled no special facilities **Pets** accepted **Closed** never
Proprietors Thierry and Pascaline Humez

THE NORTH-EAST

COLMAR

LE COLOMBIER

~ TOWN HOTEL ~

7 rie de Turenne, 68000 Colmar (Haut-Rhin)
TEL 03 89 23 96 00 **FAX** 03 89 23 97 27
E-MAIL info@hotel-le-colombier.com **WEBSITE** www.hotel-le-colombier.com

L E COLOMBIER HAS RELATIVELY few bedrooms in a largish building – a former convent, converted ten years ago to a hotel. Original stone features
sprout, *de rigeur*, in the public spaces (notably the staircase), but we
thought the bar area showed imagination, with a freestanding wood fire
screened by glass, throwing off dancing flames and a comfortable heat
from a mere three or four logs. Quite original, too, is the breakfast room,
with cane and metal chairs. Upstairs, we tried not to let the aromatherapy
oils wafting through the ventilation system dull our senses. The bedrooms
are spacious and well cared for; but the curtains and bedspreads are dull.
The corridors are smart, but, well, like hotel corridors, and the bedrooms
don't quite dispel that antiseptic feel of town hotels where the designer
has been let loose, no expense spared. Even so, No. 21 is great, with painted ceiling beams and parquet floor. The price of breakfast can be a barom-
eter in such places: here, it's a fair one for a buffet with
choices – you can pay more for bad coffee and croissants in humbler
hotels. So, we conclude that Le Colombier is a fair deal, and a good base in
Colmar, home of the amazing Issenheim altarpiece.

~

NEARBY Musée des Cappuchins; Alsace wineries.
LOCATION near town centre, well signposted; car parking in street
FOOD breakfast
PRICE €€
ROOMS 24; 19 double and twin, 3 single, one triple, one family, all with bath (8
Jacuzzi) or shower; all rooms have phone, TV, air conditioning, minibar, safe,
hairdrier
FACILITIES sitting room, bar, breakfast room, courtyard
CREDIT CARDS AE, DC, MC, V
CHILDREN welcome **DISABLED** 2 specially adapted rooms **PETS** accepted
CLOSED never
MANAGER Anne Sophie Heitzler Gerard

THE NORTH-EAST

COURCELLES-SUR-VESLE

CHATEAU DE COURCELLES
~ COUNTRY HOTEL ~

8 rue du Château, 02220 Courcelles-sur-Vesle (Aisne)
TEL 03 23 74 13 53 **FAX** 03 23 74 06 41
E-MAIL reservation@chateau-de-courcelles.fr **WEBSITE** www.chateau-de-courcelles.fr

IN PAST YEARS WE HAVE RATED this expensive Relais & Château hotel as a
back-up address rather than a main entry, and that's what it would
remain except for consistently good reports from readers. They talk of an
especially warm welcome, beautiful rooms and impressive food (Michelin
star),and we too think that the management do something quite special
here, probably helped by there being only 11 bedrooms, plus four suites
and three apartments. It's a graceful, not intimidatingly large, 17thC
château set in a small park in a peaceful backwater of the Vesle between
Reims and Soissons; and, of course, it has a history – Napoleon and
Rousseau were guests. Some might consider the drawing room a tad too
heavy for their taste, with many betasseled lampshades, and predictably
deep-red, traditionally patterned wallpaper. But the roomy bedrooms
have, at their best, a certain freshness, with good use of paint on the panelling; one has an unusual terracotta floor. You could be calm-but-busy
here for two or three days, with a long list of facilities and things to do
nearby. 'Rooms and grounds a pleasure to be in', state recent guests.

~

NEARBY Reims; Epernay; Abbaye St Jean-des-Vignes; Laon.
LOCATION from Reims N31 direction Soissons; Courcelles-sur-Vesles is in about 30
km (NB, don't confuse it with Courcelles, 10 km from Reims); signposted in
village; car parking
FOOD breakfast, lunch, dinner; room service
PRICE ©©©©
ROOMS 18; 11 double and twin, 4 suites, 3 apartments, all with bath; all rooms
have phone, TV, minibar, hairdrier
FACILITIES sitting room, 3 dining rooms, swimming pool, tennis, sauna, jogging
track, bicycles
CREDIT CARDS AE, DC, MC, V **CHILDREN** welcome
DISABLED one specially adapted room **PETS** accepted **CLOSED** never
MANAGER Ivan-Paul Cassetari

THE NORTH-EAST

L'EPINE

AUX ARMES DE CHAMPAGNE
~ VILLAGE HOTEL ~

avenue de Luxembourg, 51460 L'Epine (Marne)
TEL 03 26 69 30 30 **FAX** 03 26 69 30 26
E-MAIL aux.armes.de.champagne@wanadoo.fr **WEBSITE** www.auxarmesdechampagne.com

THIS WOODEN-SHUTTERED flower-decked roadside inn has long been, in the capable and caring hands of its owners, Jean-Paul and Denise Pérardel, an outstanding example of its type. The building is attractive but not memorable, the position, though enjoying a fine view of L'Epine's flamboyant Gothic cathedral, is marred somewhat by being on the road, but it's the standards inside that count, and they are notably high. Though it has been continually improved and refurbished over the years, the hotel still exudes a refreshing lack of pretension. Bedrooms, in wings behind the main building, are either fairly small and countrified in style, or larger and more 'country house' style; all are 'comfortable and impeccable'. Sixteen more straightforward rooms are located in a modern annexe 200 metres down the road.

A good night's sleep and a warm welcome notwithstanding, the main attractions of Aux Armes de Champagne are the renowned cuisine (Michelin star) and the very fine cellar. Philipppe Zeiger is hopefully keeping up the standards of his predecessor, Gilles Blandin, in the kitchen, where the modern cooking with regional touches is consistently appreciated. This is a popular overnight stopping place, especially for people en route to Alsace or the Alps and beyond from the Channel Tunnel.

~

NEARBY cathedral; Champagne country.
LOCATION in L'Épine, 8 km E of Châlons-sur-Marne on N3 to Metz; car parking
FOOD breakfast, lunch, dinner
PRICE €€€
ROOMS 37 double and twin, all with bath or shower; all rooms have phone, TV, minibar, hairdrier
FACILITIES sitting room, bar, restaurant, garden, tennis, mini-golf
CREDIT CARDS AE, DC, MC, V **CHILDREN** accepted
DISABLED no special facilities **PETS** accepted **CLOSED** early-Jan to mid-Feb
PROPRIETORS Jean-Paul and Denise Pérardel

THE NORTH-EAST

HESDIN-L'ABBE

HOTEL CLERY

~ COUNTRY MANSION ~

rue du Château, 62360 Hesdin-l'Abbé (Pas-de-Calais)
TEL 03 21 83 19 83 **FAX** 03 21 87 52 59
E-MAIL chateau-hotel.clery@najeti.com **WEBSITE** www.hotelclery-hesdin-labbaye.com

A dignified façade dominates the fine tree-lined approach to this once private house, properly called Château d'Hesdin l'Abbaye. But there is no need to be intimidated: this is not a stuffy place. There is a very fine Louis XV wrought-iron staircase, but essentially the style is bright and light in harmonious pastel tones, understated and modern. It continues to please our readers: '...exceptionally friendly and attentive staff makes this a very pleasant place to stay', runs our latest report. The hotel already has an established British trade; the excellent golf at nearby Hardelot and St Omer is an attraction in addition to its proximity to the Channel.

Though many are small, bedrooms are freshly decorated, with plenty of individual touches; don't overlook the larger ones in the cottage annexe, especially if you are a family. In the main house there is an attractive bar, and a sitting room with upholstered chairs and a log fire – a welcome sight when arriving at the hotel on a cold, foggy day. There are three dining rooms in all; one in a conservatory is particularly attractive. Food is 'good, but not exceptional, though housekeeping is immaculate', says our inspector. The hotel is one of several owned by Jean-Jacques Durand's Najeti company. All in all, excellent value for money.

~

NEARBY Hardelot, golf and beach (9 km); Le Touquet (15 km).
LOCATION in tiny rural village, 9 km SE of Boulogne; 1 km from exit 28 (A16); ample car parking
FOOD breakfast, dinner
PRICE €€€
ROOMS 22 double and twin, all with bath or shower; all rooms have phone, TV
FACILITIES sitting room, dining room, bar, garden, tennis, bicycles
CREDIT CARDS AE, DC, MC, V **CHILDREN** welcome
DISABLED no special facilities **PETS** not accepted
CLOSED Jan; restaurant closed Sat lunch
MANAGER Caroline Lefour

THE NORTH-EAST

ILLHAEUSERN

HOTEL DES BERGES

~ VILLAGE HOTEL ~

4 rue de Collonges, 68970 Illhaeusern (Haut-Rhin)
TEL 03 89 71 87 87 **FAX** 03 89 71 87 88
E-MAIL hotel-des-berges@wanadoo.fr **WEBSITE** www.hotel-des-berges.fr

THIS IS THE HOTEL that goes with the famous Auberge de l'Ill, one of just three French restaurants that have kept their three Michelin stars for more than 20 years. Hotel and *auberge* stand a little apart in a garden on the little River Ill (*berges* means river banks). Like most class acts, the Berges is understated. The softly spoken manager, Marco Baumann, is laid back, in a charming way, but be sure that he knows his business. It's all in superb taste, full of natural materials – kelims, much use of wood, almost nothing metallic or shiny, with admirable attention paid to connecting areas. It feels, and is, like a private house. The five double bedrooms, all different, use many a fine fabric in soft colours. In summer you can breakfast on a barge in the river. Apart from punting, there's (intentionally) little to do, except mellow out, attended by eight discrete staff. Marc Haeberlin's food at the *auberge* remains a memorable experience. Though in the highest echelon, both restaurant and hotel are very much a family affair (Marco is Haeberlin's brother-in-law, and the great Paul Haeberlin, Marc's father, remains *chef de cuisine*) and they are surely all the better for it.

~

NEARBY Alsace wineries; Riquewihr; Colmar.
LOCATION on edge of village; car parking
FOOD breakfast (lunch, dinner in Auberge de l'Ill)
PRICE ⓔⓔⓔⓔⓔ
ROOMS 5 double and twin, all with bath, one apartment; converted fisherman's cottage; all rooms have phone, TV, video, air conditioning, minibar, safe, hairdrier
FACILITIES sitting areas, bar, lift, terrace, garden, river punt
CREDIT CARDS AE, DC, MC, V
CHILDREN welcome **DISABLED** specially adapted apartment
PETS accepted
CLOSED hotel and restaurant closed Mon, Tues; hotel closed Feb
MANAGER Marco Baumann

THE NORTH-EAST

INXENT

AUBERGE D'INXENT
~ VILLAGE INN ~

318 rue de la Vallée, 62170 Inxent (Pas-de-Calais)
TEL 03 21 90 71 19 **FAX** 03 21 86 31 67
E-MAIL auberge.inxent@wanadoo.fr

WE CAME ACROSS THIS SIMPLE AUBERGE quite by chance as we were driving through the pretty valley of the Course (follow the signposted Route des Sept Vallées if you want to discover the delightful countryside behind Boulogne). The whitewashed building, decorated with blue and white shutters, stands on the D127 (so there is some road noise, though not much) near the quiet village of Inxent and has been an auberge for over 100 years. Though the present owners, Jean-Marc and Laurence Six, have been in residence for only eight of those years, and have thoroughly refurbished since they took over, it feels as though little has changed. (M. Six, by the way, previously a *sommelier* in Lille, bought the auberge on the proceeds of a prize he won for collecting Perrier bottle tops.)

It was lunchtime when we arrived, and we ate well – hearty regional food, perfectly in tune with the surroundings. In the entrance hall, an old range stands on a hearth surrounded by coloured tiles, and to one side is the simple dining room, with a log fire to warm you on chilly days. Bedrooms are sweet and neat, with pretty bathrooms and beamed ceilings. Outside, the attractive garden leads down to the river Course, where M. Six farms the trout that he serves in the restaurant.

~

NEARBY Vallée de la Course; Boulogne-sur-Mer; Le Touquet.
LOCATION on D127 between Montreuil-sur-Mer and Desvres; car parking
FOOD breakfast, lunch, dinner
PRICE €
ROOMS 5 double and twin, all with bath; TV on request
FACILITIES sitting room, restaurant, breakfast room, garden
CREDIT CARDS MC, V
CHILDREN accepted **DISABLED** no special facilities **PETS** accepted
CLOSED Tue, Wed and late Jun to mid-Jul; Jan
PROPRIETORS Jean-Marc and Laurence Six

THE NORTH-EAST

ARNOLD

～ VILLAGE HOTEL ～

98 route des Vins, 67140 Itterswiller (Bas-Rhin)
TEL 03 88 85 50 58 **FAX** 03 88 85 55 54
E-MAIL arnold-hotel@wanadoo.fr **WEBSITE** www.hotel-arnold.com

HERE IS A CLEVER PACKAGE OF HOTEL, restaurant and shop – a blend of the best of the old and the new, aimed at today's traveller, who appreciates a traditional ambience but wants everything convenient. The accommodation is in a pleasing timber and yellow-painted Alsatian house standing in its own vineyards. There is no restaurant or bar here, just a small breakfast room, and the place feels *sotto* because of it. Bedrooms have rough-cast, yellow-washed plaster walls, some with new panelling and bright cotton bedspreads. Bathrooms are a similar standard. The best have long views of vineyards and hills.

For a happy buzz, just go fifty paces up the road to the Arnold's restaurant, where local residents mingle with hotel guests and the hearty Alsatian food is way above average. Here, as in the hotel, everything seems to run on rails – yet there's nothing functional about it. To achieve this effect you need a head for the market, attention to detail and a liking for people: all of which, not surprisingly, are qualities of the friendly owner, Bruno Simon. The Arnold has its own wines: try the Oscar Riesling, available in restaurant and shop.

～

NEARBY The Alsatian wine route; Colmar; Strasbourg.
LOCATION on edge of village, with restaurant almost opposite; car parking just off road
FOOD breakfast, lunch dinner
PRICE €€
ROOMS 29; 24 double and twin, 3 triple, one family, one apartment, all with bath or shower; all rooms have phone, TV, minibar
FACILITIES sitting room, bar, restaurant, local produce boutique, terrace, small garden, wine tastings
CREDIT CARDS AE, MC, V
CHILDREN welcome
DISABLED one specially adapted room **PETS** by arrangement
CLOSED Christmas; restaurant closed Mon (Sun dinner out of season)
PROPRIETOR Bruno Simon

THE NORTH-EAST

LAPOUTROIE

LES ALISIERS
~ COUNTRY HOTEL ~

5, rue Foude, 68650 Lapoutroie (Haut-Rhin)
TEL 03 89 47 52 82 **FAX** 03 89 47 22 38
E-MAIL hotel-restaurant.lesalisiers@wanadoo.fr **WEBSITE** www.alisiers.com

AN ENGLISH COUPLE report that they have been back to this converted farmhouse three times – 'which speaks for itself'. You approach along a narrow, steeply winding road to get a 'wonderful surprise' on arrival. The picturesque building with 'an Alpine feel' has a splendid setting and great views to the village below and across a wooded valley to the Vosges hills.

Food, in the hands of chef Marcel Lanthermann, is the strong card, with a 'sophisticated' set menu centred on local ingredients and dishes. Michelin awards a Bib Gourmand for good food at moderate prices. Floor-to-ceiling windows in the dining room exploit the view: try to get the table in the pole position to enjoy this to the full. Most rooms are simple – 'comfortably rustic' – and spotlessly clean, but some are small. The five newly created 'design' rooms are the best and most comfortable. The Degouys are proud of what they do and go out of their way to make guests feel welcome. Staff are eager to please and prices are very fair.

If you like a relaxed, family atmosphere, then Les Alisiers is for you. A member of the Hôtels au Naturel Group, which believes in respecting the environment and using local ingredients.

~

NEARBY Vosges walking; cross country skiing.
LOCATION in own grounds, off the N415 in direction of St-Die, 3 km from Lapoutroie's centre – signposted from the church; car parking
FOOD breakfast, lunch, dinner
PRICE €€
ROOMS 18; 17 double and twin, one single, all with bath; all rooms have phone
FACILITIES sitting room, bar, restaurant, terrace, garden
CREDIT CARDS MC, V
CHILDREN welcome
DISABLED some specially adapted rooms
PETS by arrangement
CLOSED Christmas, Jan, one week end Jun
PROPRIETORS Jacques and Ella Degouy

THE NORTH-EAST

MONTREUIL

CHATEAU DE MONTREUIL
∾ CHATEAU HOTEL ∾

4 chaussée des Capucins, 62170 Montreuil (Pas de Calais)
TEL 03 21 81 53 04 **FAX** 03 21 81 36 43
E-MAIL chateaudemontreuil@wanadoo.fr **WEBSITE** www.chateaudemontreuil.com

MONTREUIL, CHATEAU DE: charming host, exceptional food, great advice on local shopping for food and wine. Comfortable, well equipped rooms. Not cheap. Wife of patron: English.' Military man, our reporter; as usual verdict spot on; other readers concur. A typical comment: 'you would go far to find a better place to stay in the north of France'.

This substantial, luxurious country house, dating from the 1930s, is a well-established favourite with British travellers, who make up most of the resident guests. The house is immaculately done out, with great taste throughout. Shower cubicles have been added to bathrooms, and the kitchen recently underwent a complete refit. Bedrooms are splendid – decorated with flair and furnished with character; those on the top floor are very spacious, but the first floor rooms give better views of the beautiful English-style gardens. There is a snug brick-and-beams bar, an airy glass-fronted sitting room and an elegant dining room. Although you're quite close to the town centre, the setting is quiet, the gardens secluded.

Christian Germain's cooking aims high and hits the target (the restaurant does not rely on English custom but has a loyal French following). Breakfast ('home-made everything') is delicious.

∾

NEARBY ramparts (still intact), citadel; Le Touquet (15 km); golf.
LOCATION in quiet part of town, 38 km S of Boulogne, off N1; ample car parking
FOOD breakfast, lunch, dinner; room service
PRICE €€€
ROOMS 14; 12 double and twin, 2 family, all with bath; all rooms have phone, TV, air conditioning, minibar, safe, hairdrier
FACILITIES sitting room, restaurant, bar, terrace, garden
CREDIT CARDS AE, DC, MC, V
CHILDREN welcome **DISABLED** 3 rooms on ground floor
PETS not accepted
CLOSED mid-Dec to end Jan
PROPRIETORS Christian and Lindsay Germain

THE NORTH-EAST

OSTHOUSE

A LA FERME

~ VILLAGE GUESTHOUSE ~

10, rue du Château, 67050 Osthouse (Haut-Rhin)
TEL 03 90 29 92 50 **FAX** 03 90 29 92 51
E-MAIL hotelalaferme@wanadoo.fr **WEBSITE** www.hotelalaferme.com

WE DISCOVERED THIS PLACE just after it had opened in 2001, and thought then that it was one of the most interesting new enterprises in Alsace – a view we still hold. The former 18thC farm building, its outside painted a brilliant powder blue – a contemporary twist to the traditional Alsatian colour – stands just off the village centre in its garden. Inside, no expense has been spared to turn it into Brigitte and Jean-Philippe Hellmann's ideal modern-traditional lodging. The homely old proportions have been artfully preserved to keep the private house feel. Walls are panelled or roughly plastered with a pale wash. Wooden oak floors smartly pull it all together. Bedrooms – the smallest we saw was spacious – are enticing, with striped cotton fabrics, fat duvets, white-painted furniture: homely but uncluttered rustic-chic. The suite is elegant and roomy, the bathrooms sparkling, all marble. You get a view of old farm buildings from the bedrooms and a huge gastronomic breakfast (special bread, smoked salmon, *presskopf* terrine) served in the small lounge or on the terrace. Room rates are very reasonable. For lunch or dinner, stroll to the Hellmanns' restaurant, A l'Aigle d'Or, four minutes away, where Jean-Philippe, the chef, offers traditional dishes presented in clean, contemporary style.

~

NEARBY Strasbourg; Alsace vineyards; Colmar; golf at Plobsheim (8 km).
LOCATION in village; ask hotel for directions; car parking
FOOD breakfast
PRICE €€
ROOMS 7; 6 double, one single, all with bath or shower; all rooms have phone, TV, minibar
FACILITIES sitting area, breakfast room, terrace, garden
CREDIT CARDS MC, V
CHILDREN welcome **DISABLED** 2 specially adapted rooms
PETS accepted
CLOSED never; restaurant closed Mon, Tue
PROPRIETORS Brigitte and Jean-Philippe Hellmann

THE NORTH-EAST

AUX TROIS ROSES
~ VILLAGE HOTEL ~

19, rue Principal, 67290 La Petite-Pierre (Bas-Rhin)
TEL 03 88 89 89 00 **FAX** 03 88 70 41 28
E-MAIL hotel.3roses@wanadoo.fr **WEBSITE** www.aux-trois-roses.com

THIS OLD-FASHIONED HOTEL is tucked away near the northern border of Alsace, in the Northern Vosges, in the middle of an atmospheric medieval village – but could almost be in the country, so quiet can seem these Alsatian communities. Its (18thC) face to the street is pleasing: creeper-covered, shuttered and balconied, tumbling with geraniums in summer, just the size you might expect of a charming small hotel, and the small-scale feel continues in reception, divided into warmly panelled alcoves. Check curtains and Alpine chalet-style fittings and furnishings are all very cosy and calming. It gets less charming as you move away from the central public area: several spacious dining rooms spread out beyond – and, to one side, an indoor swimming pool.

Though bedrooms are meant to be in the process of refurbishment, a recent guest tells us that her family's, though comfortable and clean, were very dated ('worn carpets, faded, flowery wallpaper, chipped wood-look plastic doors, '70s style radios'). She was, however, won over by the warmth and kindness of Messieux Geyer (older and younger), especially towards the children, and by the 'superb' food. 'Within minutes of getting to this hotel we felt at home and sitting out on the patio, sipping Reisling and watching the sun go down over the trees will be one of the enduring memories of our holiday.'
~

NEARBY Northern Vosges walking; Alsace wineries.
LOCATION in village main street; car parking in garages and on street
FOOD breakfast, lunch, dinner
PRICE €
ROOMS 42 double, twin and family, all with bath or shower; all rooms have phone, TV, hairdrier
FACILITIES sitting areas, dining rooms, bar, lift, indoor swimming pool, solarium, terrace, table tennis
CREDIT CARDS AE, DC, MC, V
CHILDREN accepted **DISABLED** no special facilities **PETS** accepted **CLOSED** never
PROPRIETOR Philippe Geyer

The North-East

Seigneurs de Ribeaupierre
~ VILLAGE HOTEL ~

11, rue du Château, 68150 Ribeauvillé (Haut-Rhin)
Tel 03 89 73 70 31 **Fax** 03 89 73 71 21

SITUATED AT THE EDGE of this picture-perfect wine town, this is a hotel that you will enjoy if you like escaping into warm, enveloping interiors and a hushed atmosphere, where everything runs on rails. Two sisters, Marie-Madeleine and Marie-Cécile Barth, have softened and brightened exposed stone and gnarled beams with classy fabrics at the windows, cheerful tablecloths in the vaulted breakfast room and, in the intimate *salon*, armchairs arranged so that everyone gets their share of the glow from the raised corner fireplace. Bedrooms come in many sizes, adding to the private house feel. There is a sprinkling of antiques, duvet covers in pretty fabrics, and pools of light from well-placed table lamps. In the sitting area of a suite, two sofas overflow with generously stuffed cushions in co-ordinating fabrics. Not the place for a stag party. Some rooms are non-smoking, and, you may not be surprised to hear, *animaux ne sont pas admis*. We think it's a fair deal for the prices charged - breakfast is included in the room rate. No restaurant; recommended Ribeauvillé eating places are Winstub Zum Pfifferhuis (serious food, no smoking) and l'Auberge Zahnacker; also Chambard at Kaysersberg.

~

NEARBY Alsace Route de Vin; Hunawihr; Colmar (19 km).
LOCATION from Grand'rue, head for place de la Sinne and bear right; hotel on corner near church of St Grégoire; car parking
FOOD breakfast
PRICE €€
ROOMS 10; 7 double, 3 suites, all with bath or shower; all rooms have phone
FACILITIES breakfast room
CREDIT CARDS AE, DC, MC, V
CHILDREN welcome
DISABLED access difficult
PETS not accepted
CLOSED Christmas to Mar
PROPRIETORS Marie-Madeleine and Marie-Cécile Barth

THE NORTH-EAST

JEAN DE BRUGES
~ VILLAGE HOTEL ~

18, Place de l'Eglise, 80135 St-Riquier (Somme)
TEL 03 22 28 30 30 **FAX** 03 22 28 00 69
E-MAIL jeandebruges@wanadoo.fr **WEBSITE** www.hotel-jean-de-bruges.com

THIS IS WHAT you think a good small French hotel ought to be – and so often isn't. Location: in a big square, right beside a medieval abbey, with amazing façade. Exterior: a smallish, handsome 17thC house in white Picardy stone. Public rooms: full of unpretentious style. Bedrooms: white walls, wrought-iron bedsteads, with homely, painted cane bedside tables, no jarring colour schemes or standard-issue floral wallpaper; even the smallest has the loo separate from the bath or shower. Bathrooms: gleaming. Can there be a catch? It's hard to fault, except perhaps on price, which is not unfair, but pushes at the top end of its range.

Actually, it's not strictly a French hotel, but Belgian. The engaging (and savvy) Bernadette Stubbe-Martens and her lawyer husband came here from Bruges in 1995 and created the place from a ruin. Even if you don't stay, have a drink in the beautifully light *salon de thé*, which doubles as dining room and breakfast room. (English readers, note the grandfather clock showing the time in London.) If warm, spill outside on to the terrace for a better view of that church façade, and explore the town, with its unexpectedly interesting shops.

~

NEARBY Côte d'Opale; Fôret de Crécy; Somme battlefields.
LOCATION in church square, 10 km NE of Abbeville; car parking
FOOD breakfast
PRICE €€
ROOMS 11, 10 double and twin, one apartment, all with bath or shower; all rooms have phone, TV, hairdrier, minibar; 2 have air conditioning
FACILITIES sitting room, bar, tea room/dining room, lift, terrace
CREDIT CARDS AE, DC, MC, V
CHILDREN welcome
DISABLED no special facilities
PETS accepted
CLOSED Christmas, Jan, Mon
PROPRIETOR Bernadette Stubbe-Martens

THE NORTH-EAST

TROYES

LE CHAMP DES OISEAUX

20, rue Linard Gonthier, 10000 Troyes (Aube)
TEL 03 25 80 58 50 **FAX** 03 25 80 98 34
E-MAIL message@champdesoiseaux.com **WEBSITE** www.champdesoiseaux.com

THE CITE, OR HISTORIC CENTRE of Troyes, is a symphony of amazing timber-framed buildings dating back to the Middle Ages, and this hotel gives you a ringside seat. It is an exceptionally skilful restoration using traditional techniques of two dwellings dating from the 15th and 16th centuries, on a peaceful cobbled side street.

The courtyard is a charming feature of the interior, where you can eat in warm weather. Looking into it are the bedrooms, artfully carved out of irregular spaces. Here, a bed raised on a platform; there a bathroom slipped in under closely sloping beams, and a loo dramatically perched up flights of steps. Some of the rooms are small, and some guests report noise as other visitors enter or leave their rooms, but all are decorated in clean good taste to contrast with the heavy, beamy features: simple white bedspreads, white-painted tables, and well-judged, emphatically patterned or coloured fabrics. There's a sitting room in the cellar and an artfully decorated breakfast room. No restaurant, but Mme Boisseau will give you the inside track on local eating places. 'Excellent in every way', runs our latest report from a satisfied customer.

NEARBY cathedral; archbishop's palace with museum of modern art.
LOCATION city centre; garage car parking
FOOD breakfast
PRICE €€€
ROOMS 12; 9 double and twin, 3 suites, 10 with bath, 2 with shower; all rooms have phone, TV
FACILITIES 2 sitting rooms, bar, breakfast room, courtyard
CREDIT CARDS AE, DC, MC, V
CHILDREN accepted
DISABLED one specially adapted room
PETS accepted
CLOSED never
PROPRIETOR Monique Boisseau

THE NORTH-EAST

LA TOUR DU ROY
~ TOWN HOTEL ~

45 rue Général Leclerc, 02140 Vervins en Thiérache (Aisne)
TEL 03 23 98 00 11 **FAX** 03 23 98 00 72
E-MAIL chatotel@chatotel.com **WEBSITE** www.chateauxethotels.com

PLACES LIKE THIS often disappoint: the imposing manor house exterior (commanding the town's ramparts), the historic associations, the romantic fortified tower — could so easily be gift wrapping for pretentious food and dubious bedrooms. Well, to be honest, some of La Tour's bedrooms are middle-aged and predictable, with jarring colour schemes; but that doesn't stop it being something special. In fact, it has a certain quirky panache: mainly because of the circular bedrooms in the 11thC tower (one approached through the bathroom, with double tub); but also on account of the flowery wash basins; of the lobster tank jostling the solid manor house furniture in the lobby; the huge stained glass windows; the fortified wall exposed in the dining room; and here and there an interesting Art Nouveau chair to contrast with parquet, tapestries and panelling.

The Desvignes run things with enthusiasm. Madame cooks, while the assistant manager, Anglophile Eric de Robaulx, is a character – "Tell your English readers I've got Scottish ancestry – the Beamishes". In short, a hotel that is eccentric, endearing and more than a bit patchy, but with its heart in the right place. It pleases some and not others, equally understandably. We received two letters about it within the same week, one highly amused, the other highly indignant. See what you think.

~

NEARBY Laon (36 km); St-Quentin (50 km).
LOCATION 36 km NE of Laon, on N2 between Paris and Brussels; underground car parking
FOOD breakfast, lunch, dinner
PRICE €€€
ROOMS 22; 13 double, twin and triple, 8 suites, one apartment, all with bath; all rooms have phone, TV, air conditioning, minibar
FACILITIES sitting room, dining room, swimming pool
CREDIT CARDS AE, DC, MC, V **CHILDREN** welcome **DISABLED** 2 specially adapted rooms
PETS accepted **CLOSED** never **PROPRIETORS** Desvignes family

THE NORTH-EAST

WIERRE-EFFROY

LE BEAUCAMP

~ COUNTRY GUESTHOUSE ~

62720 Wierre-Effroy (Pas-de-Calais)
TEL 03 21 30 56 13 **FAX** 03 21 32 17 95
E-MAIL contact@lebeaucamp.com **WEBSITE** www.lebeaucamp.com

L E BEAUCAMP CALLS ITSELF, with perfect precision, a *'demeure de charme'*.
Imagine the most demure of French *gentilhommeries*, with slate roof
and pale blue shutters, set back from the road in its own unpretentious little park. Inside, guests have the run of the house. It consists of an elegant,
light-filled *salon* with Swedish style furniture, cosy breakfast room and
spacious kitchen (where you are welcome to make a drink or a snack) and
five pretty bedrooms, while the owners live in the adjoining wing.

We've been keeping our eye on this place since M. and Mme Bernard
told us that they were handing the running of their hotel, Ferme du Vert,
to their son and daughter-in-law (see following page), and renovating Le
Beaucamp, the childhood home of Anny Bernard-Martinet, to become
both their own house and, as a retirement project, *chambres d'hôtes*. We
went to see it in its pre-renovated state and again when it was completed,
up and running, and it has been lovingly brought back to life.

Everything feels fresh here, from the new paint, polished wooden
floors, *pink toile de jouey* curtains and white furniture to the breakfast,
with produce – hams, cheese, eggs, fruit – from the local farm. You can
dine at Ferme du Vert.

~

NEARBY Côte d'Opale; Boulogne (11 miles); Calais (16 miles).
LOCATION A16 exit Marquise-Rinxent, follow signs to Wierre-Effroy; Le Beaucamp
is down a private drive off D232 Wierre-Effroy to Boulogne road; car parking
FOOD breakfast
PRICE €
ROOMS 5 double and twin, all with bath
FACILITIES sitting room, breakfast room, kitchen, garden
CREDIT CARDS MC, V
CHILDREN accepted
DISABLED no special facilities **PETS** not accepted **CLOSED** never
PROPRIETORS Anny and Jo Bernard

THE NORTH-EAST

WIERRE-EFFROY

FERME DU VERT

~ FARM GUESTHOUSE ~

62720 Wierre-Effroy (Pas-de-Calais)
TEL 03 21 87 67 00 **FAX** 03 21 83 22 62
E-MAIL ferme.du.vert@wanadoo.fr **WEBSITE** www.fermeduvert.com

There are two farm guesthouses at the village of Wierre-Effroy, the Ferme du Vert and the Ferme Auberge de la Raterie. From the outside, they both have the same sort of charm: farm buildings arranged around a delightful courtyard, dominated by the farmhouse itself, in each case a pleasing, long, low, shuttered building. Animals range freely. Ferme du Vert, however, is our clear favourite because the bedrooms are in simple good taste – white walls, beams, adequate, homely furnishings – rather than jarring colour schemes. No. 16 is good fun, with plenty of space. Ferme du Vert also offers genuine peace – much of the Raterie is given over to conference facilities. There is a homely *salon*, and across the courtyard is the simple, recently redecorated restaurant, with its big, inviting open fireplace and country look. Visitors report 'tasty home cooking', singling out the soup and duck cooked in beer. There's plenty to amuse you here, and they make their own cheese. Ferme du Vert is now run by the owners' son and his wife, as the elder Bernards now run a stylish B&B in their nearby family home, Le Beaucamp (see previous page).

~

NEARBY Côte d'Opale; Boulogne (11 miles); Calais (16 miles).
LOCATION A16 exit Marquise-Rinxent, follow signs to Wierre-Effroy, hotel well signposted up track; car parking
FOOD breakfast, lunch, dinner
PRICE €
ROOMS 16; 11 double, one single, four triple/family, all with bath or shower; all rooms have phone, TV; some have minibar
FACILITIES sitting room, bar, breakfast room, dining room, table tennis, putting, short tennis, bicycles
CREDIT CARDS MC, V
CHILDREN welcome
DISABLED 3 rooms on ground floor **PETS** accepted
CLOSED mid-Dec to mid-Jan
PROPRIETORS M. and Mme Bernard

THE NORTH-EAST

BERGHEIM

CHEZ NORBERT

VILLAGE HOTEL

*9 Grand'rue, 68750 Bergheim
(Haut-Rhin)*
TEL 03 89 73 31 15
FAX 03 89 73 60 65
E-MAIL labacchante@wanadoo.fr
FOOD breakfast, Sun lunch, dinner
PRICE €
ROOMS 12
CLOSED Mar, one week Nov

ONE OF OUR MOST knowledge-able reporters recommends this hotel and restaurant (La Bacchante) on the (rather busy) main street of charming Bergheim. Behind the big wooden gates, you're at once removed from the traffic, in a charming, mellow courtyard: plenty of flowers and greenery, outdoor seating and tables in sunny corners. Inside, the atmospheric restaurant is centre-stage: they reckon on packing the customers in here, under the low-slung beams, on one of which perches a row of bulbous *eau de vie* bottles: The Alsatian cooking is locally popular, and *maître sommelier* Norbert Moeller and *sommelière* Sabine Schalck have an interesting wine cellar. Bedrooms, some under the eves, are simple and neat.

BOULOGNE-SUR-MER

LA MATELOTE

TOWN HOTEL

70/80 blvd Ste-Beuve, Boulogne-sur-Mer (Pas-de-Calais)
TEL 03 21 30 33 33
FAX 03 21 30 87 40
E-MAIL tolestienne@nordnet.fr
WEBSITE www.la-matelote.com
FOOD breakfast, Sun lunch, dinner **PRICE** €€ **ROOMS** 29
CLOSED hotel never; restaurant Christmas, New Year, Sun dinner, Mon lunch

RED AND GOLD IS THE THEME at La Matelote, and you won't forget it. It's everywhere, from the façade (right opposite Nausicaa marine life centre) to the last bedroom. Immaculately turned out, the hotel has grown up in the last five years around Tony Lestienne's prestigious restaurant of the same name. With its uniform decoration and purpose-made mahogany furniture and fittings it has a rather masculine air, but the colour scheme does create a feeling of warmth and no one would mind spending time in one of the well-equipped bedrooms (with pristine bathrooms), especially in the winter months. Save money by taking a 'standard' room; they are just the same as the 'prestige' rooms only a bit smaller and you can spend your savings on Lestienne's sublime, and superbly presented, food.

THE NORTH-EAST

CHAUNY

LA TOQUE BLANCHE

TOWN RESTAURANT-WITH-ROOMS

24 ave Victor Hugo, 02300 Chauny
TEL 03 23 39 98 98 **FAX** 03 23 52 32 79 **E-MAIL** info@toque-blanche.fr **FOOD** breakfast, lunch, dinner **PRICE** €€ **ROOMS** 7
CLOSED restaurant closed Sat lunch, Sun dinner, Mon

In the St Quentin area, where we are perenially frustrated for places worth putting in the guide, this is a useful stopover if you want to spend some money on good, sophisticated food *(escalopes de foie gras au vinaigre de framboise; etuvée de homard au Sauternes)* served with some ceremony in a smartish dining room. Bedrooms and bathrooms are comfortable and newly decorated, but not all our readers will warm to the colours or the style. There's a large and pleasant garden, though it's adjacent to some industrial units. Friendly owners, Vincent (the chef) and Véronique Lequeux. About two hours' drive from Calais.

LE CROTOY

LES TOURELLES

SEASIDE HOTEL

2-4 rue Pierre Guerlain, 80550 Le Crotoy (Somme)
TEL 03 22 27 16 33
FAX 03 22 27 11 45
E-MAIL lestoureslles@nhgroupe.com
WEBSITE www.lestourelles.com
FOOD breakfast, lunch, dinner
PRICE € **ROOMS** 27
CLOSED 3 weeks Jan

ONCE THE HOME OF PARFUMIER Pierre Guerlain, Les Tourelles stands on the Somme estuary, famed for its pearl grey light. It's very odd, at least from the outside, painted dark red and topped by two blue-capped, rocket-like turrets. Not so inside, where a pared-down version of seaside chic, so beloved of *nouvelle vague* coastal hotels, has been applied, with wooden floors, driftwood sculptures and natural materials in the airy bedrooms. This is a happy-go-lucky place, perfect for children who can even sleep together in a special dormitory. The food is no more serious, but it is carefully cooked and presented.

THE NORTH-EAST

FUTEAU

A L'OREE DU BOIS

RESTAURANT-WITH-ROOMS

Courupt, 55120 Futeau (Meuse)
TEL 03 29 88 28 41
FAX 03 29 88 24 52
E-MAIL oreedubois@free.fr
WEBSITE www.oreedubois.fr
FOOD breakfast, lunch dinner;
PRICE €€
ROOMS 14
CLOSED Jan

WE'VE BEEN AWARE OF this rural restaurant-with-rooms on the borders of Champagne and Lorraine in the attractive Argonne region for some years, but have only recently seen it for ourselves after an enthusiastic reader exhorted us to do so. It's a calm, quiet place (Relais du Silence), well-cared for by its owners, chef Paul Aguesse and his wife Roselyne. Paul's contemporary food is the thing here, served in an elegant-rustic dining room with beamed ceiling, old dresser and picture windows with panoramic views over the valley, lovely at sunset. The bedrooms, though, feel dowdy by comparison; best are the newer ones.

GIRMONT VAL D'AJOL

AUBERGE DE LA VIGOTTE

CONVERTED FARMHOUSE

Girmont Val d'Ajol, 88340
Gerardmer (Vosges)
TEL 03 29 61 06 32
FAX 03 29 61 07 88
E-MAIL courrier@lavigotte.com
FOOD breakfast, lunch, dinner
PRICE € **ROOMS** 19
CLOSED Nov to mid-Dec;
restaurant closed Tue, Wed

WE'VE HEARD GOOD THINGS about this gentle country auberge, 2,000 ft up in the Vosges hills, amid the thick conifer forests, meadows, streams and ponds of this little visited but lovely region. An enterprising young couple, the Bouguerne-Arnould's, (Mme is an English teacher) are responsible for bringing this old farmhouse back to life and creating a calm ambience deep in the heart of nowhere. Rooms are simple but pretty, with walls washed in pastel colours and a pleasant assortment of furniture and beds, some modern and some antique. Dinner features dishes such as *ravioles de St Jacques sauce corail au gingembre* and *pieds de cochon aux morilles*. There's an attractive terrace with wonderful views.

The North-East

Chartreuse du Val St Esprit

CHATEAU HOTEL

*1 rue de Fourquières, 62199
Gosnay (Pas-de-Calais)*
Tel 03 21 62 80 00
Fax 03 21 62 42 50
E-mail levalsaintesprit@
lachartreuse.com
Website www.lachartreuse.com
Food breakfast, lunch, dinner
Price €€€ **Rooms** 63 **Closed** never

W^E DON'T OFTEN recommend a hotel for its corridors, but the ones here are remarkably elegant, especially the main one on the ground floor of this recently redecorated 18thC château. though even those in the two annexes are very *soignée* and give the place a lift. Bedrooms and reception rooms are more predictable, though smart, Set in a rural pocket, albeit flat and hemmed in by industrial Béthune, the former charterhouse is surprisingly lovely and has great presence. Though privately owned and very gracious, it doesn't escape a rather corporate air. It supports no less than three restaurants with food that is firmly above average, and prices – for rooms and food – much less than you would expect for a four-star place.

Le Cerf

VILLAGE INN

*30 rue du Général-de-Gaulle, 67520
Marlenheim (Bas-Rhin)*
Tel 03 88 87 73 73
Fax 03 88 87 68 08
E-mail info@lecerf.com
Website www.lecerf.com
Food breakfast, lunch, dinner
Price €€€
Rooms 13
Closed never; restaurant closed
Tues, Wed

A^LL THE SIGNS are that the Cerf is as compelling as ever for visitors who like the cooking of Alsace as much as its wines. Michel Husser carries on the gastronomic tradition of father Robert; Michelin awards two stars for such house specialities as *presskopf de tête de veau en croustille, sauce gribiche* and *choucroute au cochon de lait et foie gras fumé*. Bedrooms are not particularly luxurious, but are well furnished and thoroughly comfortable, with thoughtful extra touches such as a plate of homemade petits fours and fresh fruit. There is a cobbled courtyard for drinks and breakfast.

THE NORTH-EAST

MONTREUIL-SUR-MER

AUBERGE LA GRENOUILLERE

RESTAURANT-WITH-ROOMS

La Madelaine-sous-Montreuil,
62170 Montreuil (Pas-de-Calais)
TEL 03 21 06 07 22
FAX 03 21 86 36 36
E-MAIL Auberge.de.la.
Grenouillere@wanadoo.fr
FOOD breakfast, lunch, dinner
PRICE €€€ **CLOSED** Jan, Wed
(except Jul, Aug), Tue

Though patron Roland Gauthier and his son Alexandre, who is now the chef, no longer hold a Michelin star, we continue to receive high praise for the food at this low Picardy-style farmhouse, known to many as the Froggery. It's serious, classic stuff and lunch on the riverside terrace is a delight, rather overshadowing the gleaming brass and polished wood of the restaurant, complete with murals of Fontaine's fable of the frog who ate until he exploded, painted in the 1930s. The bedrooms are excellent, with attractive bathrooms. One is a tiny, rustic cottage. Don't be put off by all those English voices: this is a serious French enterprise.

OTTROT

L'AMI FRITZ

VILLAGE HOTEL

8 rue des Châteaux, Le Haut,
67530 Ottrot (Haut-Rhin)
TEL 03 88 95 80 81
FAX 03 88 95 84 85
E-MAIL ami-fritz@wanadoo.fr
WEBSITE www.amifritz.com
FOOD breakfast, lunch, dinner
PRICE €€
ROOMS 22
CLOSED never

CLIMBING UP THE SLOPES OF Mont Odile in the charming Wine Route village of Ottrot, you come to the picture-postcard façade of hotelier and chef Patrick Fritz's establishment, with its pale ochre walls and shuttered windows, under which a profusion of brightly coloured geraniums cascade from window boxes. Inside, it's equally romantic, if a bit formal, with a smart restaurant (you can also eat on the terrace) and downstairs, a *wienstube* where in chilly weather dinners can be taken in front of a roaring fire. Mainly traditional Alsatian food is served, best accompanied by Ottrot's own red wine. Bedrooms are smart and comfortable. All a little overdone for our taste, but you get a good night's sleep and in our opinion the bill at the end is very fair value.

THE NORTH-EAST

BERCEAU DE VIGNERON

TOWN HOTEL

10 place Turenne, 68230
Turckheim (Haut-Rhin)
TEL 03 89 27 23 55
FAX 03 89 27 41 21
E-MAIL hotel-berceau-du-vigneron@wanadoo.fr
WEBSITE www.berceau-du-vigneron.com **FOOD** breakfast
PRICE € **ROOMS** 16
CLOSED Jan to mid-Feb

WE LIKE the location of this pretty, shuttered hotel: it's built into the ramparts of the Disneyesque medieval town of Turckheim, by the impressive gates. The handsome, traditional Alsatian building has been completely renovated to give a smart-rustic style – clay floors, beams, wooden pillars, country furniture and check tablecloths in the breakfast room. Bedrooms are carefully furnished, and the best have a gracious air with full, floor length curtains and co-ordinated fabrics. A very useful budget address along the Route de Vin, we feel: your impressions would be welcome. Breakfast only is served, but there's a restaurant – Auberge du Veilleur – close by.

BOYER LES CRAYERES

CHATEAU HOTEL

64 boulevard Henry Vasnier, 51100
Reims (Marne)
TEL 03 26 82 80 80
FAX 03 26 82 65 52 **E-MAIL** crayeres@relaischateaux.com
WEBSITE www.gerardboyer.com
FOOD breakfast, lunch dinner; room service
PRICE €€€€€ **ROOMS** 16
CLOSED Christmas to mid-Jan

GERARD BOYER (before his retirement one of the finest chefs in the land) had a good starting point for his famous restaurant: a graceful turn-of-the-century mansion, situated in a spacious park almost at the heart of Reims and surrounded by the *caves* of the famous champagne names. There are a grand staircase, enormous windows, marble columns and tapestries, a wood panelled, candlelit dining room, and, of course, sumptuous bedrooms, individually decorated. As for the superb wines and the food, which continues to merit three Michelin stars under chef Thierry Voisin, our advice is to starve yourself in preparation. Boyer Les Crayères is now run by Xavier Gardinier.

THE WEST

HOTELS IN THE WEST

Our west of France region has three major components of interest to visitors. First there is the Loire valley and its immediate surroundings, including the atmospheric Sologne, south of Orléans, as well as the valleys of the Loire's two major tributaries, the Cher and the Indre. Not surprisingly in a region so rich in history and magnificent architecture, with a cultivated landscape, some important vineyards and a fine cuisine, the greatest cluster of charming small hotels is here. The second area of interest is the hilly Limousin, fading into the northern fringes of Périgord, around Angoulême and Limoges. And finally there is the hinterland of the Atlantic coast, including the canals of Poitou-Charente.

The Loire cuts a swathe across the centre of France, linking the important cities of Angers, Tours and Orléans; the last was the country's artistic and intellectual capital in medieval times. Strung out between the three are the famous royal châteaux, including the Renaissance jewels of Chambord and Chenonceau. Some of our Loire hotels are housed in châteaux that are cast in the same mould: **Château de Pray** at Amboise (page 116), **Château des Briottières** at Champigné (page 123), **Château de Rochecotte** at St-Patrice (page 141) and **Domaine de la Tortinière** at Montbazon-en-Touraine (page 130). They might look intimidating from the outside, but are generally run with the kind of warm informality that particularly appeals to us. You can also stay at the splendid yet welcoming **Château de Chissay** (tel 02 54 32 32 01).

Just because you're in the Loire, however, doesn't mean that you have to stay in a château and there are many more intimate charming small hotels as well: for example, the family-friendly **Manoir de Clénord** at Mont-près-Chambord (page 129), **Le Bon Laboureur**, an extended coaching inn at Chenonceaux (page 124), **La Tonnellerie**, a solid village house with a country atmosphere in Tavers near Beaugency (page 142), cosy **L'Auberge de Combreux** (tel 02 38 46 89 89), **Moulin Fleuri** at Montbazon, a 16thC watermill (tel 02 47 26 01 12), or, further south on the Indre near Loches, another converted mill, **Le Moulin L'Etang** (page 128).

There are a couple of magnificent châteaux hotels, **de La Verrerie** (at Oizon, page 134) and its smaller neighbour, **d'Ivoy** (at Ivoy le Pré, page 127) to the east on the fringes of the Massif Central. To the south there's another pocket of hotels around Châteauroux including the charming **L'Hermitage** on the river at Buzançais (page 121), renowned for its food.

Travelling south, in the Limousin, where the hills are gentle precursors to the dramatic cliffs and gorges of the Massif Central, we recommend another couple of châteaux: turreted **Renaissance De Nieuil**, (page 133), which has been in the same family for years, and **Ste-Catherine** at Montbron (page 131), once owned by Empress Joséphine, and a relaxed place to stay, more like a country house than a château.

Finally, to the west, where great rollers break on the long sandy beaches of the windswept Atlantic coast, we have a clutch of hotels, from a simple *auberge* in Pons (**Auberge Pontoise**, page 144) to a delightful *chambres d'hôte*, **Domaine de Rennebourg** at St-Denis-du-Pin (page 137). There is also the rustic riverside **Auberge de la Rivière** at Fontenay-le Comte (tel 02 51 52 32 15) and the informal **Hostellerie de l'Abbaye** in medieval Celles-sur-Belle (tel 05 49 32 93 32). Further north the glorious **Château de la Gressière** (tel 02 51 74 60 06) has an idyllic setting above the sea.

THE WEST

AMBOISE

MANOIR LES MINIMES
~ RIVERSIDE CHATEAU ~

34, Quai Charles Guinot, 37400 Amboise (Indre-et-Loire)
TEL 02 47 30 40 40 **FAX** 02 47 30 40 77
E-MAIL manoir-les-minimes@wanadoo.fr **WEBSITE** www.manoirlesminimes.com

THE SETTING IS PERFECT – an 18thC manor proudly facing one of the widest stretches of the Loire – the service impeccable and the bedrooms among the most elegant we have seen in the region. Our reporter worried that it was perhaps a touch too polished, but the house and its setting won her over with their peace and their charm.

The bedrooms each have their own character, and the bathrooms are enormous: havens of white, with shining surfaces and expansive towels. The furnishings throughout are a wonderful mix of antique mahogany *armoires* (if you're looking for a pleasant diversion, search for the secret drawers), Chinese vases and well-placed 18thC landscapes, with a couple of welcome eccentricities such as a harp in the drawing room. The owner, Eric Deforges, certainly cares about his guests, and the 14 rooms make the hotel small enough to remain intimate despite the polish. We felt most at home in the traditional bedrooms on the third floor, with their exposed dark oak beams, intricately carved wardrobes and simple cream carpets. If you're feeling flush, the corner suite (No. 10) is the most spectacular, with views from two sides over château and river.

There is no restaurant, but you are within walking distance of the centre of Amboise. Breakfast on the terrace is recommended: make sure you try the plump, warm *pain au chocolat*. The hotel is exclusively non-smoking.

NEARBY Tours (25 km); Blois (34 km); Loire châteaux; golf.
LOCATION on the banks of the Loire, on the D751; car parking
FOOD breakfast
PRICE €€
ROOMS 14; 13 double and twin, one suite, all with bath or shower; all rooms have phone, TV, air conditioning, hairdrier **FACILITIES** sitting room, dining room, terrace
CREDIT CARDS AE, DC, MC, V **CHILDREN** accepted
DISABLED access possible to one bedroom **PETS** accepted
CLOSED Feb, sometimes Nov
PROPRIETOR Eric Deforges

THE WEST

AMBOISE

CHATEAU DE PRAY

~ CHATEAU HOTEL ~

route de Chargé, 37400 Amboise (Indre-et-Loire)
TEL 02 47 57 23 67 **FAX** 02 47 57 32 50
E-MAIL chateau.depray@wanadoo.fr **WEBSITE** www.praycastel.online.fr

IF YOU ARE FOND OF Loire wines and, by and large, would prefer not to walk up and down hills, then the main road between Amboise and Chargé is just the place for a stroll. Every few yards there are *caves* hollowed from the soft stone of the bluffs that line the course of the river. Further back, and higher, the Château de Pray's Renaissance façade looks down towards the river, flanked by two stout 13thC turrets. The effect is a little like the belle of the ball sandwiched between a pair of dowager aunts. Managed by chef Ludovic Laurenty and his wife, this is an agreeable, friendly spot in a sur-prisingly pastoral setting. Monsieur Laurenty's short, seasonal menus, pre-sented in a dining room with an imposing stone fireplace, are a delight and draw in not only locals but also guests staying at a neighbouring *manoir* that has no restaurant of its own.

The bedrooms, all with excellent bathrooms, are smart and appealing. They are not furnished in heavy baronial style (although two or three of them have four-posters) but all have their fair share of antique furniture and walls hung with paintings that are appreciably better than average. The immaculate courtyard is a suntrap and the lawns below the château look a likely place for that aperitif you've been thinking about all day.

~

NEARBY Tours (25 km); Blois (34 km); Loire châteaux; golf.
LOCATION 3 km E of Amboise on the D751 beyond junction with the N10; car parking
FOOD breakfast, lunch, dinner
PRICE €€€-€€€€
ROOMS 19; 13 double, 3 twin, 2 triple, one family, all with bath or shower; all rooms have phone, TV, hairdrier
FACILITIES sitting room, dining room, bar, terrace, garden, swimming pool
CREDIT CARDS AE, DC, MC, V **CHILDREN** accepted
DISABLED access difficult
PETS not accepted
CLOSED early Jan to mid-Feb; restaurant Tue dinner, Wed
MANAGER Ludovic Laurenty

THE WEST

ANGLES SUR L'ANGLIN

LE RELAIS DU LYON D'OR

~ VILLAGE INN ~

4 rue d'Enfer, 86260 Angles sur l'Anglin (Vienne)
TEL 05 49 48 32 53 **FAX** 05 49 84 02 28
E-MAIL thoreau@lyondor.com **WEBSITE** www.lyondor.com

ANGLES SUR L'ANGLIN IS, by any measure, a very attractive village indeed. Perched on a hill, its medieval houses look out over the substantial ruins of both castle and abbey to the river below. Carvings discovered recently in caves near the river show that people have been coming here for around 15,000 years but these early visitors' misfortune was that Guillaume and Heather Thoreau didn't arrive until 1994. They took a semi-derelict post house and transformed it, inside and out, making a delightful hotel with a highly successful restaurant that beats any big-city equivalent with the freshness and quality of its (local) ingredients, and wins the service match hands down with its warmth and friendliness. A large room with a high, beamed ceiling and a baronial stone fireplace at one end, it is still warm and intimate. Local wines are well represented on the short, excellent wine list, and there is a wide selection of half bottles so you can ring the changes.

The decoration is Heather's department, and her art and influence show in every room, where the original architectural features have been painstakingly restored. The bedrooms are all different, decorated in warm colours and with fine fabrics, and all reveal Heather's skill with paint-effects (she runs courses). The bathrooms are works of art themselves.

~

NEARBY La Roche-Posay (12 km); jardin des 'Rosiers'; Poitiers (51 km).
LOCATION in centre of village; car parking
FOOD breakfast, lunch, dinner
PRICE €-€€
ROOMS 11; 8 double and twin, one triple, 2 family suites, 5 with bath, 6 with shower; all rooms have phone, TV
FACILITIES sitting room, restaurant, health centre
CREDIT CARDS AE, MC, V **CHILDREN** accepted
DISABLED one specially adapted suite
PETS accepted **CLOSED** Jan to Mar
PROPRIETORS Heather and Guillaume Thoreau

THE WEST

BANNEGON

AUBERGE DU MOULIN DE CHAMERON

∽ CONVERTED MILL ∽

Bannegon, 18210 Charenton-du-Cher (Cher)
TEL 02 48 61 83 80 **FAX** 02 48 61 84 92
E-MAIL moulindechameron@wanadoo.fr **WEBSITE** www.moulindechameron.fr.st

THE MOULIN DE CHAMÉRON is a curious animal, and difficult to categorize. At the heart of it is the original 18thC watermill – now a combination of country museum, displaying ancient tools of the trade, and charmingly intimate and traditional restaurant, with the old fireplace as its focal point. But the bedrooms are housed across the garden in a pair of unremarkable modern buildings of rather towny appearance – comfortable, but thin on charm. So should it be thought of as a restaurant-with-rooms? We think to do so would be to underestimate its appeal as a place to stay for more than a one-night stopover (though one reporter found the peace marred by the noise of early morning departures) – at least in summer, when the wooded garden and neat pool come into play, along with the restaurant's romantic tented dining terrace beside the mill stream. Jean Merilleau's cooking is excellent: dinner might include trout served with a *fondue* of endives, oxtail cooked in wine, followed by a chocolate *fondant aux aromates*, and we've heard that there is a well-stocked and wide-ranging cellar.

Try for one of the bedrooms with its own small terrace, where in fine weather you can breakfast to birdsong. ∽

NEARBY Meillant castle (25 km); Noirlac abbey (30 km).
LOCATION in countryside between Bannegon and Neuilly, 40 km SE of Bourges; car parking
FOOD breakfast, lunch, dinner
PRICE €-€€
ROOMS 14; 8 double, 5 twin, 8 with bath, 5 with shower, one family with bath; all rooms have phone, TV
FACILITIES 2 sitting rooms, bar, 2 dining rooms, garden, swimming pool, table tennis, fishing **CREDIT CARDS** AE, MC, V **CHILDREN** welcome
DISABLED no special facilities **PETS** accepted
CLOSED mid-Nov to early Mar; restaurant low season Mon and Tue lunch
PROPRIETORS M. Rommel and M. Merilleau

THE WEST

LE BLANC

DOMAINE DE L'ETAPE

～ MANOR HOUSE HOTEL ～

route de Bélâbre, 36300 Le Blanc (Indre)
TEL 02 54 37 18 02 **FAX** 02 54 37 75 59
E-MAIL domainetape@wanadoo.fr **WEBSITE** www.domaineetape.com

THE DOMAINE DE L'ETAPE IS, quite literally, at the end of the road deep enough in the countryside to satisfy the most desperate need to escape the city. A 19thC mansion in 250 hectares of woods and fields, it also has a large lake, which you're welcome to fish, and, three minutes' walk away, the outbuildings of a home farm, complete with horses and chickens. All this is presided over by Mme Seiller with the kind of genial tranquillity that comes of years of practice (more than 30 of them in her case). The house has been in her family for 125 years, and when she started the hotel she had just seven bedrooms. There are now 35 but within that total there are three distinct types. Those in the hotel itself are undoubtedly the best on offer, comfortably and informally decorated. Then there is a pleasant two-storeyed modern building, with rooms on the ground floor that open directly to the garden. Lastly there are some very rustic rooms down on the farm, which are long on character, but short on comfort. Hard-wearing and cheap, they tend to be popular with families. Back in the main building there is a panelled dining room that opens out to the terrace and a handsome Louis Philippe *salon*. Family friendly.

～

NEARBY La Roche-Posay (30 km); jardin des 'Rosiers'; Poitiers (60 km); golf; canoeing.
LOCATION 5 km SE of Le Blanc off the D10 to Bélâbre; car parking
FOOD breakfast, lunch, dinner
PRICE €-€€
ROOMS 35; 14 double, 17 twin, 3 triple, one family, 30 with bath, 5 with shower; all rooms have phone, TV, minibar, hairdrier
FACILITIES sitting room, 2 dining rooms, terrace, garden, fishing, riding
CREDIT CARDS AE, DC, MC, V **CHILDREN** accepted
DISABLED access possible
PETS accepted
CLOSED never
PROPRIETOR Mme Seiller

THE WEST

BRIOLLAY

CHATEAU DE NOIRIEUX

~ MANOR HOUSE HOTEL ~

26 route du Moulin, 49125 Briollay (Maine-et-Loire)
TEL 02 41 42 50 05 **FAX** 02 41 37 91 00
E-MAIL noirieux@relaischateaux.com **WEBSITE** www.chateaudenoirieux.com

'A GEM OF A HOTEL, situated at the western end of the Loire châteaux-belt; whereas most hotels on the Loire tourist trail are over-priced and under-enthusiastic, this one gets most things right and is thoroughly professional in the nicest way.' So says one of our most conscientious reporters. Since he's started so well, we'll let him finish.

'Dating from the 17th century, with art deco additions in 1927, it opened as a hotel in 1991. It is set in magnificent grounds, with views down to the Loire. It is outstandingly comfortable; a good test was that during three days of almost continuous rain we always felt cosseted. The *salons* are beautifully furnished and comfortable, the dining room light and airy, with a terrace for fine weather. Bedrooms are split between the main building and two others – all well furnished, some quite opulently.

'The cuisine is inventive and of a high standard. The wine list is exemplary, with prices that don't take your breath away. We received a warm welcome, and all the staff were unfailingly helpful and courteous. The château is not cheap, but is excellent value in every respect.'

~

NEARBY Angers (12 km); Loire châteaux; golf.
LOCATION in countryside off D52 (junction 14 off A11); car parking
FOOD breakfast, lunch, dinner
PRICE €€€-€€€€
ROOMS 19 double with bath; some rooms have phone, TV, minibar, hairdrier
FACILITIES sitting room/bar, dining room, Jacuzzi, garden, swimming pool, tennis
CREDIT CARDS AE, DC, MC, V
CHILDREN accepted
DISABLED 2 ground floor bedrooms
PETS accepted
CLOSED Feb, Nov; restaurant Sun dinner, Mon mid-Oct to May
MANAGERS Gérard and Anja Côme

THE WEST

BUZANCAIS

L'HERMITAGE
~ RIVERSIDE HOTEL ~

route d'Argy, 36500 Buzançais (Indre)
TEL 02 54 84 03 90 **FAX** 02 54 02 13 19

On the otherwise unremarkable fringe of Buzançais, with its back to the road, lies a small, charming creeper-clad hotel. After turning into the yard (lockable garages are available) you walk under a short, covered land bridge into delightful and unexpectedly large grounds. Beyond the gravel outside the front door, lawns slope gently down to the shade of the weeping willows on the bank of the Indre – you are welcome to bring your fishing-pole and try your luck.

Owned and run for years with hospitality and flair by chef Claude Sureau and his wife, the hotel was sold in 2004. We trust that the new owner, Mme Sainson, is following in her predecessor's footsteps, producing menus that offer tremendous value, attracting as many locals as visitors, and varying not just from season to season but also from day to day depending on what looks tempting in the market. The hotel has two dining rooms, for summer and winter, with the land bridge connecting the summer dining room, in its own attractive (air conditioned) garden pavilion, to the main building. It has a small terrace for those who would rather dine outside. The bedrooms are quite modest in size, but light and fresh and most have a view over the gardens. More reports please.

NEARBY Châteauroux (27 km); Loches (45 km); golf; riding.
LOCATION on outskirts of town on D11 to Argy, beside the Indre; car parking
FOOD breakfast, lunch, dinner
PRICE €
ROOMS 14; 6 double, 6 twin, 6 with bath, 6 with shower, 2 single with shower; all rooms have phone, TV, hairdrier
FACILITIES sitting area, 2 dining rooms, terrace, garden, fishing
CREDIT CARDS MC, V
CHILDREN accepted
DISABLED not suitable **PETS** accepted
CLOSED 2 weeks mid-Sep
PROPRIETOR Alice Sainson

THE WEST

CANGEY

LE FLEURAY
~ MANOR HOUSE HOTEL ~

Cangey, 37530 Amboise (Indre-et-Loire)
TEL 02 47 56 09 25 **FAX** 02 47 56 93 97
E-MAIL lefleurayhotel@wanadoo.fr **WEBSITE** www.lefleurayhotel.com

READERS CONTINUE TO WRITE to us in praise of this 'delightful place' whose two key attractions are a warm welcome and relaxed atmosphere, courtesy of the Newingtons, the lively and committed English owners; and the peaceful, indeed isolated, rural setting in open fields. (Keep faith in the signposting from Cangey – it's more than 6 km outside the village.) Combined, these qualities are at a premium in the Loire (major sights and vineyards are within half an hour) and together with fair prices for prettily and freshly decorated rooms with views (the best with small outdoor sitting areas) explain the place's obvious popularity. There is a handsome new conservatory and a particularly attractive terrace for summer dining, and when we visited in high season there was a good-humoured buzz in the dining room from a cross-section of nationalities. The staff, several English students on long vacation, were at full stretch. Don't expect a 'French eating experience'. Despite positive readers' letters about the cooking, we have found in the past that the menu changes little, and that the food, though satisfying and well-presented, lacks panache.

At certain times, guests are expected to eat dinner in the hotel – check when booking if the obligatory half pension terms are operating.

~

NEARBY Châteaux: Amboise, Chaumont, Chenonceaux, Tours; Vouvray (vineyards).
LOCATION on D74, 12 km NE of Amboise, 7 km from A10 exit 18; car parking
FOOD breakfast, dinner
PRICE €€
ROOMS 15 double and family, all with bath or shower; all rooms have phone, hairdrier
FACILITIES sitting room, restaurant, terrace, garden
CREDIT CARDS MC, V
CHILDREN welcome
DISABLED specially adapted rooms available **PETS** accepted
CLOSED late Feb, late Oct to early Nov, Christmas and New Year
PROPRIETORS Newington family

THE WEST

CHAMPIGNE

CHATEAU DES BRIOTTIERES

~ CHATEAU HOTEL ~

49330 Champigné (Maine-et-Loire)
TEL 02 41 42 00 02 **FAX** 02 41 42 01 55
E-MAIL briottieres@wanadoo.fr **WEBSITE** www.briottieres.com

LIFE'S HURLY-BURLY has never made it through the gates, let alone up the wooded drive, of this serene château. Two hundred years of unbroken ownership by the same family have kept the atmosphere as well as the contents and appearance of this house wonderfully intact. François de Valbray, the present relaxed owner, has thought of everybody. If you want the undiluted charm and grace of the château, you can stay in it, dine beneath the gaze of the ancestors (by arrangement), relax in the *grand salon* and generally use the place like home (including a game of billiards after dinner if you're so inclined). Bedrooms and bathrooms vary in size but all offer style and comfort.

If you're travelling in a party, or are worried about how your children and your blood pressure will thrive in this antique-laden environment, then take some or all of the old *fruitier*: this thoroughly comfortable house is close to the main building, and has its own more utilitarian sitting room. Outside there are 40 hectares of woods, lawn and lake to protect you from the farmland beyond. If you just want to get married, you can take the imposing old stable block but expect to have to arrive along the back drive and leave (quietly) the same way to avoid disturbing other guests. A gem.

~

NEARBY Angers (24 km); abbeys of Solesmes and Fontevrault; Loire châteaux; golf.
LOCATION 3.5 km N of Champigné on the D190; car parking
FOOD breakfast, dinner (by arrangement)
PRICE ©©©-©©©©
ROOMS 15; 10 double and twin with bath, 5 double and twin with shared bath in *gîte*; 10 rooms have phone
FACILITIES sitting rooms, billiards room/library, dining room, terrace, garden, swimming pool
CREDIT CARDS AE, DC, MC, V **CHILDREN** accepted
DISABLED access difficult
PETS accepted **CLOSED** New Year, Feb
PROPRIETORS François and Hedwige de Valbray

THE WEST

CHENONCEAUX

LE BON LABOUREUR

~ VILLAGE HOTEL ~

6 rue du Docteur-Bretonneau, 37150 Chenonceaux (Indre-et-Loire)
TEL 02 47 23 90 02 **FAX** 02 47 23 82 01
E-MAIL laboureur@wanadoo.fr **WEBSITE** www.bonlaboureur.com

AFTER 200 YEARS OR SO as close neighbours of the Château de Chenonceau, the Jeudi family knows a thing or two about receiving visitors. The first priority, of course, is to have somewhere to put them. So, as the popularity of this 18thC coaching inn increased (the châteaux of Amboise, Chambord and Chaumont are all close by), it has absorbed several other buildings, expanding sideways and even across to the other side of the road. A swimming pool in the pleasant garden and a tree-shaded terrace for outside dining have increased its appeal, and two sitting rooms and a capacious bar offer plenty of uncrowded space indoors. A pair of dining rooms, one an elegant period room and the other a more relaxed area, gives you a chance to ring the changes and, if travelling with children, to lengthen their leashes a little.

It would be difficult to shorten the supply chain for many of the vegetables used in the hotel's competent kitchen: their own kitchen garden is right next door. Several of the generally light, attractive bedrooms are well set up as family rooms, with those in 'The Manor' furthest from the general bustle of the hotel. An amiable spot.

NEARBY Tours (35 km); Amboise (14 km); Loire châteaux; golf.
LOCATION in the middle of the village, 200 m from the château; car parking
FOOD breakfast, lunch, dinner
PRICE €€€
ROOMS 28; 24 double and twin, 4 apartments, all with bath or shower; all rooms have phone, TV; some have air conditioning
FACILITIES sitting room, 2 dining rooms, bar, terrace, garden, swimming pool, helipad
CREDIT CARDS AE, DC, MC, V **CHILDREN** welcome
DISABLED 2 specially adapted rooms **PETS** accepted
CLOSED mid-Nov to mid-Dec, early Jan to mid-Feb; restaurant mid-Oct to Apr Wed lunch, Thu
PROPRIETORS M. and Mme Jeudi

THE WEST

CHINON

HOTEL DIDEROT
～ TOWN MANSION ～

4 rue Buffon, 37500 Chinon (Indre-et-Loire)
TEL 02 47 93 18 87 **FAX** 02 47 93 37 10
E-MAIL hoteldiderot@wanadoo.fr **WEBSITE** www.hoteldiderot.com

SURPRISINGLY FEW HOTELS have been in these pages since the first edition while generating a steady stream of entirely complimentary reports. 'Excellent' and 'superb' are typical verdicts of the Diderot, to which most visitors can't wait to return. Although the popular French-Cypriot owner, Theo Kazamias, sold the hotel to Laurent and Françoise Dutheil in April 2003, little seems to have changed here, not even the moderate prices. Laurent worked for M. Kazamias for seven years, while Françoise was Chef de Réception at the Château de Marçay, a smart Relais et Châteaux hotel down the road. They have carried out some renovation, but have ensured its spirit remains untouched. Although we haven't visited yet, the Dutheils sound just as charming and helpful as their predecessors.

Creeper-covered and white-shuttered, it is a handsome town house set in a courtyard. Its exotic collection of trees – including fig and banana – makes the courtyard an appealing spot for sitting out and there are plenty of tables and chairs to encourage you. Breakfast (served on the shady terrace or in a rustic room with tiled floor and massive beams) is exceptionally tasty – thanks to Laurent's home-made preserves (more than 50 varieties), which you can buy to take home with you. Bedrooms are simply furnished, but are spotlessly clean and some have fine views.

～

NEARBY châteaux: Azay-le-Rideau (20 km), Langeais (30 km).
LOCATION in middle of town; limited car parking
FOOD breakfast
PRICE €
ROOMS 28; 26 double and twin, 2 family, all with bath or shower; all have phone
FACILITIES bar, breakfast room, courtyard
CREDIT CARDS AE, DC, MC, V
CHILDREN welcome
DISABLED some ground floor bedrooms **PETS** not accepted
CLOSED one week Christmas, mid-Jan to mid-Feb
PROPRIETORS Laurent and Françoise Dutheil

THE WEST

CHOUZÉ-SUR-LOIRE

LE CHATEAU DES REAUX

~ CHATEAU HOTEL ~

Chouzé-sur-Loire, 37140 Bourgueil (Indre-et-Loire)
TEL 02 47 95 14 40 **FAX** 02 47 95 18 34
E-MAIL reaux@club-internet.fr **WEBSITE** www.chateaureaux.net

ON THE NORTH BANK of the Loire, between its confluences with the Indre and Vienne, this was the first Renaissance château to be built in the Valley of the Kings. The builder, Jean Briçonnet, was the first mayor of Tours and his family went on to build Chenonceau and Azay-le-Rideau. Built on the foundations of a 1,000-year-old keep, and surrounded by a moat, alternating brickwork with the white stone of Touraine produced its startling red and white geometric exterior. The plainer neo-classical element was added some 250 years later and the most recent addition, by the great-great-grandfather of the present owners, reverted to the original chequerboard design.

Jean-Luc and Florence de Bouillé obviously cherish this national monument (just look at the care lavished on the glorious *salons*) and have encyclopædic knowledge of its history. Bedrooms may vary in size but not in authenticity, their old, beamed interiors freshened rather than obscured by modern decoration. Whatever else you do, take a walk up the magnificent staircase inside one of the towers – perhaps to work up an appetite before settling down to a dinner designed to show you the best produce the region can offer (only available for groups of 10 people or more, and must be booked in advance). There are four more modest bedrooms in a cottage in the grounds – at cheaper prices.

~

NEARBY Chinon (13 km); Tours (38 km); Saumur (26 km); Loire châteaux; golf; riding; canoeing.
LOCATION just E of Chouzé-sur-Loire off the N152, 4 km S of Bourgueil; car parking
FOOD breakfast; lunch and dinner for groups by arrangement
PRICE €€-€€€
ROOMS 16; 12 double and twin, 4 suites, all with bath; all rooms have phone, TV, hairdrier **FACILITIES** sitting room, dining room, bar, meeting room, garden, tennis
CREDIT CARDS AE, DC, MC, V **CHILDREN** accepted
DISABLED access difficult **PETS** not accepted **CLOSED** Christmas
PROPRIETORS Jean-Luc and Florence de Bouillé

THE WEST

IVOY-LE-PRE

CHATEAU D'IVOY

~ CHATEAU HOTEL ~

18380 Ivoy-le-Pré (Cher)
TEL 02 48 58 85 01 **FAX** 02 48 58 85 02
E-MAIL chateau.divoy@wanadoo.fr **WEBSITE** http://perso.wanadoo.fr/chateau.divoy

O N A DAMP, COLD DAY at the beginning of April, at the end of a long wet drive through the woods that surround it, and despite its 400-odd years of age, this château was warm. That makes it one of a very select band indeed and also signals the care that Mme Gouëffon-de Vaivre takes with her guests' comfort. Built in the early 16th century, it was home to Mary Stuart's purser, who fled here from Edinburgh after Lord Darnley's murder, and later to General Lord Drummond, commander of the Royal Ecossais, and his family. All the bedrooms are large and they, and their superb bathrooms, look out over the lawns and park at the back of the château. Like the rest of the rooms, they are all stunning examples of Mme Gouëffon-de Vaivre's art: she is a professional interior designer whose first task was to rescue the dining room from the jungle established there by the previous owner as a habitat for his beloved insects. Ferns have now given way to Spode and hearty breakfasts.

Each bedroom is named and themed accordingly. 'Kipling' for example has colonial furniture surrounding a Victorian Anglo-Indian bed draped with a mosquito net. You can almost hear the distant skirl of pipes as you walk into 'Lord Drummond' with its ceiling-scraping four-poster. Downstairs, a grand *salon* and library are yours to enjoy.

~

NEARBY Aubigny-sur-Nère (19 km); Bourges (47 km); Gien (48 km); golf; canoeing.
LOCATION off D12, 5 km E of La Chapelle d'Angillon, through a park, 300 m on the right after the church; car parking
FOOD breakfast
PRICE €€€
ROOMS 6; 5 double, 4 with bath, one with shower, one twin with bath; all rooms have phone, TV **FACILITIES** sitting room/bar, library, breakfast room, terrace, garden, swimming pool, croquet, helipad
CREDIT CARDS MC, V **CHILDREN** accepted over 14
DISABLED access difficult **PETS** not accepted **CLOSED** never
PROPRIETORS M. and Mme Gouëffon-de Vaivre

THE WEST

LOCHES

LE MOULIN L'ETANG

~ CONVERTED MILL ~

Chanceaux-près-Loches, 37600 Loches (Indre-et-Loire)
TEL 02 47 59 15 10
E-MAIL moulinletang37@aol.com **WEBSITE** www.moulinetang.com

SUE HUTTON AND ANDREW PAGE have moved mill. They found this 16thC watermill by accident and fell in love with it. We haven't had an opportunity to visit yet, but we know it must be pretty special to entice them away from the undeniable attractions of Le Moulin (page 147) just 12 km away. Le Moulin L'Etang stands in a 3-hectare wooded garden containing a large lake, waterfall, river and the original mill pond, which has been converted into a natural swimming pool. With their usual division of responsibilities, Sue has transformed the interior with flair, filling both public rooms and bedrooms with antique furniture, paintings and rugs, complemented by elegant pale colour schemes, whilst Andrew continues to cook dinner with skill and care.

Sue and Andrew treat their guests as if they had just struggled ashore after a shipwreck and needed quickly, but in no particular order, a drink, a bath, hot soup, sticking plaster for their cuts, another drink, food, maps, news from home, advice on local shops, shampoo, weather forecast – and just about anything else you can think of. And, as if that weren't enough, like skilled tailors they size you up before deciding which of their four appealing, comfortable rooms would suit you best.

~

NEARBY Loches (2 km); Tours (45 km); Poitiers (74 km).
LOCATION 2 km N of Loches off the N143; car parking
FOOD breakfast, dinner
PRICE €
ROOMS 4 double with bath
FACILITIES sitting room, dining room, terrace, garden, swimming pond
CREDIT CARDS not accepted
CHILDREN accepted
DISABLED not suitable
PETS accepted
CLOSED Dec to Feb
PROPRIETORS Andrew Page and Sue Hutton

THE WEST

MONT-PRES-CHAMBORD

MANOIR DE CLENORD

～ COUNTRY BED-AND-BREAKFAST ～

route de Clénord, 41250 Mont-près-Chambord (Loir-et-Cher)
TEL 02 54 70 41 62 **FAX** 02 54 70 33 99
E-MAIL info@clenord.com **WEBSITE** www.clenord.com

A QUIET, FAMILY-FRIENDLY 18thC manor house, surrounded by 25 hectares of woods, with a little river nearby and an attractive swimming pool, makes the Manoir de Clénord a popular spot with people keen to avoid the formality of many of the hotels in the region. The river, Le Beuvron, is a tributary of the Loire and took its name from the native beavers which still live along its course.

Christiane Clément-d'Armont has recently moved to the South of France, handing over the reins of the business to her niece Jacqueline Denormandie and her husband Pascal, who aim to make their guests feel as welcome and at home as Christiane always did. Guests have the run of the house, including the use of a large drawing room (with an open fire in winter) furnished with the emphasis more on comfort than on show, which really sets the style for the rest of the house. The bedrooms are large, for the most part, with fine, old, solid furniture of the sort one's grandparents might have in their spare bedroom – no items of frail elegance playing hostage to childish misfortune.

If you plan to stay here, do something about it in good time: there are plenty of regulars who fill up the diary early in the season.

～

NEARBY Blois (9 km); Loire châteaux; Tours (69 km).
LOCATION in woods 4 km SW of Mont-près-Chambord on the road to Clénord; car parking
FOOD breakfast
PRICE €€
ROOMS 8; 5 double and twin, 3 suites, all with bath or shower
FACILITIES sitting room, breakfast room, terrace, garden
CREDIT CARDS MC, V
CHILDREN accepted
DISABLED access difficult **PETS** accepted
CLOSED mid-Nov to mid-Mar
PROPRIETOR Christiane Clément-d'Armont

THE WEST

DOMAINE DE LA TORTINIERE
~ CHATEAU HOTEL ~

37250 Montbazon-en-Touraine (Indre-et-Loire)
TEL 02 47 34 35 00 **FAX** 02 47 65 95 70
E-MAIL contact@tortiniere.com **WEBSITE** www.tortiniere.com

PERCHED HIGH ABOVE the Indre, this attractive, turreted château has a clear view across its own sloping meadows and the river to the tower of Montbazon, and is close to the line of the old Roman road that led from there to Tours. Built in 1866 by the widow of Armand Dalloz (who created France's civil code), it took its name from the old manor that preceded it and first became a hotel in 1955. It is run with charm and energy by Xavier Olivereau and his wife Anne, who show the kind of attention to detail and genuine concern for the comfort of their guests that is almost a forgotten art elsewhere.

The ground floor hall and *salon* are panelled and plastered, with parquet floors dotted with oriental rugs, empire chairs and generously upholstered, comfortable sofas. The winter restaurant shares this floor and has a cosy section inside one of the house's twin towers. The other tower hides a winding staircase and an underground passage to the spare and cool summer restaurant in the old orangery beneath a formal terrace. In dry weather the tables drift outside under awnings to get the full benefit of the magical setting. Bedrooms are a satisfying combination of taste and money: both elegant and comfortable. Some are not in the château proper but these are, if anything, of an even higher standard.

~

NEARBY Tours (9 km); Chenonceaux (33 km); Amboise (38 km).
LOCATION 2 km N of Montbazon on the N10 towards Tours and left on the D287; car parking
FOOD breakfast, lunch, dinner
PRICE €€
ROOMS 29; 22 double and twin, 7 suites, all with bath; all rooms have phone, TV, hairdrier; some have air conditioning
FACILITIES sitting room, 2 dining rooms, terrace, garden, swimming pool, tennis, fishing **CREDIT CARDS** DC, MC, V **CHILDREN** accepted
DISABLED 2 specially adapted rooms **PETS** accepted
CLOSED late Dec to Mar
PROPRIETORS Olivereau family

THE WEST

MONTBRON

CHATEAU SAINTE-CATHERINE

～ CHATEAU HOTEL ～

route de Marthon, 16220 Montbron (Charente)
TEL 05 45 23 60 03 **FAX** 05 45 70 72 00
E-MAIL chateau.st.catherine@free.fr **WEBSITE** www.chateausaintecatherine.com

THE TARDOIRE VALLEY is a pretty one, but the area around Montbron, east of Angoulême, is off the beaten tourist track and we presume this is why we hear so little from readers about this fine old house, once the residence of the Empress Joséphine.

The approach, along a winding drive through splendid wooded grounds, is appropriately imposing and the house – built in a pale, irregular stone – looks handsome but austere. Inside it is a different story: despite fine furnishings and immaculate housekeeping, there is none of the expected pretension, and a relaxed, informal atmosphere prevails.

Rooms are decorated and furnished with proper regard for both style and comfort: the dining rooms (one leads into the other) have tapestries on the walls, and a carved wooden mantlepiece stands over an old fireplace; the two sitting rooms are inviting and relaxing. Most of the individually furnished and thoroughly comfortable bedrooms have views of the surrounding parkland; they do vary in size, and the prices reflect this. One menu and an 'interesting' *carte* are offered, where the majority of dishes are from nearby Périgord. There has been a change of owner since our last edition, so reports please.

～

NEARBY Angoulême (30 km); Brie (40 km); Rochechouart (40 km).
LOCATION in park off D16, 4 km SW of Montbron, E of Angoulême; car parking
FOOD breakfast, lunch, dinner
PRICE €€€
ROOMS 14; 10 double and twin, 4 suites, all with bath or shower; all rooms have phone, TV
FACILITIES 2 sitting rooms, 2 dining rooms, bar, garden, swimming pool
CREDIT CARDS AE, DC, MC, V
CHILDREN accepted
DISABLED no special facilities **PETS** accepted
CLOSED never
PROPRIETOR Mme Crocquet

THE WEST

MONTRICHARD

CHATEAU DE LA MENAUDIERE

~ CHATEAU HOTEL ~

BP15-Chissay-en-Touraine, 41401 Montrichard (Loir-et-Cher)
TEL 02 54 71 23 45 **FAX** 02 54 71 34 58
E-MAIL chat-menaudiere@wanadoo.fr **WEBSITE** www.chateaumenaudiere.com

THERE SEEM TO BE FEW Loire châteaux that are not connected in some way with Jean Briçonnet, the first mayor of Tours, and Menaudière is not one of them. Built originally in 1443 on a rocky outcrop known as La Kaërie (which gave the château its first name), it replaced a manor owned by Briçonnet's family and continued in their ownership until 1624. This association also puts Menaudière in the heartland of the Loire châteaux, with Chenonceau, Amboise, Chambord and Chaumont all within striking distance. It has had its ups and downs, and, architecturally speaking, its additions and subtractions. One surviving element which preserves its charm is a stout, round tower, now completely divorced from the main building, which has three bedrooms served by a stone spiral staircase.

Elsewhere the fairly frequent changes of ownership have gradually worn away the original contents of the château so, although the walls are historic, there are few ancestors gazing down from them, and some of the more modern furniture sits a little uneasily in its ancient surroundings. However, the staff are friendly and efficient, the bedrooms spacious and well equipped, and the two in-house restaurants offer the hungry traveller a wide range of choices supported by an extensive wine list.

~

NEARBY Chenonceaux (11 km); Loire châteaux; golf.
LOCATION to the right off the D115, 2 km from Montrichard towards Amboise; car parking
FOOD breakfast, lunch, dinner
PRICE €€
ROOMS 27 double, twin and triple, 20 with bath, 7 with shower; all rooms have phone, TV, minibar
FACILITIES sitting room, 2 dining rooms, meeting room, bar, terrace, garden, swimming pool, tennis **CREDIT CARDS** AE, DC, MC, V **CHILDREN** accepted
DISABLED not suitable **PETS** accepted
CLOSED mid-Nov to Mar; restaurant Sun dinner, Mon low season
MANAGER Geneviève Segui

THE WEST

NIEUIL

CHATEAU DE NIEUIL

~ CHATEAU HOTEL ~

route de Fontafie, 16270 Nieuil (Charente)
TEL 05 45 71 36 38 **FAX** 05 45 71 46 45
E-MAIL chateaunieuilhotel@wanadoo.fr **WEBSITE** www.chateaunieuilhotel.com

'OUR ROOM WAS extremely comfortable, even though it was one of their smaller ones, and one of the best-value rooms of our holiday,' says a reporter on this fairy-tale Renaissance château, making the point that high prices can be worth paying if you get something special in return. Steep-roofed, turreted, and surrounded by parkland stretching away beyond its formal garden and ornamental 'moat', it is the picture of elegance. Inside, it is appropriately furnished, with exquisite antiques, porcelain and tapestries. Some of the bedrooms are exceedingly grand.

It could be embarrassingly pretentious. But the delight of the place is that it is not at all pretentious or intimidating. The château has been in the Bodinaud family for over 100 years, and the hotel is very much a family concern. Mme Bodinaud (an ex-design lecturer) does all the interior decoration and oversees the cooking, earning a Michelin star for her imaginative food, while her husband administers a collection of 300 cognacs.

In winter a cosy log fire is lit in the restaurant, La Grange aux Oies, while in summer tables are set out on the pretty terrace. The Bodinauds' shared interest in art led to the opening of a gallery several years ago.

~

NEARBY Angoulême (40 km); Limoges (65 km).
LOCATION in wooded park, 2 km E of Nieuil; car parking
FOOD breakfast, lunch, dinner
PRICE €€€€
ROOMS 14; 11 double, 3 suites, all with bath; all rooms have phone, TV, minibar, air conditioning, hairdrier
FACILITIES sitting room, 2 restaurants, bar, meeting room, garden, swimming pool, tennis, fishing
CREDIT CARDS AE, DC, MC, V
CHILDREN accepted
DISABLED access possible to one bedroom and suite **PETS** welcome
CLOSED Nov to late Apr; restaurant 'La Grange aux Oies' Sun, Mon dinner
PROPRIETORS Jean-Michel and Luce Bodinaud

THE WEST

OIZON

CHATEAU DE LA VERRERIE
~ CHATEAU HOTEL ~

Oizon, 18700 Aubigny-sur-Nère (Cher)
TEL 02 48 81 51 60 **FAX** 02 48 58 21 25
E-MAIL laverrerie@wanadoo.fr **WEBSITE** www.chateau-france.com/-verrerie.fr

IF YOU DRIVE NORTH from Bourges for 50 km, you will arrive at Aubigny-sur-Nère without having encountered a single corner worthy of the name. Long after the Romans left, the Scots arrived in 1422 in the shape of John Stuart, Count of Darnley, on whom a grateful Charles VII of France had bestowed the estates of Aubigny for his help against the English during the Hundred Years' War. Stuart's grandson built the first elements of this handsome château about 80 years later. The Duke of Richmond sold it three and a half centuries after that to an ancestor of the present owner, Count Béraud de Vogüé. This is the house where he was born and where he and his family now live.

Their welcome is as warm as the setting is magical: lawns, lake and woods keep the rest of the world at bay while you hunt, shoot, fish, ride, row, practise archery or just sit under a tree with a book and absorb some of the history that surrounds you through peaceful osmosis. The bedrooms are satisfyingly large, the furniture antique and the decoration fresh. Bathrooms are baronial and guests have a drawing room of their own to use as they please. Breakfast comes to you in your room, and you can take your other meals at the excellent restaurant housed in a 17thC cottage just outside the body of the keep. The wine list reminds you effortlessly that you are between Sancerre and the Loire.

~

NEARBY Gien (29 km); Bourges (45 km).
LOCATION 11 km SE of Aubigny (follow signs) off the D89; car parking
FOOD breakfast, lunch, dinner
PRICE €€€
ROOMS 12; 11 double and twin, one suite, all with bath; all rooms have phone
FACILITIES sitting rooms, library, meeting rooms, restaurant, bar, terrace, garden, boating, fishing, helipad; hunting, shooting, archery and riding (by arrangement)
CREDIT CARDS AE, MC, V **CHILDREN** accepted **DISABLED** not suitable
PETS accepted **CLOSED** mid-Dec to mid-Feb; restaurant Tue and Wed lunch
PROPRIETOR Comte Béraud de Vogüé

THE WEST

ONZAIN-EN-TOURAINE

DOMAINE DES HAUTS DE LOIRE

∼ MANOR HOUSE HOTEL ∼

41150 Onzain (Loir-et-Cher)
TEL 02 54 20 72 57 **FAX** 02 54 20 77 32
E-MAIL hauts.de.loire@wanadoo.fr **WEBSITE** www.domainehautsloire.com

THE CRUNCH OF freshly-raked gravel gives you something of a clue as you walk towards the front door of Domaine des Hauts de Loire – and even if you've arrived by helicopter (some do, by the way) you have to walk the last bit like the rest of us. Inside this former hunting lodge, built in 1860, the Bonnigal family have created a very stylish, very luxurious hotel. Travellers on a modest budget should just sigh and pass by. The wooden floors here have a deeper shine, the carpets deeper pile and the oriental rugs lie thicker on the ground than most other places you are likely to visit. A regiment of keen young staff keeps everything just so under the watchful eye of Mme Bonnigal – and this includes maintaining the marked trails through the woods, each with helpful signs to let you know how long it should take to walk. Fresh flowers are everywhere (with a rose on each of the yellow-clad tables in the beamed dining room) and in fine weather the French windows are thrown open to let in the country air.

The food is everything you could hope for, as is the wine list. The smartly decorated, antique-filled bedrooms are divided between the house itself and a nearby row of cottages, where the most spectacular is a beamed loft with a gigantic picture window and a bathroom to die for.

∼

NEARBY Blois (20 km); Amboise (20 km); Loire châteaux.
LOCATION 2 km from Onzain off the D1 before Mesland; car parking
FOOD breakfast, lunch, dinner
PRICE €€€€
ROOMS 33; 19 double, 14 twin, all with bath; all rooms have phone, TV, minibar, hairdrier; some have air conditioning
FACILITIES sitting room, dining room, breakfast room, terrace, garden, swimming pool, tennis, helipad
CREDIT CARDS AE, DC, MC, V **CHILDREN** accepted
DISABLED access possible **PETS** not accepted
CLOSED Dec to mid-Feb; restaurant Mon, Tue
PROPRIETORS M. and Mme Bonnigal

THE WEST

ST-CHARTIER

CHATEAU DE LA VALLEE BLEUE

~ CHATEAU HOTEL ~

route de Verneuil, St-Chartier, 36400 La Châtre (Indre)
TEL 02 54 31 01 91 **FAX** 02 54 31 04 48
E-MAIL valleebleue@aol.com **WEBSITE** www.valleebleue.com

THE YOUNG GASQUETS took over this handsome château in 1985, just in time to make an appearance in the first edition of this guide, and have been assiduously improving it ever since – a barn and stables have been renovated to provide extra space, and most recently five bedrooms have been revamped and a new suite created. A report from a British resident in France with young children sums up the Vallée Bleue precisely: 'Here is complete commitment. Service was friendly and discreet – the children treated like young adults. The restaurant was one of the best we've eaten in.' Another report praises the 'large, airy' rooms and votes it 'the nicest hotel that we stayed in'; however, a more recent reader mentions that 'the room was a little tired looking', though it proved 'a charming place to stay'.

Inside, the atmosphere of the house is, as always, warm and easy. Fresh flowers and a cosy log fire in the spacious entrance hall set the tone, and personal touches are in evidence in every room, including memorabilia of Georges Sand and Chopin, whose doctor built the château. It overlooks gardens front and back, giving all the bedrooms – big, and comfortably furnished with antiques – a pleasant outlook; just visible, beyond cows grazing in the fields, are the terracotta rooftops of the village. Public rooms are gracious and charming, furnished with solid antiques and looking on to the garden. Cooking, under the aegis of a new chef, is regionally based.

~

NEARBY Tour de la Prison; Sarzay (10 km); Nohant (5 km).
LOCATION just outside hamlet, on D69 9 km N of La Châtre; car parking
FOOD breakfast, lunch, dinner
PRICE €€
ROOMS 15; 13 double and twin, 2 suites, all with bath or shower; all rooms have phone, TV, minibar, hairdrier
FACILITIES sitting room, 2 dining rooms, meeting room, fitness room, garden, swimming pool, bowling **CREDIT CARDS** MC, V **CHILDREN** welcome
DISABLED 3 ground floor rooms **PETS** not accepted **CLOSED** mid-Nov to early Mar
PROPRIETOR Gérard Gasquet

THE WEST

DOMAINE DE RENNEBOURG
～ COUNTRY GUESTHOUSE ～

17400 St-Denis-du-Pin (Charente-Maritime)
TEL 05 46 32 16 07 **FAX** 05 46 59 77 38

IN DEEP COUNTRYSIDE, the Domaine de Rennebourg is a mother-and-daughter enterprise born, like so many others, out of a desire to escape the extinction by a thousand divisions that Napoleonic inheritance laws visit on family estates. And what a success it has been. The long stone house forms one side of the classic large grassed courtyard so characteristic of the yeoman farms of the region, and beyond it is a garden big enough to lose yourself in. The rooms inside are freshly painted and as welcoming as Michèle and Florence Frappier themselves. Utterly in keeping with the architecture, they are lifted way above the ordinary by innumerable little flashes of inspiration – artistic and humorous – and all look as if they are wearing their Sunday best.

Inside one of the outbuildings that form a second side of the yard, like a cross between a waxworks and a section of the Victoria & Albert Museum, is Florence's astonishing collection of dresses, accessories and assorted fripperies from the central 40 years of the 19th century. Another houses the sort of wet weather games centre for children that despairing parents elsewhere would go down on bended knee to have access to. You'd think there would have to be a catch somewhere, but Michèle's kitchen apparently effortlessly produces food that is inventive, plentiful and, despite including aperitif and wine, seems to defy rational economic analysis.

～

NEARBY Niort (38 km); La Rochelle (60 km); tennis.
LOCATION in deep countryside off the N150, 6 km N of St Jean-d'Angély; car parking
FOOD breakfast, dinner
PRICE €
ROOMS 7 double and twin with bath or shower
FACILITIES sitting room, dining room, terrace, garden, swimming pool
CREDIT CARDS not accepted **CHILDREN** welcome
DISABLED access possible **PETS** accepted
CLOSED never
PROPRIETORS Michèle and Florence Frappier

THE WEST

ST-GAULTIER

LE MANOIR DES REMPARTS

~ MANOR GUESTHOUSE ~

14 rue des Remparts, 36800 St-Gaultier (Indre)
TEL and **FAX** 02 54 47 94 87
E-MAIL willem.prinsloo@wanadoo.fr

PEOPLE WHO CHERISH the fond belief that rooms photographed to illustrate interior design magazines don't exist in real life will be forced to change their minds by Ren Rijpstra's treatment of this 18thC manor house. The quiet town has long since flowed round and incorporated the house, but behind high walls it sits in its own green oasis with a gravelled courtyard in front and a walled garden behind. To one side of the yard is a barn that now houses a cool dining room, but the real treat starts inside where, without disturbing the building's original form, furniture, fabrics and lighting work with carefully considered colours to show the rest of us how it can be done. Floors and fireplaces are original and a particularly fine, broad oak staircase rises in easy stages to the four bedrooms. Nor are creature comforts forgotten: the beds may be old and the fine linen antique, but the mattresses are new, the bathrooms are difficult to leave and the drawing room is a comfortable book-lined haven.

Despite all the thought and energy spent on the house there seems to be an inexhaustible supply left to benefit the guests. Breakfasts are famous: fresh fruit juice, yoghurt, cereals, eggs from their own hens, homemade jams, local cheeses and tea that has never been in a bag. The experience of a recent guest confirms our opinion: 'It was wonderful – the attention to detail and the warmth and comfort'. Dinners are by arrangement – and well worth arranging. There's a no smoking rule, even in the garden.

~

NEARBY Châteauroux (30 km); Poitiers (76 km); golf.
LOCATION in town (ask for directions when you book); car parking
FOOD breakfast, dinner (by arrangement)
PRICE €€
ROOMS 4; 3 double, one suite, all with bath
FACILITIES sitting room, dining room, terrace, garden **CREDIT CARDS** MC, V
CHILDREN accepted **DISABLED** not suitable **PETS** not accepted
CLOSED mid-Dec to early Jan
PROPRIETOR Ren Rijpstra

THE WEST

ST-HILAIRE-DE-COURT

CHATEAU DE LA BEUVRIERE

∼ CHATEAU BED-AND-BREAKFAST ∼

St-Hilaire-de-Court, 18100 Viezon (Cher)
TEL 02 48 75 14 63 **FAX** 02 48 75 47 62

THE APPROACH IS THROUGH glorious wooded grounds, part of this 11thC château's Cher valley estate, which has survived virtually untouched since the Middle Ages. A splendid example of the period's architecture, its round towers topped by conical slate roofs, the small-scale château is as appealing inside as it is out. Put a foot through the door and you will immediately sense its intimacy and welcome. Château seems too grand a name to describe it. The pleasantly decorated public rooms are filled with family furniture, and our reporter was particularly taken with the mellow breakfast room with its upholstered Empire armchairs and immaculate tables. Mme de Brach is now running the hotel on her own and has closed the dining room.

The peaceful bedrooms overlook the gardens, and although they're all different, each has something to recommend it. Some have beds tucked into wood-panelled alcoves; in others the bed is on a mezzanine floor, with a sitting area below – not suitable for the unsure of foot, as the staircase is steep. Another reporter was enchanted with her room in one of the turrets. She was also impressed by the reasonable prices, but warned that the owner speaks little English. Our only disappointment was the siting of the swimming pool, a touch too close to the hotel – but that's a quibble.

∼

NEARBY Bourges (39 km); Viezon (7 km); golf.
LOCATION off the D96 W of St-Hilaire near the Cher; car parking
FOOD breakfast
PRICE €
ROOMS 15 double and twin with bath; all rooms have phone; 2 have minibar
FACILITIES sitting area, bar, dining room, terrace, garden, swimming pool, tennis
CREDIT CARDS AE, DC, MC, V **CHILDREN** accepted
DISABLED access difficult
PETS accepted
CLOSED late Dec to mid-Mar; restaurant Sun dinner, Mon Sep to June
PROPRIETOR Mme de Brach

THE WEST

LE LOGIS SAINT-MARTIN

~ COUNTRY HOTEL ~

chemin de Pissot, 79400 St-Maixent-l'Ecole (Deux-Sèvres)
TEL 05 49 05 58 68 **FAX** 05 49 76 19 93
E-MAIL courrier@logis-saint-martin.com **WEBSITE** www.logis-saint-martin.com

LE LOGIS ST-MARTIN is a wonderful surprise. A couple of minutes' drive down a worryingly suburban road leading off the N11 as it leaves St-Maixent-L'Ecole brings you suddenly to the green, wooded bank of the river Sèvre, opposite an island served by a footbridge. For ten years Bertrand and Ingrid Heintz have been running this long, low 17thC stone house as a hotel-restaurant of uncompromisingly high standards. The first thing you will notice is that the hotel staff don't ever appear in the restaurant, and vice versa. Monsieur Heintz would rather his people mastered their trades one at a time, and any confusion would mar his passion for tip-top service.

The beamed restaurant is an enticing room washed in muted yellows and glinting with silver and crystal; they have a first-rate new chef in Guy Robin, and there is a steady stream of local people who make a pilgrimage from town, along the river bank, to eat here. This close to Cognac you can easily bring your excellent meal to a satisfactory conclusion; there is also a generous list of teas and coffees to choose from, and the cigars are pretty good as well. The very comfortable well-lit bedrooms are no disappointment: elegantly redecorated in yellow and blue, they all look out over the peaceful river or garden.

~

NEARBY Niort (24 km); Poitiers (48 km); golf; riding; fishing.
LOCATION on western edge of town beside the river Sèvre, S of the N11; car parking
FOOD breakfast, lunch, dinner
PRICE €€
ROOMS 11; 10 double and twin, one suite, 5 with bath, 6 with shower; all rooms have phone, TV, hairdrier
FACILITIES sitting room, restaurant, meeting room, terrace, garden, helipad
CREDIT CARDS AE, DC, MC, V **CHILDREN** accepted
DISABLED access difficult **PETS** not accepted
CLOSED Jan; restaurant Mon, lunch on Tue and Sat
PROPRIETORS Bertrand and Ingrid Heintz

THE WEST

ST-PATRICE

CHATEAU DE ROCHECOTTE
~ CHATEAU HOTEL ~

St-Patrice, 37130 Langeais (Indre-et-Loire)
TEL 02 47 96 16 16 **FAX** 02 47 96 90 59
E-MAIL chateau.rochecotte@wanadoo.fr **WEBSITE** www.chateau-de-rochecotte.fr

TALLEYRAND BOUGHT ROCHECOTTE in 1825 for his favourite niece, the Duchesse de Dino. Originally a rather stark 18thC castle with glorious views over the Loire Valley to the Château d'Usée, she gave it an Italianate look by adding pillars, pergolas and terraces, extended it in the same style to make room for their many friends and even harnessed the hydraulic technology of the moment to pipe water to the suites and kitchens. In 1986 Monsieur Pasquier bought it for his wife and daughters. They then renovated it with great attention to detail, and have continued faithfully in the house's tradition of 'hands on' hospitality: large though it is, there seems to be at least one member of the family in sight at all times.

Many of the pictures, chandeliers, tapestries and pieces of furniture originally installed by the Duchesse are still where she put them, undisturbed by the intervening owners. But this is no museum: the smart *salons* are there to be used and enjoyed and more modern pieces mingle comfortably with the old. The bedrooms are all individually decorated to an exacting standard, with carpets, wall-coverings and fabrics teamed together, and quite sensibly priced by floor area. Talleyrand preferred the calm of Rochecotte to his own, ritzier, Valençay: it's not difficult to see why.

~

NEARBY Langeais (8 km); Tours (33 km); Chinon (24 km).
LOCATION in village, between Tours and Saumur on N152, then D35; car parking
FOOD breakfast, lunch, dinner
PRICE €€€
ROOMS 34; 31 double and twin, 3 suites, all with bath; all rooms have phone, TV, hairdrier
FACILITIES 2 sitting rooms, dining room, meeting room, lift, terrace, garden, swimming pool **CREDIT CARDS** AE, DC, MC, V
CHILDREN accepted
DISABLED access difficult **PETS** accepted
CLOSED early Feb to early Mar, 2 weeks early Dec
PROPRIETORS Pasquier family

THE WEST

LA TONNELLERIE

~ VILLAGE HOTEL ~

12 rue des Eaux-Bleues, Tavers, 45190 Beaugency (Loiret)
Tel 02 38 44 68 15 **Fax** 02 38 44 10 01
E-MAIL tonelri@club-internet.fr **WEBSITE** www.tonelri.com

THE FLOW OF READERS' REPORTS on this fine 19thC wine merchant's house has dried to a trickle (perhaps because the cheapest rooms are no longer cheap) but its attractions seem to us to remain undiminished.

The hotel, in the small village of Tavers, close to the Loire and not far from Beaugency, is set around a central courtyard-garden which is at the heart of its appeal. There are shady chestnut trees and a pretty little swimming pool; tables for summer meals stand on the lawn and further away from the house on terrace areas.

The country atmosphere extends indoors to the two dining rooms, both looking on to the garden; one in 'winter garden' style, the other handsomely rustic, with a tiled floor and mellow woodwork. The cooking is *nouvelle* in style but recognizes the traditions of the region, and is above average in its execution.

Over the years Mme Pouey has steadily improved the hotel, most recently adding four 'apartment/suites' (pastel walls, flowery drapes, polished antiques, smart tiled bathrooms) and refurbishing other bedrooms.

Nearby Beaugency (3 km); Loire châteaux: Chambord (25 km), Blois (30 km).
Location in middle of village, W of Beaugency; car parking
Food breakfast, lunch, dinner
Price €€€
Rooms 20; 5 double, 7 twin, 3 suites, 5 apartments, all with bath; all rooms have phone, TV, hairdrier
Facilities sitting room, 2 dining rooms, lift, garden, swimming pool, tennis
Credit cards AE, MC, V
Children welcome
Disabled ground floor rooms available
Pets accepted
Closed early Jan to Mar
Proprietor Marie-Christine Pouey

THE WEST

AVAILLES-EN-CHATELLERAULT

LE PIGEONNIER DU PERRON

COUNTRY HOTEL

86530 Availles-en-Châtellerault (Vienne) TEL 05 49 19 76 08
FAX 05 49 19 12 82 E-MAIL accueil
@lepigeonnierduperron.com
WEBSITE www.lepigeonnierdu
perron.com FOOD breakfast, lunch,
dinner PRICE € ROOMS 15
CLOSED never

A READER DREW our attention to this delightful place between Poitiers and Tours. A sprawling 15thC stone farmhouse that once belonged to the philosopher René Descartes, it and its barn have been expertly converted into a hotel, opened in 2002 by the Thiollets. (It's his family home.) According to our reader, they 'did everything to make us feel welcome and comfortable'. She describes the rooms as 'sympathetically and simply furnished in the utmost good taste', and the food as 'wholesome and imaginatively presented ... breakfast was the best ever in France'.

CHAUMONT-SUR-THARONNE

LA CROIX BLANCHE DE SOLOGNE

VILLAGE INN

*5 place de l'Eglise, 41600
Chaumont-sur-Tharonne (Loir-
et-Cher)* TEL 02 54 88 55 12
FAX 02 54 88 60 40 E-MAIL lacroix
blanchesologne@wanadoo.fr
FOOD breakfast, lunch, dinner
PRICE € ROOMS 18 CLOSED never

WHEN WE LAST VISITED La Croix Blanche, we found a cosy *auberge* in a 15thC building, furnished with gleaming country antiques and floral fabrics. But, as we went to press, we received a worryingly negative report from readers, who were not made welcome and complained of desperately slow service at dinner: their food (Périgordian and good) finally arrived 'after two hours waiting'. On the positive side, there is a delightful flower-filled garden where you eat in summer, the dining room is attractively rustic, and the country-style bedrooms are comfortable, though some of the decoration is a bit heavy-handed. More reports please.

THE WEST

PONS

AUBERGE PONTOISE
TOWN HOTEL

*23 avenue Gambetta, 17800 Pons
(Charente-Maritime)*
TEL 05 46 94 00 99 **FAX** 05 46 91 33 40
E-MAIL auberge.pontoise@
wanadoo.fr **FOOD** breakfast, lunch,
dinner **PRICE** € **ROOMS** 22 **CLOSED** 5
weeks Dec to Jan; restaurant Sun
dinner and Mon low season

I**T'S ALL CHANGE** at this simple hotel in an old biscuit factory. In 2003 François-Xavier Dessaint became the new owner, with Eric Roulaud promoted to chef, having served as second-in-command to previous owner-chef Frédéric Massiot. His skill has safeguarded the *auberge*'s reputation for excellent regional cuisine; try his homemade *foie gras* and one of the fish dishes. The decorative overhaul started by the Massiots is now complete, with *soigné* dining room, cosy bar, modest, but fresh bedrooms with new bathrooms, and a flowery patio for summer dining. It still offers great value for money. Pons, a medieval hill town on the Compostella pilgrim route, stands above the Cognac countryside and is well worth the visit.

ST-JEAN-ST-GERMAIN

LE MOULIN
CONVERTED MILL

*St-Jean-St-Germain, 37600
Loches (Indre-et-Loire)*
TEL 02 47 94 70 12
FAX 02 47 94 77 98
E-MAIL lemoulinstjean@club-
internet.fr **WEBSITE**
www.lemoulinstjean.com
FOOD breakfast
PRICE € **ROOMS** 6
CLOSED never

L**ONG-TIME OWNERS**, Andrew Page and Sue Hutton have left Le Moulin to run another mill guesthouse nearby (see page 128), leaving this lovely place in the hands of another English pair, John Higginson and Barbara Maxwell. Novice hoteliers and still finding their feet according to one reporter, they only provide breakfast (served in the pretty conservatory or on the veranda overlooking the mill stream), but assure us that there are plenty of local restaurants. On its own little tree-lined isthmus at the edge of St-Jean village, the mill is a heart-warming sight at the end of your journey. There is a little river beach when the winter rains are over and a swimming pool for those who prefer not to share with perch and tadpoles.

THE EAST

HOTELS IN THE EAST

OUR EASTERN FRANCE region takes in Burgundy, Franche-Comté and most of the Alps, each different in character, but all exceptionally rewarding areas for lovers of food and the great outdoors.

The attractions of Burgundy are well known, especially to the gourmet and wine-lover. If you have begun to suspect that standards have slipped in French cooking of late, your faith will surely be restored in this region, where you will find its famous regional dishes cooked to perfection. There are plenty of glossy, sophisticated hotels in these parts, but also good examples of our favourite sort of places such as the traditional village *auberge* or old coaching inn, where the chef/*patron* is a fine cook (perhaps with a Michelin star) and the bedrooms are spotless, comfortable, unpretentious and inexpensive enough to excuse that bottle of Gevrey-Chambertin. Try, for example, the **Hôtellerie du Val d'Or** in Mercurey (page 169), the **Hostellerie du Château** in Châteauneuf-en-Auxois (page 155), the cheerful **Le Vaendangerot** at Rully (tel 03 85 87 38 76), or the charming nine-room **Auberge du Pot d'Etain** at L'Isle-sur-Serein (tel 03 86 33 88 10). Nearby, the luxurious **Château de Créancey** is at the other end of the price scale (tel 03 80 90 57 50). For a marvellous gastronomic tour of the cuisine of the whole region, don't miss lunch or dinner at **Le Cep** in Fleurie-en-Beaujolais (no rooms).

Most people come to Burgundy to tour the world-famous vineyards and to see the Romanesque architecture, but there are peaceful lesser-known corners which have much to offer, such as Fontaine-Française and the Vingeanne valley north-east of Dijon; the Brionnais (see **La Reconce**, Poisson, page 174, or try **Les Récollets** at Marcigny, under new management, tel 03 85 25 05 16) and the rolling pastures and woodland north of Nevers (see **Ferme Auberge du Vieux Château**, Oulon, page 173).

Franche-Comté comprises the high valley of the Saône whose wide rolling country has a rustic simplicity, and the wild, untamed slopes of the Jura mountains. Amongst the handful of recommendations we have in these parts is the elegant **Hôtel Castan** in Besançon (page 152). If it's full, you could also try **Château d'Amondans** (tel 03 81 86 53 14), with a lovely 16thC interior, or the very traditional, very French **Le Lac** at Malbuisson (tel 03 81 69 34 80).

Travelling south-west, before you reach Lyon, where we have two new hotels (pages 165 and 166), we can recommend the **Ostellerie du Vieux Pérouges** (tel 04 74 61 00 88), one of the oldest inns in the country, and, south of Lyon in Chonas-l'Amballan, **Domaine de Clairfontaine** (tel 04 74 58 81 52) in a beautiful 18thC house with a serene setting and a Michelin-starred restaurant.

In the right hands, Alpine chalets and former farmhouses make perfect charming small hotels: our selection includes sophisticated old favourites such as **La Croix-Fry** at Manigod (page 167) and the **Bois Prin** at Chamonix (page 154), a new find, **Les Grands Montets** at Argentière (page 147), as well as much simpler places such as **Chalet Rémy** at St-Gervais (page 184) and **Coin Savoyard** at Combloux (page 156), in the guide for the first time. We can also recommend **Le Chamois d'Or** (tel 04 79 06 00 44), a friendly two-star 10 minutes walk from the centre of Val d'Isère, and the English-owned **Auberge Camelia** in Aviernoz (tel 04 50 22 44 24), both very fairly priced. A summer visit to any of these hotels, when the bustle of winter sports is exchanged for a much more gentle atmosphere, is highly recommended.

THE EAST

ANTHY-SUR-LEMAN

AUBERGE D'ANTHY
~ VILLAGE HOTEL ~

74200 Anthy-sur-Léman (Haute-Savoie)
TEL 04 50 70 35 00 **FAX** 04 50 70 40 90
E-MAIL info@auberge-anthy.com **WEBSITE** www.auberge-anthy.com

OUR FIRST CHARMING SMALL HOTEL on the French shore of Lake Geneva, and a notable discovery. Ignore the mess of shopping warehouses as you approach on the N5 between Thonon and Geneva. As you turn on to the minor road that leads to Anthy-sur-Léman, things improve. Anthy, a former farming community, is charming, and the *auberge* is a pleasing, mostly wooden building at the centre of the village, with its old hoist still preserved high under an eave. Owners Catherine and Alain Dubuloz renewed their family property (an inn since 1927) in 1997, with much more than average imagination and taste. Bedrooms are clean and uncluttered, simply decorated with white, protruding beams providing a dash of character. The dining areas are large and lively, especially the main one with its restful, diffuse lighting from a translucent ceiling.

The food is outstanding. Unusual dishes such as *cabri* (kid) *en cocotte* are regularly offered alongside mouthwatering staples such as fillets of perch fresh from the lake, sliced so thinly that they roll into shell-like parcels. The wine list displays the same imagination and care. A thoroughly genuine place, where (at present) the French, rather than tourists go. The bar area next to the dining room is very much for the locals: as we left early on Sunday morning, in they came for their breakfast: a glass of white wine, a Gauloise, a croissant and a couple of black coffees. Walk down to the rocky pier on the lake before dinner. Fair prices.

~

NEARBY Lac Léman; Geneva (25 km); Evian (15 km); Portes du Soleil ski resorts.
LOCATION 25 km from Geneva in peaceful village centre; parking on road outside
FOOD breakfast, lunch, dinner **Price** ⓔ
ROOMS 16, 14 double, 2 triple, all with bath; all rooms have phone, TV
FACILITIES sitting area, bar, restaurant, lift, garden, terrace, bicycles, sailing boat
CREDIT CARDS AE, DC, MC, V **CHILDREN** welcome **DISABLED** one specially adapted room
PETS accepted **CLOSED** hotel never; restaurant 2 weeks Jan
PROPRIETORS Claude and Catherine Dubuloz

THE EAST

LES GRANDS MONTETS

∽ MOUNTAIN HOTEL ∽

340 chemin des Arbérons, 74400 Argentière (Haute-Savoie)
TEL 04 50 54 06 66 **FAX** 04 50 54 05 42
E-MAIL info@hotel-grands-montets.com **WEBSITE** www.hotel-grands-montets.com

IN A TRADITIONAL SAVOYARD VILLAGE in the Chamonix Valley, this is a larger hotel than we might normally choose for the guide (it has 48 rooms), but it still manages to seem intimate and welcoming. An advantage of its size is that it can offer a splendid indoor swimming pool, massage and spa complex, which provides a welcome way to relax aching joints after a day on the slopes. It also has an attractive bar with a walk-around fireplace (get there early though to be sure of getting a prime spot by the flames). There is no dining room, but there are plenty of local eating places.

The rooms are being done up gradually in classic chalet style: try and get one of the freshly decorated ones (particularly Nos 104 or 103 with fireplaces and views over Mont Blanc). The new family rooms have wooden *lit clos* for children: they will love climbing through a heart to their own hidden bed area. There are also some duplexes and interconnecting rooms. The hotel is located by the 'tots' slopes and the Ecole de Ski Français, as well as some of the most challenging runs in the Alps – so it offers excellent access for skiers of all levels.

∽

NEARBY Chamonix (10 km); Mont Blanc; Megève (42 km); Vallorcine (10 km); Montenvers train.
LOCATION in centre of village N of Chamonix; ample car parking
FOOD breakfast
Price ⓔⓔⓔ-ⓔⓔⓔⓔ
ROOMS 48 double, twin and family, all with bath or shower; all rooms have phone, TV, minibar, hairdrier; some have air conditioning
FACILITIES bar/sitting room, breakfast room, spa, indoor pool,
CREDIT CARDS AE, DC, MC, V **CHILDREN** accepted
DISABLED some ground floor rooms available
PETS accepted
CLOSED May, Jun, mid-Sep to mid-Dec
PROPRIETORS Stella and Alain Blanc-Plaque

THE EAST

ARNAY-LE-DUC

CHEZ CAMILLE
~ TOWN HOTEL ~

1 place Edouard-Herriot, 21230 Arnay-le-Duc (Côte-d'Or)
TEL 03 80 90 01 38 **FAX** 03 80 90 04 64
E-MAIL chez-camille@wanadoo.fr **WEBSITE** www.chez-camille.fr

ARMAND POINSOT'S EXCELLENT COOKING (traditional but light) is only one attraction of this captivating hotel whose position at a crossroads in the centre of Arnay makes it the town's most notable feature. The dark, dull corridors give no hint of the appeal of the bedrooms, which come as a delightful surprise: some are compact, others spacious; many are beamed and all are full of character: antiques, pretty floaty curtains, armchairs. Bathrooms are simple, but acceptable. One family room has two bedrooms; another room in the roof is tiny but appealing. Cheaper rooms are available in the Claire de Lune annexe.

Downstairs there is a large, comfortable lobby/sitting room, but the heart of the hotel is its dining room, fashioned, conservatory-style, from a covered coutyard, with a leafy tree in the middle. To one side is the kitchen, open to view, and, adjoining, the pâtisserie. "It's interesting for the guests to see the kitchen staff at work", says M. Poinsot, "and just as interesting for the staff to see the guests." His team appears to be faultless: one feels he has perfected the art of running a traditional French restaurant. The waitresses wear long white aprons and floral skirts, the food is delicious, the service smooth. This is the France we love to find.

NEARBY Beaune (36 km); Saulieu (29 km).
LOCATION in town centre; car parking and garage
FOOD breakfast, lunch, dinner
Price €
ROOMS 11 double and twin, all with bath; all rooms have phone, TV, minibar, hairdrier
FACILITIES 2 sitting rooms, restaurant, cellar
CREDIT CARDS AE, DC, MC, V **CHILDREN** welcome
DISABLED no special facilities **PETS** accepted
CLOSED never
PROPRIETOR Armand Poinsot

THE EAST

AUXERRE

PARC DES MARECHAUX
~ TOWN MANSION ~

6 avenue Foch, 89000 Auxerre (Yonne)
TEL 03 86 51 43 77 **FAX** 03 86 51 31 72
E-MAIL contact@hotel-parcmarechaux.com **WEBSITE** www.hotel-parcmarechaux.com

IN MARCH 2002, THE LECLERCS took over this substantial 1850s house, which was restored from near-dereliction by a previous owner. It still enjoys clear support from readers, one of whom describes it as 'a delight' and would 'strongly recomend it'. The welcoming ambience, confident style and solid comfort of the house would do credit to any professional hotelier. For a bed-and-breakfast establishment, the public rooms are exceptionally comfortable; as well as the sitting room, the smart little bar looking over the garden is appreciated.

The large bedrooms are beautifully done out in restrained colours, and handsomely furnished using warm wooden beds and chests in traditional styles. Although the rooms on the noisy roadside have been soundproofed of late, one overlooking the garden – the secluded, leafy 'park' from which the hotel takes its name – is preferable. Some have French windows opening directly on to the garden.

Breakfast, which can be taken outside in summer – as an alternative to the pretty breakfast room – is 'excellent', and includes fresh orange juice and 'more copious options to bread and croissants, should you wish'. Light meals are also served in your room, in the dining room or on the terrace.

NEARBY cathedral, abbey church of Saint-Germain; Chablis (20 km).
LOCATION signposted in Auxerre, close to middle of town; car parking
FOOD breakfast, light meals
PRICE €€
ROOMS 25; 19 double and twin, 2 single, 4 family, all with bath; all rooms have phone, TV
FACILITIES sitting room, bar, dining room, lift, garden, swimming pool
CREDIT CARDS AE, DC, MC, V
CHILDREN welcome **DISABLED** 3 rooms on ground floor
PETS accepted **CLOSED** never
PROPRIETORS M. and Mme Leclerc

THE EAST

CHATEAU DE VAULT DE LUGNY
~ COUNTRY HOTEL ~

11 rue du Château, 89200 Avallon (Yonne)
TEL 03 86 34 07 86 **FAX** 03 86 34 16 36
E-MAIL hotel@lugny.com **WEBSITE** www.lugny.com

PRESS A BUTTON and the iron gates open automatically; once through, the front door comes into view across the sweep of lawn. This hotel is constantly winning awards, and offers an undeniably stunning atmosphere and location – a wonderful moated château complete with 13thC dungeon, stone staircases, enormous beds and winter dinners in front of a magnificent fire-place. The extensive, well-wooded grounds include a stretch of trout fishing, a tennis court and a medieval defensive tower.

Inside, this ambience is faithfully preserved: it's a very handsome house, but Elisabeth Audan's good taste has kept the decoration not too smart, not too informal: it has the feel of a private home. There are two rather grand bedrooms, filled with impressive antiques; the rest are more homely, but spacious and comfortable.

Dinner is taken house-party style at a table large enough to allow a couple to talk between themselves, but if you prefer to sit at a separate table for complete privacy, you can. The food is rich and delicious, and presented in restrained good taste: not dolled up, but in the style of real home cooking. If in doubt, try the classic Burgundy menu. But, for all its appeal, it is one of the most expensive hotels in this guide, and a recent inspector found the service dismissive on occasion. More reports please.

~

NEARBY Avallon (4 km); Vézelay (10 km).
LOCATION 4 km W of Avallon, 1 km N of Pontaubert, on D427 outside village of Vault de Lugny; ample car parking
FOOD breakfast, lunch, dinner; room service
PRICE €€€€€
ROOMS 12 double and twin, all with bath; all rooms have phone, TV, minibar, hairdrier, safe **FACILITIES** sitting room, bar, dining room, garden, tennis, fishing
CREDIT CARDS AE, DC, MC, V **CHILDREN** welcome
DISABLED rooms on ground floor **PETS** accepted **CLOSED** mid-Nov to early Feb
PROPRIETOR Elisabeth Audan

THE EAST

AVALLON

MOULIN DES TEMPLIERS

~ BED-AND-BREAKFAST CONVERTED MILL ~

Vallée du Cousin, Pontaubert, 89200 Avallon (Yonne)
TEL 03 86 34 10 80 **FAX** 03 86 34 03 05
E-MAIL jean.liberatore@freesbee.fr **WEBSITE** www.hotel-moulin-des-templiers.com

WHEN WE LAST TURNED UP HERE we were met by a sorry sight: the place had been flooded during a freak deluge, and the waters of the Cousin still lapped menacingly close to the sodden walls of the building. If you ask, Anne and Jean will doubtless show you how high the water reached, but by now there will be few other signs of the havoc it caused.

We have always felt affection for this modest stopover, now in the capable hands of dynamic young owners, the Liberatores. They have freshened the quaint bedrooms, which have white rough plastered walls, flowery wallpaper on the ceilings, dark old polished doors, and tiny bathrooms (with separate loos) tucked into odd corners. Bedrooms on the first floor are compact – the smallest is minute – while those on the second floor are slightly larger.

Records of a mill on this spot as far back as the 12th century can be found in the National Archives. It was used by the Templars as a resting place on the pilgrimage to Santiago della Compostella, but was burned by the Huguenots in 1571, along with the Templars' chapel. Today it makes an idyllic spot on the banks of the normally charming little river, which runs along an unspoiled wooded valley. Breakfast is served in one of two tiny rooms, or on the riverside terrace on fine days.

~

NEARBY Avallon (4 km); Vézelay (13 km).
LOCATION just outside Pontaubert, signposted, in Cousin valley; with car parking across road
FOOD breakfast
PRICE €
ROOMS 15 double and twin, all with bath (small) or shower; all rooms have phone
FACILITIES 2 breakfast rooms, sitting room, bar, terrace
CREDIT CARDS AE, DC, MC, V **CHILDREN** accepted
DISABLED not suitable **PETS** accepted **CLOSED** Dec to mid-Feb
PROPRIETORS Anne and Jean Liberatore

THE EAST

BESANCON

CASTAN

~ TOWN HOTEL ~

6 square Castan, 25000 Besançon (Doubs)
TEL 03 81 65 02 00 **FAX** 03 81 83 01 02
E-MAIL art@hotelcastan.fr **WEBSITE** www.hotelcastan.fr

AN EXEMPLARY HOTEL with lovely, individually furnished bedrooms that are full of elegance and character, with antiques, oil paintings, gilt mirrors, chandeliers, and parquet floors strewn with rugs. Each one is displayed on the excellent website; you are invited to fax or phone your booking stating your preferred choices – a tough decision. For those without internet: all ten are lovely, but of the cheaper ones (which are a bargain) we particularly like Trianon, with original panelling, Bonaparte and Victor Hugo (who was born in this lovely town). The building is an 18thC *hôtel particulier* with a verdant courtyard, filled in summer with flowers, palms and climbing plants, around which its three wings are wrapped. It was bought in a derelict state by dentist Gérard Dintroz and his wife as their private home, but being larger than they needed, they decided to convert part of it into a small hotel. Madame Dintroz is in charge, along with a small friendly staff, while her husband, recently retired from dentistry, follows his passion for collecting antiques – particularly old armour – all over the world; a great bonus for his guests. He is so knowledgeable and enthusiastic, it is well worth seeking him out for a chat if he's home. Breakfast, served on charming china, either in your room or in the panelled breakfast room, lives up to expectations with home-made jams and other products.

~

NEARBY Vieille Ville; Citadelle; Natural History Museum.
LOCATION on small square in town centre; follow signs for Vieille Ville and La Citadelle; limited private car parking
FOOD breakfast
PRICE €€
ROOMS 10 double and twin, all with bath; all rooms have phone, TV, minibar, hairdrier; half have air conditioning
FACILITIES sitting area, breakfast room, courtyard
CREDIT CARDS AE, MC, V **CHILDREN** accepted **DISABLED** 2 rooms on ground floor
PETS accepted **CLOSED** Christmas and New Year, first 3 weeks Aug
PROPRIETOR Gérard Dintroz

THE EAST

LAMELOISE
~ TOWN HOTEL ~

36 place d'Armes, 71150 Chagny (Saône-et-Loire)
TEL 03 85 87 65 65 **FAX** 03 85 87 03 57
E-MAIL reception@lameloise.fr **WEBSITE** www.lameloise.fr

JACQUES LAMELOISE AND HIS WIFE maintain with ease the reputation of this calm, shuttered house, established by his father Jean, as one of the best restaurants in France. A haven of sophisticated yet low-key luxury, it comes as something of a surprise in the middle of workaday Chagny (despite its proximity to the Côte d'Or, wine is not produced in Chagny). Entering from the scruffy place d'Armes, you are suddenly amongst bronzed people in designer clothes and gold jewellery. The refurbished reception lobby is modern and slick, with red sofas and soft lighting. The bedrooms are very attractive and comfortable, no two the same, and furnished with charming fabrics and antiques, with the obligatory marble bathrooms.

The classical, dignified, yet not exorbitant restaurant, is of course at the heart of things, and still retains three Michelin stars and 19/20 from Gault Millau. You are hardly likely to be staying in the adjoining hotel unless you are treating yourselves to lunch or dinner here. The food is rooted in the cuisine of Burgundy, with the best Burgundy wines to accompany. Breakfast, as you can imagine, is superior. Despite its elevated status and its sophistication, Lameloise, which began humbly enough, retains its solid and traditional roots.

~

NEARBY Beaune (16 km); Côte de Beaune.
LOCATION in town centre; car parking and garage
FOOD breakfast, lunch, dinner
PRICE €€€
ROOMS 17 double and twin, all with bath; all rooms have phone, TV, hairdrier; most have air conditioning **FACILITIES** sitting room, bar, restaurant, lift
CREDIT CARDS AE, DC, MC, V **CHILDREN** accepted
DISABLED access possible **PETS** accepted
CLOSED mid-Dec to mid-Jan; hotel and restaurant closed Wed, Thu until 5 pm; restaurant closed Mon lunch
PROPRIETORS Lameloise family

THE EAST

CHAMONIX

AUBERGE DU BOIS PRIN

~ CHALET HOTEL ~

69 chemin de l'Hermine, Les Moussoux, 74400 Chamonix (Haute-Savoie)
TEL 04 50 53 33 51 **FAX** 04 50 53 48 75
E-MAIL info@boisprin.com **WEBSITE** www.boisprin.com

DESPITE INCREASING COMPETITION, the Bois Prin remains our favourite spot in, or at least near, Chamonix. This is partly because of the stunning views – the kind that would have driven the 19thC Romantics crazy – across the valley to the spires and glaciers of Mont Blanc, but also because (as recent visits attest), it is a deeply cosseting place to stay.

The Bois Prin is a traditional, dark-wood chalet, in a pretty, flowery garden close to the foot of the Brévent cable-car, on the north side of the deep, steep-sided Chamonix valley. The Carriers have run the hotel since it was built (by Denis Carrier's parents) in 1976. The first impression may be of a surprising degree of formality, with crisply dressed staff. But in fact you quickly find that the informal and friendly approach of the young owners sets the tone. Bedrooms face Mont Blanc, and are lavishly furnished, with rich fabrics, carved woodwork (much of it Denis's own work) and a sprinkling of antiques; the best have private terraces. Food is excellent, with a good choice of menus and a 'wonderful' cheeseboard. 'Luxurious...yet at the same time homely and cosy' praises our reporter.

~

NEARBY Mont Blanc and Le Brévent.
LOCATION on hillside, NW of town; ample car parking and garages
FOOD breakfast, lunch, dinner; room service
PRICE €€€-€€€€
ROOMS 11; 9 double and twin, 2 family, all with bath; all rooms have phone, TV, minibar, hairdrier
FACILITIES dining room, lift, sauna, spa, terrace, garden
CREDIT CARDS AE, DC, MC, V
CHILDREN welcome
DISABLED no special faciliti
PETS accepted
CLOSED mid-Apr to early May, Nov
PROPRIETORS Denis and Monique Carrier

THE EAST

CHATEAUNEUF-EN-AUXOIS

HOSTELLERIE DU CHATEAU
~ VILLAGE HOTEL ~

Châteauneuf-en-Auxois, 21320 Pouilly-en-Auxois (Côte d'Or)
TEL 03 80 49 22 00 **FAX** 03 80 49 21 27
E-MAIL infos@hostellerie-chateauneuf.com **WEBSITE** www.hostellerie-chateauneuf.com

THIS PICTURESQUE *hostellerie*, cleverly converted from a 15thC presbytery close to the château, is in keeping with the delightful, and very quiet, medieval village around it: old stone walls, quiet rustic rooms and terraced gardens. In the beamed, picture-windowed restaurant, wholesome Burgundian dishes are the order of the day. 'Very good value', says a recent report. Another enthusiastic reader tells us that they felt relaxed and at ease as soon as they walked through the door on a cold, snowy day. 'Warm and welcoming...small, brick-walled reception/bar, warming log fires and a comfortable seating area. In the dining room I ate a Charolais steak good enough to kill for. Our large family room was attractively decorated and overlooked the château. It was clean and the bathroom was perfectly adequate'.

Another reader endorses these comments. 'A delightful hotel. The surrounding village is most picturesque, and there are lovely views over the plain from its hilly vantage point. The staff were helpful and the accommodation comfortable. The food was delicious – perhaps the best meal of our trip.' Please note that the hotel is closed on Mondays and Tuesdays, except in July and August.

~

NEARBY Pouilly-en-Auxois (10 km); Dijon (45 km).
LOCATION in hamlet, next to château, 10 km SE of Pouilly-en-Auxois; street car parking
FOOD breakfast, lunch, dinner
PRICE €
ROOMS 17; 15 double and twin, one single, one suite, all with bath; all rooms have phone
FACILITIES 2 sitting rooms, dining room, terrace, garden
CREDIT CARDS AE, DC, MC, V **CHILDREN** welcome
DISABLED not suitable **PETS** accepted
CLOSED Dec to mid-Feb, Mon, Tue except Jul, Aug
PROPRIETOR André and Florence Hartmann

THE EAST

COMBLOUX

COIN SAVOYARD
~ MOUNTAIN HOTEL ~

300 route de la Cry, 74920 Combloux (Haute-Savoie)
TEL 04 50 58 60 27 **FAX** 04 50 47 95 57
E-MAIL lecordonant@wanadoo.fr **WEBSITE** www.coin-savoyard.com

THE AFFLUENT MOUNTAIN RESORT of Combloux is close to Chamonix but much quieter, so you have the advantage of the stunning surroundings without the crowds. As with almost all alpine resorts, there is wonderful walking in summer and wonderful skiing in winter. Although it is not right at the foot of the slopes, there is a little *navette* which arrives every 15 minutes in season to take skiers there, so you don't have to suffer a walk with aching limbs at the end of the day.

This is a truly welcoming place to stay. The house used to be a farm, which belonged to Colette's grandparents, then her parents, who opened a few rooms to guests, and now it is hers. With their wood-clad walls and ceilings and wooden furniture, the bedrooms are rustic without being cloying. A few of them (Nos 3, 5 and 6) look out over the village church with its pealing bells, and the mezzanine rooms are perfect for families.

Recommended by Gault Millau, the cuisine is based on well-prepared ingredients that come fresh from the market. Expect plenty of hearty fondues, all served in the splendid wooden bar and restaurant, though in summer you can have lunch beside the swimming pool in the original orchard. Altogether, an unpretentious, rewarding find.

~

NEARBY Chamonix (30 km); Mont Blanc; Megève (6 km); Annecy (77 km).
LOCATION in heart of village, N of Megève; limited car parking
FOOD breakfast, lunch, dinner
PRICE €
ROOMS 10; 7 double and twin, 3 mezzanines, all with bath; all rooms have phone, TV
FACILITIES dining room, bar, spa, garden, swimming pool
CREDIT CARDS AE, DC, MC, V
CHILDREN accepted
DISABLED not suitable **PETS** accepted
CLOSED mid-Sep to mid-Dec, mid-Apr to Jun
PROPRIETORS Colette and Philippe Astay

THE EAST

CURTIL-VERGY

LE MANASSES

~ VILLAGE HOTEL ~

rue Guillaume de Tavanes, 21220 Curtil-Vergy (Côte-d'Or)
TEL 03 80 61 43 81 **FAX** 03 80 61 42 79

WHAT BETTER WAY to spend an overnight stop in Burgundy than in the heart of a working vineyard in the Hautes Côtes de Nuits? Indeed the Prince of Wales saw fit to stay here for several days, painting and walking (see the little display cabinet). And a steady stream of readers' letters continues to praise Le Manassès warmly, from the 'beautiful view over the valley' to the Chaley family's 'great personal touch'. 'Everything we asked for was done immediately, and they all gave the impression that they enjoyed looking after us.'

They keep the hotel very *propre*: neat as a pin and furnished with great care and taste, and it offers excellent value for money. Most of the rooms are located in the same building as the reception/breakfast room, while five more luxurious – and larger – rooms have been added in a converted stone building across the courtyard. Charming co-ordinated fabrics make these rooms particularly pretty. All the rooms have marble bathrooms. Back in the main building the Chaleys have installed a wine museum, where tools and bottles from the past are displayed, and where, each evening, wine tastings are conducted for their guests. Breakfast is exemplary, with local jams and cheeses, *assiette charcuterie, jambon persillé,* and *pain d'épices,* even a glass of wine if you should wish. Perhaps best of all is the view: green valley, wooded hillside, no other buildings in sight. No dinner, but the Chaleys will recommend good restaurants.

NEARBY Beaune (24 km); abbeys of St Vivant and Citeaux.
LOCATION in village, 24 km NW of Beaune; car parking
FOOD breakfast
PRICE €-€€
ROOMS 12 double and twin, all with bath; all rooms have phone, fax, TV, air conditioning, minibar, hairdrier **FACILITIES** breakfast room, wine museum
CREDIT CARDS AE, DC, MC, V **CHILDREN** accepted
DISABLED not suitable **PETS** accepted **CLOSED** Dec to Mar
PROPRIETORS Yves, Françoise and Cécile Chaley

THE EAST

FLAVIGNY-SUR-OZERAIN

L'ANGE SOURIANT
~ VILLAGE BED-AND-BREAKFAST ~

rue Voltaire, 21150 Flavigny-sur-Ozerain (Côte-d'Or)
TEL 03 80 96 24 93 **FAX** 03 80 96 24 93
E-MAIL ange-souriant@wanadoo.fr **WEBSITE** www.ange-souriant.com

Browsing through the guest book at this wonderful *chambre d'hôte* reveals comments such as, 'We liked it here so much that we have now bought a house in the village'. You will appreciate the lovely fortified village of Flavigny-sur-Ozerain, the setting for the film *Chocolat*, all the more after a night in one of Will Barrueto's cosy bedrooms, with their oak beams, white walls, flowing fabrics, well-restored antiques and private home feel (no telephones or televisions). A Peruvian American, he certainly knows how to make you feel welcome. His breakfasts, served in the dining room or on fine mornings in the charming courtyard, are legendary. What you get depends on where you come from – hams and cheeses for the Swiss or Germans, croissants for the French, eggs for the English. He is a thoughtful and serene host, and will give you an excellent walking tour of the village, if you have time.

Dinner is not provided but there are two good restaurants in the village: our inspector recommends the *crêperie* in the old monastery. Summer sees open-air cinema and various processions and festivals. Both B&B and village certainly make it worth a stay of more than one night.

~

NEARBY Semur-en-Auxois (17 km); Avallon (55 km); Dijon (58 km); Alise -Ste-Reine (7 km); Abbaye de Fontenay.
LOCATION in village, 5 km E of D905 via D9; car parking nearby
FOOD breakfast
PRICE €
ROOMS 4; 2 double with bath or shower, one family suite with 2 bedrooms and shared bath
FACILITIES sitting room, breakfast room, courtyard
CREDIT CARDS MC, V
CHILDREN welcome
DISABLED not suitable **PETS** not accepted
CLOSED Oct to Mar
PROPRIETOR Will Barrueto

THE EAST

FLEURVILLE

CHATEAU DE FLEURVILLE

~ VILLAGE HOTEL ~

71260 Fleurville (Saône-et-Loire)
TEL 03 85 27 91 30 **FAX** 03 85 27 91 29
E-MAIL chateaufleurville@free.fr **WEBSITE** www.chateau-de-fleurville.com

WELL-PLACED FOR A STOPOVER on the route south, equidistant between Tournus and Mâcon, Fleurville is hemmed in on one side by the A6 *autoroute*, and on the other by the N6, with the railway line running alongside, and yet this 16th-17thC residence in wooded parkland is peaceful and pleasant enough for more than just a night's stay. M. Lehmann, who bought the hotel just before publication of our last edition, has been busy renovating it ever since: it was growing dangerously unkempt just before he took over. Our only word of warning is that he may be too enthusiastic a restorer – we like our châteaux with just the right degree of faded elegance, and some of the old rooms and wallpapers were wonderful. But M. Lehmann is welcoming and warm, and intends to make this one of the best and most affordable family châteaux in the area, so he is keeping prices down. The new bedrooms are stylish and sleek – we especially like the red room, with its four-poster bed and huge mahogany wardrobe, and the smaller but beautiful tower room leading off the stone spiral staircase.

Celebrated chef Serge Nodot has been brought in to create the food, and its success is confirmed by numerous articles in the French press. The *filet de boeuf charolais* (practically a crime not to try while in Burgundy) is exceptional here.

~

NEARBY Tournus (15 km); Mâcon (15 km); vineyards; Romanesque churches and abbeys.
LOCATION just off RN6, halfway between Tournus and Mâcon; car parking
FOOD breakfast, lunch, dinner
PRICE €€
ROOMS 15; 14 double and twin, one suite, all with bath; all rooms have phone, TV; refurbished rooms have minibar, hairdrier
FACILITIES sitting room, dining room, breakfast room, bar, terrace, garden, swimming pool, bicycles **CREDIT CARDS** AE, DC, MC, V **CHILDREN** welcome
DISABLED limited access possible **PETS** accepted **CLOSED** mid-Nov to early Feb
PROPRIETORS France and Pascal Lehmann

THE EAST

GEVREY-CHAMBERTIN

LES GRANDS CRUS

~ VILLAGE HOTEL ~

route des Grands Crus, 21220 Gevrey-Chambertin (Côte-d'Or)
TEL 03 80 34 34 15 **FAX** 03 80 51 89 07

THE WALLS ARE VERTICAL and plastered, the exposed beams are straight and smooth, the windows are easily opened casements: this is a modern hotel, built as recently as 1977, and so not as immediately charming as many older places in these pages. But the Grands Crus has been done out in traditional Burgundian style, with quarry-tiled floors, lime-washed walls, tapestry fabrics and a carved-stone fireplace, and it drips with geraniums in summer – so to a degree at least it combines the charm of the old with the comfort of the new. The welcome, however, could be improved: never exactly ebullient, it can involve a fair amount of Gallic *froideur*.

The bedrooms are not the last word in stylish decoration, but they are peaceful, spacious and thoughtfully furnished, and look out over the famous Gevry-Chambertin vineyards, which sweep away in all directions. A better-than-average breakfast is served in the small flowery garden in fine weather; if you're confined indoors, there may be delays because of a shortage of space in the breakfast room, off reception.

There are plenty of restaurants nearby for other meals, including some notably good ones.

~

NEARBY Dijon (10 km); Beaune; abbeys of St-Vivant and Citeaux.
LOCATION in village, 10 km SW of Dijon; car parking
FOOD breakfast
PRICE €
ROOMS 24 double and twin, all with bath; all rooms have phone, hairdrier
FACILITIES sitting room, garden
CREDIT CARDS MC, V
CHILDREN welcome
DISABLED no special facilities
PETS accepted
CLOSED Dec to Mar
PROPRIETOR Marie-Paule Farnier

THE EAST

GOUMOIS

TAILLARD

~ CHALET HOTEL ~

25470 Goumois (Doubs)
TEL 03 81 44 20 75 **FAX** 03 81 44 26 15
E-MAIL hotel.taillard@wanadoo.fr **WEBSITE** www.hoteltaillard.com

AN INTERMITTENT FLOW of appreciative comments about this pretty chalet in a wooded valley on the Swiss border continues to arrive in our office. They like the wonderful views, the delightful garden, the comfortable, affordable rooms, the friendly atmosphere, and (not least) the food. 'Delicious, if slightly repetitive', is the latest word on the latter subject, while others have been unqualified in their praise of the 'beautifully presented' dishes. The dining room makes the most of the view, with elegantly laid tables placed around bay windows, thrown open in summer. The colourful garden gives way to green pastures and then thickly forested hills which stretch over the border. In summer you can take in the breathtaking view over a coffee and croissants on the terrace, eyeing up the inviting swimming pool while you do so.

The house has its roots in the 18th century, and has been owned and run as a hotel by the same family since 1875. The present M. Taillard is an artist, and some of his paintings decorate the walls. Bedrooms are comfortable and carefully furnished with a mixture of pieces, some antique. The welcome, as one reader comments, is 'low-key but genuine'.

~

NEARBY Switzerland; Mombaillard (45 km).
LOCATION in elevated position in Doubs valley overlooking Goumois; car parking
FOOD breakfast, lunch, dinner
PRICE €€
ROOMS 22; 14 double and twin, 8 family, all with bath; all rooms have phone, TV
FACILITIES sitting room, dining room, billiards room, fitness/Jacuzzi, terrace, garden, swimming pool
CREDIT CARDS AE, DC, MC, V
CHILDREN welcome
DISABLED no special facilities
PETS accepted
CLOSED mid-Nov to mid-Mar
PROPRIETORS Taillard family

THE EAST

GRÉSY-SUR-ISERE

LA TOUR DE PACORET
~ COUNTRY HOTEL ~

Montailleur, Grésy-sur-Isère, 73460 Fontenex (Savoie)
TEL 03 80 21 23 23 **FAX** 03 80 21.29 10
E-MAIL info@hotel-pacoret-savoie.com **WEBSITE** www.hotel-pacoret-savoie.com

IT'S THE LOCATION, SURROUNDED by unspoiled country with fine mountain views from the upper windows, that makes this simple hotel special. An old stone watchtower, it was built on the summit of a hill in the 14th century for the Dukes of Savoy and later passed on to the Duc de Pacoret. All the bedrooms allow you to savour the views over the Isère valley and the fields of corn around it. It's a truly peaceful spot. The hotel is a Relais de Silence, run by informal young owners, supported by a willing, courteous staff. A splendid black stone spiral staircase leads up to the rather dull but comfortable and individually decorated bedrooms, each named after a different flower. On the ground floor the smartish dining and sitting rooms are decorated with rich tapestry wallhangings. But best of all is the vine-clad terrace, its tables covered in Provençal cloths, and the large garden with its tempting swimming pool; non-swimmers can play *boule*.

There are few more inviting places to sit than the shady terrace, from where you can watch the gently snaking river and see as far as the Alps' distant, snow-capped peaks. Tables are laid out here in warm weather under the vine or parasols. Half-board is obligatory, but it's no hardship when the setting is so appealing and, according to reports, the cooking and service excel. Specialities include traditional Savoyard dishes.

~

NEARBY Albertville (12 km); Chambéry (39 km); Annecy (58 km); golf.
LOCATION in hamlet, 1.5 km NE of Grésy; car parking
FOOD breakfast, lunch, dinner; half-board obligatory
PRICE €€€
ROOMS 9 double, twin and single, all with bath or shower; all rooms have phone, TV
FACILITIES sitting room, dining room, meeting room, garden, terrace, swimming pool, helipad
CREDIT CARDS MC, V **CHILDREN** accepted
DISABLED not suitable **PETS** accepted
CLOSED Nov to Easter; restaurant Tue lunch Sep to Aug, Wed lunch Sep to Jul
PROPRIETORS Gilles and Laurence Chardonnet

THE EAST

CHATEAU D'IGE

~ CHATEAU HOTEL ~

71960 Igé (Saône-et-Loire)
TEL 03 85 33 33 99 **FAX** 03 85 33 41 41
E-MAIL ige@chateauxhotels.com **WEBSITE** www.chateaudige.com

THIS TURRETED, creeper-covered château, fortified in 1235 and built by a little river on the edge of the Mâcon hills, has preserved its medieval atmosphere despite its conversion into a luxury hotel. Spiral staircases winding up into the turrets, stone-flagged floors, a huge open hearth in the massively beamed dining room, dark, narrow corridors, vast old beds and antique furnishings all contribute to the sense of time standing still. Next year it will be losing its Relais et Châteaux status – perhaps it is not quite polished enough for membership, perhaps they are asking for too much money to be spent on upgrades – but in our inspector's opinion, it is worth travelling any distance to stay in. You are served breakfast in a light-filled conservatory overlooking lovely flowery gardens by a woman who has worked here for 25 years – that is all you need to know about the wonderful welcome you receive, and just how difficult a place this is to leave.

There are a few special bedrooms: one at the foot of the lovely gardens, for extra peace, and two that are not advertised because they are small, but incredibly good value. The restaurant, the stone-vaulted La Tour du Parc, is ably run by Olivier Pont, whose soufflés have to be seen to be believed.

~

NEARBY Mâcon (15 km); Cluny (13 km); Romanesque churches and abbeys; vineyards.
LOCATION in village, signposted, 15 km NW of Mâcon; ample car parking and garage
FOOD breakfast, lunch, dinner; room service
PRICE €€
ROOMS 14; 8 double and twin, 6 suites, all with bath; all rooms have phone, TV, hairdrier
FACILITIES sitting room, bar, 2 dining rooms, terrace, garden
CREDIT CARDS AE, DC, MC, V
CHILDREN welcome
DISABLED no special facilities **PETS** accepted
CLOSED Dec to Mar; restaurant closed Mon to Fri lunch
PROPRIETOR Françoise Lieury Germond

THE EAST

LEVERNOIS

LE PARC

~ VILLAGE BED-AND-BREAKFAST ~

Levernois, 21200 Beaune (Côte-d'Or)
TEL 03 80 24 63 00 **FAX** 03 80 24 21 19
E-MAIL hotel.le.parc@wanadoo.fr **WEBSITE** http://perso.wanadoo.fr/hotel.le.parc

BEAUNE HAS A DEARTH of reasonably priced accommodation, and so Le Parc, just five kilometres away, is an especially welcome address. In a pleasant rural setting, it's an attractive old white shuttered *maison bourguignonne*, its walls thickly draped in creeper. Here is the cosy little reception area, with wicker armchairs, fringed lampshades and potted plants, with a bar behind. There is also a breakfast room, although in fine weather you can sit at tables in the pretty gravelled courtyard, flanked on the other side by another attractive building. This houses some of the hotel's 25 bedrooms, larger than those in the main part. All the bedrooms are simple but prettily decorated, with odd bits of furniture picked up here and there – nothing standardized – and rather low, skimpy looking beds.

From the outside, the hotel is lent a deceptively smart, even exclusive appearance by the long white wrought-iron fence which runs along the village pavement between the two buildings. At the rear, the courtyard opens on to a large, peaceful and informal garden.

Mme Oudot is friendly and efficient. She has recently opened a charming new hotel, Le Clos, at Montigny-les-Beaune (tel 03 80 25 97 98 fax 03 80 25 94 70), another useful address in the Beaune area.

~

NEARBY Beaune (5 km); Côtes de Beaune.
LOCATION in village, 5 km SE of Beaune; ample car parking
FOOD breakfast
PRICE €
ROOMS 25 double and twin, 6 with bath, 19 with shower; all rooms have phone, TV
FACILITIES sitting area, bar, breakfast room, courtyard, garden
CREDIT CARDS MC, V
CHILDREN welcome
DISABLED 5 rooms on ground floor
PETS not accepted
CLOSED Dec, Jan
PROPRIETOR Alain and Christiane Oudot

THE EAST

COUR DES LOGES
~ CITY HOTEL ~

2-8 rue du Boeuf, 69005 Lyon (Rhône)
TEL 04 72 77 44 44 **FAX** 04 72 40 93 61
E-MAIL contact@courdesloges.com **WEBSITE** www.courdesloges.com

THE BUILDING ALONE is worth a visit if you happen to be in the old town (which itself is a UNESCO World Heritage site): the hotel has been created within four Renaissance houses that once belonged to the Lord of Burgundy, Claude de Beaumont. A dramatic central courtyard is enclosed by arcades that reach up three storeys, and Italian arches and Moorish colours abound, reflecting the fact that Italian merchants and spice traders also made their home here over the centuries. These touches help to make the Cour des Loges such a successful combination of the historic and the modern. Refitting it has been the latest project of avid hotel collectors Jocelyne and Jean-Louis Sibuet (see pages 171 and 294), and has produced a very stylish hotel without recourse to the stark sterility that can spoil contemporary hotel architecture. The rooms are luxurious without being overdone. Our favourites – luckily the cheapest – are two storeyed, with the sitting room and bathroom at entry level, and stairs up to a bed-platform, like a little ship's cabin.

Not surprisingly, the restaurant, Les Loges, serves excellent food, but equally delicious and less expensive, the snacks served in the elegant bar are imaginatively chosen and presented, and make a welcome change in this part of France, where good bars and simple, well-prepared international food can be hard to find.

~

NEARBY Vieux Lyon; Palais de Justice; place du Change; Gare St Paul.
LOCATION on a pedestrian street in the heart of Vieux Lyon; car parking
FOOD breakfast, lunch, dinner
PRICE ⑤⑤⑤⑤
ROOMS 62 double, twin, suites and apartments, all with bath; all rooms have phone, TV, air conditioning, minibar, safe, hairdrier **FACILITIES** sitting room, dining rooms, bar, meeting rooms, spa, sauna, indoor swimming pool, roof garden
CREDIT CARDS AE, DC, MC, V **CHILDREN** accepted
DISABLED limited access **PETS** not accepted **CLOSED** never
PROPRIETORS Jocelyne and Jean-Louis Sibuet

THE EAST

LA TOUR ROSE
~ TOWN HOTEL ~

22 rue du Boeuf, 69005 Lyon (Rhône)
TEL 04 78 37 25 90 **FAX** 04 78 42 26 02
E-MAIL tourrose@slh.com

PHILIPPE CHAVENT is a Lyon chef with a Michelin star – and something of a Renaissance man. In St-Jean, the old quarter, he has recreated the atmosphere of the residences of the great Florentine bankers and merchants by turning a 17thC building into something extraordinary. There are 12 bedrooms, each designed to illustrate a period in the long history of Lyon's silk industry. One is decorated with Fortuny pleats, another with Art Deco patterns designed by Dufy, and all are draped, from floor to ceiling, in silk, taffeta, velvet and other textiles. (Bathrooms are modern, with stone floors and walls, and are fitted with shiny stainless steel basins.)

The heart of the hotel is a pink tower and there are balustraded galleries, ornamental ponds with waterfalls, and terraced gardens. The fireplace in the bar was rescued from a condemned château and there is an original 13thC wall of a *jeu de paume* (real tennis) court. Panelling in the bar comes from the law courts at Chambéry. The dining room is in the 13thC chapel of what used to be a convent, with a cobbled terrace and a fabulous glass extension which opens to the sky in the summer. We can still recommend this place, but with reservations: a recent letter paints a picture of a very overpriced hotel in need of some attention. The room was 'so very uninviting, dreary looking, not very large and dark'; dinner was 'not wonderful, despite their Michelin star...It was not good value for money, and we are left feeling very disappointed'.

~

NEARBY Vieux Lyon; Palais de Justice; place du Change; Gare St Paul.
LOCATION in the heart of Vieux Lyon, car parking; ask hotel for details of car access
FOOD breakfast, lunch, dinner
PRICE €€€€€-€€€€€€
ROOMS 12; 6 double and twin, 6 suites, all with bath; all rooms have phone, TV, minibar, hairdrier
FACILITIES 3 sitting rooms, bar, dining room, lift, terraces
CREDIT CARDS AE, DC, MC, V **CHILDREN** accepted **DISABLED** no special facilities
PETS accepted **CLOSED** never **PROPRIETOR** Philippe Chavent

THE EAST

MANIGOD

CHALET HOTEL DE LA CROIX-FRY
~ CHALET HOTEL ~

rue du Col de la Croix-Fry, Manigod, 74230 Thônes (Haute-Savoie)
TEL 04 50 44 90 16 **FAX** 04 50 44 94 87
E-MAIL hotelcroixfry@wanadoo.fr **WEBSITE** www.hotelchaletcroixfry.com

'ABSOLUTELY GORGEOUS' was the verdict of one of our reporters, and our most recent visit confirms the star rating of this wooden mountain chalet at the highest point of an alpine col, with a terrace overflowing with flowers. Run, with great pride, by a third generation of Veyrats – the chalet was once shared in the summer by the family and their cows – the hotel is cosy and welcoming. A wood fire burns on cool evenings and the sofas and armchairs gathered around the hearth are covered in sheepskin. The bedrooms are attractively rustic – even in the modern annexe-chalets, which provide adaptable family accommodation with kitchenettes. But what really impresses us is the evident pride of the family and their endless efforts to maximize a guest's stay. The Veyrats love running their hotel and the pleasure shows.

The restaurant, serving nourishing mountain food, has spectacular views of peaks and valleys. Mme Guelpa-Veyrat's brother, Marc, is one of Savoy's culinary celebrities, but the *tarte aux myrtilles* from her kitchen has many admirers. In summer the Veyrats invite their guests to picnic in the pastures with their cows and to swim in the pool; in winter the invitation is to ski.

~

NEARBY Vallée de Manigod; Thônes (10 km); Annecy (26 km).
LOCATION on the col, 5 km NE of Manigod, on D16, 6 km S of La Clusaz; car parking
FOOD breakfast, lunch, dinner; half-board obligatory
PRICE €€€
ROOMS 12 double, duplex, one and two-bedroom suites, all with bath (suites with Jacuzzi bath); all rooms have phone, TV, terrace or balcony
FACILITIES sitting room, bar, gym, terrace, garden, swimming pool
CREDIT CARDS AE, MC, V
CHILDREN accepted
DISABLED no special facilities **PETS** not accepted
CLOSED mid-Sep to mid-Dec, mid-Apr to mid-Jun
PROPRIETOR Marie-Ange Guelpa-Veyrat

THE EAST

LE COIN DU FEU
~ CHALET HOTEL ~

route du Rochebrune, 74120 Megève (Haute-Savoie)
TEL 04 50 21 04 94 **FAX** 04 50 21 20 15
E-MAIL contact@coindufeu.com **WEBSITE** www.coindufeu.com

IT'S DIFFICULT TO KNOW which of the Sibuets' Megève hotels to highlight, but our inspector picks out this one, citing it as the 'most authentic'. You could also stay at Les Fermes de Marie (tel 04 50 93 03 10) or Le Mont Blanc (tel 04 50 21 20 02) and experience the same exclusive sense of rustic sophistication; here you have the advantage of being a little away from the hustle and bustle of the attractive and elegant village centre. It feels like a private chalet, and makes a seductive place to return to after a day's skiing or walking in the mountains: in fact it's rather difficult to leave in the first place.

Le Coin du Feu has all the right ingredients for a fantasy about living in the mountains: masses of old wood – walls, floors, beamed and panelled ceilings, even a carved wooden fireplace in the sitting room – pretty fabrics (smart checks and tartans mixed with Provençal), soft lighting, snug, duvet-covered beds hidden in alcoves behind curtains (as was the tradition in these chalets), indulgent afternoon tea in front of a crackling fire, friendly and efficient service, and good honest food served in the popular restaurant. A slick interpretation of Alpine charm for the smart set.

~

NEARBY skiing; walking; Chamonix valley.
LOCATION on outskirts of town, near Rochebrune téléphérique, signposted; car and garage parking
FOOD breakfast, lunch, dinner
PRICE €€
ROOMS 23 single, double and twin and suites, all with bath; all rooms have phone, TV, minibar, hairdrier
FACILITIES sitting room, dining room, bar, lift, terrace
CREDIT CARDS AE, DC, MC, V
CHILDREN welcome
DISABLED no special facilities **PETS** accepted
CLOSED Apr to mid-Jul, late Aug to mid-Sep
PROPRIETORS Jocelyne and Jean-Louis Sibuet

THE EAST

MERCUREY

HOTELLERIE DU VAL D'OR

∽ VILLAGE HOTEL ∽

Grande-Rue, 71640 Mercurey (Côte-d'Or)
TEL 03 85 45 13 70 **FAX** 03 85 45 18 45
E-MAIL valdor.cogney@infonie.fr **WEBSITE** www.hotellerie-val-dor.com

BEFORE HE TOOK OVER this friendly early 19thC coaching inn on the main street of the prestigious but rather dull wine village of Mercurey, Dominic Jayet worked for long-time owners, Jean-Claude and Monique Cogny, first as a waiter then as *sommelier*. He has been here since April 1988 and is totally dedicated to the place. After the Cognys left, little time was wasted in embarking on a thorough overhaul, and this once modest inn has emerged sharp and stylish with impeccable accommodation and a first-rate kitchen: despite a change of chef – the current one is Pascal Charreyras – it keeps its Michelin star. Although we haven't witnessed the new regime first-hand, or had any feedback yet, M. Jayet is eager to maintain the original family atmosphere and to involve his own family in the business. So far, he has succeeded in keeping rates considerably lower than many other hotels in this region, where culinary excellence and exorbitant prices so often go hand-in-hand.

Downstairs, there are two dining rooms, one rustic, with beamed ceiling, large fireplace and wooden furniture, the other more intimate and elegant, and a bar with neat tables and chairs. The pristine bedrooms are all slightly different, thoughtfully decorated in contrasting colours – blue and yellow or pink and green – and have new bathrooms and beds.

∽

NEARBY Château de Germolles (10 km); Buxy (20 km).
LOCATION in middle of village, 9 km S of Chagny; car parking
FOOD breakfast, lunch, dinner
PRICE ⓔⓔ
ROOMS 13; 10 double and twin, 2 family, one single, all with bath or shower; all rooms have phone, TV, hairdrier; 10 have air conditioning
FACILITIES 2 dining rooms, sitting room/bar, garden
CREDIT CARDS MC, V **CHILDREN** accepted
DISABLED no special facilities **PETS** not accepted
CLOSED Mon and Tue lunch
PROPRIETOR Dominic Jayet

THE EAST

LES CHARMES
~ TOWN HOTEL ~

10 place du Murgur, 21190 Meursault (Côte-d'Or)
TEL 03 80 21 63 53 **FAX** 03 80 21 62 89

ON THE FACE OF IT, the charm of Les Charmes is mostly in the shady walled garden, so big it's almost a small park. At the far end, or by the pool, you could be far from it all, instead of at the heart of this world-famous Burgundy town. But there's more. This 18thC *maison bourgeoise* is a world of its own, once you're through the gates. The outside breakfast area, hard by the front door, under a glass and metal awning is, well, charming. The breakfast room just inside is tiny and the only indoor sitting space also contains the reception desk. But somehow it all hangs together: the patina of the creaky parquet, the neat tiled entrance passage, the antiques and quality repros all quietly tell you that things are done nicely here, in a spinsterish sort of way. Les Charmes is a charming small hotel in the sense that its negative features, such as the dark warren of upstairs corridors, don't spoil things much. One small bedroom we looked at was bleakish; another borderline; another (large, with exposed beams) full of character: be sure to ask for a *chambre meublée à l'ancienne*, rather than *en moderne*. If you like integrity and a genuine French experience, you'll like Les Charmes.

~

NEARBY Beaune (8 km); Côte de Beaune; Château de Rochepot.
LOCATION in town centre; car parking
FOOD breakfast
PRICE ⓔⓔ
ROOMS 14 double and twin, all with bath; all rooms have phone, TV, minibar
FACILITIES sitting room, breakfast room, terrace, garden, swimming pool
CREDIT CARDS MC, V
CHILDREN accepted
DISABLED one specially adapted room
PETS not accepted
CLOSED Dec to Mar
PROPRIETOR Marie-Luce Haut

THE EAST

MEURSAULT

LES MAGNOLIAS

~ TOWN HOTEL ~

8 rue Pierre Joigneaux, 21190 Meursault (Côte-d'Or)
TEL 03 80 21 23 23 **FAX** 03 80 21.29 10
E-MAIL lesmagnolias@mageos.com **WEBSITE** www.les-magnolias.fr

IN A PLEASANTLY QUIET LOCATION, but only a few minutes' walk from the centre of the village celebrated for its white wine, Les Magnolias is a polished and unusually stylish bed-and-breakfast hotel.

Opened in 1988 by Englishman Antonio Delarue (sadly we didn't meet him, although we are told he is charming), Les Magnolias consists of a group of old houses – once the home of a local *vigneron* – set behind high entrance gates around a small gravelled courtyard full of magnolias, old roses and fig trees. Reception is in one corner; while the bedrooms are located in two separate buildings, three rooms and a suite in one, eight rooms in another. Downstairs is a sweet little sitting room – the only public room in the hotel (breakfast is laid out at a circular table in your room). The bedrooms are a delightful surprise, with the feel of a private house. Each one is large and pretty, and individually decorated with some panache – a chaise-longue here, a carved *armoire* there, flowery fabrics, floaty curtains, plates and prints on the walls. There are fresh flowers in the bedrooms and little posies in the bathrooms. In fine weather you can take breakfast in the courtyard.

~

NEARBY Beaune (8 km); Côte de Beaune; château de Rochepot.
LOCATION close to town centre; car parking
FOOD breakfast
PRICE ⓔⓔ
ROOMS 12;11 double and twin, one suite, 10 with bath, 2 with shower; all rooms have phone, hairdrier
FACILITIES sitting room, courtyard
CREDIT CARDS AE, MC, V
CHILDREN accepted
DISABLED 2 rooms on ground floor
PETS not accepted
CLOSED Dec to Mar
PROPRIETOR Antonio Delarue

THE EAST

NITRY

AUBERGE DE LA BEURSAUDIERE
～ VILLAGE HOTEL ～

89310 Nitry, Bourgogne (Yonne)
TEL 03 86 33 69 69 **FAX** 03 86 33 69 60
E-MAIL auberge.beursaudiere@.wanadoo.fr **WEBSITE** www.beursaudiere.com

WE SHOULD TELL YOU from the start what you might dislike about this place: the waitresses are in traditional dress, and each of the bedrooms is themed along a particular local craft or *métier* – from the simple *Lavandière* (washerwoman) to the grander *Vigneron* (wine grower). But our inspector found it delightful rather than contrived. 'It all works perfectly,' she says. 'What you find is a very thoughtful, charming, family-run concern, where, if the staff are not related, they seem to be godparents to each other's children.' Each of the rooms is wonderfully decorated with well-chosen pieces of furniture (including some antiques) that fit the relevant theme, and all are very good value. Particularly recommended is *L'Ecrivain* (the writer) and either of the two bedrooms in the *pigeonnier*.

The restaurant is well established – pretty much run as a separate concern. It is very popular and prone to crowds of tourists, but there is a long wooden table and open fire, and the vaulted cellars make an excellent location for the majority of the tables. And the food is delicious. Unusually for France, the restaurant does not close at 2 or 3pm after lunch, but stays open all day.

～

NEARBY Avallon (23 km); Vézelay (31 km); Auxerre (36 km).
LOCATION in village, 1 km N of Nitry exit off A6; car parking
FOOD breakfast, lunch, dinner
PRICE €-€€
ROOMS 11 double and twin, all with bath or shower; all rooms have phone, TV, minibar
FACILITIES dining room, breakfast room, terrace, garden, children's play area
CREDIT CARDS AE, DC, MC, V
CHILDREN welcome
DISABLED 3 ground floor rooms
PETS accepted
CLOSED never
PROPRIETOR Serge Lenoble

THE EAST

OULON

FERME AUBERGE DU VIEUX CHATEAU

~ FARM GUESTHOUSE ~

58700 Oulon (Nièvre)
Tel and **Fax** 03 86 68 06 77

We don't include many *fermes auberges* in our guide: they are often too uncomfortable; but we can't resist this one. You won't find much more basic accommodation than offered here – not only are the bedrooms small, but they are unpleasantly box-like and lack anything much more than a bed and a place to put your clothes. But the farm itself and the setting is simply idyllic, and it's unlikely that you would ever find this beautiful, undulating corner of Burgundy unless you were heading here.

The turreted old farm lies just outside the charming village of Oulon in a fold of green hills that stretch out on all sides. We arrived unannounced one lunchtime and were treated to one of those simple but perfect French meals that are becoming more and more of a memory than a reality. In the beamed, stone-walled dining room, we were presented with the family's own *foie gras*, as well as *côte d'agneau, pommes dauphinoise*, a tray of cheese and home-made crystallized fruit; at the next door table, farmworkers were enjoying their lunch, too. Afterwards, seduced by the place, we walked in the countryside and, despite the bedrooms, decided to stay the night. Before leaving we bought a bottle of home-made *crème de cassis*. This is a great place for young children, with farm animals, a swimming pool, and outdoor dining in summer.

~

Nearby Nevers (35 km); Vézelay (60 km).
Location just outside Oulon, 7 km NE of Prémery; car parking
Food breakfast, lunch, dinner
Price €
Rooms 9; 8 double, one family, 3 with shower and W.C., 3 with shower only, 3 with communal bathroom
Facilities dining room, courtyard, terrace, swimming pool
Credit cards MC, V **Children** welcome
Disabled not suitable **Pets** accepted
Closed Dec to Mar
Proprietors Fayolle-Tilliot family

THE EAST

POISSON

LA RECONCE

~ VILLAGE HOTEL ~

Le Bourg, 71600 Poisson (Saône-et-Loire)
TEL 03 85 81 10 72 **FAX** 03 85 81 64 34
E-MAIL la.reconce@wanadoo.fr

THE STRANGELY-NAMED VILLAGE of Poisson lies on the borders of Charolais (famous for its white cattle) and Brionnais (noted for its Romanesque churches), both beautiful, little visited stretches of rolling countryside. When farmers walked their cattle to market in St Christophe-en-Brionnais (still held every Thursday), they stopped to rest at the village inn, La Poste, which for more than 30 years has been the restaurant, specializing in Charolais beef and fish, of Denise and Jean-Noel Dauvergne. Some 10 years ago they bought the handsome house next door and converted it into a hotel. The parquet flooring in each room is original; apart from that, however, the rooms are standardized and modern, but with more comfort and attention to detail than one expects at this price. Lavatories are separate from bathrooms, and there are desks and plenty of mirrored cupboard space, with well-equipped bathrooms. Recent reports endorse its charms.

A door in the lobby of La Reconce connects with the bar of La Poste, where locals gather. The restaurant is altogether more *soignée*, with apricot walls, pale wicker chairs and white tablecloths, and a tank of tropical fish. In summer it is delightful to eat in the little garden under the shade of paulownia trees. The hands-on chef, M. Dauvergne, rarely emerges from the kitchen, while dainty and elegant Madame runs things at the front.

~

NEARBY Romanesque churches in Brionnais; Charolais.
LOCATION in village centre, opposite church, 8 km S of Paray-le-Monial; car parking
FOOD breakfast, lunch, dinner
PRICE €
ROOMS 7; 6 double and twin, one suite, 3 with shower, 4 with bath; all rooms have phone, TV, minibar, hairdrier
FACILITIES breakfast room, bar, dining room, verandah, garden
CREDIT CARDS AE, MC, V **CHILDREN** accepted
DISABLED one specially adapted suite **PETS** accepted
CLOSED Mon, Tue, except Aug
PROPRIETORS Dauvergne family

THE EAST

St-Boil

AUBERGE DU CHEVAL BLANC
~ VILLAGE HOTEL ~

71390 St-Boil (Saône-et-Loire)
Tel 03 85 44 03 16 **Fax** 03 85 44 07 25

IN LOVELY COUNTRYSIDE close to the Charolais region, a good stopover en route between the vineyards of Burgundy and Beaujolais. The owners, Martine and Jany Cantin (he is Burgundian, but spent time at the famous Closerie de Lilas in Paris before opening up here in the late 1980s) have augmented the village *auberge* (where there are three very simple bedrooms) by providing further bedrooms in a handsome *maison bourgeoise* across the road. In its grounds is an attractive swimming pool surrounded by a swathe of green lawn. Although the house is charming, with a lovely wooded staircase, bedrooms unfortunately pay little attention to its 18thC period. They are perfectly acceptable, but without much character. Those on the top floor have exposed beams and two have *oeil de boeuf* windows. Downstairs is the breakfast room for hotel guests. In a little separate building there is a useful apartment, again functional, consisting of two bedrooms, kitchenette and bathroom (adapted for use by the disabled).

Back across the road, the restaurant, which has a good local reputation, is soothing and sophisticated, decked in pale green and cream, with a shady courtyard where you can dine in summer.

~

Nearby Cluny (28 km); Côte Chalonais vineyards.
Location on D981, on main street in village between Chalon and Cluny; with car parking
Food breakfast, lunch, dinner
Price €
Rooms 13 double and twin, 10 with shower, 3 with bath, one apartment with bath; all rooms have phone, TV
Facilities sitting room, breakfast room, bar, restaurant, courtyard, swimming pool
Credit cards AE, DC, MC, V
Children accepted
Disabled specially adapted apartment **Pets** accepted
Closed mid-Feb to mid-Mar; restaurant closed Wed
Proprietors Jany and Martine Cantin

THE EAST

SAVIGNY-LES-BEAUNE

LE HAMEAU DE BARBORON

~ COUNTRY HOTEL ~

21420 Savigny-les-Beaune (Côte-d'Or)
TEL 03 80 21 58 35 **FAX** 03 80 26 10 59
E-MAIL lehameaudebarboron@wanadoo.fr **WEBSITE** www.hameau-barboron.com

THIS MUST BE THE MOST lost and alone hotel in Burgundy, yet Beaune is only ten kilometres away. To reach the converted 16thC farmhouse, you drive along a single-track road through a narrow wooded valley, which finally opens out into a wide grassy meadow. Barboron lies amidst a vast *domaine de la chasse*, and wild boar are hunted here, as they have been for centuries, every Saturday between October and February.

The lovely old farm buildings, grouped around a courtyard, have been impeccably restored, as has the interior. It's all in magazine-perfect, rustic chic good taste – perhaps too perfect. Even the staff kitchen, seen through glass doors from the reception hall, looks like a carefully arranged set piece. A table in reception is artfully strewn with glossy magazines, all opened at pages showing other perfect rustic chic interiors. There are stone walls, exposed beams, natural fabrics and lovely unusual floors – wood and terracotta tiles, with a hunting horn motif engraved on each of the terracotta ones. Bedrooms are spacious, elegant and restful. It's a long way to go, and a lot of money, for what amounts to a simple bed-and-breakfast place, however chic, but the peace and sense of isolation are hard to beat. And to give yourselves something to do in the evening you drive off in search of that perfect restaurant.

~

NEARBY Beaune (10 km); Côte de Beaune.
LOCATION 3 km from Savigny-les-Beaune, follow signs in village; car parking
FOOD breakfast
PRICE €€
ROOMS 12; 9 double and twin, 3 duplex sleeping 4, all with bath; all rooms have phone, TV, minibar
FACILITIES breakfast room, terrace
CREDIT CARDS AE, MC, V **CHILDREN** accepted
DISABLED one specially adapted room **PETS** accepted
CLOSED never
PROPRIETOR Odile Nominé

THE EAST

VÉZELAY

LE PONTOT
~ TOWN MANSION ~

place du Pontot, 89450 Vézelay (Yonne)
TEL 03 86 33 24 40 **FAX** 03 86 33 30 05

MOST VISITORS to this rambling fortified house – the only hotel inside the walls of the old town of Vézelay, just a short walk from the famous basilica – are captivated by its combination of character and luxury. Rebuilt after the Hundred Years War, it was added to in the 18th century. Since 1984 the American owner, architect Charles Thum, and manager Christian Abadie have skilfully converted the building into a rather special bed-and-breakfast. (Who needs a restaurant when the famous Espérance lies just down the road?) The bedrooms include a large Louis XVI apartment, with canopied beds, fireplace and private dressing room; and another with stone paving, 16thC beamed ceiling and antique, country-style furnishings.

Breakfast is served on gold-encrusted, royal blue Limoges porcelain. On cool days it is eaten in front of a blazing fire in the handsome, panelled Louis XVI *salon*; but in summer you sit outside in the delightful walled garden. Recent reports confirm that visitors continue to be entranced by Le Pontet's gracious ambience, hospitable staff, historic setting and fair prices.

~

NEARBY St-Père-sous-Vézelay (2 km); Avallon (15 km).
LOCATION in middle of town; with car parking
FOOD breakfast
PRICE €€€€
ROOMS 10; 9 double and twin, one single, all with bath; all rooms have phone
FACILITIES sitting room, bar, breakfast room, terrace, garden
CREDIT CARDS DC, MC, V
CHILDREN accepted over 10
DISABLED not suitable
PETS accepted
CLOSED Nov to Easter
MANAGER Christian Abadie

THE EAST

VILLENEUVE-SUR-YONNE

LA LUCARNE AUX CHOUETTES

~ RESTAURANT-WITH-ROOMS ~

quai Bretoche, 89500 Villeneuve-sur-Yonne (Yonne)
TEL 03 86 87 18 26 **FAX** 03 86 87 22 63
E-MAIL lesliecaron-auberge@wanadoo.fr **WEBSITE** www. lesliecaron-auberge.com

THOSE WHO REMEMBER the delectable *Gigi* will have perked up when reading the e-mail and website addresses of this hotel, and indeed it is the actress Leslie Caron who owns 'The Barn Owl's Window'. She noticed the riverside property – a row of four 17thC derelict houses by the side of a graceful old bridge – on her way in and out of town from her nearby home, and renovated and opened them as a restaurant with four rooms in 1993. It makes a reasonable, moderately priced place in which to stop the night, not least because of the interesting little town of Villeneuve-sur-Yonne and the tranquil riverside setting.

There are just four rooms: three suites and a double room. They are all different and all decorated by Miss Caron, with pretty fabrics, canopied beds, an assortment of furniture, some antique, beamed walls, rugs on the floors, and nooks and crannies. They are, however, we felt, showing signs of wear and tear in places. Some are reached by dramatically steep old staircases, and the sense of being in a really old building predominates (Americans love it). The restaurant, in a 17thC warehouse with high vaulted ceiling, stone walls, roaring fire and fabric-covered chairs, is the heart of the operation (and you can eat by the river under large white parasols). The chef, Daïsuke Inagaki, is Japanese, but sticks to mainly French cuisine, with a few oriental touches.

~

NEARBY Porte de Joigny; Sens (14 km); Auxerre (45 km).
LOCATION in middle of town, by bridge, 14 km S of Sens; car parking
FOOD breakfast, lunch, dinner
PRICE €€-€€€
ROOMS 4; 3 suites, one double, all with bath; all rooms have phone, TV
FACILITIES bar, restaurant, terrace, bathing, fishing, boating, bicycles
CREDIT CARDS MC, V
CHILDREN accepted **DISABLED** not suitable **PETS** accepted
CLOSED Sun dinner, Mon except Jul and Aug
PROPRIETOR Leslie Caron

THE EAST

VILLA LOUISE

MANOR HOUSE HOTEL

21420 Aloxe-Corton (Côte-d'Or)
TEL 03 80 26 46 70
FAX 03 80 26 47 16
E-MAIL hotel-villa-
louise@wanadoo.fr
WEBSITE www.hotel-villa-louise.fr
FOOD breakfast, light dinner
PRICE €€
ROOMS 12
CLOSED never

WE REGRET HAVING TO DEMOTE this lovely 17thC mansion, which has long featured in these pages, from a long to a short entry after negative reports concerning both the welcome and the condition of the rooms. Véronique Perrin is now running her grandmother's house alone, and we would welcome more reports. It has a splendid setting next to the Château in this tiny village, a place of pilgrimage for lovers of great white wines, and is full of old timber work and beamed ceilings, with a large airy salon, which opens out on to the park and vineyards, and a garden dotted with attractive tables and chairs. Véronique, who makes her own wine, has redecorated the public rooms with flair. New indoor pool and solarium.

LE CEP

TOWN HOTEL

*27 rue Maufoux, 21206 Beaune
(Côte-d'Or)*
TEL 03 80 22 35 48 **FAX** 03 80 22 76 80
E-MAIL resa@hotel-cep-beaune.com
WEBSITE www.hotel-cep-beaune.com
FOOD breakfast, lunch, dinner
PRICE €€
ROOMS 61
CLOSED never

ALTHOUGH IT IS somewhat larger than our usual limit, we include Le Cep because it is a good hotel with plenty of character, and the best address in the centre of Beaune. A stone's throw from the Hôtel-Dieu, it has sumptuously furnished public rooms and attractive – though mostly quite small – bedrooms, with antique furniture and beams. Breakfast ('excellent; much more than just croissants') is served in the vaulted former wine cellar or, in summer, in the pretty arcaded Renaissance courtyard. Although only breakfast is served, most guests dine in the restaurant next door. The Bernard family and their staff are genuinely friendly and hospitable. Off the lovely courtyards, five new suites have been created.

THE EAST

CHAGNY

CHATEAU DE BELLECROIX

CHATEAU HOTEL

71150 Chagny (Saône et Loire)
TEL 03 85 87 13 86 **FAX** 03 85 91 28 62 **E-MAIL** info@chateau-bellecroix.com
WEBSITE www.chateau-bellecroix.com
FOOD breakfast, lunch, dinner
PRICE €€ **ROOMS** 20
CLOSED mid-Dec to mid-Feb, Wed Oct
to end May; restaurant Mon lunch,
Wed, Thur lunch

IMPRESSIVELY TOWERING, mellow exterior walls, covered with creeper; a charming hostess, Delphine Gautier, who took over from her mother a few years ago; a roomy but friendly dining room, whose good reproduction panelling gives it a Scottish baronial feel; just off it is a snug little sitting room, done in smart contemporary papers and fabrics. The larger of the bedrooms have massive walls, antique tiled floors and eclectic furnishings. If you like the 'castle experience', these will probably outweigh the drawbacks: some dull smaller bedrooms and traffic noise from the adjacent main road – though only heard outside.

CHAROLLES

HOTEL DE LA POSTE

TOWN HOTEL

*place de l'Eglise, 71120 Charolles
(Saône-et-Loire)*
TEL 03 85 24 11 32 **FAX** 03 85 24 05 74
E-MAIL contact@la-poste-hotel.com
WEBSITE www.la-poste-hotel.com
FOOD breakfast, lunch, dinner
PRICE € **ROOMS** 17 **CLOSED** mid-Nov to Dec, Sun dinner, Mon

A PRIME EXAMPLE of a provincial hotel and restaurant doing a sound job. Its long-time chef/*patron*, moustachioed Daniel Doucet, has now been joined by his son Frédéric in the kitchen, which dishes out a mean *côte de boeuf charolais à deux temps*. The white-painted building is immaculately maintained, as is the smart bar/*salon*, and the pale yellow panelled dining room is postively ritzy by small town standards. It is also possible to dine in the flowery internal courtyard. Bedrooms are unexceptional but smartly done out, with an occasional lapse of taste here and there. There are five new air conditioned rooms in a villa opposite the hotel, whose attractive garden overlooks the river. A useful address if you are passing.

THE EAST

CLUNY

HOTEL DE BOURGOGNE

TOWN HOTEL

place de l'Abbaye, 71250 Cluny (Saône-et-Loire)
TEL 03 85 59 00 58 **FAX** 03 85 59 03 73 **E-MAIL** contact@hotel-cluny.com
WEBSITE www.hotel-cluny.com
FOOD breakfast, lunch, dinner
PRICE €€ **ROOMS** 17
CLOSED Dec to Feb, Tue and Wed Feb; restaurant Tue, Wed

AFTER MANY YEARS, this is still our favourite Cluny hotel. It's close to the abbey (in fact it was built in 1917 on abbey ground), facing Cluny's large main square. We particularly like the calm but friendly atmosphere. There's a charming, long, low-ceilinged sitting room with a creaky polished floor, and a graceful dining room with large open fire and an arresting black-and-white tiled floor. Frédéric Carayon's three menus offering mainly Burgundian specialities draw many a non-resident. Off reception is a neat little bar, and a sunny courtyard gives yet another dimension to the public areas. Bedrooms are generally unexceptional, but comfortable. Owners Nathalie and Michel Colin are young and friendly.

CORDON

LE CORDONANT

MOUNTAIN HOTEL

47400 Cordon (Haute-Savoie)
TEL 04 50 58 34 56
FAX 04 50 47 95 57
FOOD breakfast, lunch, dinner
PRICE €
ROOMS 16
CLOSED Sep to mid-Dec, May to early Jul

THIS HOTEL IS AT 1000m above sea level: the air goes straight to the bottom of your lungs. There are, of course, plenty of mountain chalets similar to this one, but M. Pugnat has spent last year renovating, creating a very smart small hotel (at least, on the inside; outside it still has a charmingly 1970s Alpine not-so-chic feel, with pink and brown wooden boards adorning the walls). The bedrooms are small but comfortable, and there is a first-rate spa and incredible views. Breakfast is served outside if the weather permits, and you can bet your eggs will be fresh. This place offers excellent value, and does not try to be anything other than a good, family-run mountain chalet.

THE EAST

AUBERGE DES CHASSEURS

COUNTRY HOTEL

Naz Dessus, 01170 Echenevex (Ain)
TEL 04 50 41 54 07
FAX 04 50 41 90 61
FOOD breakfast, lunch, dinner
PRICE €€€ **ROOMS** 15
CLOSED mid-Nov to Mar

AT THE FOOT of the Jura mountains, facing the Alps (with views over Lake Geneva to Mont Blanc), this is an attractive converted farmhouse with a warm welcome. It has been in the family of its owner, Dominique Lamy, since the mid-19th century, and thanks to the attentions of a Swedish decorator is now dressed in a Scandinavian-inspired coat of paint effects which includes patterned beams, painted ceilings, and doors adorned with flowers and inscriptions. The satisfying food in the stylish dining room is complemented by an excellent, well-priced wine list. The pool, the lovely flowery terrace and the very reasonable prices are a bonus.

AU GAY SEJOUR

COUNTRY HOTEL

Le Tertenoz de Seythenex, 74210 Faverges (Haute-Savoie)
TEL 04 50 44 52 52
FAX 04 50 44 49 52 **E-MAIL** hotel-gay-sejour.com@wanadoo.fr
FOOD breakfast, lunch dinner
PRICE € **ROOMS** 11 **CLOSED** mid-Nov to mid-Dec; restaurant Sun dinner, Mon

A SIMPLE, honest and much admired inn which stands in a secluded spot not far from Lac d'Annecy en route to the major ski resorts. The sturdy 17thC former farmhouse has been in the dedicated hands of the Gay family for generations; chef/*patron* Bernard Gay was taught to cook by his grandmother and will one day hand over the running of the place to his son, who is training as a chef. Food is at the heart of the house, with plenty of fish dishes, both from local lakes and the sea, as well as regional specialities such as truffles in season. Bedrooms are simple and spotless, with pine panelled walls and straightforward modern furnishings. There are beautiful views from the terrace; peace and quiet is assured.

THE EAST

LYON

HOTEL DES ARTISTES

CITY HOTEL

8 rue Gaspard André, 69002 Lyon (Rhône)
TEL 04 78 42 04 88
FAX 04 78 42 93 76
E-MAIL hartiste@club-internet.fr
WEBSITE www.hoteldesartistes.fr
FOOD breakfast **PRICE** €-€€€
ROOMS 45 **CLOSED** never

THIS HOTEL COMES WITH A LONG HISTORY: located next to the Théâtre des Célestins, it has housed various well-known actors and singers over the years. Ask the staff for stories about them. Well placed by the Saône and the bridges over to Vieux Lyon, you will be in easy walking distance of the sights. There are surprisingly big bathrooms in the redecorated rooms, although otherwise the feel is smart but unexceptional. Room 204 (not redecorated so slightly cheaper) is very large, and therefore great value. No bar or restaurant, but a pretty Mediterranean-style breakfast room, and a lovely friendly staff who are mines of information on where to eat and shop locally. A reliable bet for a stop in downtown Lyon.

MAILLY-LE-CHATEAU

LE CASTEL

VILLAGE GUESTHOUSE

2 place de l'Eglise, 89660 Mailly-le-Château (Yonne)
TEL 03 86 81 43 06
FAX 03 86 81 49 26
E-MAIL lecastelmailly@aol.com
WEBSITE www.lecastelmailly.com
FOOD breakfast, lunch, dinner (by arrangement)
PRICE €€ **ROOMS** 6
CLOSED never

A RECENT INSPECTION REVEALED a change of ownership at this hotel. The new owners, Dominique and Elisabeth Meuterlos, are a lovely couple, who want their guests to feel part of the family: you eat around one big table, they buy local wine for all to drink, and encourage you to chat and to get to know one other. They are carrying out much-needed renovations, gradually doing up all the bedrooms and creating fewer, but larger, family suites, with disabled access on the ground floor. However the main areas – sitting and dining rooms – still feel uncomfortably in need of repair, so be warned that the hotel is basic, even though the welcome is genuine. Reports would be appreciated.

THE EAST

PULIGNY-MONTRACHET

MONTRACHET
TOWN HOTEL

*10 place des Marronniers, 21190
Puligny-Montrachet (Côte-d'Or)*
TEL 03 80 21 30 06
FAX 03 80 21 39 06
E-MAIL info@le-montrachet.com
WEBSITE www.le-montrachet.com
FOOD breakfast, lunch, dinner
PRICE €€€
ROOMS 32
CLOSED Dec

THE CENTRE of Puligny-Montrachet, place des Marronniers, is laid to grass and surrounded by chestnut trees and by the outlets of local wine-growers. The handsome stone-built hotel overlooks the square, and though the interior lacks character, and (we thought) is priced somewhat on the high side, it makes a useful stopover while touring the vineyards. Opened in the 1980s, it is furnished in a smart though rather functional way, with the same chairs (modern version of the traditional tapestry) used throughout the public rooms. 22 rooms are located in the main building, the others in a separate building across the street. The spacious, calm restaurant, serving local specialities, has a Michelin star. In summer you can sit on the pretty front terrace.

SAINT-GERVAIS

CHALET REMY
CHALET HOTEL

*Le Bettex, 74170 St-Gervais
(Haute-Savoie)*
TEL 04 50 93 11 85
FAX 04 50 93 14 45
FOOD breakfast, lunch, dinner
PRICE €
ROOMS 19
CLOSED early Nov to late Dec

IN SHARP CONTRAST to the glossy chalet hotels of nearby Megève (see page 171), this chalet is as simple – and as genuine – as you could hope to find, with all the associated charm. With breathtaking views across to Mont Blanc, it's a traditional stone and log 18thC farmhouse which retains its original woodwork. The interior seems to have been frozen in time for at least 50 years. A central staircase leads to a rectangular gallery with bedrooms off it. These, all wood, are tiny and very simple but warm, with comfortable beds, and the communal bathrooms are *très propre*. Traditional, satisfying dishes are served in a candlelit dining room, and there's a fine terrace with views overlooking the garden and mountains.

THE EAST

VAL-DE-MERCY

AUBERGE DU CHATEAU

RESTAURANT-WITH-ROOMS

3 rue du Pont, 89680 Val-de-Mercy (Yonne)
TEL 03 86 41 60 00
FAX 03 86 41 73 28
E-MAIL delfontainej@wanadoo.fr
FOOD breakfast, lunch, dinner
PRICE € **ROOMS** 5
CLOSED mid-Jan to Mar; restaurant Sun dinner, Mon

WE INCLUDE this hotel in a little riverside village deep in the quiet countryside in the hope that it is as nice as it looks from the outside. We were recommended it *en passant* while in the area, but sadly when we turned up it was unexpectedly closed. Still, a good poke round gave us every intention of returning – it looked very promising, stylish yet informal, with an elegant restaurant fashioned from two rooms and a pretty courtyard for summer dining. Bedrooms, we are told, have parquet floors, old roses on the curtains and a good smattering of antiques. The menu looked tempting ... the chef/*patron* proudly told us (on the phone) that he had been trained by Michel Roux in England ... reports please.

VEYRIER-DU-LAC

LA DEMEURE DE CHAVOIRE

LAKESIDE HOTEL

route d'Annecy-Chavoire, 74290 Veyrier-du-Lac (Haute-Savoie)
TEL 04 50 60 04 38
FAX 04 50 60 05 36
E-MAIL demeure.chavoire@wanadoo.fr
WEBSITE www.demeuredechavoire.com
FOOD breakfast, snacks
PRICE €€€
ROOMS 13 **CLOSED** never

THERE HAS BEEN a change of ownership at this hotel, situated on the shores of Lake Annecy and, conveniently, on the main road to the ski resorts. Although we haven't been able to inspect recently, on our last visit, we found it an impeccably kept, charming place set in a pretty garden, a happy combination of traditional elegance and modern comforts. Every room has been thoughtfully and richly furnished, and the bedrooms are all individually decorated in romantic style. They are named after local beauty spots and famous writers – you may sleep in the Jean-Jacques Rousseau suite. Reception rooms have marquetry floors, panelled walls and embossed ceilings. Plenty of good taste and calm. Reports please.

THE SOUTH-WEST

HOTELS IN THE SOUTH-WEST

THE LIMOUSIN HILLS represent the watershed between the basins of the Charente and the Loire, to the north, and that of the Garonne and its tributaries, to the south; and the start of our South-West region.

With Atlantic beaches, the expanses of the Landes, the Basque country, the Pyrenees and the Spanish border, and fine examples of medieval towns, villages and fortified *bastides,* this is a region rich in diversity, tradition and history. You can also eat memorably - the area is renowned throughout France for its gastronomy and is fiercely proud of its reputation.

For many visitors, the valleys of the Dordogne and the Lot represent an ideal, not only of France but of life itself – life in a kind climate and a fertile landscape. Correspondingly, our concentration of hotels here is second only to that of Provence. Our recent researches for this edition have revealed a welcome stability amongst these hotels; old favourites – for example, the **Moulin de l'Abbaye** (page 197) at Brantôme, **Manoir de Hautegente** at Coly (page 202), **La Pélissaria** at St-Cirq-Lapopie (page 219) and **Domaine de la Rhue** at Rocamadour (page 217) – remain consistent, while we have added some interesting new addresses, such as **Le Jardin d'Eyquem** at St-Michel-de-Montaigne (page 226) and **Domaine de St-Géry** at Lascabanes (page 209). We can also recommend **Les Tendoux** at Issigeac (tel 05 53 24 30 00), where the congenial hosts have found the perfect balance between pampering and privacy. Further south, the peaceful, rolling countryside of Gascony, its gastronomic delights and its fortified *bastides* have become much better known to holidaymakers of late and this is reflected in the number of interesting hotels we have discovered there: **Domaine de Bassibé** (page 236) and **Château de Projan** (page 215) to name but two.

Only a handful of addresses in the Bordeaux wine region and the strange, immense expanses of the Landes, but useful ones. In the marvellous landscape of the Pyrenees, we again find consistency, with such old favourites as **Arcé** at St-Etienne-de-Baïgorry still on top form after five generations in the same hands (page 223) and **Arraya** at Sare after three (page 228). Useful new addresses include **Maison Garnier** at Biarritz (page 194), **Petit Hotel Labottierre** at Bordeaux (page 196) and **Domaine de l'Aragon** at Herrere (page 207).

The hotels in this guide represent the pick of the region, but there are many other excellent addresses. For wider coverage, see *Charming Small Hotel Guides* Southern France.

THE SOUTH-WEST

AGNAC

CHATEAU DE PECHALBET

~ COUNTRY HOUSE HOTEL ~

47800 Agnac (Lot-et-Garonne)
TEL and FAX 05 53 83 04 70
E-MAIL pechalbet@hotmail.com **WEBSITE** www.pechalbet.free.fr

WHEN HENRI PEYRE and his wife, Françoise, fled from the crowded shores of the Riviera in 1995 in search of somewhere quiet in the country, their initial idea was to provide *chambres d'hôte* with breakfast only. But they found that guests were most reluctant to tear themselves away from the huge rooms and peace of this beautiful 17thC château to go out to eat in restaurants at the end of the day and last year Mme Peyre gave in to pressure and now cooks dinner. 'It's very pleasant,' says her husband. 'We all gather on the terrace to watch the sunsets, then eat by candelight and talk and talk. It's sometimes very difficult to get our guests to bed.' Prices are kept deliberately low to encourage people to come for several days, or even weeks, at a time. There is a huge amount of space – rooms, furnished with charming antiques, are enormous and all open on to the terrace – and the house has an intriguing history. Sheep graze in the park, when autumn comes around logs crackle in the massive stone fireplace and there is mushrooming in the woods. For guests M. Peyre has his own list of what he claims are entirely secret places that he has discovered himself to be visited nearby, and he and his wife offer the warmest of welcomes. Reports please.

~

NEARBY Eymet (4 km); Bergerac (25 km).
LOCATION on 40-hectare country estate; signposted S of Eymet on D933 to Miramont; ample car and garage parking
FOOD breakfast, dinner
PRICE €
ROOMS 5 double and twin, all with bath or shower
FACILITIES 2 sitting rooms, bar, dining room, terrace, gardens, swimming pool
CREDIT CARDS not accepted
CHILDREN welcome
DISABLED no special facilities **PETS** accepted
CLOSED Dec to Apr
PROPRIETOR Henri Peyre

THE SOUTH-WEST

AINHOA

OHANTZEA
~ VILLAGE HOTEL ~

64250 Aïnhoa, (Pyrénées-Atlantiques)
TEL 05 59 29 90 50 **FAX** 05 59 29 89 70

A WARM WELCOME AWAITS in this unpretentious, seriously Basque hotel dating back to the 17th century and in the same family for the past three centuries. The timbered and shuttered building in the centre of a picturesque village is typical of the region. Inside, you step back in time, with bare, worn wooden flooring, beamed ceilings, old pictures, shelves of antique kitchen utensils, copper kettles, pewter jugs – and no concession to modern materials or ornament. French windows look out on to the garden from the spacious dining room. Bedrooms are large and convey the same mood of established solidarity and family farmhouse comfort. Mme Ithurria modestly explains that 'this is not a modern house and we have no formula, except to provide the atmosphere of a family home and fair prices'. It is not surprising that it is much patronized by our readers. The food, too, caters to old-fashioned tastes with large helpings of succulent baby lamb and other local products. Great value for money.

The area is renowned for its mild climate; Edmond Rostand, author of *Cyrano de Bergerac*, came here to take the spa waters and liked it so much that he built a house nearby, Villa Arnaga (open to visitors on the D932).

NEARBY Spanish border (2 km); Villa Arnaga; St-Pée-sur-Nivelle (10 km); Sare (10 km).
LOCATION in middle of village, 10 km SW of Cambo-les-Bains; car parking
FOOD breakfast, lunch, dinner
PRICE €
ROOMS 10; 8 double and twin, 2 family, all with bath; all rooms have phone
FACILITIES sitting room, dining room, garden
CREDIT CARDS AE, DC, MC, V
CHILDREN welcome
DISABLED no special facilities
PETS accepted
CLOSED mid-Nov to mid-Feb
PROPRIETOR Marcel Ithurria

THE SOUTH-WEST

LE SQUARE

~ VILLAGE HOTEL ~

5/7 place de la Craste, 47220 Astaffort (Lot-et-Garonne)
TEL 05 53 47 20 40 **FAX** 05 53 47 10 38
E-MAIL Latrille.Michel@wanadoo.fr **WEBSITE** www.latrille.com

WARM OCHRE AND SIENNA-WASHED EXTERIORS, blue shutters and striped awnings on a little *place* filled with roses and pergolas really make you feel you are heading south. There have been recent improvements at this charming little hotel since Agen chef Michel Latrille and his wife, Sylvie, took over. Now there is a satisfying combination: M. Latrille's excellent traditional local cuisine and stylish, comfortable, spacious bedrooms with shining bathrooms, all set off by Mme Latrille's vivacity. No expense has been spared on the high quality renovation of two adjoining houses and the smart Kenzo fabrics, painted furniture, modern uplighting and glistening tiled bathrooms are pleasingly fresh and uplifting. This little hotel is just the right size and the Latrilles have created an easy informality, while assuring that there are no slips in their standards. Nooks and crannies of the hotel are filled with interesting detail; a small Moorish-style patio with olive tree helps to give the impression you are not far away from the road to Spain and there's a large, leafy outside terrace on the first floor for eating on summer evenings. Outside, dogs bark, old men play *boules* and children scamper in the square.

~

NEARBY Agen (18 km); *bastides*; Garonne river.
LOCATION in village centre; garage and street car parking
FOOD breakfast, lunch, dinner
PRICE €€
ROOMS 14; 12 double and twin, 2 suites, 11 with bath and 3 with shower; all rooms have phone, TV, air conditioning, minibar, safe, hairdrier
FACILITIES sitting room, dining room, lift, terrace
CREDIT CARDS MC, V
CHILDREN accepted
DISABLED one specially adapted room
PETS accepted
CLOSED one week in May; 3 weeks in Nov
PROPRIETORS Michel and Sylvie Latrille

THE SOUTH-WEST

BARCUS

CHEZ CHILO
~ VILLAGE HOTEL ~

64130 Barcus (Pyrénées-Atlantiques)
TEL 05 59 28 90 79 **FAX** 05 59 28 93 10
E-MAIL martine.chilo@wanadoo.fr

IT IS WELL WORTH making a detour to enjoy the delights of this small hotel on the borders of the verdant Basque and Béarn country. The expertise of three generations has created a place of welcome, comfort and wonderful food. The attractive building harmonizes with the surrounding village, with a delightful garden and children's play area, and a discreetly located swimming pool with mountain views. The rooms have all been recently refurbished, and are bright and friendly without extravagance. Downstairs is an L-shaped dining room with open fireplace, a large sitting room with a bar, reminiscent of an English country inn, and a main dining room with picture windows on to the garden. This is the setting for a memorable meal. Early each morning the freshest and best of local produce is delivered straight from the market, ready to be transformed by Pierre Chilo into dishes of exceptional refinement and quality. This is a refreshing, reasonably-priced, efficient and very enjoyable stopping-place for the traveller and Martine and Pierre Chilo specialize in a warm Basque welcome. Note that they have recently acquired another hotel, the Bidegain, with period Basque interior, in nearby Mauléon (tel 05 59 28 16 05).

~

NEARBY Pau (50 km); the Spanish border.
LOCATION in village, on D24 between Oloron Ste-Marie and Mauléon; ample car parking
FOOD breakfast, lunch, dinner
PRICE €-€€€
ROOMS 10; 7 double and twin, 3 family, 6 with bath (3 Jacuzzi), 4 with shower
FACILITIES sitting room/TV room, bar, restaurant, terrace, garden, swimming pool
CREDIT CARDS AE, DC, MC, V
CHILDREN welcome
DISABLED one specially adapted room
PETS accepted
CLOSED Jan
PROPRIETORS Pierre and Martine Chilo

THE SOUTH-WEST

BIARRITZ

MAISON GARNIER

~ TOWN GUESTHOUSE ~

29 rue Gambetta, 64200 Biarritz (Pyrénées-Atlantiques)
TEL 05 59 01 60 70 **FAX** 05 59 01 60 80
E-MAIL maison-garnier@hotel-biarritz.com **WEBSITE** www.hotel-biarritz.com

A SHORT WALK up from the two main beaches brings you to an old part of the town which belongs to the locals and seems unconnected with surfers and seaside congress venues. It is here that Jean-Christophe Garnier has transformed a neglected old family hotel into the pleasantest place to stay in Biarritz at a reasonable price. With a background in hotel administration, he has applied his professional skill and experience down to the smallest detail with the result that you will find everything you need and nothing you don't. The rooms are uncluttered, with comfortable beds, fittings which are in the right place and work, superb showers (always a triumph to find showers which work perfectly), practical storage facilities.

The dining room is light and pleasant; only breakfast is served but this starts with freshly pressed orange juice and includes a buffet selection of fresh breads and croissants, jams and coffee, so that you don't have to wait or ask for more. The sitting area is stylishly different with a fireplace and interesting pictures on the walls. Wooden floors, white walls and light fabrics lend an almost colonial air which is very attractive. Monsieur Garnier knows what he is doing, and is doing it well.

~

NEARBY market; seafront; golf; town centre.
LOCATION follow signs for Centre Ville, place Clémenceau, then left by Bank Inchauspé (large white building) into rue Gambetta; car parking in street
FOOD breakfast
PRICE €-€€
ROOMS 7 double and twin, all with shower; all rooms have phone, TV
FACILITIES sitting room, dining room
CREDIT CARDS AE, DC, MC, V
CHILDREN accepted
DISABLED no special facilities
PETS accepted
CLOSED never
PROPRIETOR Jean-Christophe Garnier

THE SOUTH-WEST

BORDEAUX

CHAMBRE EN VILLE
~ CITY HOTEL ~

Rue Bouffard, 33000 Bordeaux
TEL 05 56 81 34 53 **FAX** 05 56 81 34 54

THIS COMES CLOSE to our idea of a perfect city centre hotel - small (just five rooms), elegant (Dutch owner Ruud Vandepol used this building previously as an art gallery, so his paintings and furniture are dotted everywhere), and relaxed (this feels more as if you have an apartment downtown, as no evening meals are served, and you reach your room via a coded doorway at night). A wonderful stone staircase spirals its way through the centre of the building, with the rooms well spaced out over three floors - and there is no lift, so do beware. It is not especially child-friendly - take your own travel cot if need be - but children will love the location, as will you, on Rue Bouffard, the chic antique district, close to the Musée des Beaux Arts and the wonderful pedestrianised heart of Bordeaux. Each room is individually decorated - we like the Bordelaise, with its antique writing table, or the Nexus next door, which is perhaps the most sumptuous. Breakfast is served on the long mahogany table downstairs, with generous jugs of orange juice and pastries.

~

NEARBY Bordeaux.
LOCATION central Bordeaux
FOOD breakfast
PRICE €€
ROOMS 5; including 3 suites
FACILITIES dining room
CREDIT CARDS AE, DC, MC, V
CHILDREN accepted
DISABLED no disabled access
PETS no
CLOSED never
PROPRIETORS Ruud Vandepol and Reme Labory

THE SOUTH-WEST

BORDEAUX

PETIT HOTEL LABOTTIERE
~ TOWN HOTEL ~

14 rue Francis Martin, 33000 Bordeaux
TEL 05 56 48 44 10 **FAX** 05 56 48 44 14

BORDEAUX IS A PLACE in flux: the old squares are being restored, the quays reclaimed and a new tramline laid down that will transform the city. The hotels, however, don't seem to be keeping pace with this sense of optimism. Or so we had imagined, until we came across this - a rare chance to stay in what is effectively a living museum. Classified as a *Monument Historique*, this neo-classical house has been lovingly restored by its current owners, having been bought in 1960 and saved from demolition. The result is almost as much an exhibition as hotel, with every period detail painstakingly researched and rendered (there's an original Rubens, the sister of which is hanging in the Louvre), and two bedroom suites in a separate annexe, all furnished with perfect examples of *époque* furniture. The entire place displays just the right degree of shabbiness. There's no restaurant, but this is Bordeaux, where eating is an art form and the breakfasts are generous to a fault, all served on antique silver (as Madame says, *'c'est un vrai repas'*). Small touches make your stay even more special - the minibar, for example, is included in the price – and we were presented with the local delicacy of Brébis cheese and black cherry jam on arrival. This is a truly special place, where you are invited to share in someone's personal vision made real.

~

NEARBY Bordeaux Centre.
LOCATION Jardin Publique
FOOD breakfast
PRICE €€€
ROOMS 2
FACILITIES terrace, garden, exhibition
CREDIT CARDS AE, MC, V
CHILDREN accepted
DISABLED no disabled access **PETS** accepted
CLOSED never
PROPRIETORS Liliane and Michel Korber

THE SOUTH-WEST

BRANTOME

MOULIN DE L'ABBAYE
～ CONVERTED MILL ～

1 route de Bourdeilles, 24310 Brantôme (Dordogne)
TEL 05 53 05 80 22 **FAX** 05 53 05 75 27
E-MAIL moulin@relaischateaux.com **WEBSITE** www.relaischateaux.com

'ALTHOUGH WE ARRIVED rather late (8.30 pm), without a booking and clad in leather, we were welcomed with open arms. We stayed in one of their buildings across the river, and were upgraded to a junior suite (without asking) on the top floor which had a fabulous view to the Moulin. There was a huge bathroom with a circular marble bathtub. The room was tastefully decorated in colonial style. We would love to have stayed there longer and felt it was worth the money.' So write a very satisfied pair of motorcyclists about this exquisite little mill.

The setting is the thing. The shady riverside terrace, illuminated in the evening, is an idyllic place for a drink or a meal while admiring Brantôme's unusual angled bridge, the tower of the abbey or the swans gliding by. Wonderful views over the river and the old houses of one of the prettiest villages in France are also to be had from many of the bedrooms – all comfortably furnished, some with four-poster beds and antiques, others in more modern style.

Traditional Périgord dishes with a creative touch earn the restaurant 16/20 from Gault-Millau and a star from Michelin. The dining room makes a pleasant setting for this excellent cuisine in cooler weather, although we can raise no enthusiasm for the 'Monet-style' colour scheme.

NEARBY Antonne-et-Trigonant (3 km); Bourdeilles (10 km).
LOCATION on edge of town, 20 km N of Périgueux; garage parking across road
FOOD breakfast, lunch, dinner; room service
PRICE €€€-€€€€
ROOMS 17 double and twin, 3 apartments, all with bath; all rooms have phone, TV, air conditioning, minibar, hairdrier
FACILITIES sitting room, restaurant, terrace
CREDIT CARDS AE, DC, MC, V **CHILDREN** welcome
DISABLED no special facilities **PETS** accepted
CLOSED Nov to May
MANAGER Bernard Dessum

THE SOUTH-WEST

CHEZ MARCEL
~ VILLAGE INN ~

rue du 11 Mai 1944, 46100 Cardaillac (Lot)
TEL 05 65 40 11 16 **FAX** 05 65 40 49 08

BUILT AS AN *auberge* and stables in the mid-19th century and now the local bar-restaurant of a small village north of Figéac, this has been run for the past three years by Bernard Marcel, who took it over on the death of his father, André. Time has barely touched it and from the minute you find yourself among the red-and-white gingham tablecloths and lace curtains of the handsome ground floor rooms you are enveloped by the authentic rustic charm of days gone by. The barely believable prices and unspoiled simplicity of the place have proved a winner for the Marcel family, but some small changes are planned, though nothing that could be described as radical. Mme Marcel, Gisèle, who speaks English, is slowly adding to the delightful collection of country antiques in the bedrooms and her husband is contemplating the possibility of replacing the plastic curtain in the shower with a glass door, but he's not in any hurry. Nothing to frighten the horses, so that Chez Marcel fans, of which there are many, will not get any unwelcome shocks when they return. The chef, Jacky Fabre, has been there for 22 years and bread comes in fresh from the baker just up the road. There's plenty of life in the bar in the evenings and a pretty little village to visit.

~

NEARBY Figéac (9 km); Cahors (60 km); valley of the Lot.
LOCATION in country village; car parking in large public car park and street
FOOD breakfast, lunch, dinner
PRICE €
ROOMS 5; 4 double and 1 triple; all rooms have washbasins and share shower and WC on landing
FACILITIES restaurant, bar, terrace
CREDIT CARDS MC, V
CHILDREN accepted
DISABLED no special facilities **PETS** accepted
CLOSED 2 weeks in Feb
PROPRIETOR Bernard Marcel

THE SOUTH-WEST

HOSTELLERIE FENELON
~ VILLAGE INN ~

46110 Carennac (Lot)
TEL 05 65 10 96 46 **FAX** 05 65 10 94 86
E-MAIL contact@hotel-fenelon.com **WEBSITE** www.hotel-fenelon.com

Mme RAYNAL WAS, with her characteristic attention to detail, busy gardening and planting out geraniums in the plentiful window boxes on this jolly-looking, family-run, colourful *logis*, with red roof and red-and-white striped awnings, when we called. She likes the place to be a riot of flowers and her warm welcome and the friendly and unobtrusive service of her staff have won her many admirers among our readers. Traditionalists will be happy to know that son, Philippe, is now in the kitchen and continues his father's highly commended and generous *cuisine du terroir*. In the middle of the Haut-Quercy, Carennac is a delightful, riverside medieval village, full of charm, and quite a few of Mme Raynal's neat, clean bedrooms – conventionally decorated with reproduction furniture and flowery prints – look over the pointed Périgordan roof of a little gingerbread house on the banks of the Dordogne river. The beamed restaurant, too, overlooks the river, though meals are also served on the paved terrace at the front of the hotel, which is shielded from the quiet road by a tall hedge. Use of the swimming pool is reserved for guests. Excellent value for money and a homely ambience make this a perfect staging post for touring the area.

~

NEARBY Carennac priory; Rocamadour (30 km); Gouffre de Padirac (10 km).
LOCATION in village centre; ample car parking
FOOD breakfast, lunch, dinner
PRICE €
ROOMS 15 double and twin, all with bath or shower; all rooms have phone, TV
FACILITIES sitting room, dining room, bar, terrace, garden, swimming pool
CREDIT CARDS DC, MC, V
CHILDREN accepted
DISABLED access difficult
PETS accepted
CLOSED mid-Jan to mid-Mar
PROPRIETORS M. and Mme Raynal and sons

THE SOUTH-WEST

LE MOULIN DU ROC

~ CONVERTED MILL ~

24530 Champagnac-de-Bélair (Dordogne)
TEL 05 53 02 86 00 **FAX** 05 53 54 21 31
E-MAIL moulinroc@aol.com **WEBSITE** www.moulinduroc.com

THIS DELECTABLE OLD WALNUT-OIL MILL with its Michelin-starred restaurant belongs to that rare breed of hotels that gives you the sense of being pampered without costing a fortune. The setting on the banks of the Dronne is truly romantic: the gardens are lush, secluded, shady and bursting with colour. A Japanese-style bridge crosses the river enabling you to reach a grassy area with scattered seating and discreetly positioned swimming pool and tennis court. Inside the rough-stone 17thC building, oak beams, stone fireplaces, mill machinery, rich fabrics and a wealth of antiques – oil paintings, silverware and solid Périgord dressers – combine with abundant flower arrangements to create an intimate yet highly individual style. Some may find it slightly heavy. The same cannot be said of the food: in the land of *foie gras*, Alain Gardillou manages to build on culinary traditions to produce remarkably light and inventive dishes. Breakfasts, too, are a treat, with home-baked rolls, fresh fruit, eggs and yoghurt, beautifully served. Bedrooms vary in size, but do not disappoint. Many are pretty, cosy and filled with their share of antiques; several have four-posters. Others have recently been redesigned to create fewer, more spacious rooms, including large, immaculate bathrooms. However, a recent guest felt that 'it had really become a restaurant with rooms which made the price that we had to pay outrageous'.

NEARBY Brantôme (6 km); Bourdeilles (15 km).
LOCATION in village, on D82 and D83, 6 km NE of Brantôme; car parking
FOOD breakfast, lunch, dinner
PRICE €€€
ROOMS 13; 8 double and twin, 4 junior suites, 1 suite, all with bath or Jacuzzi; all rooms have phone, TV, minibar, hairdrier, 8 rooms have air conditioning
FACILITIES sitting room, restaurant, terrace, garden, covered swimming pool, tennis
CREDIT CARDS DC, MC, V **CHILDREN** welcome
DISABLED 2 rooms on ground floor **PETS** accepted
CLOSED Jan to Mar, restaurant on Tues
PROPRIETORS M. and Mme Gardillou

THE SOUTH-WEST

CIBOURE

LEHEN TOKIA
~ SEASIDE GUESTHOUSE ~

chemin Achotarreta, 64500 Ciboure (Pyrénées-Atlantiques)
TEL 05 59 47 18 16 **FAX** 05 59 47 38 04
E-MAIL info@lehen-tokia.com **WEBSITE** www.lehen-tokia.com

THE UNUSUAL NAME means 'first house' in the strange language of the Basques, whose origins still baffle the experts. A splendid example of neo-Basque architecture, it was built in 1925 by the architect Hiriart who is credited with coining the expression 'art deco'. The house embodies many features in this style, notably stained-glass windows by Jacques Grüber, and is a *Monument Historique*. It is certainly special.

On a recent visit we found that the new proprietor, Yan Personnaz, has done much to make the house lighter, fresher and more welcoming and comfortable without sacrificing any of its spirit or charm. It still feels like a home, an atmosphere enriched by its display of personal belongings, books and paintings. All the rooms have been refurbished, and each one is different (see the hotel's excellent website). Only breakfast is served, but other meals can be delivered by a local caterer. The rose garden and pretty summerhouse and terrace look out to the ocean whilst retaining an intimate seclusion. Ideal for golfing enthusiasts: there are seven courses within a radius of 15 kilometres, and golfing trips can be organized.

~

NEARBY St-Jean-de-Luz; Spanish border; Biarritz (16 km).
LOCATION in Ciboure, across river Nivelle from St-Jean-de-Luz, well signposted in residential street withing walking distance of beach and town centre; street car parking
FOOD breakfast
PRICE ⓔⓔ
ROOMS 7; 6 double and twin, 1 suite, 5 with bath, 2 with shower; all rooms have phone, TV, minibar
FACILITIES sitting rooms, terrace, garden, swimming pool
CREDIT CARDS AE, DC, MC, V
CHILDREN accepted
DISABLED access difficult **PETS** not accepted
CLOSED mid-Nov to mid-Dec
PROPRIETOR Yan Personnaz

THE SOUTH-WEST

COLY

MANOIR D'HAUTEGENTE

~ MANOR HOUSE HOTEL ~

Coly, 24120 Terrasson (Dordogne)
TEL 05 53 51 68 03 **FAX** 05 53 50 38 52
E-MAIL hotel@manoir-hautegente.com **WEBSITE** www.manoir-hautegente.com

A READER ONCE DESCRIBED this creeper-clad manor house as 'so good that I wouldn't tell you about it if it were not already in the guide'. The house, set in beautiful wooded grounds in the heart of the Périgord Noir, has been in the Hamelin family for about 300 years, and is now run by Edith Hamelin and her son Patrick. It was built as a forge in the 13thC, later became a mill (using the stream that runs beside it), was then embellished and turned into a family residence and was finally converted into a hotel – but with the feeling of a private house skilfully retained. Public rooms and the spacious, comfortable bedrooms are imaginatively decorated with family antiques and paintings.

Dinner in the pretty vaulted dining room is a five-course affair – 'first-class cooking' which inevitably includes home-produced *foie gras*, another of the Hamelins' commercial successes. The present chef, Ludovic Lavaud, is a particular find. Wines are reasonably priced.

In the pleasant grassy grounds there is a smart pool that gets plenty of sun. There is also a pond, and fishing is available on the local river. The Hamelins are natural hosts and a warm welcome awaits guests to their family home.

~

NEARBY châteaux; Lascaux (15 km); Sarlat (25 km).
LOCATION in countryside, 6 km SE of Le Lardin on D62, in own grounds; ample car parking
FOOD breakfast, dinner
PRICE €€
ROOMS 15 double and twin, all with bath; all rooms have phone, TV, hairdrier
FACILITIES sitting room, dining room, terrace, garden, swimming pool
CREDIT CARDS AE, DC, MC, V
CHILDREN welcome
DISABLED 2 rooms available
PETS accepted
CLOSED Nov to Easter
PROPRIETORS Edith Hamelin and Patrick Hamelin

THE SOUTH-WEST

CONDOM

TROIS LYS

~ TOWN HOTEL ~

38 rue Gambetta, 32100 Condom (Gers)
TEL 05 62 28 33 33 **FAX** 05 62 28 41 85
E-MAIL hoteltroislys@minitel.net **WEBSITE** www.gascogne.com/htroislys

T HIS BEAUTIFULLY RESTORED 18thC town house is an old favourite of ours for its restrained elegance both externally and within. It is a real oasis of calm and quiet despite its location in the centre of a busy market town. Its new owner, Pascal Miguet, is as dedicated as his predecessor and draws on long experience working in international hotels. A charming new dining room gives a feeling of space and at the same time initimacy, as does the friendly new bar. The hotel is now air-conditioned throughout. In summer the entrance courtyard which leads off the pedestrian precinct is decorated with shrubs and flowers, and set with chairs and tables. You can eat here when the weather permits. The kitchen specializes in fresh local produce cooked with care and expertise, but without pretension.

Despite another new feature, a fully-equipped meeting room, the Trois Lys continues to feel more like a home than a hotel. All is light and restful, with Versailles parquet floors, original moulded wood panelling – and a perfect wide stone staircase with wrought iron balustrade. The bedrooms are in keeping, each with a different colour scheme, with antique or reproduction furniture. Outside there is a large swimming pool and terrace, discreetly hidden behind a wall, and shaded.

~

NEARBY Cathédrale St-Pierre; Musée d'Armagnac.
LOCATION in town centre, car parking
FOOD breakfast, lunch, dinner
PRICE €€€
ROOMS 10; 9 double and twin, 1 single, 8 with bath, 2 with shower; all rooms have phone, TV, air conditioning, hairdrier
FACILITIES dining room, terrace, swimming pool
CREDIT CARDS V
CHILDREN welcome
DISABLED access difficult **PETS** accepted
CLOSED never
PROPRIETOR Pascal Miguet

THE SOUTH-WEST

LES EYZIES-DE-TAYAC

LE MOULIN DE LA BEUNE

~ VILLAGE HOTEL ~

24620 Les Eyzies de Tayac (Dordogne)
TEL 05 53 06 93 39 **FAX** 05 53 06 94 33
E-MAIL souliebeune@perigord.com **WEBSITE** www.moulindelabeune.com

LES EYZIES can be a crowded place – one of the most visited villages in France, so it is said – but signs to the Moulin take you down a track and under the bridge that is the main road to a hidden leafy little enclave on the banks of the Beune, where all you can hear is the sound of rushing water. This is an elegant little hotel, where with simple good taste, Mme Soulié puts together old and new with charming results. In the red-tiled entrance hall, logs crackle in the large stone fireplace to mingle with the sound of the river; there are umbrellas by the door for guests. You look out on to a verdant, shaded, waterside terrace. Rooms are decorated with light, restful colours and there are architectural prints of Versailles on the walls of the corridor. For those who absolutely must see a TV, there is one in the small breakfast room downstairs. The visitors' book is full of tributes: 'everything one loves to encounter – courtesy, good taste, style, high standards and warmth...an enchanted place'. In the evenings, you walk over a little bridge to the restaurant in another part of the restored water mill, where the old wheel still turns and M. Soulié prepares his *Perigordan* specialities. Budget prices, a sublime setting, and easy parking make this a perfect base.

~

NEARBY National Museum of Prehistory; caves; troglodytic village; *bastides*.
LOCATION in village centre; car parking
FOOD breakfast, lunch, dinner
PRICE ⓔ
ROOMS 20 double and twin, 14 with bath, 6 with shower; all rooms have phone
FACILITIES small sitting room, dining room, terrace, garden
CREDIT CARDS AE, MC, V
CHILDREN welcome
DISABLED no special facilities
PETS accepted
CLOSED Nov to Apr
PROPRIETORS Annick and Georges Soulié

THE SOUTH-WEST

FOURCES

CHATEAU DE FOURCES
~ CHATEAU HOTEL ~

32250 Fourcès (Gers)
TEL 05 62 29 49 53 **FAX** 05 62 29 50 59
E-MAIL chatogers@aol.com **WEBSITE** www.chateau_Fources.com

THE ORIGINS OF THIS FORTIFIED CASTLE are traced back to the 12th century. It stands guarding the entrance to a circular *bastide* (very popular with tourists in summer) with typical half-timbered houses and covered arcades near the river Azoue. Thanks to the energy, dedication and flair of its present owner, Patrizia Barsan, it has been meticulously restored and transformed into a delightful hotel which successfully blends the requirements of modern man into an ancient setting. The massive stone masonry of the high walls and turret – in excellent condition – dominate, but they are softened by Renaissance mullion windows which allow in plenty of light. The central square spiral staircase was one of the first to be built in France. By some miracle an efficient lift has been installed, and leads to charmingly arranged bedrooms. A sitting room opening on to a terrace has vestiges of an old wine press. Stairs lead down to a spacious dining room where a good choice of menus is on offer. Breakfast can be served in your room if you wish. The château is surrounded by a park bordering the river which is fringed by magnificent stands of weeping willow. The swimming pool sits beside a covered terrace. Mme Barsan is a memorable hostess. Reports please.

~

NEARBY Condom (13 km); *bastides.*
LOCATION 5.5 km NE of Montréal via RD29; car parking
FOOD breakfast, lunch, dinner
PRICE €€-€€€
ROOMS 17; 12 double and twin, 5 suites, all with bath; all rooms have phone, TV, minibar, safe
FACILITIES sitting room, bar, dining room, billiard room, lift, terrace, swimming pool, fishing
CREDIT CARDS AE, DC, MC, V **CHILDREN** accepted
DISABLED no special facilities **PETS** accepted
CLOSED Oct to Dec
PROPRIETOR Mme Barsan

THE SOUTH-WEST

GRENADE-SUR-L'ADOUR

PAIN ADOUR ET FANTAISIE

~ RIVERSIDE HOTEL ~

14-16 place des Tilleuls, 40270 Grenade sur l'Adour (Landes)
TEL 05 58 45 18 80 **FAX** 05 58 45 16 57
E-MAIL pain.adour.fantaisie@wanadoo.fr

WHEN DIDIER OUDILL left for the Café de Paris, Biarritz, he was succeeded as chef/*patron* of this distinguished hotel/restaurant by Philippe Garret, who has worked here since its creation. Both served under Michel Guérard at Eugénie-les-Bains and this tutelage is evident as much in the taste and quality in the design and furnishings of the rooms as in the refinement and authority of the cuisine and service. One half of the building was an 18thC *maison de maître* and boasts a superb stone staircase and fine oak panelling and carved fireplace in part of the dining room. The other half is 17th century, with original arcading on to the market square and half-timbered walls. Much care has gone into selecting appropriate antique furniture and the atmosphere is enhanced with original paintings and fine mirrors. On the south side is a handsome wide terrace overhanging the river: a very romantic setting for a summer's evening, with elegantly-laid tables and green-and-white parasols. Bedrooms are spacious; the best are furnished in a modern style and have views over the river, and whirlpool baths. They have fanciful names, such as Clair de Lune. The food is much vaunted – M. Garret has a Michelin star.

~

NEARBY Pau (60 km); Mont-de-Marsan (14 km); Biarritz.
LOCATION 15 km SE of Mont-de-Marsan on river Adour; car parking and garage
FOOD breakfast, lunch, dinner
PRICE €€
ROOMS 11 double, all with bath; all rooms have phone, TV, hairdrier; 8 have air conditioning, minibar, safe, whirlpool bath
FACILITIES sitting room, restaurant, terrace
CREDIT CARDS AE, DC, MC, V
CHILDREN accepted
DISABLED one ground floor room
PETS accepted
CLOSED 2 weeks Feb, Sun dinner, Mon in winter, Wed
PROPRIETOR Philippe Garret

THE SOUTH-WEST

HERRERE

DOMAINE DE L'ARAGON
~ COUNTRY HOTEL ~

Route de Pau, 64680 Herrere
TEL 05 59 39 24 63 **FAX** 05 59 39 24 84
E-MAIL info@domaine-aragon.com **WEBSITE** www.domaine-aragon.com

FOUND AT THE FOOT of the Pyrenees, this 19thC country house makes an ideal base for walkers and those who enjoy mountain biking. Whilst exploring the area you will also discover the rich gastronomic history of the region, including the Jurancon's wines, Ossau valley cheese, traditional *poule au pot* and *garbue*. The hotel has bicycles you can borrow. Alternatively you could make use of the sitting room with its comfortable sofas and log fire.

The house is surrounded by large grounds filled with magnificent, old trees. If the weather permits, you can have your breakfast or supper out here. Not that the baroque dining room isn't a memorable experience - guests have been known to take photos in order to show their friends. The style and elegance found here is echoed throughout the hotel: notice especially the frescoed sitting room and the nine bedrooms with pretty flowered curtains and dark wood furniture. The views from the rooms are also worth a mention - they all look over the grounds and the best look out on to the mountains. This hotel has been taken over by new owners and is new to our guide, so reports would be welcome.

~

NEARBY Parc national des Pyrénées, Pau (25 km).
LOCATION on RN134 between Oloron-Ste-MArie (7 km) and Pau, at the entrance of Herrere, car parking available
FOOD breakfast, dinner (by reservation)
PRICE ⓔ
ROOMS 9; 3 with bath, 6 with shower; all rooms have phone, TV
FACILITIES breakfast/dining room, sitting room, library, terrace, park, seminar room
CREDIT CARDS MC, V
CHILDREN welcome
DISABLED no special facilities **PETS** accepted
CLOSED never
PROPRIETOR Eva Kratky and Helmut Fritz

THE SOUTH-WEST

LACAVE

CHATEAU DE LA TREYNE

~ CHATEAU HOTEL ~

Lacave, 46200 Souillac (Lot)
TEL 05 65 27 60 60 **FAX** 05 65 27 60 70
E-MAIL treyne@relaischateaux.com **WEBSITE** www.relaischateaux.com/treyne

W E'VE HAD OUR EYE on this little château beside the Dordogne since an
inspector came back a few years ago with a report littered with
emphatically underscored adjectives – 'gorgeous... impeccable... exceptionally comfortable'. Of course, it is not cheap; perhaps we should be
grateful that elevation to Relais et Châteaux status has not pushed
prices up further.

Michèle Gombert-Deval's house has made a splendid small hotel. It
starts with the advantage of a beautiful position, in woods on a low cliff cut
by the meandering river Dordogne. But the compelling attraction of the
château is the near-ideal balance struck between the impressiveness of a
fortified manor house and the intimacy of a genuine home. The building
dates from the early 14th century, but was substantially rebuilt in the
1600s; it is now tastefully equipped with a happy mix of furnishings –
comfy sofas in front of an open fire, as well as grand antiques.

There are long walks to enjoy in the grounds, and a very beautiful formal garden before which you can take breakfast. Excellent regional food is
served – on the delightful terrace perched above the river in good weather.

~

NEARBY Souillac (6 km); Rocamadour; Sarlat.
LOCATION 3 km W of village on D43, 6 km SE of Souillac; in large grounds beside
river; ample car parking
FOOD breakfast, lunch, dinner; room service
PRICE €€€€
ROOMS 16; 14 double and twin, 2 suites, all with bath; all rooms have phone, TV,
air conditioning, hairdrier
FACILITIES 3 sitting rooms, dining room, bar, billiard room, lift, terrace, garden,
swimming pool, tennis
CREDIT CARDS AE, DC, MC, V
CHILDREN welcome **DISABLED** access difficult **PETS** accepted
CLOSED mid-Nov to Easter
MANAGER Philippe Bappel

THE SOUTH-WEST

LASCABANES

LE DOMAINE DE SAINT-GERY

~ COUNTRY GUESTHOUSE ~

46800 Lascabanes (Lot)
TEL 05 65 31 82 51 **FAX** 05 65 22 92 89
E-MAIL duler@saint-gery.com **WEBSITE** www.saint-gery.com

FROM THE MOMENT you are welcomed into M. and Mme Duler's captivating *maison d'hôte* you know that this is going to be a special experience. The Dulers go out of their way to ensure that their guests feel completely at ease, far from the cares of the world. Nothing is too much trouble.

The farm buildings – constructed of gleaming white limestone, typical of the Quercy Blanc region – have been painstakingly restored over the years. Likewise, the guest rooms are decorated with great flare; they retain their rustic charm, but this is very gracious country living. One room occupies a vaulted, stone cave, while another features an inglenook fireplace. All are endowed with family heirlooms of distinction.

The Domaine is no longer a working farm. Instead the Dulers now concentrate on preparing top quality local produce, including prize-winning *foie gras* and succulent cured hams and sausages, which they proudly serve at their dinner table. Meals are taken together, usually at a magnificent table on the balcony, where M. Duler eagerly shares his passion for food and wine. To work up a suitably robust appetite, there are 12 km of footpaths around the property and a good-sized swimming pool. Bookings are only taken by phone or letter.

~

NEARBY Lauzerte (18 km); Cahors (18 km).
LOCATION on estate 500 m from Lascabanes; ample car parking
FOOD breakfast, dinner
PRICE €€€
ROOMS 5; 4 double and twin, 1 duplex suite, all with bath; all rooms have phone
FACILITIES sitting room, terrace, grounds, swimming pool, farm shop
CREDIT CARDS V
CHILDREN welcome
DISABLED no special facilities
PETS accepted
CLOSED Nov to April
PROPRIETORS M. and Mme Duler

THE SOUTH-WEST

LECTOURE

HOTEL DE BASTARD

～ COUNTRY TOWN MANSION ～

rue Lagrange, 32700 Lectoure (Gers)
TEL 05 62 68 82 44 **FAX** 05 62 68 76 81
E-MAIL hoteldebastard@wanadoo.fr **WEBSITE** www.hotel-de-bastard.com

LECTOURE RISES ON A HILL overlooking the beautiful valley of the Gers. It is a town of rich archaeological finds and fine architecture. So it is fitting that its best hotel stands proudly displaying all its 18thC elegance as a former private mansion. A paved upper terrace is a lovely setting for summer meals. Protected by a semi-circle of warm stone buildings, it has views over the unspoiled countryside. A lower level includes a swimming pool, and plenty of room to relax around it, with a new *salon*/bar in a separate building. Judiciously placed trees, shrubs and flowers add to the picture.

Gascony has a well-deserved reputation for its local produce – *foie gras*, duck and goose in all its forms, vegetables, fruit (including superb melons and prunes) – but rarely are they presented with such imagination and variety as here. 'The best place to eat for miles around', says one knowledgeable local resident. The dining room is made up of three *salons*, each opening into the other and full of light. Inside the hotel is decorated in sympathy with its 18thC character, with polished wood floors and pretty antique furniture. Bedrooms are mostly small; ask for one on the first floor (*premier étage*), rather than on the second, with its mansard roof. They are, however, along with the food, very good value for money.

～

NEARBY Musée Lapidaire; tannery; *bastides*; Auch (35 km).
LOCATION in town, 35 km N of Auch; car parking and garage
FOOD breakfast, lunch, dinner
PRICE €
ROOMS 29; 24 double and twin, 3 triple, 2 suites, all with bath or shower; all rooms have phone, TV, hairdrier
FACILITIES sitting room, bar, restaurant, terrace, swimming pool
CREDIT CARDS AE, DC, MC, V
CHILDREN welcome
DISABLED no special facilities **PETS** accepted
CLOSED mid-Dec to Feb
PROPRIETOR Jean-Luc Arnaud

THE SOUTH-WEST

MARTEL

RELAIS SAINTE-ANNE

～ VILLAGE HOTEL ～

rue de Pourtanel, 46600 Martel (Lot)
TEL 05 65 37 40 56 **FAX** 05 65 37 42 82
E-MAIL Relais.Sainteanne@wanadoo.fr **WEBSITE** www.relais-ste-anne.com

OCCUPYING A FORMER GIRL'S CONVENT SCHOOL, the Relais Ste-Anne is one of those understated hotels which you could quite easily walk past without noticing its presence. Inside the arched entrance – marked by a discrete sign on a narrow backstreet – lies a delightfully shaded and flower-filled courtyard with some fine specimen trees and plenty of room to spread out between the neatly clipped box hedges.

The same attention to detail is echoed in the bedrooms scattered among the 19thC buildings and a modern, but unobtrusive annexe. Each room is individually styled, from dusky tones to warm Provençal yellows and blues, or the 'English' room with its cosy floral prints, striped wallpaper and plump cushions. Several have individual terraces or balconies and most are generously proportioned, with king-size beds, although the cheapest rooms above reception are on the small side.

The owners are considering opening a restaurant across the road, but for the moment concentrate their energies on providing a top-notch breakfast with local walnut bread and homemade jams. Or, if you want more, eggs, cheese and *charcuterie*. In fine weather breakfast is served on a raised terrace overlooking the gardens – an idyllic setting.

～

NEARBY Souillac (14 km); Rocamadour (20 km).
LOCATION on S side of village; car parking
FOOD breakfast
PRICE €€
ROOMS 15; 13 double and twin, 1 single, 1 triple, all with bath or shower; all rooms have phone, TV, hairdrier
FACILITIES sitting room, terrace, garden, swimming pool
CREDIT CARDS AE, DC, MC, V
CHILDREN accepted
DISABLED one specially adapted room **PETS** not accepted
CLOSED mid-Nov to Apr
PROPRIETOR M. Bettler

THE SOUTH-WEST

MAUROUX

HOSTELLERIE LE VERT

~ FARMHOUSE HOTEL ~

Mauroux, 46700 Puy l'Evêque (Lot)
TEL 05 65 36 51 36 **FAX** 05 65 36 56 84

L E VERT goes from strength to strength. The attractions of this secluded 17thC farmhouse have been greatly increased by the construction of a swimming pool. Whatever the changes, however, it will doubtless remain the kind of hotel you look forward to returning to at the end of the day; it also looks set to become the kind you're disinclined to leave at all.

There is just a small side door to lead you inside. Within, all is original stone walls and beams ('just about perfect', comments a reader). The dining room opens out on to a terrace with wide views; through an arch at one end is a small sitting room – ideal for an aperitif. The bedrooms are all comfortably and tastefully modernized, and have lovely views. The largest are quite grand and furnished with antiques. But the most attractive are in the little annexe a couple of yards from the entrance – the lower one stone-vaulted, the upper one beamed, with a marble floor. The garden has chairs and tables, and is improving in colour despite dry summers. The owners are a friendly and hard-working couple – M. Philippe cooks (interestingly and competently), Mme Philippe serves (and also speaks excellent English).

~

NEARBY Bonaguil (15 km); Biron (35 km); Monpazier (50 km).
LOCATION in countryside, off D5 10 km SW of Puy-l'Evêque, 10 km SE of Fumel; ample car parking
FOOD breakfast, lunch, dinner
PRICE €
ROOMS 7 double and twin, all with bath or shower; all rooms have phone, TV
FACILITIES sitting room, dining room, terrace, garden, swimming pool
CREDIT CARDS AE, MC, V
CHILDREN welcome
DISABLED no special facilities
PETS accepted
CLOSED mid-Nov to mid-Feb
PROPRIETORS Eva and Bernard Philippe

THE SOUTH-WEST

MIMIZAN

AU BON COIN DU LAC

~ LAKESIDE HOTEL ~

34 avenue du Lac, 40200 Mimizan (Landes)
TEL 05 58 09 01 55 **FAX** 05 58 09 40 84
WEBSITE www.jp-caule.com

OUR LAST VISIT found changes underway at this well-loved hotel, and we are holding our breath that they will prove to be beneficial. An English owner has taken over, and is intending to renovate completely, adding new bedrooms and a swimming pool. Jean Pierre Caule, thankfully, will remain as chef, and is going for his second Michelin star, so be prepared to enjoy the fruits of his labours. However, he and his wife have decided to bow out of the day-to-day running of the hotel.

We hope this doesn't disappoint the many readers who have enjoyed this place for its slightly old-fashioned charm. The new owner is a long-term fan, and intends to preserve the unpretentious service, relaxed atmosphere and gastronomic menu that has kept so many coming back. The location, beside a large freshwater lake, surrounded by pine trees, is one of the main attractions. Apparently the ultimate aim is to become a Relais et Chateaux, so go soon if you want to enjoy the service without the prices.

~

NEARBY Bordeaux (98 km); Arcachon (65 km); Dax (70 km).
LOCATION on edge of lake, 2 km N of Mimizan; car parking
FOOD breakfast, lunch, dinner
PRICE €-€€€
ROOMS 4 (summer 2004, going to 15 summer 2005)
FACILITIES sitting room, restaurant, terrace, garden
CREDIT CARDS AE, MC, V
CHILDREN accepted
DISABLED rooms on ground floor
PETS not accepted
CLOSED never
PROPRIETOR Chris Antich

THE SOUTH-WEST

PAUILLAC

CHATEAU CORDEILLAN-BAGES

∾ CHATEAU HOTEL ∾

route des Châteaux, 33250 Pauillac (Gironde)
TEL 05 56 59 24 24 **FAX** 05 56 59 01 89
WEBSITE www.cordeillanbages.com

To BE TRUTHFUL, we wondered whether to keep this in the guide - is it too well established and admired to be truly charming? But time and again we are happily seduced by the building itself, which is perfectly proportioned for a country hotel: elegant but not imposing, with honeyed stone and one of the best gravel driveways you will find anywhere. And the staff are incredible - nothing is ever too much trouble, and you are never made to feel overawed by the encyclopaedic wine list, or the Michelin-starred food that chef Thierry Marx creates on a nightly basis. We suggest that you try the intensely succulent local *gambas*, supplied from a little port higher up the Garonne called St. Vivien. The bedrooms can be at times disappointing for a four-star hotel - the suites are wonderful, but the standard rooms lack character, although we are told these are all being redone this year. Cordeillan-Bages stands head and shoulders above the rest in this wonderful corner of the world: world-famous vineyards such as Lynch Bages, Mouton-Rothschild and Chateau Lafite are close by.

∾

NEARBY Pauillac.
LOCATION on the Route des Chateaux in Nothern Medoc
FOOD breakfast
PRICE €€€
ROOMS 30
FACILITIES dining room
CREDIT CARDS AE, DC, MC, V
CHILDREN accepted
DISABLED limited access
PETS no
CLOSED never
PROPRIETOR John-Michel Cazes

The South-West

Projan

Chateau de Projan

~ Chateau guesthouse ~

32400 Projan (Gers)
Tel 05 62 09 46 21 **Fax** 05 62 09 44 08
e-mail chateaudeprojan@libertysurf.fr

WHEN GLOBETROTTING art lover Bernard Vichet acquired this historic château he had a dream of creating something which would bring a breath of life into hotel-keeping. His key words are 'welcome, art and conviviality'. An entry in the guest book reads 'from the moment we entered I knew I was in a very special home – the cultural quality was so exciting for me', indicating how he has succeeded. The setting is magnificent, with panoramas of timeless natural beauty, the château sedate and sure in its classic grace. Inside all is light and airy, and harmoniously juxtaposes the old with the new. One enters a hall to be faced by a superb antique wooden staircase hung with highly colourful modern paintings and a floor featuring bright contemporary mosaic in marble and granite of symbolic geese taking flight. For conviviality there is a grand piano, a lovely terrace and belvedere for dancing, and a library of art books open to all. The bedrooms each display original paintings by different modern artists. The château is run with expertise by Christine Poullain. In autumn, her husband Richard runs weekend courses on how to buy and prepare fattened ducks for the table – appropriate for the home of *foie gras*.

~

Nearby Aire sur l'Adour (15 km); Eugénie-les-Bains; Pyrenees.
Location in own grounds, on rocky spur overlooking the two Lees valleys, 15 km S of Aire sur l'Adour, signposted off D134 to Sarron; car parking
Food breakfast, dinner on request
Price €-€€
Rooms 8 double and twin, all with bath or shower
Facilities sitting room, restaurant, library, terrace, garden
Credit cards MC, V
Children accepted
Disabled no special facilities
Pets accepted
Closed Fri Jan to May
Manager Christine Poullain

THE SOUTH-WEST

PUYMIROL

LES LOGES DE L'AUBERGADE
∽ VILLAGE HOTEL ∽

52 rue Royale, Puymirol (Lot-et-Garonne)
TEL 05 53 95 31 46 **FAX** 05 53 95 33 80
E-MAIL trama@aubergade.com **WEBSITE** www.aubergade.com

'*EXCELLENCE PAR EXCELLENCE*' enthused a visitor to this handsome former residence of the Counts of Toulouse, dating from the 13th century and in a little fortified village. The lodestones to Puymirol are chef Michel Trama (two Michelin stars) for his superb food, wine and cigars, and his wife Maryse, with whom he has created this international-class hotel-restaurant. The building has stone walls, high ceilings, beams, a 17thC oak staircase and is decorated with impeccable style. The extensive kitchens are impressive and full of activity with M. Trama very much in personal charge. A special feature is a large smoking room with a glass-fronted, fully humidified cabinet containing a collection of the very best Cuban cigars – not for show but for smoking.

A terrace garden, leading off the dining room, has attractive canvas sun-shades and is discreetly illuminated through trees and bushes after dark. Bedrooms, in contemporary style, are large and elegant, and bathrooms have whirlpool baths. The overall feeling inside is one of light and airiness, predominantly white (much original stone), with white furniture offset with green and the colours of the abundant floral decorations.

∽

NEARBY Agen (17 km); Moissac (32 km); Villeneuve-sur-Lot (31 km).
LOCATION in middle of small fortified village, 20 km E of Agen; car parking and garage
FOOD breakfast, lunch, dinner; room service
PRICE ⓔⓔⓔ-ⓔⓔⓔⓔ
ROOMS 10 double and twin, all with whirlpool bath or massage shower; all rooms have phone, TV, video, air conditioning, minibar, hairdrier
FACILITIES sitting room, restaurant, terrace
CREDIT CARDS AE, DC, MC, V
CHILDREN accepted
DISABLED 2 rooms on ground floor
PETS accepted
CLOSED 5 weeks Feb-Mar
PROPRIETORS Michel and Maryse Trama

THE SOUTH-WEST

ROCAMADOUR

DOMAINE DE LA RHUE
∼ CONVERTED STABLES ∼

46500 Rocamadour (Lot)
TEL 05 65 33 71 50 **FAX** 05 65 33 72 48
E-MAIL domainedelarhue@wanadoo.fr **WEBSITE** www.domainedelarhue.com

ON OUR MOST RECENT VISIT we came away more enthusiastic than ever about this truly charming place. A former stable block next to the handsome, family-owned château, it's set in peacefully rolling countryside, down a long drive, where you're assured complete silence. Above all, the Jooris are exceptional hosts: they have time for everyone, even when demands press in. Helpful and good humoured, they never intrude: the atmosphere is always good.

Their formula is simple: they serve no meals other than breakfast and light lunches (on request) by the pool, but guests are welcome to make themselves at home and spend the day relaxing by the pool if they feel like it. There's a proper reception area and large sitting areas for guests' use. Rooms are comfortable and pretty; several are ideal for families, some with kitchenettes and their own garden entrances.

Eric Jooris is a hot-air balloon pilot and will take guests for flights, weather permitting. With Gallic nonchalance, he calmly pushes away branches as the basket brushes against them on the way up out of Rocamadour's deep gorge. But he's very safe. If you like that sort of thing, don't miss a flight. In short, a brilliant place.

∼

NEARBY Rocamadour (7 km); Padirac (15 km); Carennac (20 km).
LOCATION in countryside, on N140 7 km N of Rocamadour; car parking
FOOD breakfast, light lunch
PRICE €€
ROOMS 14; 12 double and twin, 2 family, 12 with bath, 2 with shower; all rooms have phone, fan; some rooms have minibar, kitchenette, hairdrier
FACILITIES sitting room, terrace, swimming pool
CREDIT CARDS V
CHILDREN accepted
DISABLED no special facilities **PETS** accepted
CLOSED mid-Oct to Easter
PROPRIETORS M. and Mme Jooris

THE SOUTH-WEST

CHATEAU LARDIER

~ COUNTRY HOUSE HOTEL ~

route de Sauveterre, Ruch, 33350 Castillon-la-Bataille (Gironde)
TEL 05 57 40 54 11 **FAX** 05 57 40 72 35
E-MAIL chateau.lardier@free.fr **WEBSITE** www.chateau.lardier.free.fr

THE PAGES PRODUCE their own AOC Bordeaux Rouge and Rosé (bottles attractively displayed everywhere and available to accompany your own supper cooked on the barbecue by the pool) from the vineyards that surround this elegant 17th/18thC house, with its rows of white shutters and long ivy-clad stone façade. Relaxed and informal, it is the kind of place that is immediately welcoming, with spacious, airy ground floor rooms, bedrooms with views over neat rows of vines and a pleasant garden area at the rear next to the pool. If you don't want to go out in the evenings to eat locally, there's a communal barbecue under the chestnut tree and swings for children. Rooms, reached up a wide, stone staircase, are simple and basic, but antique beds have pretty cotton covers and tables have marble tops. There's a good choice of sleeping arrangements, with extra beds available, and it is hard to beat for value, given the swimming pool and the other amenities. Peace, quiet and birdsong are in abundance. A set of large sitting and games rooms is set aside on the ground floor for guests. There are plenty of country lanes to explore and walks through the vineyard at the end of a long, hot day by the pool.

~

NEARBY Castillon-la-Bataille (10 km); Dordogne river; St-Emilion (20 km).
LOCATION among vineyards; ample car parking
FOOD breakfast
PRICE €
ROOMS 7; 5 double and twin, 2 triple, 3 with bath, 4 with shower; all rooms have phone, TV
FACILITIES 2 sitting rooms, billiard room, terrace, garden, swimming pool
CREDIT CARDS MC, V
CHILDREN welcome
DISABLED no special facilities
PETS accpeted
CLOSED Nov to Mar
PROPRIETORS Jean-Noël and Evelyne Pagès

THE SOUTH-WEST

ST-CIRQ-LAPOPIE

LA PELISSARIA

〜 VILLAGE INN 〜

St-Cirq-Lapopie, 46330 Cabrerets (Lot)
TEL 05 65 31 25 14 **FAX** 05 65 30 25 52
E-MAIL lapelissariahotel@minitel.net **WEBSITE** www.perso.wanadoo.fr/hoteldelapellissaria

RECENT REPORTS LEAVE US IN NO DOUBT that the Matuchets' distinctive little hotel is as compelling as ever. The 13thC house clings to the steep hillside on the edge of the lovely medieval hilltop village of St-Cirq-Lapopie. It was lovingly restored by the Matuchets themselves, and its quirky character is such that you descend the stairs to the bedrooms which look out on to the tiny garden and enjoy stunning views over the Lot valley. The bedrooms – two of them detached from the house, down the garden – are light, airy and comfortable, with close attention to detail in the furnishings. Three large bedrooms, with two double beds in each, are located in an old house next door to the main one. The place is simply and artistically decorated, its thick stone walls painted white, with old wooden beams and tiled floors.

Although Mme Matuchet no long cooks dinner, there are plenty of good restaurants in St-Cirq-Lapopie to which the couple will direct you. Breakfast is served *alfresco* or in your room if you prefer.

M. Matuchet, who is a musician, provides a pleasant musical background with tapes of his own music. The *salon* is graced by a piano and various stringed instruments.

〜

NEARBY Peche-Merle caves and museum; Cahors (35 km).
LOCATION in village, 30 km E of Cahors; car parking difficult
FOOD breakfast
PRICE €€
ROOMS 10; 8 double and twin, 6 with bath, 2 with shower, 2 suites with bath; all rooms have phone, TV
FACILITIES sitting room, dining room, terrace, garden, small swimming pool
CREDIT CARDS MC, V
CHILDREN welcome
DISABLED one suitable bedroom **PETS** accepted
CLOSED mid Oct-mid April
PROPRIETORS Marie-Françoise Matuchet

THE SOUTH-WEST

ST-CIRQ-LAPOPIE

AUBERGE DU SOMBRAL

~ VILLAGE INN ~

place Sombral, St-Cirq-Lapopie, 46330 Cabrerets (Lot)
TEL 05 65 31 26 08 **FAX** 05 65 30 26 37

A LITTLE DOLL'S HOUSE of a hotel in this romantic medieval village on a crag overlooking the river, which is one of the major beauty spots of the Lot valley and proud of its reputation as 'Pearl of the Quercy'. Mme Hardeveld is normally to be found behind her desk in the entrance hall, which is also a cosy small *salon* for guests with a bar. Delicious smells waft out of M. Hardeveld's kitchen and copious duck and truffle dishes are served in the beamed restaurant, where table lamps and a wood fire cast a warm glow on the copper saucepans and paintings by local artists hanging on the walls. Rooms, reached by a twisting wooden staircase, are simple, smallish and unpretentious; there are pansies in the window boxes and glimpses through the curtains of narrow cobbled alleyways and stone and half-timbered buildings. Mme Hardeveld, who has been running her little *auberge* for 30 years, says there is just no room for televisions or fancy fittings to the bathrooms. But the essentials are there and they are pretty and spotlessly clean. Staff are friendly. Drinks and cups of coffee may be enjoyed at the metal tables on the pavement terrace along the front of the building. But – a warning – parking can be frustrating here.

~

NEARBY Cahors (30 km); Château de Cénevières (1 km).
LOCATION in village centre; public car parking in square
FOOD breakfast, lunch, dinner
PRICE €
ROOMS 8 double and twin, all with bath or shower; all rooms have phone
FACILITIES small sitting room, restaurant, bar, terrace
CREDIT CARDS DC, MC, V
CHILDREN welcome
DISABLED no special facilities
PETS accepted
CLOSED mid-Nov to Apr
PROPRIETORS Monique and Gilles Hardeveld

THE SOUTH-WEST

L'ABBAYE

~ VILLAGE HOTEL ~

rue de l'Abbaye, 24220 St-Cyprien (Dordogne)
TEL 0553 29 20 48 **FAX** 05 53 29 15 85
E-MAIL hotel@abbaye-dordogne.com **WEBSITE** www.abbaye-dordogne.com

THE NEARBY ABBEY OF THE AUGUSTINS gave this handsome, large, stone, 18thC house its name and you enter through an archway off the street. Mme Schaller is anxious to explain that anyone with a car should drive straight in and will then be shown the way to the private car park behind the main house. St-Cyprien is another of the little jewels of the Périgord Noir and rooms at the front of the hotel have views down towards the Dordogne and across the roofs of the village. The Schallers have been welcoming guests to the Abbaye for 30 years and are delightful hosts. M. Schaller is an expert on local history and takes groups of guests out on guided tours. But there is much history in the house itself – the sitting room was once the 16thC kitchen and still has its original sink and bread oven. The big, bright, red-tiled, yellow dining room and small breakfast room open on to the south-facing terrace, where you can sit at small tables under the lime and acacia trees. Madame likes her antique French beds and there's an assortment of Louis-styles to choose from. Most rooms are in the main house; those at the front have the best views, those at the back or in two smaller, buildings (reached through gardens) may be quieter.

~

NEARBY Perigueux (55 km); Sarlat; Le Bugue; châteaux.
LOCATION in medieval village; car parking
FOOD breakfast
PRICE €€€
ROOMS 23 double and twin, 13 with bath, 10 with shower; all rooms have phone, hairdrier, TV, minibar, safe
FACILITIES sitting rooms, dining room, bar, terrace, garden, swimming pool
CREDIT CARDS AE, MC, V
CHILDREN accepted
DISABLED not suitable
PETS accepted
CLOSED mid-Oct to mid-Apr
PROPRIETORS Yvette and Marcel Schaller

THE SOUTH-WEST

HOSTELLERIE DE PLAISANCE

~ VILLAGE HOTEL ~

place du Clocher, 33330 St-Emilion (Gironde)
TEL 05 57 55 07 55 **FAX** 05 57 74 41 11
E-MAIL hostellerie.plaisance@wanadoo.fr **WEBSITE** www.hostellerie-plaisance.com

NEWLY RENOVATED, this creamy stone hotel in the immaculately preserved wine village of St-Emilion had been open only a few months when we visited; landscaping of the terrace was not yet finished but it has aspirations, we learned, to be a Relais et Château hotel and the new owners also have a *premier grand cru classé* vineyard. The setting – in a little square with terrace and garden looking over old stone houses to vines beyond – is perfect, though parking is liable to be a headache in the high season. The comfortable surroundings, however, should alleviate some of the pain, and the china alone – all Limoges – makes this exquisite little place worthy of note. Bathrooms are – of course – spanking new, with glossy taps, a bath pillow, fresh freesias, piles of fluffy towels, bathrobes, heated towel rail and generous helpings of toiletries (even a nail file). Rooms – some have terraces – have matching wallpaper and fabric, good quality lamps and reproduction furniture, but our inspector was dismayed to find no lining paper in the chest of drawers. First-rate breakfasts with freshly squeezed orange juice and huge white cups of coffee. Manager M. Rizzotti is from the Oustau de Beaumanière in Les Beaux-de-Provence. Reports, please.

~

NEARBY Bordeaux (40 km); vineyards; Dordogne region (40 km).
LOCATION in upper section of village; free parking outside hotel from 6.30 pm to 11 am, otherwise in public parking spaces
FOOD breakfast, lunch, dinner; room service
PRICES ©©©-©©©©
ROOMS 14; 13 double and twin, 1 single; 12 with bath, 1 with shower; all rooms have phone, TV, air conditioning, hairdrier; some have minibar, safe
FACILITIES sitting room, dining room, bar, lift, terrace
CREDIT CARDS AE, DC, MC, V
CHILDREN welcome
DISABLED no special facilities **PETS** accepted
CLOSED Jan
MANAGER M. Martial Rizzotti

THE SOUTH-WEST

ST-ETIENNE-DE-BAIGORRY

ARCE

～ RIVERSIDE HOTEL ～

64430 St-Étienne-de-Baïgorry (Pyrénées-Atlantiques)
TEL 05 59 37 40 14 **FAX** 05 59 37 40 27
E-MAIL reservations@hotelarce.fr **WEBSITE** www.hotel-arce.com

A FAVOURITE OF OUR INSPECTORS AND OUR READERS, recently redecorated and refurbished to maintain its impeccable standards. The setting – by a river in a typical Basque village – is a magical one, best appreciated from the dining terrace, which juts out over the water and is sheltered by a canopy of chestnut trees. Nestled there, one feels both intimate and secluded and nothing could be more pleasant than a relaxed breakfast by the water's edge. Inside, the public rooms are spacious: a smart dining room with picture windows, and a beamed library with books in a variety of languages. The green, white and red colours of the Basque flag predominate. Some of the bedrooms are impressively large, with apartment-sized sitting areas; others open on to small terraces with mountain views. A sizeable blue-tiled swimming pool is hidden in a green enclosure on the far side of a wooden bridge across the river.

Management of the hotel is now in the capable hands of the fifth generation of the family Arcé. The much-appreciated cooking emphasizes fresh local ingredients, with an interesting wine list at reasonable prices. There is plenty to do in the area – walking, fishing, cycling, riding, canoeing – and the Atlantic coast is only half an hour away.

～

NEARBY Pyrenees; Spanish border; Atlantic coast.
LOCATION in village, 10 km W of St-Jean Pied-de-Port; car parking
FOOD breakfast, lunch, dinner
PRICE €€
ROOMS 23; 22 double and twin, 20 with bath, 2 with shower; 1 single with shower; all rooms have phone, TV, hairdrier
FACILITIES sitting rooms, dining room, library, games room, terrace, garden, swimming pool, tennis
CREDIT CARDS DC, MC, V **CHILDREN** welcome
DISABLED one ground floor room **PETS** accepted
CLOSED mid-Nov to mid-Mar
PROPRIETORS Arcé family

THE SOUTH-WEST

LA DEVINIERE
~ SEASIDE GUESTHOUSE ~

5 rue Loquin, 64500 St-Jean-de-Luz (Pyrénées-Atlantiques)
TEL 05 59 26 05 51 **FAX** 05 59 51 26 38

LA DEVINIERE is discreetly tucked away in a pedestrian precinct with nothing more than a modest signboard artistically spelling out the name in Basque green. Other than that, there is little to betray that this house is in fact a hotel. Its owners describe it as a 'charming old English hotel', and that's how it feels, an elegant and traditional privately owned town house in the centre of this historic and picturesque resort. The spell is cast as soon as you enter the beautifully furnished reception area with shelves of leather-bound books and a view through to a sitting room with comfortable chairs and a grand piano. It is the creation of former lawyer Bernard Carrère and his wife, an expert in antiques.

Although there is no restaurant, a fairly new addition is that of a delightful tea room in complete harmony with the rest of the house and the concept of a hotel as a private home, surrounded by personal things. It may be for the discriminating, but nevertheless it has an air of freshness and warm welcome. A small garden lies behind the house. There is parking close by but final access is by foot – well worth the small effort.

~

NEARBY Spanish border; Biarritz (15 km).
LOCATION in pedestrian precinct in town centre; car parking nearby
FOOD breakfast
PRICE €€
ROOMS 8 double and twin, all with bath; all rooms have phone
FACILITIES sitting room, library, tea room, garden
CREDIT CARDS AE, DC, MC, V
CHILDREN welcome
DISABLED not suitable
PETS accepted
CLOSED mid-Nov to Dec
PROPRIETORS M. and Mme Carrère

THE SOUTH-WEST

St-Jean-de-Luz

PARC VICTORIA
~ TOWN MANSION ~

5 rue Cepé, 64500 St-Jean-de-Luz (Pyrénées-Atlantiques)
TEL 05 59 26 78 78 **FAX** 05 59 26 78 08
EMAIL parcvictoria@relaischateaux.com **WEBSITE** www.parcvictoria.com

THE OWNER – once a neighbour – of this gleaming white 19thC villa rescued it from demolition and spent four years restoring the house and
garden to their former glory. The place is now immaculate; the predomi-
nant feeling is of space, light and colour, both inside and out. The park
that gives the house its name has neat lawns, formal flower beds and magnificent mature cedar, pines and other specimen trees. M. Larralde
scoured antique shops to find furnishings and fittings to make his dream
come true and the hotel is filled with charming pieces. The elegant *salon*
of the main house is in the Napoléon III style, complete with chandeliers.
Alongside the generous terrace of the swimming pool stands a veranda-
style dining room and relaxation area with sunbeds and exercise equip-
ment. Bedrooms are furnished with antiques, with contemporary marble
bathrooms. Two magnificent new suites, clearly designed for the rich and
famous, have recently been added. The hotel is perhaps too grand for our
purposes, but it does its job very well, with exacting standards and an
ambience of lightness and calm. Dining in the Ivy Garden restaurant is a
delightful experience, and the food and wine are delicious

NEARBY Spanish border; Biarritz (16 km).
LOCATION exit St-Jean-de-Luz Nord from A63; at fourth traffic light, turn right,
direction Quartier du Lac; car parking
FOOD breakfast, lunch, dinner; room service
PRICE €€-€€€€
ROOMS 18; 9 double and twin, 9 suites, all with bath; all rooms have phone, TV, air
conditioning, minibar, safe, hairdrier
FACILITIES sitting room, 2 dining rooms, bar, lift, terrace, gardens, swimming pool
CREDIT CARDS AE, DC, MC, V
CHILDREN accepted
DISABLED access possible **PETS** accepted
CLOSED mid-Nov to mid-Mar
PROPRIETOR M. Larralde

THE SOUTH-WEST

St Michel-de-Montaigne

LE JARDIN D'EYQUEM

~ CASTLE HOTEL ~

24230 St Michel-de-Montaigne (Dordogne)
TEL 05 53 24 89 59
E-MAIL jardin-eyquem@wanadoo.fr **WEBSITE** www.jardin-eyquem.com

AN UNUSUAL RECOMMENDATION for us, but this is such a well thought-out idea that we felt we should not leave it out. The Le Morvans – he was a pilot, she a teacher – moved here from Paris 10 years ago to provide for others what they always hoped to find for themselves on their travels – somewhere pretty, small, calm and somewhere with a small kitchen, so that if you wanted to stay in all day you could. Both passionate about Montaigne, they have converted a farmhouse in the village where the great philosopher was born and named it after his family; in winter you can see through the trees the château of Montaigne's brother. A delightful, thoughtful air prevails. The house faces south and the swimming pool among the vines is in full sun all day. The largest apartment is the old beamed hayloft, but all are spacious with the kitchen section hidden behind cotton curtains made by Danièle, tables, chairs and even egg cups for meals, and painted furniture. When we visited, any fabrics in what could be considered dull colours were being thrown out and replaced by yellow; "for the gaiety of life" said Madame. Breakfast is served in a large ground floor room with handsome stone fireplace.

House rule: The pool must always be a quiet, peaceful place.

~

NEARBY Montaigne's Tower (short walk); St Emilion (18 km); *bastides* of Ste-Foy and Libourne.
LOCATION among vineyards on edge of village; ample car parking
FOOD breakfast
PRICE €€
ROOMS 5 apartments, double or twin, 3 with bath, 2 with shower; TV, kitchenette
FACILITIES breakfast room, terrace, garden, swimming pool
CREDIT CARDS MC, V
CHILDREN welcome
DISABLED one suitable apartment **PETS** not accepted
CLOSED Nov to Apr
PROPRIETORS Danièle and Christian Le Morvan

THE SOUTH-WEST

St-Saud-Lacoussiere

HOSTELLERIE SAINT-JACQUES

~ VILLAGE INN ~

24470 St-Saud-Lacoussière (Dordogne)
TEL 05 53 56 97 21 **FAX** 05 53 56 91 33
E-MAIL hostellerie.st.jacques@wanadoo.fr **WEBSITE** www.hostellerie-st-jacques.com

THE MORE WE LEARN about the Babayous' enterprise, the more thoroughly impressed we are by their sure understanding of holidaymakers'
needs and priorities.

The front of the creeper-clad 18thC building gives little clue to what
lies within – or, more to the point, what lies behind: the Babayous' 'summer sitting room', which consists of lovely sloping gardens, with masses of
colourful flowers, a fair-sized pool, tennis court and plenty of shade and
space for children. Inside there is an unusually large dining room/bar decorated in bright blue and yellow, with big windows which open on to the
terrace above the garden. All the bedrooms are comfortable, spacious and
attractively decorated; several can accommodate families.

The food is rich and varied; even the basic menu is probably enough to
satisfy most appetites. A buffet breakfast/brunch is served in the garden
or by the pool. Occasionally there are lively evenings with dancing and
games, or communal dinners devoted to exploration of regional cuisine.
Not your cup of tea? Just give it a try: you might be surprised.

~

NEARBY Château de Richemont; Montbrun (15 km); Brantôme (30 km);
Rochechouart (45 km).
LOCATION in quiet village, 30 km N of Brantôme; car parking
FOOD breakfast, lunch, dinner
PRICE €-€€
ROOMS 22 double and twin, 2 suites, all with bath or shower; all rooms have
phone; some have TV, minibar
FACILITIES 2 restaurants, bar, TV room, terrace, garden, swimming pool, tennis,
Jacuzzi
CREDIT CARDS AE, MC, V
CHILDREN welcome
DISABLED no special facilities **PETS** accepted
CLOSED Nov to Mar and Sun dinner, Mon
PROPRIETOR Jean-Pierre Babayou

THE SOUTH-WEST

SARE

ARRAYA

～ RIVERSIDE HOTEL ～

64310 Sare (Pyrénées-Atlantiques)
TEL 05 59 54 20 46 **FAX** 05 59 37 40 27
E-MAIL hotel@arraya.com **WEBSITE** www.arraya.com

WITH ITS TIMBERED, white-painted houses adorned with red or green shutters, Sare can claim to be the prettiest of all the extremely pretty Basque villages. In the heart of the village, this 17thC house was once an overnight resting place for pilgrims on their way across the Pyrenees to Santiago de Compostela. Behind the slightly severe frontage on the main road lies a country-style hotel of great character, now run by the third generation of the charming Fagoaga family. Inside all is spick and span and immaculately cared for – clean, airy and light, with much old, dark, burnished wood. The beamed sitting room and dining room – and every nook and cranny on stairways and landings – are filled with glorious old Basque furniture; sofas and chairs are comfortable and inviting, and flowers are everywhere.

A handsome curved wooden staircase leads to bedrooms of different sizes (some border on the small), all expertly decorated using colourful fabrics and bedspreads made by a member of the family. Some look out over the verdant garden, others have a view of the village square. The restaurant is excellent, with a well-chosen wine list; in summer meals are taken on the terrace. A new boutique on the ground floor sells local products, including delicious *gâteau basque*.

～

NEARBY Aïnhoa (10 km); St-Jean-de-Luz (14 km); Biarritz (29 km).
LOCATION in middle of village, 14 km SE of St-Jean-de-Luz; car parking
FOOD breakfast, lunch, dinner
PRICE €-€€
ROOMS 22; 20 double and twin, 19 with bath, 3 with shower; all rooms have phone, TV, safe, hairdrier
FACILITIES sitting room, restaurant, boutique, terrace, garden
CREDIT CARDS AE, DC, MC, V
CHILDREN welcome **DISABLED** ground floor rooms **PETS** not accepted
CLOSED mid-Nov to Apr; restaurant closed Sun dinner, Mon lunch
PROPRIETORS Fagoaga family

THE SOUTH-WEST

ST SEVE

DOMAINE DE LA CHARMAIE
~ COUNTRY HOTEL ~

St Seve, 33190, Gironde
TEL/FAX 05 56 61 10 72
E-MAIL lacharmaie@hotmail.com

THIS IS THE KIND OF place that makes you want to redecorate your own home. We're not sure how they manage to keep it like this, but we have been here on several occasions - even dropping in unannounced on a midweek afternoon - and always found freshly cut flowers artfully placed on tables, tarts fresh from the oven keeping warm in front of the fire, newly-pressed calico tablecloths without a spot on them. Upstairs you will find antique vases and books beside the ample beds. And wonderful touches outside, too: well kept lawns, an old stone swimming pool - believe us, you will want to move in. The owners' son Jules has obviously inherited his mother's artistic flair, and has an artisan workshop at the back of the house that would not look out of place in downtown Manhattan. This is someone's home, and you can tell. The owners may be getting a little blasé - they know they are easily the best place to stay in this southern tip of Entre Deux Mers, and on occasion you feel it - but truly, it's worth the extra effort to get here.

~

NEARBY La Reole.
LOCATION off D21 road, in village of St Seve
FOOD breakfast, dinner by arrangement
PRICE €
ROOMS 3
FACILITIES swimming pool
CREDIT CARDS MC, V
CHILDREN accepted
DISABLED no access
PETS accepted
CLOSED never
PROPRIETOR Mme Chaverou

THE SOUTH-WEST

TRÉMOLAT

LE VIEUX LOGIS

~ VILLAGE HOTEL ~

24510 Trémolat (Dordogne)
TEL 05 53 22 80 06 **FAX** 05 53 22 84 89
E-MAIL vieuxlogis@relaischateaux.com **WEBSITE** www.vieux-logis.com

WE CONTINUE TO LIST this glorious old hotel, one of the most civilized in a region with many attractive hotels, despite a recent postbag of readers' letters, which, though broadly complimentary, had some niggles too. On the complimentary side, all our correspondents marked out for special praise the 'happy and smiling, well-trained staff' and the warm atmosphere they engendered. The food, too, was praised, including the 'spectacular' buffet breakfast. Irritations included problems with hot water on a couple of occasions, tired decoration in the bedrooms and bathroooms (renovations have taken place since), and an exorbitant charge for a single brandy. All our correspondents, however, said they would return.

Owners, the Giraudel-Destords, have lived in this complex of farm and village houses for nearly 400 years. The part which is now the dining room once held pigs and wine barrels. Now all has been designer-decorated to produce comfort of a high degree. Bedrooms, some with four-posters, are done in a cosy sophisticated-rustic style; public rooms (some little used) are elegant and comfortable, with plenty of quiet nooks. The open fire in the small *salon* is much appreciated by guests. The galleried dining room looks out on to the green and flowery garden where you can breakfast.

~

NEARBY Les Eyzies-de-Tayac (25 km); Monpazier (30 km); Beynac (30 km).
LOCATION in village, 15 km SW of Le Bugue; car and garage parking
FOOD breakfast, lunch, dinner; room service
PRICE €€€€€
ROOMS 24; 18 double and twin, 6 suites, all with bath; all rooms have phone, TV, minibar, hairdrier
FACILITIES 3 sitting rooms, 2 dining rooms, bar, terrace, garden, swimming pool
CREDIT CARDS AE, DC, MC, V
CHILDREN welcome
DISABLED one specially adapated room **PETS** accepted
CLOSED never
PROPRIETOR Giraudel-Destord family

THE SOUTH-WEST

BRANTOME

LE CHATENET

MANOR HOUSE HOTEL

24310 Brantôme (Dordogne)
TEL 05 53 05 81 08
FAX 05 53 05 85 52
E-MAIL chatenet@wanadoo.fr
FOOD breakfast
PRICE €€
ROOMS 10
CLOSED Nov to Apr

WHEN WE VISITED this lovely 17thC riverside manor house to update its entry for this edition, we were sad to hear its owners, the Laxtons, tell us that they were about to hand over, after 20 years or more, to new owners. Just before going to press, however, they informed us that they had had a change of heart and decided to stay 'forever': happy news. The beauty of this noble stone *gentilhommière* (with yards of walnut panelling and a *pigonnier*) and the Laxtons' warm, welcoming ways have won them – and their dog – many friends. They have thought of everything: heated swimming pool; barbecue and garden room; linen room with washing machine; antique-filled, fabric-lined bedrooms, and excellent bathrooms.

BRANTOME

DOMAINE DE LA ROSERAIE

COUNTRY HOTEL

route d'Angouleme, 24310
Brantome en Périgord (Dordogne)
TEL 05 53 05 84 74
FAX 05 53 05 77 94
WEBSITE www. domaine-la
roseraie.com **FOOD** breakfast, din-
ner **PRICE** €€ **ROOMS** 9
CLOSED mid-Nov to mid-Mar

UNFORTUNATELY WE have received some very negative reports on this long-standing entry, some particularly critical of the bad plumbing. The Domaine de la Roseraie is a 17thC monastery swamped by flowers and plants - as the name suggests, roses can be found in abundance. All the rooms face south and contain old family furniture, are individually decorated and have independent entrances. Evelyne Roux's taste will suit those who appreciate high, comfortable beds, immaculate bathrooms, prettiness, and peace and quiet. The swimming pool is discreetly hidden behind greenery and breakfast can be taken outside at little tables. Denis Roux's local cooking is served in the evenings in the beamed dining room with stone fireplace and picture windows, or among the roses on the terrace. Reports please.

THE SOUTH-WEST

LE BUGUE

AUBERGE DU NOYER

COUNTRY HOTEL

'Le Reclaud' 24260 Le Bugue (Dordogne) **TEL** 05 53 07 11 73 **FAX** 05 53 54 57 44 **E-MAIL** aubergedunoyer@perigord.com **WEBSITE** www.perigord.com/ aubergedunoyer **FOOD** breakfast **PRICE** ⓔ **ROOMS** 10 **CLOSED** mid-Oct to Easter

A VENERABLE WALNUT TREE presiding over the gravelled forecourt gives this attractive stone-built 18thC coaching inn its name. The new proprietors no longer offer meals, but the tranquil and relaxed atmosphere remains intact. Beams, exposed stone walls and pretty floral or Dutch-style fabrics lend the rooms their rustic charm, while the books and magazines scattered around add a pleasantly homely touch. All the beds and bedding have recently been replaced and several bathrooms upgraded – though the rest are perfectly adequate and spotlessly clean. Some rooms have their own small, private terrace. A generous breakfast buffet of cereals, freshly-squeezed orange juice, fruit and assorted croissants and breads is served.

FLORIMONT-GAUMIERS

LA DAILLE

FARMHOUSE GUESTHOUSE

Florimont-Gaumiers, 24250 Domme (Dordogne) **TEL** 05 53 28 40 71 **WEBSITE** www. tourisme-ceou.com/ladaille.htm **FOOD** breakfast **PRICE** ⓔⓔ **ROOMS** 3 **CLOSED** Oct to May

 THIS UNUSUAL PLACE, in deep countryside, is one of those Dordogne establishments that combines the best of France and Britain – if you can find it (check directions in advance, it is best to first go to the village of Gaumiers). The Browns have been busy buying up land around their stone farmhouse set among very English gardens, where they've been for more than 30 years; they now have 18 private hectares of woods and fields (filled with wild flowers and orchids) for visitors to enjoy. Rooms (south-facing) are unfussy, comfortable, clean, with big cupboards, bathrooms and terraces in a modern outbuilding across the garden from the house – clean towels every day and clean sheets on third or fourth. Perfect for walkers. Good teas.

THE SOUTH-WEST

LALINDE

LE CHATEAU

RIVERSIDE HOTEL

24150 Lalinde (Dordogne)
TEL 05 53 61 01 82
FAX 05 53 24 74 60
FOOD breakfast, lunch, dinner
PRICE €€
ROOMS 7
CLOSED mid-Dec to mid-Feb

SQUEEZED ONTO THE EDGE of the Dordogne, with dense green woods on the opposite bank, the setting of this odd little turreted castle (mainly 19th century with palm tree and red shutters) is spectacular. Most of the comfortable rooms look down into the fast-running waters of the river – some have their own small balconies – and the decor is quirky and modernistic. One bathroom has a triangular bath. M Gensou, the owner/chef, rides a motorbike and stuffs snails with *foie gras* and walnut butter. We have heard the tiled entrance hall described as dowdy, but still propose Le Château for those who like water and something with a difference.

LOUPIAC

LE MURIER DE VIELS

COUNTRY HOTEL

12700, Loupiac, Aveyron
TEL 05 65 80 89 82
FAX 05 65 80 12 20
E-MAIL info@le-murier.com
WEBSITE www.le-murier.com
FOOD breakfast, lunch, dinner
PRICE € **ROOMS** 8
CLOSED never

FOUND IN THE CENTRE of a vast natural park, this 18thC Quercy stone country house is an ideal retreat for those who want to explore the surrounding countryside, or for those who simply want to enjoy the views of the Lot valley. Nearby is the medieval town of Figeac, on the Lot river, which can be reached by a 12thC pathway. Recently taken over by South African Mike Douglas, the buildings have been renovated in a rustic and yet comfortable style. This would be an excellent place to stay for a family: a separate *gite* sleeps several people and there is a large pool with terrace. Our only reservation would be the number of private functions which may spoil the feeling of seclusion in this charming location.

THE SOUTH-WEST

LA ROSERAIE

VILLAGE HOTEL

11, place Armes 24290 Montignac
TEL 04 97 08 84 48
FOOD breakfast, lunch, dinner
PRICE €
ROOMS 14
CLOSED mid-Nov to April

THIS 18THC HOUSE IS in a medieval village square which runs alongside the river Vezere (Montignac is a small village that lies on the banks of the river). The houses are grouped around a tower - the last reminder of the fortress which once belonged to the counts of Périgord. Due to the discovery of the nearby caves at Lascaux this quiet place has now become a busy tourist centre. La Roseraie is an ideal retreat from the crowds. Its pretty bedrooms are covered with flower-patterned fabrics, painted wooden furniture and have tiled floors. The bathrooms are immaculate. The terrace, overlooking a fragrant rose garden, makes the perfect setting for a drink before eating at the respected restaurant.

LE RIPA ALTA

VILLAGE HOTEL

*3 place de l'Eglise, 32160
Plaisance (Gers)*
TEL 05 62 69 30 43
FAX 05 62 69 36 99
E-MAIL ripaalta@aol.com
FOOD breakfast, lunch, dinner
PRICE € **ROOMS** 15
CLOSED never; restaurant closed
Mon in winter

NO FRILLS HERE, BUT A WARM WELCOME awaits at this country town hotel which harbours a famous chef, Maurice Coscuella, who trained alongside Bocuse and Troisgros. For more than thirty years he has regaled his guests with creative cooking using only the best of local produce. This is wine country – good quality at reasonable prices. Bedrooms are adequate although basic (one with balcony) and quiet, except on Saturday nights when the nearby disco is on. It is typically old-fashioned French, complete with bad plumbing. The hotel is popular with customers of Brittany Ferries. Plaisance is a convenient base from which to explore Gers, the land of the Musketeers, and it has a leisure park with a lake for swimming, sailing and fishing.

THE SOUTH-WEST

PUJOLS

HOTEL DES CHENES

VILLAGE HOTEL

47300 Pujols, Bel Air
TEL 05 53 49 04 55
FAX 05 53 49 22 74
E-MAIL
hotel.des.chenes@wanadoo.fr
WEBSITE www.hoteldeschenes.com
FOOD breakfast
PRICE € **ROOMS** 21 **CLOSED** never

RECOMMENDED TO US by a reader who described his stay as excellent and especially good value for money. Located in the charming village of Pujols, perched on a hill shaded by century old trees, this hotel is a real find. With panoramic views over the Lot valley, the focus is on comfort and relaxation. Rooms are clean and comfortable and there is a homely sitting room with a television. The swimming pool is surrounded by a large terrace with spectacular views, or if you prefer you could relax by the fireplace inside. This makes an ideal base for exploring one of the most beautiful villages in the area. Although only breakfast is served in the hotel, nearby is the excellent La Togue Blanche, which has a Michelin star.

ST-MARTIAL VIVEYROLS

HOSTELLERIE LES AIGUILLONS

COUNTRY HOTEL

Le Beuil, 24320 St-Martial-Viveyrols (Dordogne)
TEL 05 53 91 07 55 **FAX** 05 53 91 00 43 **E-MAIL** aiguillons@aol.com
WEBSITE www.hostellerieles aiguillons. com **FOOD** breakfast, lunch, dinner **PRICE** €
ROOMS 8 **CLOSED** Dec to Apr

THIS LITTLE *LOGIS* was built in 1993 on the ruins of a farmhouse set among the woods and fields of the Périgord Blanc – and in easy driving distance of a string of picturesque villages with Romanesque churches. Once dug in here, however, guests seem reluctant to leave the swimming pool and terrace where breakfast is served to the sound of birdsong, Christophe Beeuwsaert, who speaks English, is a dedicated, much-loved patron and there are many tributes to him – and his cooking – on the theme of 'came for one night, stayed for six' in his visitors' book. Rooms are comfortable; bathrooms are large. For those looking for high standards and tranquillity.

THE SOUTH-WEST

SEGOS

DOMAINE DE BASSIBE
COUNTRY HOTEL

32400 Ségos (Gers)
TEL 05 62 09 46 71 **FAX** 05 62 08 40 15
E-MAIL bassibe@relaischateaux.com
WEBSITE www.relaischateaux.com/bassibe
FOOD breakfast, lunch, dinner
PRICE €€€
ROOMS 18 **CLOSED** Jan to Apr

SET IN A PARK AND GARDEN running riot with cascades of flowers, the Domaine de Bassibe is an 18thC *maison de maitre* with a long two-storeyed wing, originally stables but now housing delightful suites. Alongside stands the former *chai* - another lovely stone building - once a centre of activity in this agricultural domaine and now housing the kitchens, restaurant and cellar. In the garden, La Maison des Champs, a newer construction in white and blue, contains more rooms and suites each decorated in different colours, all bright and light. Close by a stand of impressive centenarian oaks is a large pool with terrace and enclosed fitness area. This is a friendly country house where the best is offered with simplicity and warmth.

VALENCE-SUR-BAISE

LA FERME DE FLARAN
COUNTRY HOTEL

32310 Valence-sur-Baise (Gers)
TEL 05 62 28 58 22
FAX 05 62 28 56 89
E-MAIL fermedeflaran@minitel.net
WEBSITE www.gascogne.com/guide.hotels/fermeflaran.htm
FOOD breakfast, lunch, dinner
PRICE € **ROOMS** 15 **CLOSED** mid-Nov to mid-Dec, Jan

A DECENT PIT STOP on a convenient road for travellers. Typical farmhouse architecture and decoration are executed with a smart touch and plenty of efficiency. In past times the farm belonged to the community of Cistercians in the adjacent abbey which dates back to the 12th century and is now a beautifully kept venue for concerts and art exhibitions. The restaurant is always busy. Why? It serves food of above average quality at attractive prices. Meals can also be taken on the terrace in view of the well-proportioned swimming pool. Rooms are unpretentious: choose one away from the road if you can, as there can be traffic noise.

MASSIF CENTRAL

AREA INTRODUCTION

HOTELS IN MASSIF CENTRAL

FOR MANY BRITISH VISITORS, the Massif is 'unknown France' – the high, remote area between Périgord on the west and the Rhône valley on the east. For guidebook purposes, it is a rather problematic region, particularly if (like all our regions) it is defined in terms of *départements*. The points where you might consider the physical Massif to begin and end don't always coincide happily with governmental boundaries (the *département* of Ardèche, for example, falls in our South of France region, but includes territory that is physically very much part of the Massif). There is also a good case for considering this 'unspoiled France'. Of course tourism has had an impact, but it is slight compared with the impact on the much better-known areas. There are bargains to be found as a result.

The region is distinctive for the grandeur of its scenery, produced by long-extinct volcanoes, from rocky outcrops to the magnificent mountain ranges of Monts Dômes, Monts Dore and Monts du Cantal; a landscape threaded by rivers, lakes and hot springs, around which spa towns have grown up over the centuries. Tamer, more rolling country lies to the north-west, where two of our hotels are in the *département* of Allier: **Château de Boussac** at Target (page 255) and **Le Chalet** at Coulandon (page 258), plus a new one, **Castel-Hôtel 1904** at St-Gervais d'Auvergne (page 252) in unspoiled Puy-de-Dôme. In the same *département* but to the south, **Le Radio** (tel 04 73 30 87 83) is a unique hotel in Chamalières: it was built in the 1930s in art deco style on the theme of the radio, a new invention at the time.

Travelling south, through the Massif's principal town of Clermont-Ferrand, where you can see one of the finest of the area's many Romanesque churches, we have a unique hotel, **Les Deux Abbesses** (page 251), which almost is the tiny medieval village of Saint-Arcons-d'Allier. From here, a short drive east brings you to Le Puy-en-Velay with its spectacular trio of craggy peaks. Nearby in Tence, **Hostellerie Placide** (page 256), an elegant traditional hotel, is new to this edition of the guide. To the east lies Cantal, where, after positive reports, we have reinstated **Hostellerie de la Maronne** in St-Martin as a long entry (page 254). Also in Cantal we feature the friendly **Auberge la Tomette** in Vitrac (page 257), and two new inns: **L'Auberge Fleurie** (page 247), with a first-rate kitchen, and **Auberge des Montagnes** in a wild mountain landscape (page 258). You could also try another remote, pretty inn at Boisset, **Auberge de Concasty** (tel 04 71 62 21 16), which radiates country charm and serves robust Franco-Auvergnat food.

Further south the dramatic Gorges de l'Aveyron and the Gorges du Tarn cleave the landscape, with their scattering of villages that cling precariously to the sheer rock faces. One of our hotels, **Longcol** (page 249), is set in a valley of the Gorges de l'Aveyron near Najac. We also recommend the **Hotel Restaurant du Vieux Pont** in Belcastel to the north-west (page 238), with a fine kitchen and comfortable rooms, which continues to delight our readers. In Tarn, we feature a favourite from our *Charming Small Hotel Guides*, Southern France, **Cuq-en-Terrasses** in Cuq-Toulza (page 243). Lozère to the east is the *département* at the heart of the Cévennes, where **La Lozerette** is a terrific find in Cocurès (page 240), a village on the route taken by Robert Louis Stevenson and his donkey Modestine. Here too we can recommend **Château de la Caze** (tel 04 66 48 51 01), a beautiful 15thC castle with a dramatic position, high above the Tarn, whose friendly owners ensure that it is anything but intimidating.

MASSIF CENTRAL

BELCASTEL

HOTEL RESTAURANT DU VIEUX PONT

∽ RESTAURANT-WITH-ROOMS ∽

12390 Belcastel (Aveyron)
TEL 05 65 64 52 29 **FAX** 05 65 64 44 32
E-MAIL hotel-du-vieux-pont@wanadoo.fr **WEBSITE** hotelbelcastel.com

THE NAME REFERS TO A medieval cobbled bridge linking the two components of this much-lauded restaurant-with-rooms. On one side of the
river stands a solid rough-stone house, the Fagegaltier sisters' childhood
home, now the restaurant; on the other side, the sisters have rescued a
tumbledown building next to the church to create seven comfortable, stylish bedrooms. Above, Belcastel's picture-postcard houses cling to a cliff
with a castle crowning its summit.

Michèle Fagegaltier is the manager, while her sister Nicole and Nicole's
husband Bruno Rouquier are responsible for the cooking. Their imaginative versions of local dishes, such as *boeuf de l'Aubrac à la réduction de
banyuls*, served with *un concassé de pommes de terre à la ventrèche et
au roquefort*, have won them much praise, including a Michelin star and a
Gault Millau heart and 16 points. 'Just as wonderful as last year. Welcome,
service, food and rooms without fault,' writes a reader. Through picture
windows, diners can spot trout rising if the Aveyron isn't flowing too fast.

The sisters have imparted some of their own elegance to both restaurant and hotel, and nowhere is this more evident than in the bedrooms.
They are just the kind we like; simply decorated, some with cream walls,
bedspreads and curtains, wooden floors and French windows on to the
small garden; all furnished with handpicked antiques.

∽

NEARBY Rodez (23 km); Sauveterre-de-Rouergue (26 km).
LOCATION in the village beside the river, 8 km SE of Rignac; car parking
FOOD breakfast, lunch, dinner
PRICE €
ROOMS 7 double and twin with bath or shower; all rooms have phone, TV, air
conditioning, minibar, hairdrier
FACILITIES restaurant, garden, fishing **CREDIT CARDS** MC, V **CHILDREN** accepted
DISABLED one specially adapted room **PETS** accepted **CLOSED** Jan to mid-Mar, Sun
dinner, Tue lunch and Mon Sep to Jul; restaurant Mon Jul and Aug
PROPRIETORS Michèle and Nicole Fagegaltier

MASSIF CENTRAL

CASTELPERS

CHATEAU DE CASTELPERS

~ MANOR HOUSE GUESTHOUSE ~

Castelpers, 12170 Lédergues (Aveyron)
TEL 05 65 69 22 61 **FAX** 05 65 69 25 31

YOLANDE TAPIÉ DE CELEYRON, of the old and distinguished family that owns this beautiful house, handed over the reins to her daughter, Mme de Saint-Palais, after 30 years. Our inspector found it a 'real delight' to share their home full of memories and objects of continuous history. On the stairs is a portrait of Mme Tapié's great-grandfather, an *'intendant militaire'* of Napoléon. Her grandfather (an engineer who pioneered the building of dams to harness water power and whose car licence plate was 9) restored and built on to the remains of a 17thC mill at the end of the 19th century. The result is not a grandiose château but something more like an unspoiled country house, kept as it has matured and been lived in. Its rooms are full of fine old furniture and pictures. Many of the beds are four-posters.

The taste is timeless; the charm effortless. The park is enchanting – tall trees shading a long stretch of lawn running between a river and a stream. There are swings for children. It is a 'peaceful, timeless place, happy to be just itself', in the words of our inspector. His dinner and choice of wine were excellent. The inexpensive prices, especially for weekend breaks and *table d'hôte* menus, are an added appeal.

~

NEARBY Château du Bosc; Sauveterre-de-Rouergue (20 km).
LOCATION in countryside 9 km SE of RN88, 10 km S of Naucelle; car parking
FOOD breakfast, lunch, dinner (residents only)
PRICE €
ROOMS 4; 2 double, one twin, one family, 2 with bath, 2 with shower; all rooms have phone; some have TV
FACILITIES sitting room, 2 dining rooms, garden, fishing
CREDIT CARDS AE, DC, MC, V
CHILDREN welcome if well behaved
DISABLED one ground floor room
PETS accepted
CLOSED Oct to Apr; restaurant occasional dinner or lunch
PROPRIETOR Mme de Saint-Palais

MASSIF CENTRAL

COCURES

LA LOZERETTE
~ VILLAGE INN ~

48400 Cocurès (Lozère)
TEL 04 66 45 62 12 **FAX** 04 66 45 12 93
E-MAIL lalozerette@wanadoo.fr

THE DRIVING FORCE behind this village inn is the charming Pierrette Agulhon, the third generation of her family to own and run it. Her grandmother opened the house as an *auberge*, and clearly passed her hotel-keeping skills on to her granddaughter, who manages La Lozerette with calm efficiency, helped by an able, friendly staff. Although it's on a fairly busy road (by day) on the historic route taken by Robert Louis Stevenson and his donkey Modestine, the wild mountainous landscape of the Cévennes National Park surrounds it, with signs of cultivation – vineyards and orchards – dotted here and there. The best of the views are from the large, wood-floored bedrooms. Painted in spring colours, with co-ordinating floral, checked or striped fabric, they are never fussy, but clean-cut and fresh-looking.

Several downstairs rooms have been knocked together to make the large dining room, the heart of the hotel, which, with its wood-panelled ceiling, cane chairs and cheerful yellow curtains, is cosy despite its size. The menu is regional – you might find *foie-gras de canard, chataignes, charcuterie de pays*, river trout or *ceps* on the menu – and so highly regarded that it keeps the restaurant almost permanently full. Leave your choice of wines to Pierrette, who – in addition to her other talents – is a qualified *sommelier*.

~

NEARBY corniche des Cévennes; gorges du Tarn; Mende (42 km).
LOCATION in village, 6 km NE of Florac; car parking
FOOD breakfast, lunch, dinner
PRICE €
ROOMS 21; 20 double and twin, one single, all with bath or shower; all rooms have phone, TV
FACILITIES 2 sitting rooms, restaurant, bar, garden
CREDIT CARDS AE, DC, MC, V **CHILDREN** accepted
DISABLED one specially-adapted room **PETS** accepted **CLOSED** early Nov to Easter
PROPRIETOR Pierrette Agulhon

MASSIF CENTRAL

CONQUES

SAINTE FOY
~ VILLAGE HOTEL ~

Conques, 12320 St-Cyprien-sur-Dourdou (Aveyron)
TEL 05 65 69 84 03 **FAX** 05 65 72 81 04
E-MAIL hotelsaintefoy@hotelsaintefoy.fr **WEBSITE** www.hotelsaintefoy.fr

HOTEL SAINTE-FOY is a lovingly restored, partly timbered 17thC inn which takes its name from the great abbey church directly opposite (with a remarkable tympanum and treasury). It is in the lovely, old village of Conques, and for centuries it has been one of the main stopping places for pilgrims on the route to Santiago.

Marie-France and Alain Garcenot have been the proprietors since they took over from an aunt in 1987. In 1993 it was promoted to four stars. Today they are justifiably proud of their achievement, but the facilities that allow its four-star rating are not the sole basis of the hotel's appeal.

The house has been beautifully furnished with close attention to detail and to preserving the character of the building. Glowing wood is everywhere. The large two-part sitting room is particularly well furnished with antiques. Bedrooms are highly individual, tasteful and large, with views either over the church or the flowery courtyard garden.

You can dine here or in the intimate but pleasantly spacious rooms inside. The increasingly inventive cooking (daily changing menus rooted in the local *terroir*) gets impressive reviews.

~

NEARBY Rodez (36 km); Figeac (44 km).
LOCATION in the heart of the village; car parking
FOOD breakfast, lunch, dinner; room service
PRICE €€€
ROOMS 17; 15 double, 2 suites, all with bath; all rooms have phone, hairdrier; suites have air conditioning; TV on request
FACILITIES sitting room, 3 dining rooms, bar, conference room, interior patio, 2 terraces
CREDIT CARDS AE, DC, MC, V
CHILDREN accepted
DISABLED one specially adapted room
PETS accepted **CLOSED** mid-Oct to Easter
PROPRIETORS Marie-France and Alain Garcenot

MASSIF CENTRAL

CORDES-SUR-CIEL

LE GRAND ECUYER
~ MEDIEVAL INN ~

79 Grand Rue Raimond VII, 81170 Cordes-sur-Ciel (Tarn)
TEL 05 63 53 79 50 **FAX** 05 63 53 79 51
E-MAIL grand.ecuyer@thuries.fr **WEBSITE** www.thuries.fr

AT THE INSTIGATION OF the novelist Prosper Mérimée, this former hunting lodge of the Counts of Toulouse was classified as a historic monument in the 19th century. It has been transformed into a comfortable and dependable hotel, with stone walls, beamed ceilings and paved floors. It is furnished with heavy oak antiques and tapestry-upholstered furniture, oil paintings, suits of armour, paved floors, rich damask and velvet wall coverings, blackamoor lampholders and four-poster beds. Parts of it are rather gloomy, though the bedrooms are quiet and inviting (if you like monumental stone fireplaces), with modern bathrooms.

Cordes-sur-Ciel – a remarkably preserved 13thC fortified hilltop village, with little cobbled streets and a busy tourist attraction – is the gastronomic domain of pastry chef Yves Thuriès, who has a Michelin star and is something of a celebrity. Le Grand Ecuyer is his base, though recent visitors feel he might be doing less in the kitchen now than in the past. The service is excellent and the chandeliered, plum-coloured dining room has been conceived as a prestigious setting for his cuisine. Our reporter dined well, and was struck by the helpfulness and knowledge of the wine waiter.

~

NEARBY Fôret Grésigne; Albi (27 km); Villefranche-de-Rouergue (47 km).
LOCATION in middle of village; car parking nearby
FOOD breakfast, lunch, dinner
PRICE €€€
ROOMS 13; 10 double, 2 triple, one suite, all with bath; all rooms have phone, TV; some rooms have air conditioning
FACILITIES sitting room, 2 dining rooms, breakfast room, bar
CREDIT CARDS MC, V
CHILDREN accepted
DISABLED no special facilities
PETS accepted
CLOSED mid-Oct to Apr; restaurant lunch Mon to Fri
PROPRIETOR Yves Thuriès

MASSIF CENTRAL

CUQ-TOULZA

CUQ-EN-TERRASSES

~ COUNTRY HOTEL ~

Cuq Le Château, 81470 Cuq-Toulza (Tarn)
TEL 05 63 82 54 00 **FAX** 05 63 82 54 11
E-MAIL info@cuqenterrasses.com **WEBSITE** www.cuqenterrasses.com

FIFTEEN YEARS AGO TWO London designers bought this house as a semi-abandoned old presbytery. They worked painstakingly on the conversion and after several years produced a successful hotel. The house, in a hilltop village square, is on a series of south-facing levels – from the street downwards – with more terraces of garden tumbling down the hillside below. The present owners bought the place in 2000 and continue to run it in much the same way, confirmed by a spate of complimentary readers' letters. One reads: 'We were captivated by this charming location and hotel. We had a wonderful dinner and were extremely comfortable there'.

The entrance hall leads to the upstairs rooms via a balustraded staircase and a superb beamed ceiling, uncovered during the building work. Kitchen, dining room and beautiful outside terrace (with barbecue) for summer meals are two floors down. The swimming pool is on another terrace. All quite stunning. The decoration and furnishing are original without eccentricity – clean, fresh and colourful.

The view, particularly from the terraces, is breathtaking. It's not hard to see why the local name for this small pocket of fertile country is Le Pays de Cocagne (the land of plenty). An ideal place in which to relax and enjoy the peace.

~

NEARBY Castres (35 km); Toulouse (37 km); tennis.
LOCATION in a hilltop hamlet by the church, 2 km from Cuq-Toulza on the D45 in the direction of Aguts; car parking
FOOD breakfast, dinner (by reservation)
PRICE €€
ROOMS 8; 7 double, one suite, 6 with bath, 2 with shower; all rooms have phone, TV, hairdrier
FACILITIES dining room, terraces, garden, swimming pool
CREDIT CARDS AE, DC, MC, V **CHILDREN** accepted
DISABLED no special facilities **PETS** accepted in some rooms only
CLOSED mid-Nov to mid-Mar **PROPRIETORS** Philippe Gallice and Andonis Vassalos

MASSIF CENTRAL

LACABAREDE

DEMEURE DE FLORE

~ COUNTRY HOTEL ~

106 Route Nationale, 81240 Lacabarède (Tarn)
TEL 05 63 98 32 32 **FAX** 05 63 98 47 56
E-MAIL demeure.de.flore@hotelrama.com **WEBSITE** www.hotelrama.com/flore

THIS HOTEL IN THE FOOTHILLS of the Haut-Languedoc was opened in 1992 by Monike and Jean-Marie Tronc to realize their dream of creating a perfect hotel. Having done that, in 1999 they decided to sell to a sophisticated Italian, Francesco Di Bari, who spent almost a million francs on redecoration, creating a new restaurant, and landscaping the garden.

The 19thC *maison de maître* may be an undistinguished building, but it sits prettily in a mature, wooded *jardin anglais*, far enough from the passing RN112 to feel secluded. And within, there is a delightful ambience, mercifully unchanged since M. Di Bari took over. Stylish floral prints are set against warm, plain backgrounds. The house is full of floor-to-ceiling windows, and the general impression is light and fresh. Carefully chosen antiques and ornaments give the feel of a lived-in but cared-for family home. The eleven bedrooms are individually furnished in the same careful way, with knick-knacks and fresh flowers. You could easily be staying with friends.

Perhaps not surprisingly the cooking combines Provençal and Italian styles, and the menu changes every day depending on what's in season. In summer, 'a bite of lunch' can be had by the smart little pool or on the terrace overlooking the garden. More reports please.

~

NEARBY Castres (35 km); Albi (60 km); Toulouse (100 km); Mediterranean beaches.
LOCATION opposite service station on outskirts of village on RN112 between St-Pons and Mazamet; car parking
FOOD breakfast, lunch, dinner
PRICE €-€€€
ROOMS 11; 10 double, one suite, all with bath; all rooms have phone, TV, hairdrier
FACILITIES sitting room, restaurant, meeting room, garden, swimming pool
CREDIT CARDS MC, V **CHILDREN** accepted
DISABLED one specially adapted room **PETS** accepted **CLOSED** 3 weeks Jan
PROPRIETOR Francesco Di Bari

MASSIF CENTRAL

LA MALENE

MANOIR DE MONTESQUIOU

~ MANOR HOUSE HOTEL ~

48210 La Malène (Lozère)
TEL 04 66 48 51 12 **FAX** 04 66 48 50 47
E-MAIL montesquiou@demeures-de-lozere.com **WEBSITE** www.manoir-montesquiou.com

SET DRAMATICALLY between two sheer rock faces in the Gorges du Tarn, this attractive family-run castle-like 15thC manor house offers historical interest as well as excellent value for money. When Louis XIII ordered all rebel fortresses to be razed, the noble Montesquiou family saved their home by carrying out 'special favours' for the king, but worse misfortunes were to follow. A later fire destroyed part of the house and, during the Revolution, Gabriel de Montesquiou was imprisoned and his terrified wife hid herself in a cave; when she re-emerged she was blind.

Today, the house is having happier times. Heavily creepered, it has an inner courtyard and bedrooms in the turret, with stunning views. Larger ones have four-poster canopied beds and rich velvet upholsteries. There's much highly-polished dark furniture, which suits the surroundings, but it is an unassuming, comfortable hotel and guests are well looked after, with good humour and consideration, by owners M. and Mme Guillenet, who have been running the place and providing tasty regional fare for more than 30 years. 'Good-sized rooms, good food, very good views', reports a contented reader.

NEARBY river trips; fishing; bathing; Ste-Enimie (15 km).
LOCATION small village in the Gorges du Tarn; car parking
FOOD breakfast, lunch, dinner
PRICE €€€
ROOMS 12; 10 double and twin, 2 suites, 7 with bath, 5 with shower; all rooms have phone, TV; hairdrier on request
FACILITIES sitting room, 2 dining rooms, bar, garden, 2 terraces
CREDIT CARDS DC, MC, V
CHILDREN accepted
DISABLED access difficult
PETS accepted
CLOSED Nov to early Apr
PROPRIETORS Bernard and Evelyne Guillenet

MASSIF CENTRAL

MEYRUEIS

CHATEAU D'AYRES
~ COUNTRY HOTEL ~

48150 Meyrueis (Lozère)
TEL 04 66 45 60 10 **FAX** 04 66 45 62 26
E-MAIL contact@chateau-d-ayres.com **WEBSITE** www.chateau-d-ayres.com

THE LOVELY, STONE, mainly 18thC, white-shuttered château stands on the site of a 12thC Benedictine monastery, now in the heart of the Cévennes National Park and in its own beautiful wooded grounds, with mature sequoias and oaks. Inside it is handsome, with walnut and chestnut panelling in some rooms, vaulted ceilings and a profusion of good antiques and pictures. Bedrooms are well appointed, with elegant, traditional furniture and carved mouldings. Some of the larger rooms have interesting bathrooms – extended into round towers or elevated on a mezzanine. Staff are friendly and helpful. The food is excellent. The chef, Jacqui Joubin, specializes in Languedoc cooking using plenty of local produce. M. de Montjou is a knowledgeable *sommelier*.

The house has a relaxed, convivial atmosphere and is extremely quiet. The garden is superb, with a lake, tennis court, swimming pool made out of local stone, a small whirlpool bath, and five horses, kept specially for guests to ride. There are plenty of alluring, shady places to which you can retreat with a chair and a book on long, hot afternoons – at 750 metres, the air is fresh and pure.

~

NEARBY Meyrueis (1 km); Gorges du Tarn; Mont Aigoual (1,587 m).
LOCATION 1 km SE of Meyrueis; car parking
FOOD breakfast, lunch, dinner
PRICE €€
ROOMS 27; 21 double and twin, 6 suites, 24 with bath, 3 with shower; all rooms have phone, TV, hairdrier
FACILITIES sitting room, library, 3 dining rooms, garden, terrace, swimming pool, tennis, riding
CREDIT CARDS AE, DC, MC, V
CHILDREN accepted
DISABLED no special facilities **PETS** accepted
CLOSED mid-Dec to mid-Mar
PROPRIETOR M. de Montjou

MASSIF CENTRAL

MONTSALVY

L'AUBERGE FLEURIE
~ VILLAGE INN ~

place du Barry, 15120 Montsalvy (Cantal)
TEL 04 71 49 20 02
E-MAIL info@auberge-fleurie.com **WEBSITE** www.auberge-fleurie.com

THIS CREEPER-COVERED ROADSIDE inn in a flower-decked village looks unprepossessing from the outside, but don't be put off. It is a delightful stopover and contains one of the region's most talked-about restaurants. The young owners have recently given the *auberge* a major facelift, ensuring that its traditional features weren't destroyed in the process. Half the building is taken up by a busy *café tabac*, a lunchtime and evening watering hole for many locals. But the focal point is the restaurant, in two rustically attractive rooms, all polished wood dressers, gleaming copper, starched white tablecloths, open stone fireplace and oak beams. Contemporary touches include modern artworks and stylish grey wicker chairs. Here Jean-Pierre offers his distinctive, lively brand of Auvergnat *cuisine* in modestly priced seasonal menus, and Gisèle is host to their guests.

Nowhere is the combination of old and new more effective than in the seven charming bedrooms, where beams, ancient doors and the occasional antique bed contrast with cool white walls and linen, modern furniture, warm wood floors and pristine bathrooms. Beware, the main road can mean that these rooms are noisy. Serious hikers will revel in the choice of walks from the doorstep through the unspoilt landscape of south Cantal's Châtaigneraie country (so-called because of its ubiquitous chestnut trees).

~

NEARBY Aurillac (31 km); Conques (30 km); Gorges de la Truyère; golf.
LOCATION in village on D920 12 km N of Entraygues; car parking
FOOD breakfast, lunch, dinner
PRICE €
ROOMS 17 double and twin with bath or shower; all rooms have phone, TV
FACILITIES sitting room, dining room, café, garden
CREDIT CARDS MC, V **CHILDREN** accepted **DISABLED** access difficult **PETS** accepted
CLOSED early Jan to early Feb; restaurant Sun dinner Sep to Jul
PROPRIETORS Jean-Pierre Courchinoux and Gisèle Barbance

MASSIF CENTRAL

MOUDEYRES

LE PRE BOSSU

～ FARMHOUSE HOTEL ～

43150 Moudeyres (Haute-Loire)
TEL 04 71 05 10 70 **FAX** 04 71 05 10 21
WEBSITE www.leprebossu.fr

MOUDEYRES IS A REMOTE village of thatched stone cottages and farm buildings, high (1,200 m) in the volcanic Mézenc massif, surrounded by fields of wild flowers in the spring and mushrooms in the autumn. It is a long way off the beaten track, but our inspector found it well worth the journey: 'Rarely have I seen a more beautiful location.' It is very rugged and difficult to get to.

The conscientious Flemish owners, the Grootaerts, have worked extremely hard to create an attractive and comfortable house. To original beams, wooden floors and old-fashioned, open fireplaces, they've added antique dressers, lace curtains, wild flowers when they are available – dried flowers when they are not – and books. Pots of home-made jam and artisan products are (subtly) for sale.

Some of our reports suggest that the hospitality may occasionally lack warmth, while others enthuse over the comfort and high standard of the food. By Easter 2002, M. Grootaert should have completed his project to knock together some of the ten original bedrooms to create five splendid large double rooms and one family room. Picnic baskets are provided for lunching out. Smoking is not allowed in the dining room or bedrooms.

～

NEARBY Le Puy-en-Velay (25 km); Yssingeaux (35 km).
LOCATION on the edge of the village, SE of Le Puy, beyond Laussonne; car parking
FOOD breakfast, dinner
PRICE €€
ROOMS 6; 5 double and twin, one family, all with bath or shower; all rooms have phone
FACILITIES bar, sitting room, dining room, breakfast room, garden
CREDIT CARDS AE, MC, V
CHILDREN accepted
DISABLED no special facilities **PETS** not accepted
CLOSED Nov to Easter
PROPRIETOR Carlos Grootaert

MASSIF CENTRAL

NAJAC

LONGCOL

~ COUNTRY BED-AND-BREAKFAST ~

La Fouillade, 12270 Najac (Aveyron)
TEL 05 65 29 63 36 **FAX** 05 65 29 64 28
E-MAIL longcol@wanadoo.fr **WEBSITE** www.longcol.com

THIS SPLENDID TURRETED restored medieval farmhouse – with added buildings in the same bell-shaped slate-roofed style – is set in isolated grandeur in a forested valley of the Gorges de l'Aveyron.

Solid and dignified, the overall effect is delightful. Much skill and taste has gone into the architecture, fittings and furnishings and there are antiques in every room. Quite a few of the pieces are European, but mostly they are from Asia: huge carved and studded Indian doors, exotic wood carvings and bronzes from India, Burma and Thailand, Indian miniature paintings on silk and ivory, all cleverly lit and displayed. One could be in a luxury hotel in India. The original Belgian owner, Fabienne Luyckx, began work on the site in 1982 with her mother (who died before completion) and, although she is no longer in charge, it was her passion for Asian art and antiques that dictated the hotel's style. Added to all this is a sense of great comfort and professionalism.

There is an attractive angular swimming pool, which has views of woods, and a little walled terrace, where breakfast is served in summer. Sadly the hotel restaurant has closed, but there are plenty of eating places in the area, the nearest being 6 km away in Najac.

~

NEARBY Najac (6 km); Villefranche-de-Rouergue (20 km).
LOCATION between Monteils and La Fouillade on D638, NE of Najac; car parking
FOOD breakfast
PRICE €€
ROOMS 19 double, 17 with bath, 2 with shower; all rooms have phone, TV, minibar, hairdrier
FACILITIES sitting room, dining room, billiard room, garden, terrace, swimming pool, tennis court, fishing
CREDIT CARDS DC, MC, V **CHILDREN** welcome **DISABLED** no special facilities
PETS welcome **CLOSED** Nov to Easter; restaurant Mon, Tue and lunch Wed
PROPRIETORS Luyckx family

MASSIF CENTRAL

PONT-DE-L'ARN

LA METAIRIE NEUVE

~ FARMHOUSE HOTEL ~

81660-Pont-de-l'Arn (Tarn)
TEL 05 63 97 73 50 **FAX** 05 63 61 94 75
E-MAIL metairieneuve@wanadoo.fr **WEBSITE** www.metairieneuve.com

ALTHOUGH THE VILLAGE of Bout-du-Pont-de-l'Arn is beginning to expand, this old fortified farmhouse is set in a peaceful three-hectare oasis of well-manicured gardens sheltered by mature trees, and its mellow stone walls, creeper-clad in places, are gentle on the eye. Mme Tournier is steadily refurbishing the bedrooms in individual, smart country style, but has been careful not to lose the friendly feel of a private house. There are a host of little touches to help you feel very much at home here, the furniture is a happy combination of ancient and modern, and the bathrooms have all been renovated. Three of the bedrooms are in a converted farm workers' cottage, which has its own sitting room.

In the main house, instead of a formal *salon* there are several little sitting rooms, giving you an above-average chance of getting some space of your own to relax in. In winter the beamed dining room has an open fire, and in summer it expands into a large open-sided barn looking out over the swimming pool and garden but protected from unseasonal downpours. The cooking is principally regional, concentrating on local produce as it comes into season, and of a consistently high standard.

Don't miss the splendid collection of Spanish art in the Goya Museum in nearby Castres.

~

NEARBY Castres (19 km); Le Sidobre (30 km); Albi (60 km); golf.
LOCATION at the edge of the village just N of the N112, 3 km E of Mazamet; car parking
FOOD breakfast, dinner
PRICE €
ROOMS 17 double and twin with bath; all rooms have phone, TV, minibar
FACILITIES sitting rooms, 2 dining rooms, garden, swimming pool
CREDIT CARDS DC, MC, V
CHILDREN accepted
DISABLED access difficult **PETS** accepted
CLOSED mid-Dec to late Jan; restaurant Sun
PROPRIETOR Mme Tournier

MASSIF CENTRAL

ST-ARCONS-D'ALLIER

LES DEUX ABBESSES

~ VILLAGE HOTEL ~

Le Château, 43300 St-Arcons-d'Allier (Haute-Loire)
TEL 04 71 74 03 08 **FAX** 04 71 74 05 30
E-MAIL reservation@les-deux-abbesses.fr **WEBSITE** www.lesdeuxabbesses.com

ONCE YOU ARRIVE in St-Arcons-d'Allier, a picturesque medieval village perched above the river which gives it the second half of its name, there's no point in asking where the hotel is because you are already standing in the middle of it. Laurence Perceval-Hermet has breathed new life into a well-nigh abandoned village by converting six of the houses into 14 bedrooms for her hotel centred on the château whose origins stretch back more than a thousand years. The streets are cobbled with stones taken from the river bed and, as visitors' cars are excluded to preserve the peace and undeniable charm of the village, you and your luggage will be taken to your lodging by quad bike.

The restoration has been done sensitively, and creature comforts have been installed without marring the pleasing simplicity of the buildings. The traditional plantings in the gardens, warm stonework and glimpses of the countryside beyond the village all contribute to the atmosphere of rustic peace. Breakfast and dinner are civilized meals, eaten in the château; the latter by candlelight in the baronial dining room. Dishes at dinner are prepared using fresh local produce, flavoured with herbs from the hotel's own garden. An elegant but comfortable *salon* offers a place to linger after dinner before you walk home.

~

NEARBY Le Puy-en-Velay (47 km); St-Flour (57 km); riding; golf.
LOCATION 6 km SE of Langeac left off the D585 to Saugues; car parking
FOOD breakfast, dinner (by reservation only)
PRICE €€€€-€€€€€€; 2-night minimum stay Fri to Sun
ROOMS 14; 12 double, one twin, one single, all with bath or shower
FACILITIES sitting room, dining room, terraces, garden, swimming pool
CREDIT CARDS AE, MC, V
CHILDREN accepted over 10
DISABLED not suitable **PETS** not accepted
CLOSED Nov to May; restaurant Mon, Tue Sep to Jul
PROPRIETORS Laurence Perceval-Hermet

MASSIF CENTRAL

St-Gervais-d'Auvergne

CASTEL-HOTEL 1904
~ TOWN HOTEL ~

rue de Castel, 63390 St-Gervais-d'Auvergne (Puy-de-Dôme)
TEL 04 73 85 70 42 **FAX** 04 73 85 84 39
E-MAIL info@castel-hotel-1904.com **WEBSITE** www.castel-hotel-1904.com

THE ORIGINAL OWNER OF THIS château-style house was Monsieur de Maintenon, the husband of one of Louis XIV's mistresses. '1904' refers to the year in which it was turned into a hotel, and, remarkably the same family has owned it ever since. The present incumbent, Jean-Luc Mouty, is a gourmet chef whose delicate, interesting style of cookery pulls in the crowds from miles around. The chic dining room makes an ideal setting in which to enjoy his cuisine: light streams in through the many windows, dressed with long peach-coloured curtains, on to starched white table-cloths and a polished wood floor. In the evening, the room looks cosy, lit by table lamps and wall lights. For lighter food and a more informal setting, there's a rustic bistro, Comptoir à Moustache, which concentrates on simple regional dishes.

The rest of the hotel has a genuine old French feel. Nowhere more so than the atmospheric little bar. Though large, the beamed *salon* is an intimate room, where rugs cover the terracotta-tiled floor and a mixture of furniture includes an upright piano, a smattering of antiques and plenty of upholstered chairs. With their wooden beds and old *armoires*, the bedrooms are also charmingly traditional.

~

NEARBY Riom (39 km); Menat (18 km); Gorges de la Sioule; golf.
LOCATION in the town centre, 20 km S of St-Eloy-les-Mines; car parking
FOOD breakfast, lunch, dinner
PRICE €
ROOMS 17 double and twin with bath or shower; all rooms have phone, TV
FACILITIES sitting room, 2 dining rooms, bar, terrace
CREDIT CARDS MC, V
CHILDREN accepted
DISABLED no special facilities
PETS not accepted
CLOSED mid-Nov to Mar; restaurant Mon, Tue, Wed lunch
PROPRIETOR Jean-Luc Mouty

MASSIF CENTRAL

ST-JEAN-DU-BRUEL

HOTEL DU MIDI-PAPILLON

~ RIVERSIDE HOTEL ~

12230 St-Jean-du-Bruel (Aveyron)
TEL 05 65 62 26 04 **FAX** 05 65 62 12 97

EVERY YEAR WE RECEIVE a long hand written bulletin from Jean-Michel Papillon, the fourth generation of Papillons to run this old coaching inn, reporting on the latest developments. Readers share our enthusiasm for the place, telling us that nothing changes, the food remains 'wonderful', the welcome 'faultless', the value 'outstanding'. 'No attention to detail has been overlooked.' Our inspector, to his pleasure, finds everything just right: 'The Papillons go on doing what they have been doing for the last 150 years – providing a lively welcome, lodging and food to grateful travellers.' The hotel still bears features of its past and is the sort of traditional unpretentious *auberge* that is getting harder and harder to find; this one stands out for the quality of its food and the warmth of the welcome. There is an excellent dining room – the domain of Mme Papillon – and a view from most tables of the river and a little medieval stone humpbacked bridge. There is also a terrace (though sometimes one may not always be able to sit where one wishes). Jean-Michel Papillon cooks with vegetables from the garden and home-raised poultry, and makes his own jam, croissants, and *charcuterie*. This is the rural, family-run inn at its best. 'It was an object lesson in how a small hotel should be run and the pride which M and Mme Papillon take in their establishment is amply justified' runs our latest report.

~

NEARBY Gorges de la Dourbie (10 km); Montpellier-le-Vieux.
LOCATION by river, in village on D991, 40 km SE of Millau; car parking
FOOD breakfast, lunch, dinner
PRICE €
ROOMS 19; 8 double, 5 twin, one suite, one single, 4 family, all with bath or shower; all rooms have phone
FACILITIES sitting room, TV room, 3 dining rooms, bar, terrace, garden, swimming pool, Jacuzzi **CREDIT CARDS** MC, V **CHILDREN** welcome
DISABLED access difficult **PETS** accepted **CLOSED** mid-Nov to Easter
PROPRIETORS Papillon family

MASSIF CENTRAL

ST-MARTIN-VALMEROUX

HOSTELLERIE DE LA MARONNE
~ MANOR HOUSE HOTEL ~

Le Theil, 15140 St-Martin-Valmeroux (Cantal)
TEL 04 71 69 20 33 **FAX** 04 71 69 28 22
E-MAIL maronne@maronne.com **WEBSITE** www.maronne.com

WITH ITS SWIMMING POOL AND tennis court surrounded by lovely gardens and sweeping countryside, this handsomely furnished 19thC *maison de maître* makes a fine retreat whether you're in search of rest or recreation. So much has changed during Alain Decock's tenure that we have reinstated it as a long entry: a smart dining room with panoramic views has been built into the hillside, and bedrooms and public rooms have been given a stylish facelift. Despite its formal air, the calm, elegant sitting room, decorated in muted tones and furnished with antiques, is a particular favourite with guests. Other improvements include new bathrooms for each of the bedrooms, and a lift.

Food is taken seriously, with excellent results and a growing reputation. Madame Decock is the chef, responsible for a range of creative set menus (reaching up to *gastronomique* levels) as well as a reasonably priced *carte*. Breakfast includes freshly squeezed orange juice and delicious homemade jam.

The bedrooms and apartments are as comfortable and chic as the public rooms, with similarly subtle colour schemes. The most attractive have south-facing terraces and stunning views over the valley – easily worth the 30 or so extra euros.

~

NEARBY Salers (6 km); Aurillac (36 km); Anjony (15 km); châteaux; fishing.
LOCATION in countryside 3 km E of St-Martin on D37; ample car parking
FOOD breakfast, dinner
PRICE €€€
ROOMS 21; 17 double and twin, 4 apartments, all with bath or shower; all rooms have phone, TV, minibar; some have balcony or terrace
FACILITIES sitting room, dining room, breakfast room, meeting room, lift, garden, swimming pool, tennis court
CREDIT CARDS AE, DC, MC, V **CHILDREN** accepted
DISABLED access possible **PETS** accepted **CLOSED** Nov to Apr
PROPRIETOR Alain Decock

MASSIF CENTRAL

TARGET

CHATEAU DE BOUSSAC

~ CHATEAU HOTEL ~

Target, 03140 Chantelle (Allier)
TEL 04 70 40 63 20 **FAX** 04 70 40 60 03
E-MAIL longueil@wanadoo.fr **WEBSITE** www.chateau-de-boussac.com

INCREASED PUBLIC EXPOSURE – now in other British hotel guides as well as this one – has not affected the delicate balancing act conducted by the Marquis and Marquise de Longueil, who continue to welcome guests into their home with captivating charm.

The Château de Boussac lies between Vichy and Moulin, tucked away in the Bourbonnais – quite difficult to find. Solid, turreted and moated, the château could be a tourist sight in its own right; it is built around a court-yard, and the main reception rooms, furnished with Louis XV antiques and chandeliers, open on to a vast terrace with an ornamental lake and formal gardens. But the château is very much lived-in. By day the Marquis dons his overalls and works on the estate, but comes in to cook at least one course of the evening meal and chat to his guests. His wife looks after the rooms with care – there are fresh flowers everywhere, and the antiques are highly polished. Dinner *en famille* can be a rather formal affair, but the food is hard to fault and the Marquis, who speaks English, will make you feel at home. One reader was enchanted, and proclaimed it 'one of the highlights of our two-week trip'.

~

NEARBY Chantelle (12 km); Souvigny (35 km); Vichy (50 km).
LOCATION in countryside, off D42, NW of Chantelle; car parking
FOOD breakfast, dinner
PRICE €€€
ROOMS 5; one double, 3 twin, one suite, all with bath
FACILITIES sitting room, dining room, terrace, garden
CREDIT CARDS AE, MC, V
CHILDREN accepted if well behaved
DISABLED no special facilities
PETS accepted
CLOSED Nov to Feb (except by reservation in advance)
PROPRIETORS Marquis and Marquise de Longueil

MASSIF CENTRAL

TENCE

HOSTELLERIE PLACIDE
~ TOWN HOTEL ~

1 route d'Annonay, 43190 Tence (Haute-Loire)
TEL 04 71 59 82 76 **FAX** 04 71 65 44 46
E-MAIL placide@hostellerie-placide.fr **WEBSITE** www.hostellerie-placide.fr

IN THE SMALL, MELLOW TOWN of Tence in the lush Velay region stands this handsome former post house, built in 1900. The outside is smothered in ivy; the inside has been restored with taste and character. Pierre-Marie and Véronique are the friendly, enthusiastic owners, the fourth generation of the Placide family to be in charge here. He is a first-class chef who has raised the reputation of the restaurant, whilst she has the dual role of looking after the guests and the cellar. They make a dynamic team, who have successfully injected a youthful style into a very traditional *relais*.

The decoration is appropriate: in the elegant sitting room antiques and comfortable waxed leather furniture complement the wooden floor, beams and panelling. As we went to press. the Placides were in the process of renovating the bedrooms, smartening them up with pale walls, fresh white bedspreads and colourful checked fabric. They are all non-smoking. In the dining room, which looks on to the garden and is painted a vivid yellowy orange, the tables are covered in crisp white linen and decorated with fresh flowers. Here Pierre-Marie combines unusual flavours with delicacy and imagination on a variety of regional menus. Though not large, the garden is pretty and peaceful, a perfect spot for relaxing in a deck chair or eating breakfast in summer.

~

NEARBY Le Puy-en-Velay (47 km); Lac de Devesset; Gorges de l'Allier; fishing; golf.
LOCATION on the outskirts of town, 19 km E of Yssingeaux; car parking
FOOD breakfast, lunch, dinner
PRICE €€€
ROOMS 13 double and twin with bath or shower; all rooms have phone, TV
FACILITIES sitting room, 2 dining rooms, garden
CREDIT CARDS AE, MC, V
CHILDREN accepted
DISABLED access difficult
PETS accepted
CLOSED Jan to Apr (except Easter); Sun eve, Mon, Tue Sep to Jul

MASSIF CENTRAL

VITRAC

AUBERGE LA TOMETTE

~ VILLAGE INN ~

15220 Vitrac (Cantal)
TEL 04 71 64 70 94 **FAX** 04 71 64 77 11
E-MAIL info@auberge-la-tomette.com **WEBSITE** www.auberge-la-tomette.com

'THIS HOTEL HAS ALL THE QUALITIES of peace, welcome, attractive setting and very good food that characterize your selections,' a reader said of La Tomette – a jolly whitewashed and shuttered inn, much expanded and improved over the past 18 years, without the loss of its essential appeal. In an exceptionally pretty village in the middle of the chestnut groves of the southern Cantal, it makes a perfect base for a family holiday, with its large garden, where trees and parasols provide plenty of shade, lawns for running around, and covered and heated swimming pool. There's also a health centre with Jacuzzi, sauna and steam room.

Wood-panelling gives a rustic feel to the cosy dining room, where every day a vase of freshly picked garden flowers is placed on each of the pink-covered tables and the menus are dominated by simple, well-cooked, hearty local dishes. In summer, meals are served on a lovely terrace, part of which is covered for those who prefer to eat in total shade. In a separate building, the bedrooms are modern and clean but otherwise unexceptional. The six duplexes have a convenient lay-out for families.

~

NEARBY Maurs (21 km); Aurillac (22 km); Figeac (43 km).
LOCATION in village, 5 km S of St-Mamet-la-Salvetat; car parking
FOOD breakfast, lunch, dinner
PRICE €
ROOMS 15; 9 double and twin, 6 duplexes, all with bath or shower; all rooms have phone, TV, hairdrier
FACILITIES sitting room, dining room, sauna, terrace, garden, health centre, swimming pool
CREDIT CARDS AE, MC, V
CHILDREN accepted
DISABLED no special facilities
PETS accepted
CLOSED Jan to Apr
PROPRIETORS Odette and Daniel Chausi

MASSIF CENTRAL

COULANDON

LE CHALET
COUNTRY HOTEL

03000 Coulandon (Allier)
TEL 04 70 46 00 66
FAX 04 70 44 07 09
E-MAIL hotelchalet@cs3i.fr
WEBSITE www.hotellechalet.com
FOOD breakfast, lunch, dinner
PRICE €
ROOMS 28
CLOSED Dec to Feb

W E FIRST VISITED this modest, traditional hotel on a summer evening when its secluded, wooded, park-like garden seemed idyllic. The big fish pond (where guests are welcome to fish) is still perfect for strolling around, drink in hand, before dinner. Rooms (in the chalet-style building itself, and in converted outbuildings) vary in style and size; none is notably stylish, but the best are cheerfully comfortable (with exposed beams and bright wallpaper). Service is amiable in the dining room, where the fare includes some interesting regional specialities; Saint-Pourçain and Sancerre are special features of the wine list.

PAILHEROLS

AUBERGE DES MONTAGNES
COUNTRY HOTEL

15800 Pailherols (Cantal)
TEL 04 71 47 57 01
FAX 04 71 49 63 83
E-MAIL info@auberge-des-montagnes.com **FOOD** breakfast, lunch, dinner **PRICE** €
ROOMS 22
CLOSED mid-Oct to late Dec

T HE COUNTRYSIDE OF THE Pailherols plateau that surrounds this aptly named inn is starkly beautiful. It lies between two mountain ranges (the Aubrac and the Puys) and is magnificent walking country. It is owned and run by the warmly welcoming Combourieu family, who are fourth-generation innkeepeers. Fresh and bright, with splashes of colour here and there, the bedrooms are split between three buildings. The main one also contains the cosy beamed sitting room and bright, cheerful restaurant, which is the heart of the place and devoted to producing an excellent *cuisine de terroir*. A well-equipped games room, indoor and outdoor pools, sauna, gym, climbing wall and open-air activities on the doorstep make it

THE SOUTH

AREA INTRODUCTION

HOTELS IN THE SOUTH

MEDITERRANEAN FRANCE: sea, sun, wine, flowers, fruit, mountains, Roman remains. Heaven on earth – and with more hotel recommendations in this book than any other region of France. Our South section stretches from the border with Italy and the foothills of the Alps across Provence and the southern part of the Rhône valley into Languedoc-Roussillon to the Pyrenees, and covers the following *départements:* Alpes-Maritimes, Alpes-de-Haute-Provence, Var, Bouches-du-Rhône, Vaucluse, Gard, Drôme, Ardèche, Aude, Hérault and Pyrénées-Orientales.

Set between the wild Cévennes mountain range, the Pyrenees and the Mediterranean, Languedoc-Roussillon bears many similarities to Provence – on the other side of the Rhône – being a sun-baked land of vineyards, olive groves and dry, scrubby *garrigue.* Romanesque buildings, Roman remains and palaces of popes and cardinals are among its architectural treasures, and rugby pitches and bullrings are evidence of local passions. Far fewer good hotels here than east of the Rhône, but nevertheless we have unearthed one or two interesting new addresses.

The allure of Provence and the Côte d'Azur – sparkling sea, blue skies, the easy Mediterranean way of life, and a light that has inspired painters through the centuries – continues to work its magic. Not surprisingly, our largest concentration of recommendations is here, and the editors of this edition spent arduous (well, fairly arduous) weeks scouring its hotels, rejecting contenders (of which there were many) which, however beautifully decorated and *à la mode*, lacked personality, in favour of ones with real individuality and charm. The region is becoming ever smarter and more crowded with holidaymakers – witness the wild Lubéron, east of Avignon, now dotted with carefully restored villages, boutique hotels and slick restaurants – but it is still possible to find oases of calm even close to the tourist hotspots, as the following pages reveal.

We can also make several further recommendations throughout the area. One reporter returned recently from staying at **Le Pigonnet** in Aix-en-Provence (tel 04 42 59 02 90), full of praise for this 'lovely peaceful hotel' – though, with 52 bedrooms, it's slightly too large for a main entry. **Hostellerie La Grangette** (tel 04 90 20 00 77) is a beautifully decorated typically Provençal house just outside Velleron, a 20-minute drive east of Avignon. Just two years old, **Domaine de Bournereau** in Monteux (tel 04 90 66 36 13) is a German-owned hotel in a converted *mas* with 12 stylish modern bedrooms and a delightful garden. There is another *mas* – **Mas Dom Pater** (tel 04 90 92 01 39) – in St-Rémy-de-Provence: this one dates back to the 17th century, is distinctively decorated and has a glorious, large swimming pool. Finally, a reader warmly recommends **La Fargo** in St-Pierre-des-Champs (tel 04 68 43 12 78) in the rough, silent landscape near Lagrasse. At this simple, regional restaurant-with-rooms in a restored Catalan forge run by lovely relaxed people, you will find seasonal fire-grilled food and good-value contemporary rooms. For even wider coverage, see *Charming Small Hotels and Restaurants,* Southern France, also published by Duncan Petersen, now with restaurant recommendations as well as hotels.

THE SOUTH

AIX-EN-PROVENCE

MAS D'ENTREMONT

~ FARMHOUSE HOTEL ~

Montée d'Avignon, 13090 Aix-en-Provence (Bouches-du-Rhône)
TEL 04 42 17 42 42 **FAX** 04 42 21 15 83
E-MAIL entremont@wanadoo.fr **WEBSITE** www.masdentremont.com

THIS IS ONE OF OUR FAVOURITE HOTELS and a visit not long ago – plus complimentary reports from readers – reconfirm our earlier impressions. The hosts here are the charming M. Marignane and his family – his sister-in-law owns the Relais de la Magdeleine at Gémenos (see page 273). Low, red-roofed buildings are clustered around a courtyard – modern constructions, but using old materials. Within are wooden beams and pillars, rustic furniture, tiled floors and open fireplaces. Bedrooms are also rustic in style and comfortable. Many of the rooms are spread around the grounds in bungalows.

The setting is peaceful and the gardens a delight – with a big swimming pool shielded by cypresses, plenty of secluded corners, and a pond with a fountain, lilies and a number of lazy carp. Overlooking this is a beautiful summer dining room, with windows that slide away, effectively creating a roofed terrace – to which underfloor heating has now been added, allowing you to eat out even on a chilly day.

The food is excellent, with the emphasis on fish, fresh vegetables and a strong Provençal influence (although the chef is from Strasbourg).

~

NEARBY Aix-en-Provence; Abbaye de Silvacane (25 km).
LOCATION just off the RN7, 2 km from the centre of Aix, in large garden and grounds; car parking
FOOD breakfast, lunch, dinner
PRICE €€€
ROOMS 17; 15 double and twin, 2 family, all with bath; all rooms have phone, TV, air conditioning, minibar, hairdrier, safe
FACILITIES restaurant, gym, lift, terrace, garden, swimming pool, tennis
CREDIT CARDS MC, V **CHILDREN** welcome
DISABLED ground floor rooms available
PETS accepted
CLOSED Nov to mid-Mar; restaurant Sun dinner
PROPRIETORS Marignane family

The South

Aix-en-Provence

Hotel des Quatre Dauphins

~ Town hotel ~

54 rue Roux Alphéron, 13100 Aix-en-Provence (Bouches-du-Rhône)
Tel 04 42 38 16 39 **Fax** 04 42 38 60 19

THIS ATTRACTIVE LITTLE 19THC *maison bourgeoise*, on a quiet corner near the pretty Place des 4 Dauphins, opened as a family-run hotel more than a decade ago.

The dark green front door sports four brass dolphins and bright red geraniums grow in window boxes behind the wrought-iron bars on the ground floor. Built on three floors, there is no lift; it is simple and excellent value for money. Some original features have remained – the lovely tiled terracotta floors – and there are some nice antique pieces throughout the house, such as handsome big mirrors, little wooden tables and a pine chest in the breakfast room. The plain decoration in the rooms is pleasing: walls are painted in pale pastel shades and bedspreads and curtains are in Provençal prints. Furniture is minimal, mainly painted wood. Bathrooms are well equipped. Large, framed Impressionist posters hang in the corridors. The only public room is the breakfast/sitting room in a gentle pale yellow, with large painted wooden Provençal-style armchairs, big ceramic pots, dried flowers and pretty tablecloths. Air conditioning in the bedrooms is a welcome new addition.

It is well placed for visiting Aix on a budget, though recent reports draw attention to the inadequacies of some of the bedrooms (particularly those on the upper floors), which are small and now rather tired looking.

~

Nearby place des 4 Dauphins; Cours Mirabeau.
Location in town centre; car parking in street
Food breakfast
Price ©-©©
Rooms 13; 9 double, 3 single, one triple, 8 with bath, 5 with shower; all rooms have phone, TV, air conditioning, minibar
Facilities breakfast/sitting room
Credit cards DC, MC, V **Children** welcome
Disabled not suitable **Pets** accepted **Closed** never
Proprietor Mme Lafont

THE SOUTH

AIX-EN-PROVENCE

VILLA GALLICI

~ TOWN VILLA ~

avenue de la Violette, 13100 Aix-en-Provence (Bouches-du-Rhône)
TEL 04 42 23 29 23 **FAX** 04 42 96 30 45
E-MAIL villagallici@wanadoo.fr **WEBSITE** www.villagallici.com

MANY PEOPLE CONSIDER the four-star Relais et Châteaux Villa Gallici to be the best hotel in Aix. It is certainly beautiful, and interior-designed down to the last curtain hook. Everything, inside and out, is perfect – gardens, terraces, pool, enormous terracotta pots overflowing with flowers, white umbrellas and plenty of wrought iron. A terrace, adjoining the villa, shaded by plane trees has been converted to an outside sitting room with deep-cushioned sofas and chairs. Bedrooms are sumptuous, with marvellous French wallpapers and fabrics and elegant 18thC furniture. Most of the bathrooms are classic, and pristine white. Downstairs, a series of small, welcoming, intimate sitting rooms are filled with colour and light, prints, paintings, coffee-table books and pieces of porcelain.

Our reporter noted that the guests were as beautiful as the hotel; this is not a place for the much-loved old grey T-shirt. Perhaps there is something just a little intimidating about the grand style of the Villa Gallici for it to be entirely relaxing, but that, as always, is a matter of taste.

Be warned, the hotel is perched on top of a steep hill and, whilst the walk into Aix isn't too onerous, the climb back is – especially in high summer. Not for the infirm.

~

NEARBY Avignon (82 km); Marseille (31 km).
LOCATION in a quiet suburb, 500 m from cathedral; car parking
FOOD breakfast, lunch, dinner
PRICE €€€€€€
ROOMS 22; 18 double and twin, 4 suites, all with bath; all rooms have phone, TV, video, air conditioning, minibar, hairdrier, safe
FACILITIES sitting rooms, dining room, terrace, garden, swimming pool
CREDIT CARDS AE, DC, MC, V
CHILDREN welcome
DISABLED one specially adapted room **PETS** welcome **CLOSED** never
PROPRIETORS M. Jouve, M. Dez and M. Montemarco

THE SOUTH

ARLES

CALENDAL
~ TOWN HOTEL ~

5 rue Porte de Laure, 13200 Arles (Bouches-du-Rhône)
TEL 04 90 96 11 89 **FAX** 04 90 96 05 84
E-MAIL contact@lecalendal.com **WEBSITE** www.lecalendal.com

THIS BUSY, FRIENDLY HOTEL offers the best of both worlds: a location right next door to the great Roman arena – our inspector's room had a little balcony looking on to it – and a surprisingly large courtyard garden, a shady haven of trees (including a 400-year-old nettle tree), where on a hot day you can retreat from the dusty city. The building is 18th century, which shows through as features of the decoration, for example the rough stone walls and exposed beams downstairs. Here all the rooms have been knocked through to make one huge open-plan space, supported by pillars, with arches and steps marking the divisions between sitting and eating areas. The cosy sitting area, centred on the fireplace, is a perfect place for waiting, with armchairs and foreign-language newspapers on rods brasserie-style. You help yourself to the buffet breakfast and light lunch, which is still on offer at 5 pm.

One can't imagine being glum for long in this hotel. The colourful decoration would lift the blackest of moods. The bedrooms are different variations on a theme, mixing blues and yellows, yellows and reds or reds and greens, with pretty co-ordinating Provençal fabrics. Though small, they are well designed, with TVs on high brackets or shelves and cleverly added bathrooms, full of the fluffiest, brightest yellow towels

~

NEARBY arena; St-Trophîme; place du Forum.
LOCATION opposite Roman arena; car parking (reserve in advance)
FOOD breakfast, light lunch, tea
PRICE €
ROOMS 38 double, twin, triple and family, all with bath; all rooms have phone, TV, air conditioning, hairdrier
FACILITIES sitting area, dining areas, garden
CREDIT CARDS AE, DC, MC, V **CHILDREN** accepted
DISABLED 3 specially adapted rooms **PETS** welcome
CLOSED 3 weeks Jan
MANAGER Mme Jacquemin

THE SOUTH

ARLES

GRAND-HOTEL NORD-PINUS

~ TOWN HOTEL ~

place du Forum 13200 Arles (Bouches-du-Rhône)
TEL 04 90 93 44 44 **FAX** 04 90 93 34 00
E-MAIL info@nord-pinus.com **WEBSITE** www.nord-pinus.com

A STUNNING EXAMPLE of how a former cult hotel can, in the right hands, live again with its spirit intact but its amenities altered to suit the modern age. Anne Igou's imaginative and extravagant renovation has given back the Nord-Pinus its Bohemian past, recalling the post-war days when artists such as Picasso and Cocteau as well as bullfighters were entertained by its charismatic owners, a cabaret dancer and her husband, a famous tightrope-walking clown. The famous yellow bar, in particular, remains a homage to those times. There are other mementos, too, including a cabinet of souvenirs, huge posters advertising bullfights around the fine stairwell, as well as chandeliers, gilded mirrors and all the original wrought-iron beds. The lobby has a dramatic, slightly Moorish feel; the restaurant, a traditional brasserie, leads off it.

Bedrooms come in three sizes: the smallest are compact but charming, with Provençal fabrics and antique wardrobes; larger ones are very spacious; and the six suites are enormous, worth splashing out on, especially No. 10, the 'bullfighters' suite', from the window of which legendary matador Domínguín would greet the crowds below. The hotel is run in a laidback but professional way.

~

NEARBY Arena, Théatre Antique; St-Trophîme; Les Alyscampes.
LOCATION in town centre (follow hotel signs); garage car parking
FOOD breakfast
PRICE €€€
ROOMS 25; 19 double and twin, 6 suites, all with bath; all rooms have phone, TV, air conditioning, minibar, hairdrier
FACILITIES sitting room, bar, adjoining restaurant, breakfast room, lift, terrace
CREDIT CARDS AE, DC, MC, V
CHILDREN accepted
DISABLED access possible **PETS** accepted **CLOSED** never
PROPRIETOR Anne Igou

THE SOUTH

AVIGNON

LA MIRANDE
~ TOWN HOTEL ~

4 place de Mirande, 84000 Avignon (Vaucluse)
TEL 04 90 85 93 93 **FAX** 04 90 86 26 85
E-MAIL mirande@la-mirande.fr **WEBSITE** www.la-mirande.fr

A CLASSIC HONEY-COLOURED late 17thC façade by Pierre Mignard trans-formed La Mirande, which was built on the 14thC foundations of a car-dinal's palace, into a *hôtel particulier*. Right opposite the Palais des Papes, in a quiet cobbled square, it was seized on by the Stein family and, since 1990, has been a sumptuous hotel that looks and feels as if it had been lived in for generations by a single family endowed with money and good taste. Tiled and parquet floors, smart Provençal fabrics and chintzes, wall coverings, paint, panelling, pictures, mirrors, and furniture all come together in serene period harmony. The good news doesn't stop there: the staff are kind and courteous as well.

The central courtyard, dotted with plants and sculptures, has been cov-ered over with a glass roof, and is surrounded by a series of public rooms any one of which you'd like to wrap up and take home with you. The bed-rooms vary in size (those on the first floor being the largest) but not in their uniformly high quality. From the second-floor balconies you are treated to rooftop views across the city. Last but not least are the treats in store in the dining room: Jérôme Verrière draws eager gourmets from far and wide, and the introduction of a club table in the old kitchen for 12 to 14 people, who can take pot luck with a menu cooked over a wood-fired range, has proved a great success. And, yes, there is a garage for your car.

NEARBY Petit-Palais; Notre-Dame-des-Doms; Calvet museum.
LOCATION opposite the Palais des Papes; car parking
FOOD breakfast, lunch, dinner
PRICE €€€€€
ROOMS 20; 19 double and twin, one suite, all with bath; all rooms have phone, TV, air conditioning, hairdrier
FACILITIES sitting rooms, bar, restaurant, lift, terrace, garden
CREDIT CARDS AE, DC, MC, V **CHILDREN** accepted
DISABLED one specially adapted room **PETS** accepted **CLOSED** never; restaurant Jan
PROPRIETOR M. Achim Stein

THE SOUTH

LES BAUX-DE-PROVENCE

AUBERGE DE LA BENVENGUDO
~ COUNTRY HOTEL ~

Vallon de l'Arcoule, 13520 Les Baux-de-Provence (Bouches-du-Rhône)
TEL 04 90 54 32 54 **FAX** 04 90 54 42 58
E-MAIL @aol.com **WEBSITE** www.benvengudo.com

THE BEAUPIED FAMILY'S creeper-clad hotel just outside the village of Les
Baux, remains compelling, despite recent changes – and much more
affordable than most places in the area. The Beaupieds, who established
the hotel back in 1967, are now taking a back seat. They have appointed
Jean-Pierre Côte as the new Chef de Cuisine and joint manager with his
wife, Catherine. Rooms have the style of a private country house: a cosy
sitting room with beams, an intimate dining room and, although some of
the bedrooms are a little brash for our taste, others are homely with pretty
patterned curtains and antique furniture. A couple have four-posters.

One guest told our inspector: "This is absolutely my idea of a charming
small hotel. Just the place to spend a quiet, gentle relaxing week or 10
days. And the food is marvellous." Jean-Pierre Côte's menu changes every
day according to what is in the market. Although the garden adjoins the
road, there are no complaints of noise. The bedrooms are split between
the main building and an annexe; some have a terrace or balcony, and the
suites, with a kitchenette as well as a sitting room, are ideal for families.

The garden is delightful; there are olive groves and views of the natural
stone outcrops of the Alpilles, the 'little Alps' of this part of Provence.
Good walking country.

~

NEARBY St-Rémy-de-Provence (10 km); Arles (21 km).
LOCATION just outside the village of Les Baux-de-Provence on D78 to Fontvieille;
car parking
FOOD breakfast, dinner; half-board only from 3 nights
PRICE €€
ROOMS 20; 14 double, 6 twin, all with bath; all rooms have phone, TV, air
conditioning
FACILITIES sitting room, dining room, terrace, garden, swimming pool, tennis
CREDIT CARDS AE, MC, V **CHILDREN** accepted
DISABLED access possible **PETS** accepted **CLOSED** never; restaurant Sun
PROPRIETORS Beaupied family

THE SOUTH

LES BAUX-DE-PROVENCE

MAS D'AIGRET
~ COUNTRY HOTEL ~

13520 Les Baux-de-Provence (Bouches-du-Rhône)
TEL 04 90 54 20 00 **FAX** 04 90 54 44 00
E-MAIL contact@masdaigret.com **WEBSITE** www.masdaigret.com

THERE ARE SEVERAL HOTELS dotted peacefully below Les Baux; this one has the advantage of being the closest to the ruined fortress and its vertiginous village. It's a fairly simple place with some notable features, not least the secluded enclosed swimming pool and tranquil surrounding gardens. Lounging here – but for the rumble of traffic on busy days – you are a world away from the tourist hub of Les Baux: you can glimpse the bright colours of the tour buses through gaps in the foliage, but a real sense of privacy pervades.

As for bedrooms, go for the special ones, such as No. 16, which has a private terrace and a troglodyte bathroom incorporating a large slab of rock face, or the family apartment with a perfect little room for children. Other bedrooms in the main house are pretty if a little worn, and many have blue-shuttered French windows and balconies with wonderful views over the Provençal landscape. Downstairs, the reception rooms are *à la mode*, if not quite chic. The rock face into which the hotel is built makes another dramatic appearance in the dining room.

~

NEARBY St-Rémy-de-Provence (10 km); Arles (18 km); the Alpilles.
LOCATION on D27A, 300 m below Les Baux; car parking
FOOD breakfast, lunch, dinner
PRICE ⓔ ⓔ
ROOMS 17; 16 double, twin and triple, one apartment, all with bath; all rooms have phone, TV, air conditioning, minibar
FACILITIES sitting room, bar, dining room, terrace, garden, swimming pool
CREDIT CARDS AE, DC, MC, V
CHILDREN welcome
DISABLED not suitable
PETS accepted
CLOSED 2 weeks Jan
PROPRIETORS Frédérik Laloy and Vincent Missistrano

THE SOUTH

LA SANTOLINE
~ CONVERTED HUNTING LODGE ~

07460 Beaulieu (Ardèche)
TEL 04 75 39 01 91 **FAX** 04 75 39 38 79
E-MAIL contacts@santoline.com **WEBSITE** www.lasantoline.com

RESIDENTS OF NEARBY VILLAGES still speak of the big, old, stone Santoline as *'le château'* – a reference to its 15thC origins. As time passed, it was used as a hunting lodge and remains a secluded place well off the beaten track. With no television or other disruptions, there is little to disturb except birdsong and the occasional braying of a donkey. It is difficult to imagine a more relaxed setting. In the evenings, guests dine outside on the flower-filled terrace and watch the sun set behind the Cévennes.

Since opening their hotel in 1991, the Espenels have gathered a very loyal clientele by striking the right balance between easy-going conviviality and discreet attentiveness. Outsiders use the restaurant, which provides a daily-changing menu of regional fare and affordable wines of the Ardèche. (The inside dining room has a fine stone-vaulted ceiling and tiled floor.) Bedrooms are pretty and simple in design, with much use of natural, rustic textures – tiled or pine floors, wicker furniture, some iron bedsteads, and white plastered walls. There are thick towels in the bathrooms. Most have exhilarating views of mountains.

NEARBY Vallon-Pont-d'Arc (22 km); Gorges de l'Ardèche.
LOCATION off the D104 at La Croisée de Jalès, then the D225, 2 km from Beaulieu; car parking
FOOD breakfast, lunch, dinner
PRICE (€); half-board obligatory Jul to Sep
ROOMS 8; 7 double, one suite, all with bath; all rooms have phone, minibar; 2 have air conditioning
FACILITIES sitting room, restaurant, terrace, garden, swimming pool
CREDIT CARDS MC, V
CHILDREN accepted
DISABLED no special facilities
PETS accepted
CLOSED Oct to late Apr
PROPRIETORS M. and Mme Espenel

THE SOUTH

BEAUMONT-DU-VENTOUX

LA MAISON

~ VILLAGE RESTAURANT-WITH-ROOMS ~

84340 Beaumont-du-Ventoux (Vaucluse)
TEL 04 90 65 15 50 **FAX** 04 90 65 23 29

FROM THE OUTSIDE, La Maison looks like dozens of other pretty Provençal houses – creeper-covered stone walls, blue window-shutters and doors, white wrought-iron tables and chairs, parasols and plants in terracotta pots on a shady front terrace – but a surprise lies in store. The restaurant, opened by Michèle Laurelut in June 1993, four years before she started letting rooms, is as chic as the owner herself with the kind of sophistication that you would hardly expect to find on the edge of a sleepy rural village like Beaumont-du-Ventoux. The decoration is stylishly simple: ochre-washed plaster walls, terracotta-tiled floor and heavy cream curtains at the windows. It is furnished like a private house, with massive table lamps, cushions to sit on, well-spaced tables, and artfully arranged pictures and ornaments. The focal point is an immense stone fireplace, where a fire burns on chilly autumn nights, to be replaced by a bank of hydrangeas when the weather improves.

Michèle offers a short seasonal menu, which we considered good value at 28 euros, and you can keep your bill down if you stick to the excellent local wine. To save driving home after dinner, you could stay in one of the large, modest bedrooms (two connect), which are immaculately kept but lack the dining room's panache.

~

NEARBY Vaison-la-Romaine (12 km); Avignon (47 km).
LOCATION in village, turn left at sign just before Mairie; car parking
FOOD breakfast, lunch, dinner
PRICE €
ROOMS 3; one double with shower, one twin with shower, one twin with bath (and adjoining room)
FACILITIES restaurant, terrace, garden **CREDIT CARDS** MC, V
CHILDREN accepted **DISABLED** not suitable **PETS** accepted
CLOSED Nov to Mar; restaurant Mon and Tue Apr to Jun, Sep and Oct; lunch Mon to Sat Jul and Aug
PROPRIETOR Michèle Laurelut

THE SOUTH

BONNIEUX

AUBERGE DE L'AIGUEBRUN

~ COUNTRY HOTEL ~

Domaine de la Tour, RD 943, 84480 Bonnieux (Vaucluse)
TEL 04 90 04 47 00 **FAX** 04 90 04 47 01
E-MAIL sylviabuzier@wanadoo.fr **WEBSITE** www.aubergedelaiguebrun.com

SYLVIE BUZIER IS WARM, pretty and talented (she can paint as well as cook and decorate). Her staff are equally charming, easy-going and unobtrusively hip (her co-chef is friendly Francis Motta), They are a happy, well-knit team, and along with the hotel's setting, they engender a rare sense of peace and well-being in their beautiful house.

The hotel lies on its own in a green oasis at the end of a steep track by a waterfall in the river Aiguebrun, the only natural water in this barren region. 'When Sylvie (who previously owned a much loved restaurant near Avignon) bought it, she transformed the interior, which is now a delightful, personalized version of current Provençal decoration. Rooms are full of light: the white and cream dining room with its fresh green leaf curtains is surrounded by windows overlooking the river; the sitting room is a lovely yellow, with a well-stocked drinks tray, comfy sofas and a minah bird in an antique cage; the bedrooms are similarly full of light and colour (the family suite is excellent, with two bedrooms, one perfect for children).

The food is a highlight: a simple, delicious set menu with one or two choices using organic meat and vegetables and wild fish. Herbs and salads come from the *potager*. There is a lovely pool.

~

NEARBY Bonnieux (6 km); Lourmarin (10 km); Aix-en-Provence (45 km).
LOCATION in valley, 6 km E of Bonnieux, down a steep rutted track signposted off Bonnieux to Boux road; car parking
FOOD breakfast, lunch, dinner
PRICE €€
ROOMS 8; 4 double and twin, one single, 3 suites, all with bath; all rooms have phone, TV, hairdrier
FACILITIES sitting room, dining room, terrace, garden, potager, swimming pool bar
CREDIT CARDS MC, V **CHILDREN** accepted
DISABLED not suitable **PETS** not accepted
CLOSED mid-Nov to mid-Mar; restaurant Tues, Wed lunch
PROPRIETOR Sylvie Buzier

THE SOUTH

BONNIEUX

HOSTELLERIE DU PRIEURE

~ VILLAGE BED-AND-BREAKFAST ~

84480 Bonnieux (Vaucluse)
TEL 04 90 75 80 78 **FAX** 04 90 75 96 00
E-MAIL reservation@hotelprieure.com **WEBSITE** www.hotelprieure.com

IT HAD TO HAPPEN SOONER or later, and this attractive traditional hotel at the foot of the ramparts of one of the showpiece Luberon villages has finally surrendered to a makeover team (the pots of lavender that flank the entrance are an early giveaway). Fortunately it has been restored sympathetically, with respect for the integrity of the building, an 18thC former *hôtel-Dieu*. Through massive oak doors, a splendid wide staircase leads up to the balustraded landing and some of the original patients' rooms, whose endearingly old-fashioned wallpaper and curtains have been replaced by fresh, bright, up-to-date decoration and smart fabrics. They are furnished with handsome antiques, and many display their old beams. Some overlook the pretty walled garden at the rear, where apricot and plum trees give shade from the heat, and are quieter than those at the front, which face the road going up into the village.

Although there's no longer a restaurant, the reception staff will send out for meals if you prefer to eat in, and drinks are served in the large cheerful *salon de thé* and on the covered terrace. A swimming pool was added in 2004, and the former chapel, previously a store room, is now a boutique. Room prices are still pretty reasonable.

~

NEARBY Avignon (51 km); Aix (40 km); the villages of the Luberon.
LOCATION on a lower road of the village; car parking
FOOD breakfast; room service
PRICE €€-€€€
ROOMS 11 double and twin, with bath or shower; all rooms have phone, TV; 3 have air conditioning
FACILITIES sitting room, dining room, bar, terrace, garden, swimming pool
CREDIT CARDS MC, V **CHILDREN** accepted
DISABLED not suitable
PETS accepted
CLOSED early Nov to Mar
MANAGER Catherine Saint Guilhem

THE SOUTH

CAP D'ANTIBES

VILLA VAL DES ROSES

～ SEASIDE GUESTHOUSE ～

6 chemin des Lauriers, 06160 Cap d'Antibes (Alpes-Maritimes)
TEL 06 85 06 06 29 **FAX** 04 92 93 97 24
E-MAIL val-des-roses@yahoo.com **WEBSITE** www.val-des-roses.com

IT'S ALMOST TOO GOOD TO BE TRUE – a modestly priced hotel in Cap d'Antibes, only 30 metres from the sea. In fact, this attractive white-washed art deco villa is a four-star *chambre d'hôte* and, though we haven't yet visited ourselves, we have an excellent report of it. A couple of go-ahead young Flemish brothers, Frederik and Filip Vanderhoeven opened the villa in 2000, and are responsible for its chic decoration in a contemporary Colonial style. Downstairs, floors are cool marble, walls off-white, chairs covered in white linen. The atmosphere is soothing and relaxed. Outside, a garden full of palms (some 100 years old), a large deck sporting wicker furniture, and a swimming pool add to its charms.

The light, stylish look is carried through into the seven bedrooms, each a variation on the neutral theme. Soft cream, beige and white are complemented by natural wood floors and furniture. Some rooms have their own terrace or balcony, and some have sea views. Most are small and one is tiny, but compensates with a balcony and one of the cheapest price tags.

Breakfast is a delicious buffet of freshly-squeezed orange juice, fruit, cereals, yoghurt, cheese, salami and croissants, served on the terrace or in the conservatory. Guests can also order salads and snacks throughout the day, and there's a barbecue on Tuesday and Friday evenings.

～

NEARBY Musée Napoleonien; Musée Picasso; Cannes (12 km); Nice (20 km).
LOCATION 500 m S of Antibes, 30 m from La Salis beach; car parking
MEALS breakfast, light meals
PRICE €€
ROOMS 7; 4 double, one twin, one triple, one family, 3 with bath, 4 with shower; all rooms have TV, air conditioning, hairdrier, safe
FACILITIES sitting room, conservatory, terrace, garden, swimming pool
CREDIT CARDS MC, V **CHILDREN** accepted
DISABLED no special facilities **PETS** not accepted
CLOSED never
PROPRIETORS Frederik and Filip Vanderhoeven

THE SOUTH

CASSIS

LE CLOS DES AROMES
~ TOWN HOTEL ~

10 rue Paul Mouton, 13260 Cassis (Bouches-du-Rhône)
TEL 04 42 01 71 84 **FAX** 04 42 01 31 76
E-MAIL leclosdesaromes@wanadoo.fr **WEBSITE** www.leclosdesaromes.com

THIS IS A VERY PRETTY SMALL HOTEL, in a quiet street near the old port and run and renovated by the young, friendly and informal Bonnets. The hotel's history goes back 50 years and in the dining room there is a little oil painting of it as it was.

It is a bright, sunny place, entered either off the street into a large, attractive dining room or through the delightful paved garden. The dining room has old terracotta tiles on the floor, stripped wooden panelling on the walls, a big stone fireplace at one end, little tables with blue and yellow cloths and painted blue chairs.

Bedrooms are on the two floors above, up steep stairs. Behind simple white-painted doors, the rooms are small, but very pretty. Each one has a different colour scheme: fabrics, wallpapers and paintwork are carefully co-ordinated. Furniture is quality country-style reproduction, and ceiling fans keep them cool in the heat of the summer. Bathrooms are smallish, but spotlessly clean and sparkling white. There are two tiny rooms, with double beds, but usually let as singles. They offer hardly any room to move, but are nonetheless very appealing. The Provençal menu here is very reasonably priced, confirmed by a recent report, which also describes the food as 'excellent', and the garden, 'a very attractive place to eat'. It concludes: 'The staff could not have been more friendly or helpful. It was a lovely place to stay and offered excellent value for money.'
~

NEARBY Marseille (20 km); Aix-en-Provence (35 km).
LOCATION in a quiet side street in the old town, near the port; car parking
FOOD breakfast, lunch, dinner
PRICE €
ROOMS 8; 5 double, 2 single, one family, 3 with bath, 5 with shower; all rooms have phone **FACILITIES** dining room, terrace, garden **CREDIT CARDS** AE, MC, V
CHILDREN accepted **DISABLED** not suitable **PETS** accepted
CLOSED Oct to late Dec, Jan to mid-Feb
PROPRIETOR M. Fabrice Bonnet

THE SOUTH

CERET

LE MAS TRILLES
～ COUNTRY HOTEL ～

Le Pont de Reynes, 66400 Céret (Pyrénées-Orientales)
TEL 04 68 87 38 37 **FAX** 04 68 87 42 62
E-MAIL info@le-mas-trilles.com **WEBSITE** www.le-mas-trilles.com

LASZLO BUKK IS A Hungarian-born, Swiss-trained hotelier, whose experience includes a spell working in Canada. He and his Breton wife, whose talents are artistic, make an accomplished team. In a labour of love, they transformed this 17thC *mas* into a delightful, welcoming hotel – blending past and present and endowing it with their own very personal aura. The massive warm stone structure overlooks the fast-flowing River Tech – a tiny path brings you down to a stretch between two bends where the clear water looks almost still – an unspoiled natural sanctuary. A terrace beside the house leads down to a delightfully uncomplicated garden with lawn and swimming pool, mature trees and flowering shrubs.

Bedrooms are practical, immaculately kept and all have either a terrace or a small private garden. The atmosphere in the public rooms is informal and relaxed, so guests feel very much at home in them.

Sadly you won't find Mme Bukk's evening menu chalked up on a board as she no longer cooks her delicious dinners, but she will provide a light supper for guests if ordered in advance. Alternatively, there are numerous local restaurants. As a recent guest points out, it is essential to have a car whilst staying here.

～

NEARBY Perpignan (26 km); Castelnou (30 km); beaches.
LOCATION in countryside on the D115, 2 km from Céret in the direction of Amélie-les-Bains; car parking
FOOD breakfast, supper by arrangement
PRICE €€
ROOMS 10 double with bath; all rooms have phone, TV
FACILITIES sitting room, dining room, garden, swimming pool, table tennis, fishing
CREDIT CARDS MC, V **CHILDREN** accepted
DISABLED one specially adapted room
PETS accepted
CLOSED mid-Oct to Easter
PROPRIETORS M. and Mme Bukk

THE SOUTH

CERET

LA TERRASSE AU SOLEIL

~ COUNTRY HOTEL ~

route de Fontfrède, 66400 Céret (Pyrénées-Orientales)
TEL 04 68 87 01 94 **FAX** 04 68 87 39 24
E-MAIL terrasse-au-soleil.hotel@wanadoo.fr **WEBSITE** www.la-terrasse-au-soleil.com

THE ORIGINAL PART OF THE HOTEL was an 18thC *mas* but already a hotel when the present owners acquired it in 1980. Since then two annexes have been added for extra bedrooms and suites. The setting is lovely, higher up the mountains than nearby Céret, with splendid views over unspoiled hills.

Bedrooms vary in size, but the biggest are very spacious and all are tastefully furnished and decorated (some have their own private verandas). There is plenty of individuality in the interior design – much of it the legacy of Charles Trenet (the house at one time belonged to his agent and was a haunt of show-business personalities): unusual terracotta and ceramic tiling and imported African wood carvings, as in the huge bar. Colour and warmth in abundance introduce intimacy and cosiness not normally found in four-star hotels. Picasso is said to have sat on the terrace to enjoy the views of Mont Canigou.

The restaurant, La Cerisaie, has an enviable reputation and a young chef from Paris. At lunchtime, there is a tempting *carte brasserie* as a lighter alternative to the more serious food served at dinner. In between guests can be pampered at La Balneaire, the new health centre, which offers massages, a Turkish bath, sauna, spa and solarium.

~

NEARBY Perpignan (26 km); Castelnou (30 km); beaches.
LOCATION in Pyrenean foothills above the town, SW of Perpignan; car parking
FOOD breakfast, brunch, dinner; room service
PRICE €€€€
ROOMS 44; 39 double, 5 suites, all with bath; all rooms have phone, TV, air conditioning, minibar, hairdrier
FACILITIES sitting room, restaurant, bar, garden, health centre, swimming pool, tennis, table tennis, helipad, petanque, golf practice area
CREDIT CARDS AE, DC, MC, V **CHILDREN** accepted
DISABLED some specially adapted rooms **PETS** accepted **CLOSED** never
PROPRIETOR M. Leveille-Nizerolle

THE SOUTH

LA BONNE ETAPE

~ TOWN INN ~

chemin du Lac, 04160 Château-Arnoux (Alpes-de-Haute-Provence)
TEL 04 92 64 00 09 **FAX** 04 92 64 37 36
E-MAIL info@bonneetape.com **WEBSITE** www.bonneetape.com

'**E**XCEPTIONAL FOOD, impeccable service, beautiful pool and rooms – worth every euro' says a recent customer of this 'good stopover' – a former coaching inn in an unremarkable small town. Outside, it gives little hint of what lies within – one of the most satisfactory blends of refinement and hospitality to be found in the region. Although the kitchen lost its second Michelin star, we would re-award it if we could. Chefs Pierre and Jany Gleize (father and son) make innovative and stylish use of largely homegrown ingredients. A house speciality is Sisteron lamb (raised on mountain pastures): try it with a deep-red Vacqueyras Côtes du Rhone. Tables in the formal dining room have fresh flowers; Bach plays in the background. There are serious eaters here, many alone. The atmosphere is slightly hushed, but the waiters are helpful and friendly. There is a charming bar with painted beams. But this is no restaurant-with-rooms. Bedrooms are luxuriously comfortable – beautifully decorated with a tasteful mix of modern and antique pieces. Some have marble bathrooms. The Gleize family are warmly welcoming hosts, happily committed to their work; they also own a simpler restaurant nearby (open every day).

~

NEARBY Eglise St Donat; Sisteron (14 km).
LOCATION just off main RN85, 14 km SE of Sisteron (motorway 3 km); car parking and garage
FOOD breakfast, lunch, dinner; room service
PRICE €€€
ROOMS 19 double and twin, all with bath; all rooms have phone, TV, air conditioning, minibar, hairdrier
FACILITIES sitting room, dining room, terrace, garden, swimming pool
CREDIT CARDS AE, DC, MC, V **CHILDREN** accepted
DISABLED access possible **PETS** accepted
CLOSED hotel and restaurant late Nov to mid-Dec, Jan to mid-Feb, Mon low season; restaurant Mon, Tue and Wed lunch Oct to Mar
PROPRIETORS Gleize family

THE SOUTH

COLLIOURE

CASA PAIRAL

~ SEASIDE TOWN BED-AND-BREAKFAST ~

impasse des Palmiers, 66190 Collioure (Pyrénées-Orientales)
TEL 04 68 82 05 81 **FAX** 04 68 82 52 10
E-MAIL contact@hotel-casa-pairal.com **WEBSITE** www.hotel-casa-pairal.com

TUCKED AWAY IN A SMALL *impasse,* this quiet, elegant hotel has a magical situation just 150 metres from the busiest part of Collioure, close to the harbour and main beach with their many seaside cafés, restaurants, and narrow packed streets winding up the hill. A period-piece Catalan-style house built in the mid-19th century, it has a lush, picturesque interior garden with 100-year-old palm trees and pines shading a courtyard with tables and chairs and (somewhat apart) a swimming pool. The attractive ground-floor *salon* has a tiled floor and looks out to the courtyard and a fountain backed by oleanders and a huge magnolia. There is also a larger 1930s-style *salon* with a television and card table. The breakfast room (down a stone staircase) is captivating – and surprising; in one corner is the trunk of a vast oak tree which grows out through the roof, while opposite, large windows frame beautiful views of the garden.

Bedrooms in the main house combine old-world charm in the sleeping area with modern bathroom facilities. Our inspector was overcome by nostalgia: 'It reminded me of how good hotels used to be, but with all the up-to-date comforts. A place full of charm.' More recent reports are equally positive.

~

NEARBY Port-Vendres (4 km); Argelès-sur-Mer (6.5 km); Perpignan (27 km).
LOCATION in the centre of town 150 m from the port and beach; car parking
FOOD breakfast
PRICE €-€€
ROOMS 28 double and twin; 23 with bath, 5 with shower; all rooms have phone, TV, air conditioning, minibar, hairdrier
FACILITIES 2 sitting rooms, breakfast room, garden, swimming pool
CREDIT CARDS AE, DC, MC, V **CHILDREN** accepted
DISABLED some ground floor rooms
PETS accepted
CLOSED Nov to Apr
PROPRIETORS Mme Guiot and Mme Lormand

THE SOUTH

CORNILLON

LA VIEILLE FONTAINE

~ HILLTOP VILLAGE HOTEL ~

30630 Cornillon (Gard)
Tel 04 66 82 20 56 **Fax** 04 66 82 33 64
E-MAIL vieillefontaine@libertysurf.fr **WEBSITE** www.vieillefontaine.com

BUILT WITHIN THE WALLS of the ruined château of a medieval fortified village, with cobbled streets and ivy-clad ramparts, this little hotel is full of charm. *Patron* and chef, M. Audibert, is a Marseillais; his *gratinée de langoustines* and *chou farci à la provençale*, accompanied by the local Tavel rosé, have long been the restaurant's attractions. The hotel is the creation of Mme Audibert, a native of this once semi-abandoned village. Inspired by the Louvre pyramid, she has, with great flair, clad the exterior circular staircase to the bedrooms with an elegant glass structure, at which one can gaze in wonder over breakfast in the courtyard.

Her decorating style is simple and pretty: tiled bathrooms, Provençal fabrics, furniture from local *antiquaires*. One room contains a great chunk of the old château wall. Most have terraces; Nos 7 and 8 have views way over the top of the castle wall to the south. A steep flight of stone steps through terraced gardens leads to the pool: water gushes down from the hillside, and it is like bathing in a mountain stream.

The welcome is spontaneous and warm, and dinner on the terrace looking over the hills and vineyards of the Gard is a delight.

~

Nearby Orange (44 km); Avignon (45 km); Gorges de l'Ardèche.
Location in the heart of the village, with limited access by car; car parking outside village
Food breakfast, lunch, dinner
Price €€€
Rooms 8 double with bath; all rooms have TV, phone
Facilities sitting room, dining room, terrace, garden, swimming pool
Credit cards AE, DC, MC, V
Children welcome
Disabled not suitable
Pets accepted
Closed mid-Dec to mid-Mar
Proprietors M. and Mme Audibert

THE SOUTH

CRILLON-LE-BRAVE

HOSTELLERIE DE CRILLON LE BRAVE
~ VILLAGE HOTEL ~

place de l'Eglise, 84410 Crillon-le-Brave (Vaucluse)
TEL 04 90 65 61 61 **FAX** 04 90 65 62 86
E-MAIL crillonbrave@relaischateaux.fr **WEBSITE** www.crillonlebrave.com

THE CHARMS OF THIS luxurious hotel, occupying the old vicarage in a hill-top village, continue to inspire readers to fill our postbag with rave reviews. 'Delightful', enthuses one satisfied visitor. 'Very good restaurant, excellent service, a lovely setting and charming *patron*.' Others praise Philippe Monti's culinary expertise, and yet another applauds the wide-ranging wine list, which 'offered excellent value'. A summer bistro, serving simpler 'market food', gives guests a choice for dinner.

The rambling 16thC stone-built house is solid and calm, but most of the credit for the resounding success of the hotel must go to the aforementioned *patron*, Peter Chittick, a Canadian lawyer with exceptionally clear ideas about hotelkeeping. A considerable share goes also to the perched location, giving uninterrupted views of a heavenly landscape of olive groves and vineyards. The central trick that Mr Chittick and his collaborator Craig Miller have pulled off is to provide luxury without erasing character. Despite the designer fabrics, fitted carpets and smart bathrooms, the exposed beams, white walls and rustic furniture dominate both in the sitting rooms and the spacious bedrooms. You eat beneath stone vaults, or out on the pretty terrace, or in Le Bistrot on the ground floor and in the courtyard of a 16thC house.

~

NEARBY Mont Ventoux; Orange (35 km); Avignon (35 km).
LOCATION in village NE of Avignon, on D138 off D974; car parking
FOOD breakfast, lunch (Sat and Sun only), dinner, snacks
PRICE €€€-€€€€
ROOMS 32 double, twin and suites, all with bath or shower; all rooms have phone, minibar, hairdrier
FACILITIES 3 sitting rooms, dining room, terrace, garden, swimming pool
CREDIT CARDS AE, DC, MC, V **CHILDREN** welcome **DISABLED** access difficult
PETS accepted **CLOSED** Jan to Mar; restaurant lunch, Tue Nov to early May; bistro Oct to Apr, lunch, Mon
PROPRIETORS Peter Chittick and Craig Miller

THE SOUTH

ENTRECHAUX

LA MANESCALE

~ COUNTRY HOTEL ~

route de Faucon, Les Essareaux, 84340 Entrechaux (Vaucluse)
TEL 04 90 46 03 80 **FAX** 04 90 46 03 89

THE KING OF BELGIUM has slept here. No doubt, like so many others, he was charmed by all he found in this remote former shepherd's house up in the hills. The thoughtfulness of owners, M. and Mme Warland, permeates what could be described as a pocket-sized hotel with every comfort, and the emphasis on the privacy of guests. The smallest details are attended to here, from towels for the swimming pool to a small library for serious readers and helpfully labelled light switches. And it receives justifiably extravagant praise from our readers: 'M and Mme Warland were excellent hosts with impeccable taste and we hope that we have also become firm friends for the future'.

The house is beautifully decorated with the Warlands' own books, paintings, *objets d'art* and furniture. Stone steps and pathways connect the main building to the garden rooms, each giving privacy and views of the forest and hillsides. Two rooms are named after M. Warland's favourite painters, Tiepolo and Dali. A place for lovers of quiet and of nature, there are numerous paths through the woods for long walks. Classical music plays on the terrace at aperitif time; the views across the vineyards and valleys to Mont Ventoux in the distance are superb.

It's a steep, if short, walk from the car park to the hotel; a luggage trolley is provided.

~

NEARBY Vaison-la-Romaine (7 km); Cotes du Rhone vineyards.
LOCATION 3 km N of Entrechaux, signposted off D205 road to Faucon; car parking
FOOD breakfast
PRICE €€
ROOMS 5 double and twin, 2 with bath, 3 with shower; all rooms have phone, TV, minibar, hairdrier, safe **FACILITIES** sitting room, breakfast room, terrace, garden, swimming pool **CREDIT CARDS** AE, DC, MC, V **CHILDREN** accepted over 7
DISABLED not suitable **PETS** accepted
CLOSED end Oct to Easter
PROPRIETORS M. and Mme Warland

THE SOUTH

EYGALIERES

AUBERGE PROVENCALE

～ VILLAGE INN ～

place de la Mairie, 13810 Eygalières (Bouches-du-Rhône)
TEL 04 90 95 91 00 **FAX** 04 90 95 91 00

IN DELIGHTFUL EYGALIERES, this 18thC former coaching inn has a paved courtyard with trees and potted plants and small marble-topped tables and is well-known locally for its Provençal dishes. The horses' stone drinking troughs remain and guests' cars are safely locked away for the night in the magnificent coach house, which has a great arched gateway on to the street. There is also a spacious bar, deliberately and charmingly evocative of the 18th century.

Owner and chef Didier Pézeril and his young family extend their hospitality to rooms, some of which look out on to the courtyard, and all of which are exceptional. There are just four: quantity has been sacrificed for space and quality – simple and stylish in the best, least fussy Provençal manner, some with huge bathrooms, some with huge bedrooms. Our inspector's room had blue-washed walls, rough white cotton curtains and a paisley cover on the bed and a view out of the window of the lively Progrès café opposite. Tiled floors are attractively uneven and some rooms have traditional cupboards set in the walls. M. Pézeril's philosophy is correspondingly down-to-earth: 'We're an *auberge*, we don't have pretensions to being anything else'. The whole place oozes character.

～

NEARBY St-Rémy-de-Provence (13 km); Les Baux (23 km); the Alpilles
LOCATION in village, with car parking
FOOD breakfast, lunch, dinner
PRICE €-€€
ROOMS 4 double and twin, all with bath; all rooms have phone, TV
FACILITIES bar, restaurant, courtyard, terrace
CREDIT CARDS MC, V
CHILDREN welcome
DISABLED not suitable
PETS accepted
CLOSED mid-Nov to mid-Dec; restaurant closed Wed, Thu lunch
PROPRIETORS Pézeril family

THE SOUTH

EYGALIERES

MAS DE LA BRUNE

~ COUNTRY HOUSE BED-AND-BREAKFAST ~

13810 Eygalières (Bouches-du-Rhône)
TEL 04 90 90 67 67 **FAX** 04 90 95 99 21
E-MAIL contact@masdelabrune.com **WEBSITE** www.masdelabrune.com

IT'S A REAL PRIVILEGE to stay at Mas de la Brune, a *monument historique* and a rare example of a Renaissance mansion built in the countryside rather than a town – in this case, St-Rémy-de-Provence. Here you will find (expensive) luxury accommodation with plenty of character. The façade is embellished with stone carvings, corbels, cornices and mullioned windows, there is a spiral stone staircase with mysterious carved capitals (it's thought that the original 16thC owner may have been an alchemist), and the house sits in its own beautifully kept estate. Mme de Larouzière, who with her husband has been the proprietor for the past 10 years, is a keen gardener; the pristine landscaped grounds – including a lovely swimming pool – have fabulous views of Eygalières and the Alpilles. Their latest venture is an Alchemist's Garden, open to the public in summer.

Bedrooms are decorated in perfect country house taste, with attractively tiled bathrooms. The suite is impressive; another room incorporates the corner turret, with views across gardens and cypress trees to the village beyond, perched on its hill. The owners are charming, the staff assiduous, and the atmosphere one of calm privacy.

~

NEARBY St-Rémy-de-Provence (12 km); Avignon (27 km).
LOCATION 2 km N of Eygalières, signposted off the road to St-Rémy; car parking
FOOD breakfast
PRICE €€€€
ROOMS 10; 9 double and twin, one suite, all with bath; all rooms have phone, TV, air conditioning, minibar, safe, hairdrier
FACILITIES sitting room, breakfast room, terrace, garden, swimming pool, Alchemist's Garden
CREDIT CARDS MC, V **CHILDREN** welcome
DISABLED not suitable
PETS accepted
CLOSED Nov to Jan
PROPRIETORS Alain and Marie de Larouzière

THE SOUTH

EZE

CHATEAU EZA
~ COAST HOTEL ~

rue de la Pise, 06360 Eze (Alpes-Maritimes)
TEL 04 93 41 12 24 **FAX** 04 93 41 16 64
E-MAIL info@chateza.com **WEBSITE** www.chateza.com

WHEN AMERICAN OWNERS Patti and Terry Giles took over Château Eza, once the private home of Prince William of Sweden, they completely redecorated from top to toe. They went, in keeping with the (much-visited) village, for the medieval look, and the result – exposed brick, wrought iron, dark wood, red velvet, tapestries, brocade, suits of armour – is luxurious and not a little kitsch. A couple of donkeys, stabled in front of the hotel's reception at the bottom of the village, take your bags up to the top (your car will be parked for you), but be warned, access for anyone even vaguely infirm is arduous. Here is your bedroom, most likely with a private entrance from the street as if it were a village house, and with a private terrace overlooking the jumble of old roofs. All the rooms have views and wood-burning stoves for cool evenings. They are not especially light or spacious – they have thick stone walls, old beams, stone pillars and village house proportions – but they lack for nothing as far as decoration and comfort are concerned: draped four-poster or otherwise fancy beds, original paintings, fine antiques, splendid, perfectly equipped bathrooms. The glass-walled restaurant ('fabulous' food) is romantic, and terraces tumble down the hillside as if into the sea below. A favourite with US readers, though some recent feedback has been critical, especially of prices. Wildly expensive.

~

NEARBY Nice (12 km); Monte Carlo (8 km).
LOCATION on N7 Moyenne Corniche between Nice and Monaco; hotel approached on foot; valet car parking at edge of village
FOOD breakfast, lunch, dinner; room service
PRICE €€€€€
ROOMS 10; 7 double and twin, 3 suites, all with bath; all rooms have phone, TV, video, CD player, air conditioning, minibar, safe, hairdrier
FACILITIES restaurant, sitting rooms, bar, terraces **CREDIT CARDS** AE, DC, MC, V
CHILDREN accepted **DISABLED** not suitable **PETS** accepted **CLOSED** Nov to Apr
MANAGER Jesper Jerrik

THE SOUTH

FONTVIEILLE

LA REGALIDO

~ CONVERTED MILL ~

rue Frédéric-Mistral, 13990 Fontvieille (Bouches-du-Rhône)
TEL 04 90 54 60 22 **FAX** 04 90 54 64 29
E-MAIL contact@la-regalido-provence.com **WEBSITE** www.la-regalido-provence.com

WE CONTINUE TO BE FOND of this 19thC oil mill, a Relais et Chateaux place which manages to remain informal and friendly despite its elegant furnishings, pricey boutique and high rates – largely thanks to the presence at almost all hours of the welcoming and helpful Jean-Pierre Michel, chef-proprietor.

The Régalido has been converted into a fine *auberge* in a thoroughly Provençal style, decorated with great flair by Mme Michel. There is a charming sitting room full of flowers, and a log fire lit on chilly days. Tables are beautifully set in the elegant, peaceful, stone-vaulted dining room, and there is an atmosphere of well-being which suits the excellent cooking of Jean-Pierre. His style is classic, but he has a penchant for Provençal dishes (seafood, olive oil, herbs, garlic) – and terracotta or cast iron pots appear alongside the silver salvers. His son is now the *patissier*.

Bedrooms are individually decorated, and very comfortable, with lots of extras in the well-equipped bathrooms. Friendly staff and a pretty, flowery garden – with a terrace surrounded by mimosa and shaded by fig and olive trees – complete the picture.

~

NEARBY Montmajour Abbey; Arles (10 km); the Camargue (10 km); Tarascon (15 km).
LOCATION in middle of village, 9 km NE of Arles; with gardens and ample car parking
FOOD breakfast, lunch, dinner
PRICE €€€
ROOMS 15 double and twin, 13 with bath, 2 with shower; all rooms have phone, TV, air conditioning, minibar, hairdrier, safe
FACILITIES 2 sitting rooms, dining room, bar, terrace
CREDIT CARDS AE, DC, MC, V
CHILDREN accepted
DISABLED one specially adapted room **PETS** accepted
CLOSED Jan to mid-Feb; restaurant Mon, Tue and lunch Sat
PROPRIETOR Jean-Pierre Michel

THE SOUTH

FOX-AMPHOUX

AUBERGE DU VIEUX FOX
~ VILLAGE INN ~

place de l'Eglise, Fox-Amphoux, 83670 Barjols (Var)
TEL 04 94 80 71 69 **FAX** 04 94 80 78 38

OUR LAST ATTEMPT to revisit this old favourite ended in failure: it was cut off by snow – in spring! Reports continue to be satisfactory, however.

Fox-Amphoux, a charming little village, rich in history, has nothing to do with foxes – the name comes from its Roman origins. The inn was once a priory attached to the 12thC church, headquarters of the Knights Templar. Where owner, M. Staudinger, now has his reception desk was a sacristy, with a door leading directly into the church, the bells of which ring out every half hour. M. Staudinger is normally to be found here in his beamed reception area with his cat, and happy to talk about the life and times of Fox-Amphoux and the surrounding area.

Renovation work on all eight bedrooms is now complete, including an overhaul of the essential services. Windows have been double-glazed and satellite TVs installed; curtains and bedspreads are in fresh, bright colours. Two small rooms in the tower were once monks' cells. Bathrooms are spotless. There are comfortable leather armchairs in the *salon*; there is also a library and a billiard table. The dining room is full of character and the outside terraces have fine views over Aix and the Alpes de Haute-Provence. Fish is delivered from Marseille and there is an emphasis on fresh farm produce and country cooking, with huge helpings.

~

NEARBY Lac de Sainte-Croix; Gorges du Verdon; Thoronet Abbey.
LOCATION in centre of small perched village, 32 km N of Brignoles, 37 km W of Draguignan; public car parking in square
FOOD breakfast, lunch, dinner
PRICE €€
ROOMS 8 double and twin, 6 with bath, 2 with shower; all rooms have phone, TV, hairdrier
FACILITIES sitting room, dining room, library, billiards, 2 terraces
CREDIT CARDS AE, MC, V **CHILDREN** accepted but not encouraged
DISABLED no special facilities **PETS** accepted **CLOSED** mid-Nov to late Dec
PROPRIETORS Rudolph and Nicole Staudinger

THE SOUTH

RELAIS DE LA MAGDELEINE

~ COUNTRY HOTEL ~

13420 Gémenos (Bouches-du-Rhône)
TEL 04 42 32 20 16 **FAX** 04 42 32 02 26
E-MAIL contact@relais-magdeleine.com **WEBSITE** www.relais-magdeleine.com

'WE SIMPLY COULD NOT FAULT IT; the atmosphere, welcome and service could not have been better and the food was excellent. Even though we had one of the more expensive rooms at the front, we felt it was very good value.' So begins one of many eulogies on this lovely old *bastide*, a sentiment strongly echoed by our most recent inspector. For those of us who can't or won't pay the prices (or don't like the style) of Relais & Châteaux places, a gracious country house like this is quite a find. Last year, though, we did have just one discordant letter, questioning the price, and faulting the decoration, of a room.

It is a family affair. Daniel Marignane's mother opened the hotel in 1932, and he and his wife ran it with great dedication, charm and good humour for many years. Though recently widowed, Mme Marignane has remained in charge, together with her three sons: Philippe is the (excellent) chef, whilst Vincent and Christophe are managers. Improvements are being made all the time. Most of the bedrooms have been (charmingly) redecorated in elegant country taste, with delightful fabrics (often on the walls, too) and antiques and pictures collected by the family.

On the airy, spacious ground floor, one of the three dining rooms has been sandblasted to expose vaultings and beams in a lovely, light honey-coloured wood. In summer you eat on the romantic gravelled terrace. There's a pool – and a donkey – in the garden, and children will enjoy the giant chessboard and the ping-pong table.

~

NEARBY Cassis (15 km); Marseille (23 km); Aix-en-Provence (25 km).
LOCATION on the edge of town; ample car parking
FOOD breakfast, lunch, dinner
PRICE €€€-€€€€
ROOMS 24 double, twin and family, all with bath or shower; all rooms have phone, TV
FACILITIES sitting rooms, dining room, lift, terrace, garden, swimming pool, table tennis
CREDIT CARDS MC, V **CHILDREN** accepted **DISABLED** no special facilities **PETS** accepted
CLOSED Dec to mid-Mar **PROPRIETORS** Marignane family

THE SOUTH

GIGONDAS

LES FLORETS

~ COUNTRY INN ~

route des Dentelles, 84190 Gigondas (Vaucluse)
TEL 04 90 65 85 01 **FAX** 04 90 65 83 80

FLOWERS ABOUND AT LES FLORETS: all around the hotel on the nearby hills in spring, in pots and vases on the terrace and in the dining room, on the curtains, the lampshades and the pretty hand-painted plates, each one different. The setting, alone in a fold of wooded hills east of Gigondas and facing the dramatic Dentelles de Montmirail, is delightful, and the ambience is loved by everyone who has a hankering for traditional, family-run places. The Bernard family, who bought the hotel in 1960, have long been respected for their honest, straightforward approach, and for the good value food served in the animated dining room or on the lovely leafy terrace in summer. Now they have refurbished all the bedrooms and the once dim corridors, making this a very comfortable place in which to stay for a few days. The bedrooms remain appropriately sober but the bathrooms are a surprise – very opulent for a two-star establishment, with particularly comfortable baths, expensively tiled walls, good towels and intelligent lighting. The rooms in the garden annexe are pleasantest, with little terraces in front for breakfast; one of them is perfect for a family.

The Bernards are also wine-growers; they keep an excellent cellar, or you can drink a bottle of their own Gigondas or Vacqueras for dinner. Good walking country.

~

NEARBY Côtes-du-Rhône vineyards; Vaison-la-Romaine (15 km).
LOCATION in hills, 2 km E of Gigondas; car parking
FOOD breakfast, lunch, dinner
PRICE €€
ROOMS 15 double and twin, one family, all with bath; all rooms have phone, TV, hairdrier
FACILITIES sitting room, bar, restaurant, terrace
CREDIT CARDS AE, DC, MC, V **CHILDREN** welcome
DISABLED access possible **PETS** accepted
CLOSED Jan to mid-Mar; restaurant Mon and Tue Nov to Dec, Wed
PROPRIETORS Bernard family

THE SOUTH

GINCLA

HOSTELLERIE DU GRAND DUC
~ VILLAGE HOTEL ~

2 route de Boucheville, 11140 Gincla (Aude)
TEL 04 68 20 55 02 **FAX** 04 68 20 61 22
E-MAIL host-du-grand-duc@ataraxie.fr **WEBSITE** www.host-du-grand-duc.com

THE GRAND DUC IS THE EAGLE OWL, presiding (stuffed) over the fireplace in the beamed dining room of this delightful, modest little *logis*. A refurbished *maison de maître* (the *maître* made his living from the surrounding forests), it was opened more than a decade ago as a restaurant by the son of the Bruchet family, a chef, whose father is a wine inspector from Burgundy. The wide central hallway has original stone walls and the fine old staircase has terracotta tiles with oak nosings and wrought-iron balustrade. There's a large dining room and superb modern kitchen with a state-of-the-art German electronic oven, where they make their own bread.

The bedrooms are large, but somewhat disappointing with fussy wallpaper, which comes as an aesthetic let-down after the fine, clean lines and whitewashed walls of the dining room.

Admirers return year after year to write flattering remarks in the visitors' book: 'Gets better all the time – everything, reception, service, food and comfort is excellent.' Our inspector – wallpaper excepted – found it charming. There's a pleasant terrace, looking on to a fountain and old lime trees; in summer, you dine outside by candlelight.

~

NEARBY Perpignan (63 km); Quillan (23 km); Forêt de Fanges.
LOCATION in the village NW of Perpignan; car parking
FOOD breakfast, lunch, dinner
PRICE €
ROOMS 12 double, twin and family, all with bath or shower; all rooms have phone, TV, hairdrier, safe
FACILITIES sitting room, bar, dining room, terrace
CREDIT CARDS MC, V
CHILDREN accepted
DISABLED no special facilities
PETS accepted
CLOSED mid-Nov to mid-Mar
PROPRIETORS M. and Mme Bruchet

THE SOUTH

GRIMAUD

LE COTEAU FLEURI
～ VILLAGE HOTEL ～

place des Pénitents, 83310 Grimaud Village (Var)
TEL 04 94 43 20 17 **FAX** 04 94 43 33 42
E-MAIL coteaufleuri@wanadoo.fr **WEBSITE** www.coteaufleuri.fr

A FAN LETTER FROM A RECENT GUEST of this hotel, endorsing its charms, has prompted us to reinstate it in this edition of the guide. Built on a hillside on the edge of the fashionable village of Grimaud, the old stone house has a simple Provençal style and rambling tree-filled terraced garden.

Inside, the atmosphere is rustic, uncluttered, warmly inviting: fine, polished terracotta tiles, white walls and strikingly beautiful, large, simple arrangements of fresh flowers. The bedrooms – some small, but all comfortable – have pretty furnishings and prints, smart tiled bathrooms, and fine views. The public rooms are equally attractive and relaxing: there is a small bar, dining room and large *salon* with tiled floor and grand piano. The dining terrace, with wood-panelled roof, Provençal tablecloths, rustic wooden chairs and bougainvillea spilling over the walls, is a delightful place to be in the evening, watching the sun go down over the vineyards. Plenty of fresh fish and vegetables feature on the menu, and our reader paid tribute to the food as 'absolutely terrific' and the service as 'superb'. Both meals and rooms are very reasonably priced.

M. Minard is a relaxed *patron*, whose idea of a hotel is that it should be an overall positive experience. It's no good having a wonderful meal only to go up to bed in an ugly room. A hotel must have a soul, he says; his does.

～

NEARBY St-Tropez (10 km); Pampelonne (15 km).
LOCATION on edge of village behind chapel; car parking
FOOD breakfast, lunch, dinner
PRICE €€
ROOMS 14; 13 double and twin, one family, all with bath or shower; all rooms have phone
FACILITIES sitting room, dining room, bar, terrace, garden
CREDIT CARDS AE, MC, V **CHILDREN** welcome
DISABLED no special facilities **PETS** accepted
CLOSED 2 weeks before Christmas, 2 weeks early Jan
PROPRIETOR M. Minard

THE SOUTH

HAUT-DE-CAGNES

LE CAGNARD
~ MEDIEVAL INN ~

rue Pontis-Long, Haut-de-Cagnes, 06800 Cagnes-sur-Mer (Alpes-Maritimes)
TEL 04 93 20 73 21 **FAX** 04 93 22 06 39
E-MAIL cagnard@relaischateaux.com **WEBSITE** www.le-cagnard.com

A READER'S REPORT RAISED some doubts about this lovely hotel, perched along the ramparts of an old hill village – specifically about standards of service in the Michelin-starred restaurant. It is far from the most expensive hotel in the Relais et Châteaux group, but it is pricey enough for expectations in this department to be high. We have inspected twice since then: happily all was well on both occasions.

Le Cagnard has been sensitively converted from a series of medieval houses, most with separate street entrances. In the main house there is a stunning, vaulted dining room where you eat by candlelight. But the real knock-out is the upper dining room, leading out on to the terrace: its elaborate painted ceiling slides away at the touch of a button, opening the room to the sky.

Bedrooms vary widely: most retain a medieval feel, thanks to the preservation of features such as stone floors, and are furnished with style, but incongruous exceptions remain. Three rooms in one house have a lovely flowery garden. Access in anything other than a small car is tricky, and getting to some rooms involves a bit of awkward suitcase-lugging.

NEARBY Maison de Renoir; Château Grimaldi; Nice (15 km); Grasse (30 km).
LOCATION in middle of hill village, 2 km above main town of Cagnes; car parking 300 m away at entrance to village
FOOD breakfast, lunch, dinner; room service
PRICE €€€€-€€€€€
ROOMS 25; 15 double and twin, 10 apartments, all with bath; all rooms have phone, TV, air conditioning, minibar, hairdrier
FACILITIES dining room, bar, terrace
CREDIT CARDS AE, DC, MC, V **CHILDREN** accepted
DISABLED no special facilities
PETS accepted
CLOSED never; restaurant closed Thurs lunch and Nov to mid-Dec
PROPRIETORS Barel Laroche family

THE SOUTH

LE MAS DES GRES
~ COUNTRY HOTEL ~

la route d'Apt, 84800 Lagnes (Vaucluse)
TEL 04 90 20 32 85 **FAX** 04 90 20 21 45
E-MAIL info@masdesgres.com **WEBSITE** www.masdesgres.com

NINA AND THIERRY CROVARA run their hotel in a restored farmhouse with such a friendly, relaxed attitude that parents bring their children here from far and wide on family holidays. For the very young, high chairs are provided in the dining room and cots in the bedrooms; and for older children, there's a video machine in one of the sitting rooms, table tennis and a pool outside. Bedrooms are functional – plainly decorated with rough plaster walls and Provençal fabrics – and hard to damage. There are two sets of connecting rooms, where Nina has thoughtfully added black-out blinds to prevent an interior dawn chorus.

Before dinner, guests sit outside on the vine-covered terrace and sip the delicious iced 'orange wine' made according to Thierry's own recipe. He is the chef, and though French, trained in Nina's native Switzerland. He takes his cooking seriously and, after consultations about allergies, likes and dislikes, produces a mainly regional no-choice menu six nights a week (the Crovaras take off one night to fit in with their guests). Menu planning also takes children into account. In between courses, Thierry emerges from his kitchen to introduce himself to new guests and chat to old ones. (Guests are expected to eat dinner in the hotel.) There is some noise from the RN100 road.

~

NEARBY L'Isle-sur-la-Sorgue (6 km); Avignon (28 km); golf.
LOCATION on RN100 outside village; car parking
FOOD breakfast, dinner; light lunch by arrangement (in July and Aug)
PRICE €€
ROOMS 14 double, twin, triple and family, all with bath; all rooms have phone, CD; TV on request
FACILITIES sitting rooms, TV room, dining room, terrace, garden, swimming pool, table tennis **CREDIT CARDS** MC, V **CHILDREN** welcome
DISABLED 2 ground floor rooms **PETS** not accepted
CLOSED Dec to Mar
PROPRIETORS Nina and Thierry Crovara

THE SOUTH

LLO

ATALAYA
~ VILLAGE HOTEL ~

66800 Llo (Pyrénées-Orientales)
TEL 04 68 04 70 04 **FAX** 04 68 04 01 29
E-MAIL atalaya66@aol.com **WEBSITE** www.atalaya66.com

THIS CHARMING SMALL HOTEL in superb unspoiled mountain country had our inspector in raptures: 'Magic'. The little village of Llo straggles up the mountainside, its stone buildings imperceptibly blending into the rock. The Catalan-speaking Cerdagne is half in Spain and half in France and the border seems to be quite indistinct. A high, sun-drenched plateau of pastures and pine forests, it is popular for both summer and winter sports. The Atalaya itself appears to be growing out of the crag on either side of a mountain road and is easily missed. Ingeniously sculpted, it is enchanting, built in 1969 out of the materials of a ruined *mas* to be entirely in harmony with its natural surroundings. The distinguished cultured atmosphere inside emanates from the personality and taste of the owner, Mme Toussaint. She is charming but speaks little English.

Antique furniture and tasteful fabrics give the natural feel of a home rather than a showroom. Bedrooms are quiet, comfortable and intimate, with soft lighting. The dining room is decorated in rustic style, with gleaming antiques against stone walls. The terrace has private corners, and everywhere there are expansive, uplifting views. Superb food, rooted in the region, adds to the exhilarating sense of being on top of the world.

~

NEARBY Odeillo (10 km); Ront-Romeu (15 km).
LOCATION in the middle of the village, 2 km E of Saillagouse; car parking
MEALS breakfast, lunch, dinner
PRICE €€
ROOMS 13; 12 double, one suite, 10 with bath, 3 with shower; all rooms have TV, phone, minibar, safe
FACILITIES sitting room, dining room, bar, terrace, garden, swimming pool
CREDIT CARDS MC, V
CHILDREN accepted
DISABLED no special facilities **PETS** accepted
CLOSED early Nov to late Dec, mid-Jan to Easter
PROPRIETOR Mme Toussaint

THE SOUTH

MALATAVERNE

LE DOMAINE DU COLOMBIER

~ OLD COACHING INN ~

route de Donzère, 26780 Malataverne (Drôme)
TEL 04 75 90 86 86 **FAX** 04 75 90 79 40
E-MAIL domainecolombier@voila.fr **WEBSITE** www.domaine-colombier.com

METICULOUSLY RESTORED and full of flowers and colour, this pleasing 14thC stone building, once a stopover for pilgrims on the road to Santiago de Compostela, remains an ideal base for travellers (largely due to its position near the *autoroute* yet in the countryside). With its vine-clad façade, stone staircases, tiled roof, wrought-iron railings and penchant for flowers, this hotel really feels it is on the road to the South.

Wild flowers, gathered in the grounds, brighten every table and service is efficient and professional. When the weather is favourable (and the infamous mistral is not blowing) guests dine on the terrace, which is, again, packed with flowers and absolutely enchanting in the evening glow of lamplight. There is a large, airy restaurant with a vaulted ceiling. Flowers appear everywhere, on the tablecloths, on curtains and bedspreads and wallpaper (floral fabrics, cane furniture, china and gifts are on sale in the hotel shop). According to a couple of readers: 'Some bedrooms can seem overwhelmingly flowery, but others are more restrained.' They also commend the warm welcome, relaxed atmosphere, high standards of housekeeping and the food, both at dinner and breakfast. Their only quibbles are dirty furniture on their balcony and a disappointing minibar ('no glasses or bottle opener' and 'prices on the steep side').

~

NEARBY Montélimar (10 km); Valence (50 km).
LOCATION on private estate, off D144a from A7 to Donzère; ample car parking
FOOD breakfast, lunch, dinner
PRICE €€€
ROOMS 25; 22 double and twin, 3 suites, 23 with bath, 2 with shower; all rooms have phone, TV, air conditioning, minibar; some rooms have hairdrier
FACILITIES sitting room, restaurant, terrace, garden, swimming pool, *pétanque*
CREDIT CARDS AE, DC, MC, V **CHILDREN** welcome **DISABLED** no special facilities
PETS accepted **CLOSED** Mon Oct to Feb, mid-Feb to Mar, late Oct to early Nov
PROPRIETORS M. and Mme Chochois

THE SOUTH

MENERBES

LA BASTIDE DE MARIE

~ COUNTRY HOTEL ~

route de Bonnieux, Quartier de la Verrerie, 84560 Ménerbes (Vaucluse)
TEL 04 90 72 30 20 **FAX** 04 90 72 54 20
E-MAIL bastidemarie@c-h-m.com **WEBSITE** www.labastidemarie.com

IT WAS TRICKY TO FIND (just one discreet sign, easy to miss, announces the hotel), and even trickier leaving (the automatic gates failed to respond). Once inside, we felt at first, perhaps unreasonably, irritated by the mannered, très *Côte Sud* style of the place, complete with whole walls of purpose-built bookshelves filled with purpose-bought old books, and young men with ponytails and people with pet dogs lounging about. Next we looked round the bedrooms of the old *mas*, now photo-shoot perfect in shades of grey and cream: very smart and comfortable, with excellent bathrooms. But we remained sceptical. Then we sat down to lunch ... which turned out to be quite possibly the best food we had eaten in a long list of recent gourmet experiences, served by a courteous and friendly staff. We began to soften; we began to think about the all-inclusive price, for which you get the room, breakfast, aperitif, lunch or dinner, afernoon tea, and as much of the *domaine* wine (the hotel owns the accompanying vineyard) as you wish. And we decided that, *Côte Sud* notwithstanding, the hotel was not unfairly priced – and really rather seductive.

Opened in June 2000, La Bastide de Marie is a sister to the Coin du Feu in Megève (see page 171) and the Cour des Loges in Lyon (see page 168).

~

NEARBY Bonnieux (10 km); Avignon (40 km).
LOCATION in vineyards, 2 km E of Ménerbes, discreetly signposted; car parking
FOOD breakfast, lunch, dinner; room service
PRICE €€€€€
ROOMS 14; 8 double and twin, 6 suites, all with bath; all rooms have phone, TV, air conditioning, minibar, safe, hairdrier
FACILITIES sitting room, breakfast room, dining room, conservatory, boutique, wine shop, courtyard, terrace, garden, 2 swimming pools
CREDIT CARDS AE, DC, MC, V **CHILDREN** accepted
DISABLED not suitable **PETS** accepted
CLOSED mid-Nov to mid-Mar
PROPRIETORS Jocelyne and Jean-Louis Sibuet

THE SOUTH

MINERVE

RELAIS CHANTOVENT
~ VILLAGE HOTEL ~

17 Grande Rue, 34210 Minerve (Hérault)
TEL 04 68 91 14 18 **FAX** 04 68 91 81 99

MINERVE, AN OLD CATHAR REFUGE, is that rare thing – a 14thC fortified hilltop town unspoiled, as yet, by the tourist business. Tourists there are, but the industry has not yet taken over and the small town continues to have an ongoing organic life which is very appealing. With only two narrow streets up and down, cars have to be left below. It is no effort (except for the handicapped) and well worth the inconvenience.

The hotel is really in three parts. There is a restaurant and stunning terrace looking across a deep gorge to a layered limestone cliff populated by birds and with vineyards on the top level. Then there's a separate building with bedrooms and, around the corner in the next street, an old village house, restored with care and charm, with sitting room and fireplace, furnished in period harmony.

All the decoration is done with attention to detail, but no fuss – light walls, uncluttered, attractive etchings and paintings. The Evenous – he is a Breton and an expert in preparing abundant local produce for the table – are a dedicated couple, with taste and finesse and a real love for their home. However we were sorry to hear recently from one well-travelled reporter, who was unimpressed with her room and unable to use the sitting room. More reports please.

~

NEARBY Carcassonne (45 km); Narbonne (32 km); St-Pons (29 km).
LOCATION in small historic town NW of Carcassonne with no access by car; car parking outside town
FOOD breakfast, lunch, dinner
PRICE €
ROOMS 10 double, one with bath, 9 with shower
FACILITIES sitting room, dining room, terrace
CREDIT CARDS MC, V **CHILDREN** accepted
DISABLED not suitable **PETS** accepted
CLOSED mid-Dec to mid-Jan
PROPRIETORS M. and Mme Evenou

THE SOUTH

MOUGINS

MANOIR DE L'ETANG
~ COUNTRY MANOR HOUSE ~

66 allée du Manoir, 06250 Mougins (Alpes-Maritimes)
TEL 04 92 28 36 00 **FAX** 04 92 28 36 10
E-MAIL manoir.letang@wanadoo.fr **WEBSITE** www.manoir-de-letang.com

'THE OVERALL FEEL to this place', writes our latest inspector, 'is expensive and discreet'. A quiet, orderly, elegant retreat from the bustle of fashionable Mougins, its imposing entrance is found in a residential suburb; thereafter a winding drive leads to the extremely pretty 19thC manor house. Pale stone, white shutters, a thick covering of virginia creeper. Inside, the reception area doubles as sitting room, with an open fireplace, strong colours and country furniture. The adjoining restaurant with its intense yellow walls overlooks the swimming pool, and there is a tiled dining terrace for summer eating. Views are low-key: gentle, green, rolling Southern countryside. The colourful garden is filled with different Mediterranean plants and trees.

Bedrooms, split between several buildings, are individually decorated and stylishly *à la mode*, with fresh fabrics, white walls, wood floors and contemporary wrought-iron and pale wood furniture; some are large with private terraces. Crisp Egyptian cotton sheets cover the beds and bathrooms are attractively tiled.

The management is 'hands-on' and the staff attentive and friendly. There is an Italian restaurant, Il Lago, which is generally well regarded.

~

NEARBY Cannes; Grasse; Picasso Museum at Vallauris (10 km).
LOCATION in extensive grounds, on Antibes road, 2 km from town centre; car parking
FOOD breakfast, lunch, dinner
PRICE €€€
ROOMS 21; 17 double and twin, 4 suites, all with bath; all rooms have phone, TV, air conditioning, minibar, safe
FACILITIES sitting area, restaurant, spa, terrace, garden, swimming pool
CREDIT CARDS AE, DC, MC, V **CHILDREN** accepted
DISABLED 2 specially adapted rooms **PETS** not accepted
CLOSED Nov to Mar
PROPRIETOR Mme Richards

THE SOUTH

LA BASTIDE DE MOUSTIERS

~ COUNTRY HOUSE HOTEL ~

La Grisolière, 04360 Moustiers-Ste-Marie (Alpes-de-Haute-Provence)
TEL 04 92 70 47 47 **FAX** 04 92 70 47 48
E-MAIL contact@bastide-moustiers.com **WEBSITE** www.bastidedemoustiers.com

THIS IS THE MADELEINE of chef and hotelier supremo Alain Ducasse. In a
pale pink restored 17thC *bastide* overlooking green meadows on the
edge of a village near the dramatic Verdon gorge, he has created his own
remembrance of times past. His country house for lovers of Provence is a
resounding triumph; delicious smells of cooking come from the kitchen all
day. Chefs, in their whites, can be seen collecting salad and fresh herbs
from a vegetable garden which is a work of art in itself. The *bastide* and
the discreet swimming pool are surrounded by beds of lavender and each
of the 12 romantically decorated bedrooms evokes a colour or an image of
Provence. To sit on the terrace in the morning air with a bowl of *café au
lait*, fresh bread from the village bakery and home-made rhubarb jam
among green glazed pots overflowing with white petunias is a moment to
be treasured. Dinner is just as memorable; traditional dishes with plenty
of olive oil and garden vegetables. You might find *millefeuille de blettes
braisées au parfum de sauge* or *agneau de Beauregard piqué de sarriette
et rôti à la broche*. Upstairs, the sheets are being turned down as you eat.

~

NEARBY Moustiers ceramics; Lac de Ste-Croix; gorges.
LOCATION within walking distance of Moustiers; car and garage parking
FOOD breakfast, lunch, dinner; room service
PRICE €€€€
ROOMS 12; 11 double and twin, one suite, all with bath; all rooms have phone, TV,
air conditioning, minibar, hairdrier
FACILITIES sitting room, dining room, bar, terrace, garden, swimming pool, riding
CREDIT CARDS AE, DC, MC, V
CHILDREN welcome
DISABLED access possible
PETS not accepted
CLOSED never
PROPRIETOR Alain Ducasse

THE SOUTH

NICE

LE GRIMALDI

~ TOWN BED-AND-BREAKFAST ~

15 rue Grimaldi, 06000 Nice (Alpes-Maritimes)
TEL 04 93 16 00 24 **FAX** 04 93 87 00 24
E-MAIL zedde@le-grimaldi.com **WEBSITE** www.le-grimaldi.com

NOT TO BE CONFUSED with the rather dreary-looking Nice Grimaldi just down the road, this upmarket and stylish little hotel was opened in 1999. Englishwoman Joanna Zedde and her French husband gutted the fairly basic hotel that already occupied the elegant 1920s town house with its white shutters and wrought-iron balconies, aiming for something altogether smarter. The location – a lively area of stylish shops, bars and restaurants – is ideal, and the beach is only a ten-minute walk.

The ground floor is occupied by a large reception area decorated in bright reds and yellows which doubles as breakfast room, bar and sitting room; it is full of fresh flowers and leafy plants. The comfortable bedrooms are all tastefully (and not too fussily) decorated with co-ordinating Soleido fabrics and wallpapers set against cool white. Some are done out in vibrant sun colours, others are more restrained in shades of blue and green and the delicate wrought-iron furniture fits in well. There are two types of room; the 'Superiors' have sufficient space for an invitingly squashy sofa. Bright yellow towels make a splash in the immaculate all-white bathrooms. A classy B&B.

~

NEARBY Vieux Nice; Opéra; beach.
LOCATION on street just W of Vieux Nice; public car parking nearby (50 m)
FOOD breakfast
PRICE €€
ROOMS 46 double and twin, all with bath; all rooms have phone, TV, air conditioning, minibar, safe, hairdrier
FACILITIES bar/breakfast room/sitting room, lift
CREDIT CARDS AE, DC, MC, V
CHILDREN accepted
DISABLED no special facilities
PETS accepted
CLOSED never
PROPRIETOR Joanna Zedde

THE SOUTH

NICE

LA PEROUSE

TOWN HOTEL

11 quai Rauba-Capeu, 06300 Nice (Alpes-Maritimes)
TEL 04 93 62 34 63 **FAX** 04 93 62 59 41
E-MAIL lp@hroy.com **WEBSITE** www.hroy.com/la-perouse

YOU WILL FIND LA PEROUSE at the eastern end of the seafront, right beneath Nice's Château. Its position, hard up against the cliff face, is not its most appealing asset. Only the reception is on the street; all the rest is out back.

The reception area sets the tone; a welcoming little space done out in country fabrics and rustic furniture. The rest of the hotel – it was fully refurbished several ago – follows suit, with a mix of Provençal and country fabrics, pale floor tiles, bleached wood and wrought-iron furniture, warm sunny colours, country prints. Rustic terracotta tiles in the bathrooms, stone colours, fluffy white tiles. All rooms have a balcony or terrace of some kind; some are huge, especially those on the top floor; some have fabulous views over the sea.

The communal terrace lies right under the overhanging cliff and has a small heated pool. There is also a roof terrace with an outdoor Jacuzzi, small fitness suite, sauna and solarium. The breakfast room is pretty, with sofas and tables laden with the day's papers. You can eat meals under the lemon trees in summer and, according to two fastidious recent reporters, the food is very distinguished, though prices are steep. The hotel is immaculately maintained with a very friendly staff and management.

NEARBY Château; port; Vieux Nice; Marché aux Fleurs; beach.
LOCATION on seafront; valet car parking in public car park
FOOD breakfast; lunch and dinner mid-May to mid-Sep
PRICE €€€€
ROOMS 62; 58 double and twin, 4 suites, all with bath or shower; all rooms have phone, TV, air conditioning, minibar, safe, hairdrier
FACILITIES dining room, breakfast room, bar, fitness room, lift, terraces, swimming pool **CREDIT CARDS** AE, DC, MC, V **CHILDREN** accepted
DISABLED access difficult **PETS** accepted
CLOSED never
MANAGER Laure Giometti

THE SOUTH

NICE

WINDSOR
~ TOWN HOTEL ~

11 rue Dalpozzo, 06000 Nice (Alpes-Maritimes)
TEL 04 93 88 59 35 **FAX** 04 93 88 94 57
E-MAIL reservation@hotelwindsornice.com **WEBSITE** www.hotelwindsornice.com

THE HOTEL WINDSOR OCCUPIES an unassuming, turn-of-the-century building in a residential area of Nice not far from shops and the station. Once in the reception hall, however, a Thai shrine takes centre stage, Indonesian hangings adorn the walls and a delicate suspended sculpture occupies one corner. The soundtrack of a space ship launch livens up the lift ride to the fifth floor which has been turned into a fitness room (eastern style) and Moroccan hammam. This place is definitely different and very *à la mode*.

Twenty of the bedrooms have been decorated by contemporary artists, mostly along clean, simple lines. Some feature white on white, others bold colours, one has a wall covered in graffiti; each is unique. One room is decorated in sand colours by an artist who imagined himself in the chamber of a pyramid. Gold stars shine out of a midnight-blue night sky and music from Lawrence of Arabia starts up when you go into the bathroom. The remaining bedrooms are more uniform with modern frescoes of Italy or oriental scenes, natural fabrics and stylish white bathrooms; some have terraces. In summer, breakfast is served in the delightful garden full of exotic trees, shrubs and flowers, in winter in the bistro-style restaurant. We hear from a recent visitor that a trip up in the lift is a 'must' for anybody visiting Nice for the first time.

NEARBY Musée Massenat; Contemporary Art Museum; Vieux Nice.
LOCATION in centre of the new town, between train station and sea; car parking
FOOD breakfast, lunch in summer, dinner
PRICE €€
ROOMS 58; 56 double and twin, 2 suites, all with bath or shower; all rooms have phone, TV, air conditioning, minibar, safe
FACILITIES restaurant, bar, fitness room, hammam, lift, terrace, garden, swimming pool
CREDIT CARDS AE, MC, V
DISABLED no special facilities **PETS** accepted
CLOSED never
PROPRIETOR Bernard Rédolfi

THE SOUTH

DOMAINE DE RIEUMEGE
~ COUNTRY HOTEL ~

route de St-Pons, 34390 Olargues (Hérault)
TEL 04 67 97 73 99 **FAX** 04 67 97 78 52
E-MAIL rieumege@wanadoo.fr

IN A LOVELY, NATURAL SETTING of hills, rock, water, trees, shrubs and soft green grass, this sensitively restored 17thC stone house is in the middle of the Haut Languedoc national park and close to Olargues, one of the villages classed as the most beautiful in France. It is a perfect place for a stroll after dinner or before breakfast. There are few hotels in this area and although there is a road nearby, little traffic noise filters through. Deep, restful calm prevails. The attractive high-ceilinged beamed restaurant retains, even after restoration, its country barn origins. (The food our inspector had was excellent, and this is confirmed by recent reports; the 'pleasant, not-too-professional service' was also much appreciated.)

Bedrooms are simply furnished with respectable antique pieces – and comfortable. The beamed sitting room, with open fire in cooler weather and oil lamps, is cosy, with some handsome antique furniture. A smaller separate building has been adapted to provide a luxury room and suite, complete with its own garden and private swimming pool. There is a wide range of accommodation here; three categories offer 'comfort', 'superior' and 'prestige', so there is something for all pockets. M. Henrotte and his staff are most hospitable.

~

NEARBY St-Pons (17 km); Castres (70 km); Béziers (50 km).
LOCATION in countryside 3 km outside Olargues; car parking
FOOD breakfast, lunch, dinner
PRICE €€
ROOMS 14; 10 double, 3 family, one suite, all with bath or shower; all rooms have phone; TV on request
FACILITIES sitting room, dining room, garden, swimming pool, tennis
CREDIT CARDS AE, MC, V **CHILDREN** accepted
DISABLED no special facilities
PETS accepted
CLOSED Jan to Mar
PROPRIETOR M. Henrotte

THE SOUTH

ORNAISONS

LE RELAIS DU VAL D'ORBIEU
∼ CONVERTED MILL ∼

11200 Ornaisons (Aude)
TEL 04 68 27 10 27 **FAX** 04 68 27 52 44
E-MAIL Relais.Du.Val.Dorbieu@wanadoo.fr **WEBSITE** www.chez.com/gonzalvez

THIS HOTEL HAS BEEN cleverly designed to provide everything which the overnight traveller or long-stay holidaymaker could wish for – made to measure. Extensions with red-tiled roofs have been added to the original old mill to form an integrated complex of rooms and suites, four sides of which enclose a lush, secluded cloister. Rooms are bright, modern and appealingly decorated – 15 have their own terrace. The choice of accommodation is particularly flexible for families with children, though one reporter, who came here with his family, was met with a lack of courtesy. Although parts of the hotel are old, there's no feeling of a museum but rather an efficient and comfortable hostelry. There is ample room for everyone in the spacious grounds. The swimming pool is equally serious and professional and is flanked by impressive stands of oleander. The excellent cooking – fish dishes are recommended – and wine cellar reflect the personal passion of the owner, M. Gonzalvez, the son of a *vigneron*. Quite a number of English wine merchants make this hotel their base to sample the wines of the Corbières. Another regular booking is by American cyclists who tour the region on two wheels. There's a full-time gardener and home-grown vegetables and herbs feature prominently on the menus.

∼

NEARBY Narbonne (14 km); Carcassonne (44 km).
LOCATION in countryside outside Ornaisons; car parking
FOOD breakfast, dinner
PRICE €€€€-€€€€
ROOMS 20; 14 double, 6 family suites, all with bath; all rooms have phone, TV, minibar, hairdrier
FACILITIES sitting room, dining room, meeting room, solarium, terraces, garden, swimming pool, tennis, practice golf, table tennis, *pétanque*
CREDIT CARDS AE, DC, MC, V **CHILDREN** accepted
DISABLED one specially adapted room **PETS** accepted
CLOSED Dec to Feb
PROPRIETORS M. and Mme Gonzalvez

THE SOUTH

AUBERGE DE LA MADONE
~ VILLAGE INN ~

06440 Peillon (Alpes-Maritimes)
TEL 04 93 79 91 17 **FAX** 04 93 79 99 36 **E-MAIL** madone@chateauxhotels.com
WEBSITE www.chateauxhotelsdefrance.com/madone

'**H**OW STUNNING', commented a recent visitor on seeing the setting for the first time. A 'most beautiful place' remarked another, and 'delightful' was the one-word verdict offered by a third on the top-of-the-range family-run *logis*, which happily combines a sense of special hospitality with affordable (though not low) prices. The Millos have now opened an annexe in the old part of the village – Auberge du Pourtail. Rooms here are less expensive and you eat at the Madone.

You may think that you have taken a wrong turning as you first spy Peillon, perched impossibly above, with little sign of any road leading up. Time stands still here. The medieval village consists of a few dark cobbled alleys leading up to the church, and tall stone houses looking out over rocky crests and distant forests.

The *auberge* is set just outside the walled village itself. Behind, paths lead off into the hills, past the grazing sheep with their tinkling bells; in front is the village car park and *boules* area. Within, the rather small bedrooms (with equally small balconies) are attractive and comfortable with stylish all-white bathrooms. Meals are served on the sunny terrace, under a large awning, or in the welcoming Provençal-style dining room. Cooking is above average, using organic local ingredients. An all-weather tennis court is another of the hotel's attractions.

~

NEARBY Monaco – palace, museums, exotic gardens; Nice (19 km).
LOCATION on edge of perched village, 19 km NE of Nice; ample car parking
FOOD breakfast, lunch, dinner
PRICE €€
ROOMS 19; 16 double and twin, 8 with bath, 8 with shower, 3 suites with bath; all rooms have phone, TV; 9 have hairdrier
FACILITIES sitting room, bar, TV room, 2 dining rooms, terrace, tennis
CREDIT CARDS MC, V **CHILDREN** welcome **DISABLED** access difficult **PETS** not accepted
CLOSED mid-Oct to mid-Dec, 2 weeks Jan; restaurant closed Wed
PROPRIETORS Millo family

THE SOUTH

PIOLENC

AUBERGE DE L'ORANGERIE
~ TOWN INN ~

4 rue de l'Ormeau, 84420 Piolenc (Vaucluse)
TEL 04 90 29 59 88 **FAX** 04 90 29 67 74
E-MAIL orangerie@orangerie.net **WEBSITE** www.orangerie.net

THIS CURIOUS LITTLE *auberge*, almost submerged by a jungle of greenery, is just off the main street of a small town that prides itself on its garlic festival. Owners Gérard and Micky Delarocque have given an original and imaginative 'retro' feeling to an 18thC house in a gated courtyard. The lively restaurant draws in local business people at lunchtime with dishes like *filets de rascasse à la provençale* and *noisettes de gigot d'agneau au basilic frais*. In the dining room, a collection of striking Georges de La Tour pictures are, in fact, painted by M. Delarocque, a talented copyist (and single-malt connoisseur). But the real fun starts upstairs, with Madame's evocative decoration and her charming written 'thoughts' on the theme of each room, which hang framed on the walls. The George Sand room has a portrait of the writer by Delacroix – or could it be a copy by M. Delarocque? The room named after Mme Récamier has a chaise-longue like the ones she made so fashionable. Behind the bohemianism, though, is a professional management, with orthodox ideas on things such as rules: no washing of clothes in bedrooms, for example.

Guests (minus children and pets) can also stay in the Delarocque's nearby *chambres d'hôtes* in 'La Mandarine', a Provençal farmhouse in its own grounds, with five rooms, and a pool (tel 04 90 29 69 99 fax 04 90 29 79 64 email mandarine@lamandarine.net website www.lamandarine.net).

~

NEARBY Orange (5 km); Avignon (35 km).
LOCATION in a side street off the main street; car parking
FOOD breakfast, lunch, dinner
PRICE (€); half-board obligatory in high season
ROOMS 5 double, 2 with bath, 3 with shower; all rooms have TV
FACILITIES dining room, terrace, garden
CREDIT CARDS MC, V **CHILDREN** accepted
DISABLED no special facilities **PETS** accepted
CLOSED never
PROPRIETORS M. and Mme Delarocque

THE SOUTH

LE POËT-LAVAL

LES HOSPITALIERS

～ CONVERTED CASTLE ～

Le Poët-Laval, 26160 La Bégude-de-Mazenc (Drôme)
TEL 04 75 46 22 32 **FAX** 04 75 46 49 99
E-MAIL contact@hotel-les-hospitaliers.com **WEBSITE** www.hotel-les-hospitaliers.com

READERS CONTINUE TO BE IMPRESSED by this distinctive hotel, within the ramparts of a 13thC castle and in a dominating position above the perched medieval village of Le Poët-Laval (400 m). So do we.

The attractive old stone buildings were formerly part of a stronghold of the Knights of Malta. (The Maltese cross is the hotel's emblem.) From the pool and the terrace – where meals are served in fine weather – the views across wooded countryside to hills beyond are spectacular. The very comfortable sitting room is – unusually – on the top floor and makes the most of this feature. Owner Bernard Morin's father was an art dealer and there are many original paintings in the bedrooms, as well as antique carved hardwood furniture. The restaurant also has an interesting collection of pictures. Tables are laid with fine china, white linen, and candles; service is hard to fault and the food is excellent. The menu changes daily. The welcome from the charming Morin family is warm and genuine. The eldest son, Bernard, took over the hotel from his father several years ago; he also cooks, using the freshest produce available, and the wine list reflects a comprehensive cellar. A delightful hotel that makes a lasting impression on all its guests.

～

NEARBY Montélimar (20 km); Viviers (30 km).
LOCATION at the top of the old village, 5 km W of Dieulefit; car parking nearby
FOOD breakfast, lunch, dinner
PRICE €€
ROOMS 24; 13 double, 8 twin, 20 with bath, one with shower, 3 family with bath; all rooms have phone
FACILITIES 2 sitting rooms, restaurant, bar, terrace, swimming pool
CREDIT CARDS AE, DC, MC, V
CHILDREN accepted
DISABLED no special facilities **PETS** accepted
CLOSED mid-Nov to Feb
PROPRIETOR Bernard Morin

THE SOUTH

LE PONTET-AVIGNON

AUBERGE DE CASSAGNE
~ SUBURBAN HOTEL ~

450 allée de Cassagne, 84130 Le Pontet-Avignon (Vaucluse)
TEL 04 90 31 04 18 **FAX** 04 90 32 25 09
E-MAIL cassagne@wanadoo.fr **WEBSITE** www.hotelprestige-provence.com

LE PONTET, A SUBURB OF AVIGNON – 5 km from the centre – with wide, busy roads and new housing developments, does not appear to be a place where anyone might find a hotel of any interest, let alone charm. However, behind a high wall is a former cottage of the nearby château which has been turned, with much hard work, into a remarkably comfortable and pleasant hotel, with a locally renowned one-Michelin-star kitchen, chef from Bocuse, and an abundant wine cellar. At dinner, our inspector counted 20 different cheeses on the tray and 45 Côtes du Rhône reds on the wine list. In somewhat confined grounds, the hotel also manages, with clever use of lawns, paths and landscaped gardens, to create an impression of space and even rusticity. Everything is immaculately well tended; the cypress trees look as if someone brushes and combs them every night.

Bedrooms in the garden bungalows are large and pretty, with fresh Provençal prints; each one has its own terrace, with table and chairs, where guests can breakfast in dressing gowns – and do. Rooms 16 and 17 are almost in the swimming pool and delightfully secluded and quiet in the evenings, when the restaurant – a popular gathering place – buzzes with locals as well as residents. A recent plaudit commends the 'first class' accommodation, facilities, Michelin-starred food and 'warm welcome'.

~

NEARBY Avignon (4 km); Aix-en-Provence (82 km); Arles (36 km).
LOCATION in a quiet suburban side road; car parking
FOOD breakfast, lunch, dinner
PRICE €€€€-€€€€
ROOMS 40 double and twin, 38 with bath, 2 with shower; all rooms have phone, TV, air conditioning, minibar, hairdrier, safe
FACILITIES 2 sitting rooms, restaurant, bar, gym, sauna, garden, swimming pool, tennis, table tennis, boules **CREDIT CARDS** AE, DC, MC, V **CHILDREN** welcome
DISABLED 3 specially adapted rooms **PETS** accepted
CLOSED never
PROPRIETORS M. Gallon, M. Trestour and M. Boucher

THE SOUTH

PORQUEROLLES (ILE DE)

AUBERGE DES GLYCINES

~ ISLAND HOTEL ~

place d'Armes, 83400 Ile de Porquerolles (Var)
TEL 04 94 58 30 36 **FAX** 04 94 58 35 22
E-MAIL auberge.glycines@wanadoo.fr **WEBSITE** www.aubergedesglycines.net

THERE ARE NO CARS on the island of Porquerolles and when the day trippers leave in the evening, peace prevails. This delightful small hotel is a fun, casual, bright and sunny place in the little port of Porquerolles, but within an easy walk there are rocky creeks for swimming and splendid diving spots.

Pale yellow with blue shutters, the hotel is built around an inner courtyard, which has lemon trees, wistaria (*glycines*) and a fig tree; food is served here on red Provençal tablecloths under white umbrellas. The entire hotel is decorated with bright, fresh colours and has a charming look of stylish simplicity. Downstairs, there are dried flowers and straw hats on the walls and terracotta tiles on the floor. Bedrooms are variations on a theme: clean, modern bathrooms have pale tiles and white fittings; bedrooms have matching Provençal print bedspreads and curtains. Rooms have little balconies or terraces looking into the courtyard or out towards pine and eucalyptus trees. The food, which includes plenty of fresh fish, is excellent value. Our inspector ate *loup de mer* flambéed at the table with fennel and grilled in a salt crust that was cracked open before being served. Young, friendly staff; laid-back atmosphere, though now pricey.

~

NEARBY beaches; diving; cycling and walking; national park.
LOCATION in Porquerolles village on car-free island, 5 minutes from beach; access 20 mins by ferry from La Tour Fondue (Hyères) or water taxi
FOOD breakfast, lunch, dinner
PRICE €€
ROOMS 13; 12 double and twin, one triple, 10 with bath, 3 with shower; all rooms have phone, TV, air conditioning
FACILITIES dining room, courtyard, terrace
CREDIT CARDS DC, MC, V **CHILDREN** welcome
DISABLED no special facilities **PETS** accepted
CLOSED mid- to end Jan
MANAGER Florence Venture

THE SOUTH

PORT-CROS (ILE DE)

LE MANOIR

~ SEASIDE HOTEL ~

Ile de Port-Cros, 83400 Hyères (Var)
TEL 04 94 05 90 52 **FAX** 04 94 05 90 89

PORT-CROS, THE MIDDLE OF THE THREE Iles d'Hyères, is a nature reserve on which no vehicles, not even bicycles, and no pet animals are allowed. With a resident population of no more than a handful, it is therefore entirely peaceful, and this large, green-shuttered 19thC manor house fits perfectly into its green and serene surroundings. Previously a private house, it has been run as a hotel since the late 1940s, and by its present owner, Pierre Buffet, since the 1960s. Set in lush, sub-tropical grounds by the sea, it seems much more than just a 20-minute ferry ride from the crowded coast. You feel you are in a gracious private house, and the hotel is run along house-party lines. There are several sitting rooms in which to relax, read or play cards, and the airy, comfortable white-walled bedrooms are simply but elegantly furnished with 19thC pieces of furniture; some have little terraces.

The grounds are extensive and lovely, full of palm, eucalyptus and oleander trees. There's a splendid swimming pool, beside which you can have lunch; or you can take a picnic and a ride in the hotel's motor launch to a nearby bay or cove. You must walk to the nearest sandy beach – about 25 minutes. The Provençal cooking is praised.

~

NEARBY nature trails in national park; Hyères; Toulon; Porquerolles.
LOCATION in own grounds by sea on car-free island
FOOD breakfast, lunch, dinner
PRICE €€€; half-board obligatory
ROOMS 22; 17 double and twin, 5 family, 15 with bath, 7 with shower; all rooms have phone; some have air conditioning
CREDIT CARDS MC, V
CHILDREN accepted
DISABLED rooms on ground floor
PETS not accepted
CLOSED Oct to Apr
PROPRIETOR Pierre Buffet

THE SOUTH

RAMATUELLE

LA FERME D'HERMES

~ COUNTRY BED-AND-BREAKFAST ~

route de l'Escalet, 83350 Ramatuelle (Var)
TEL 04 94 79 27 80 **FAX** 04 94 79 26 86

MME VERRIER HAS NAMED her charming hotel after her much loved late Welsh terrier – there is now a junior version in his place. Our inspector's report is positively glowing. 'This is a gorgeous spot – exquisite.'

The hotel is a recently built *mas*, now softened by the weather and creepers and surrounded by a mass of trees, shrubs, plants and greenery. Vines come up to the pool. Inside, loving attention is given to detail. Rooms are all white, with terracotta tiles on the floor – burnished with beeswax – and co-ordinated Provençal fabrics. Furniture is old, stripped pine. Each bedroom has its own private terrace and little tiled kitchenette, with gas and electric rings, oven, sink and refrigerator. Tea towels are provided and changed every day. Madame returns from the market every Saturday morning with armfuls of fresh flowers. Breakfast is the only meal served – on each private terrace – with fresh bread and pastries and home-made jams. Guests are treated as if they were part of a circle of friends, and Mme Verrier has thought of everything: alarm clock, electric mosquito repellent, daily room service, iron and ironing board, hairdrier, and even toothbrush in case you forgot yours.

~

NEARBY Ramatuelle (2 km); St-Tropez (10 km).
LOCATION in own grounds down a narrow lane 2 km from beaches; car parking
FOOD breakfast
PRICE €€€-€€€€
ROOMS 10 double and twin, all with bath; all rooms have phone, TV, kitchenette, terrace
FACILITIES sitting room, garden, swimming pool
CREDIT CARDS DC, MC, V
CHILDREN not encouraged
DISABLED no special facilities
PETS accepted
CLOSED mid-Nov to late Dec, mid-Jan to late Mar
PROPRIETOR Mme Verrier

THE SOUTH

RAMATUELLE

LA FIGUIERE
~ BEACH HOTEL ~

route de Tahiti, 83350 Ramatuelle (Var)
TEL 04 94 97 18 21 **FAX** 04 94 97 68 48

EXPECT BUMPER TO BUMPER TRAFFIC in high season along the approach road to La Figuière: it's also the only access road to famous Tahiti beach, just 500 metres away. Sounds hell? In fact the hotel is surprisingly quiet. An old farmhouse, with various wings and annexes added on, it's set back from the road in a large garden which backs on to a vineyard ... the garden is planted with fig and oleander trees and there is a large, inviting pool with plenty of sun beds. There's not much point in staying here unless you are keen on braving crowded and expensive Tahiti beach, but having tried that, many guests are happy to stay here by the pool. Many of the rooms are in fairly unattractive outbuildings, but they are simple and spotless, with white walls, co-ordinated Provençal fabrics, heavy white cotton bed-covers and the odd rustic antique. Many have private terraces which back straight on to the vines and are very quiet. A smell of beeswax lingers in the air. Bathrooms are spacious. The duplex rooms, with two beds on the upper level, suit families.

The rustic restaurant, run by different management, is in a separate building right by the pool. It serves traditional Provençal fare, and you can eat on the terrace in summer.

A caveat: we thought the management neither particularly helpful nor friendly. Reports please.

~

NEARBY Tahiti beach (500 m); St-Tropez (2.5 km).
LOCATION set back from road, 2.5 km S of St-Tropez on L'Escalet road; car parking
FOOD breakfast, lunch, dinner
PRICE ⓔⓔ-ⓔⓔⓔ
ROOMS 40; 33 double and twin, 4 triple, 3 family, 37 with bath, 3 with shower; all rooms have phone, TV, air conditioning, minibar, safe
FACILITIES sitting rooms, restaurant, terraces, garden, swimming pool, tennis
CREDIT CARDS AE, DC, MC, V **CHILDREN** accepted
DISABLED 2 specially adapted rooms **PETS** accepted **CLOSED** mid-Oct to Apr
PROPRIETOR Mme Chaix

THE SOUTH

ROQUEBRUNE

LES DEUX FRERES
~ VILLAGE RESTAURANT-WITH-ROOMS ~

06190 Roquebrune-Village Cap Martin (Alpes-Maritimes)
TEL 04 93 28 99 00 **FAX** 04 93 28 99 10
E-MAIL info@lesdeuxfreres.com **WEBSITE** www.lesdeuxfreres.com

THE BROTHERS IN QUESTION are the two large rocks which loom over this small hotel-restaurant; it stands on a little square in the unspoiled village of Roquebrune with a terrace that looks down over a tumble of villas and exotic gardens to the sea far below and, in the distance, the ghastliness of Monte Carlo.

Willem Bonestroo has a passion for large motorbikes, but that doesn't stop him running Les Deux Frères with infectious enthusiasm. The whitewashed building used to be a schoolhouse until 1965, and he has kept things refreshingly simple. The ground floor is mostly occupied by the barrestaurant, a rustic room filled with tall plants, gorgeous fresh flowers and interesting modern art. Our inspector was most impressed with the food; Provençal and French cooking with a twist – the *gambas* were marinated in ginger and served with orange peel. The quirky bedrooms are simple but full of tongue-in-cheek humour; one is nautical with porthole mirrors and oars as curtain rails, another ('The 1001 Nights') is done out in gold and midnight blue with silk curtains (a video of Aladdin is supplied) while the tiny, white Bridal Room has a canopied bed and romantic views.

NEARBY Monte Carlo (5 km); beaches (5 km); Nice (22 km).
LOCATION in centre of village; free public car parking nearby
FOOD breakfast, lunch, dinner
PRICE ©©
ROOMS 10; 8 double and 2 single, 9 with bath; all rooms have phone, TV, video, hairdrier
FACILITIES restaurant, bar, terrace
CREDIT CARDS AE, DC, MC, V
DISABLED one room on ground floor
PETS accepted
CLOSED never; restaurant closed mid-Nov to mid-Dec and Sun, Mon dinner in winter
PROPRIETOR Willem Bonestroo

THE SOUTH

ROQUEFORT-LES-PINS

AUBERGE DU COLOMBIER
∽ COUNTRY HOTEL ∽

06330 Roquefort-les-Pins (Alpes-Maritimes)
TEL 04 92 60 33 00 **FAX** 04 93 77 07 03
E-MAIL info@auberge-du-colombier.com **WEBSITE** www.auberge-du-colombier.com

DESPITE SUCH ATTRACTIONS as a large, beautifully tended garden and terraces and a lovely clean, if rather cold, swimming pool, this simple hotel succeeds in keeping its prices way down the scale. A single room without a garden view goes for less than 30 euros in winter; whether you'll judge the doubles with garden terraces to be good or bad value will probably depend on your luck with the weather; the simple, Provençal-style bedrooms are clean and comfortable; the gardens and pool are 'wonderful' (to quote one inspector).

The building is an old *mas,* low and white, whose chief attraction is certainly its setting – amid tall, shady trees, with views over wooded hills towards the sea – and the outdoor facilities that go with it. There is an especially attractive terrace for summer eating, a tennis court and plenty of space around the swimming pool for lounging. Should the weather let you down, you'll find a pleasant dining room with rustic furniture indoors. Food is a source of increasing pride here; justifiably according to our latest report. Breakfast is good, with 'some of the best pastries we've had'. The only criticisms we've heard are that rooms facing the main road can be noisy at night, and that the owner seems to find young children something of a distraction. It's probably better suited to the over-15-year-olds.

∽

NEARBY St-Paul (10 km); Grasse (15 km).
LOCATION in countryside off D2085, 15 km E of Grasse, 18 km N of Cannes; car parking
FOOD breakfast, lunch, dinner
PRICE €-€€
ROOMS 18 double and twin, 2 apartments, all with bath; all rooms have phone, TV
FACILITIES 2 dining rooms, sitting room, bar, terraces, garden, swimming pool, tennis, private nightclub
CREDIT CARDS AE, DC, MC, V **CHILDREN** tolerated
DISABLED no special facilites **PETS** accepted **CLOSED** Jan
PROPRIETOR Jacques Wolff

THE SOUTH

ROUSSILLON

MAS DE GARRIGON
~ COUNTRY VILLA ~

route de St-Saturnin d'Apt, Roussillon, 84220 Gordes (Vaucluse)
TEL 04 90 05 63 22 **FAX** 04 90 05 70 01
E-MAIL mas.de.garrigon@wanadoo.fr **WEBSITE** www.masdegarrigon-provence.com

'WE ARRIVED WITHOUT RESERVATION and were willingly accommodated; the
Provençal-style room was very comfortable, the bathroom large and
well stocked; the pool was heavenly after a long drive, and the surrounding
areas pleasant for strolling; dinner was wonderful.'

A long-time favourite of this guide, Mas de Garrigon continues to please
most of our readers, who appreciate its cosy yet sophisticated ambience,
although this year's postbag includes two letters that strike discordant
notes. House-keeping, service and bedrooms all attract some criticism.

Purpose-built by Christiane Druart in 1979, it has the feel of a traditional Provençal farmhouse, with a jumble of rough-tiled roofs facing this way
and that, as if built at random over the years. The hotel stands isolated
among pines and scrub, facing the Luberon hills. At the front is a sheltered pool sharing country views with the sunny private terraces of the
bedrooms. The place is run more on house-party than conventional hotel
lines. Guests are encouraged to browse in the well-stocked library or listen
to classical music in the *salon* – before an open fire in winter. Dinner is a
convivial affair, with guests chatting between tables in the intimate dining
room which overlooks the pool; the food, by chef Jean-Paul Minery, is delicious, with the emphasis on local ingredients (truffles in winter).

~

NEARBY Roussillon (3 km) Gordes (7 km); Village des Bories (5 km).
LOCATION signposted, in countryside on D2, 3 km N of Roussillon, 7 km E of
Gordes; car parking
FOOD breakfast, lunch, dinner
PRICE ⓔⓔ; half-board obligatory May to Oct
ROOMS 9; 7 double and twin, 2 family, all with bath; all rooms have phone, TV,
minibar, terrace **FACILITIES** sitting room, 3 dining rooms, bar, library, terrace,
swimming pool **CREDIT CARDS** AE, DC, MC, V **CHILDREN** accepted over 12
DISABLED ground floor bedrooms **PETS** accepted
CLOSED never; restaurant mid-Oct to mid-Mar
PROPRIETOR Christiane Druart

THE SOUTH

SAIGNON

AUBERGE DU PRESBYTERE
～ VILLAGE HOTEL ～

place de la Fontaine, 84400 Saignon (Vaucluse)
TEL 04 90 74 11 50 **FAX** 04 90 04 68 51
E-MAIL auberge.presbytere@wanadoo.fr **WEBSITE** www.auberge-presbytere.com

ON THE THRESHOLD OF the Luberon National Park – a relatively undiscovered area, Saignon is a hilltop village with a chequered history dating back to the 11th century. In the centre, overlooking the pretty square where the village fountain plays, this *auberge* occupies three houses, one almost completely submerged beneath an unstoppable creeper. The houses have been knocked together, to produce a quirky series of rooms downstairs, one leading off another, with those upstairs on different levels and connected by separate staircases and corridors. All have great charm, polished terracotta or wood floors, low vaulted or beamed ceilings and a combination of wicker furniture and antiques. The apparently effortless Provençal style has in fact been perfected over the past 14 years by the suavely charming half-American, half-French owner.

The restaurant is split between a cosy wood-panelled room (where smokers can take refuge) and a larger, airier non-smoking one with doors on to a little gravelled terrace. Traditional Provençal dishes are prominent on the daily-changing menu (displayed on the hotel's website after 11am) and always include fish and a vegetarian option. There is no *carte*. After dinner you can sink into one of the cream sofas beside the fireplace in the civilized sitting room or have a nightcap in the small, atmospheric bar, a popular gathering place for the village.

～

NEARBY Apt (4 km); Bonnieux (12 km); Aix (56 km).
LOCATION in the village centre; car parking nearby
FOOD breakfast, lunch, dinner
PRICE €€
ROOMS 15 double, twin and single, all with bath; all rooms have phone, hairdrier
FACILITIES sitting room, restaurant, bar
CREDIT CARDS MC, V **CHILDREN** accepted
DISABLED one specially adapted room **PETS** accepted
CLOSED early Nov to late Feb; restaurant Wed, lunch Thu
PROPRIETOR Jean Pierre de Lutz

THE SOUTH

ST-PAUL-DE-VENCE

LA COLOMBE D'OR

~ VILLAGE HOTEL ~

06570 St-Paul-de-Vence (Alpes-Maritimes)
TEL 04 93 32 80 02 **FAX** 04 93 32 77 78
E-MAIL contact@la-colombe-dor.com **WEBSITE** www.la-colombe-dor.com

WHEN PAUL ROUX (grandfather of the present owner) opened his modest inn in the 1930s, he would not have dreamed that La Colombe d'Or would become the famous and chic hotel that it is today. Many of his customers were the artists that lived and worked in St-Paul at the time, and they often paid their way with their work. It became a well-known meeting place for an arty, bohemian crowd who were joined by the emerging Riviera jet set. Today, many of the guests are well-heeled Americans, but it has not completely lost the feel of a laid-back country inn.

The art on the walls and the sculpture in the garden is extraordinary; you hardly need to visit the nearby Fondation Maeght. The wood-panelled dining rooms, where simple food is served, are hung with Picasso, Miro and Chagall. The style throughout is rustic chic and refreshingly casual; old tiled floors, natural colours and fabrics, country antiques, spectacular ceramics, plenty of plants…and art everywhere. In summer, food is served on the delightful, flower-filled terrace in the shade of ancient trees. The pool is heated year-round; for chillier days, there is a cosy sunken sitting area with leather sofas grouped around an open fire.

~

NEARBY Fondation Maeght; Nice (15 km); Grasse (25 km).
LOCATION on edge of village; valet car parking
FOOD breakfast, lunch, dinner
PRICE €€€€
ROOMS 26; 15 double and twin, 11 suites all with bath or spa bath; all rooms have phone, TV, air conditioning, hairdrier
FACILITIES dining rooms, bar, sitting rooms, terraces, garden, swimming pool
CREDIT CARDS AE, DC, MC, V
CHILDREN accepted
DISABLED access difficult
PETS accepted
CLOSED Nov, 2 weeks Jan
PROPRIETORS M. and Mme Roux

THE SOUTH

ST-PAUL-DE-VENCE

LE HAMEAU
~ COUNTRY VILLA ~

528 route de la Colle, 06570 St-Paul-de-Vence (Alpes-Maritimes)
TEL 04 93 32 80 24 **FAX** 04 93 32 55 75
E-MAIL lehameau@wanadoo.fr **WEBSITE** www.le-hameau.com

W E'VE HAD AN ENTHUSIASTIC endorsement from our latest inspector of this
cluster of red-roofed Provençal 18th and 19thC buildings that was
once a farm. 'The situation is brilliant, its back to St-Paul-de-Vence and
high enough above the main road to ensure that it's quiet.' Set in countryside, it has a lovely garden with orange and mandarin trees which give off a
heady scent in season and produce the breakfast marmalade. Bedrooms
are very stylish: elegant rustic with dark timber beams, rugs on the red-
tiled floors, some gorgeous country walnut and fruitwood antiques and
attractive fabrics. They also have beautiful bathrooms, some large, others
small and cosy. Bedrooms also vary considerably in size, as well as price,
and many have their own sun terrace or balcony. Our inspector was particularly impressed by how thoughtfully laid out his room was. A captivating
place, and very good value for money.'
  There is a cool, neat breakfast room, but it's much more fun to have
breakfast in the large terraced garden, which accommodates a smart pool.
The only improvement our inspector could suggest was to serve drinks and
light lunches by the pool. He found most of the staff charming.

NEARBY Fondation Maeght; Cagnes-sur-Mer (5 km); Nice (15 km); Grasse (25 km).
LOCATION 1 km outside village, 15 km NW of Nice; car parking
FOOD breakfast
PRICE ©©
ROOMS 17; 14 double and twin, 3 apartments, 15 with bath, 2 with shower; all
rooms have phone, TV, air conditioning, minibar, hairdrier, safe
FACILITIES breakfast room, sitting room, terrace, garden, swimming pool
CREDIT CARDS MC, V
CHILDREN accepted
DISABLED no special facilities
PETS accepted
CLOSED mid-Nov to mid-Dec, mid-Jan to mid-Feb
PROPRIETORS Lisa Burlando and Carmine Cherchi

THE SOUTH

LES BERGERIES DE PONDERACH

~ COUNTRY HOTEL ~

route de Narbonne, 34220 St-Pons-de-Thomières (Hérault)
TEL 04 67 97 02 57 **FAX** 04 67 97 29 75
E-MAIL bergeries.ponderach@wanadoo.fr **WEBSITE** www.bergeries-ponderach.com

ST-PONS-DE-THOMIERES is a pleasant little town in the Parc Régional de Haut Languedoc, in these parts an area of gentle wooded hills. This restaurant-hotel, just under a kilometre outside the town, with large grounds, a charming courtyard, and peaceful rural surroundings, has been fashioned out of an 18thC farmhouse, retaining all its character and adding many comforts. Bedrooms are smart and bright, with exposed beams. Each has its own terrace and views over the orchard and river.

M. Lentin, the proprietor, used to own an art gallery, and paintings are a major feature of the attractive drawing room and dining room. Food, however, is probably the high point: there are four menus from which to choose, the cheapest offering value for money. Fresh local produce, especially pork, takes precedence, and the wine list has an interesting selection of country wines. A recent English visitor went for one night but stayed for three – for the 'marvellous food and wonderful warm hospitality'. (M. Lentin is an Anglophile who once nearly married an English girl.) Reports confirm our view that this place offers charm and delicious food at notably fair prices. A German reader also found 'in this rural hotel an atmosphere of individuality and of culture without overdone formality or decoration', as well as 'hospitality and very friendly, attentive service'.

~

NEARBY Castres (52 km); Béziers (51 km).
LOCATION 0.8 km outside town; car parking
FOOD breakfast, lunch, dinner
PRICE €€
ROOMS 7 double with bath
FACILITIES sitting room, dining room, terraces, garden
CREDIT CARDS DC, MC, V
CHILDREN accepted
DISABLED no special facilities **PETS** accepted
CLOSED early Nov to Mar
PROPRIETOR M. Lentin

THE SOUTH

MAS DES CARASSINS
～ CONVERTED FARMHOUSE ～

1 chemin Gaulois, 13210 St-Rémy-de-Provence (Bouches-du-Rhône)
TEL 04 90 92 15 48 **FAX** 04 90 92 63 47
E-MAIL carassin@pacwan.fr

IT IS NOW FOUR YEARS SINCE Michel Dimeux and Pierre Ticot took over this
seductive small hotel, and they have been running it very successfully
since. They bought it from M and Mme Ripert, who had been in charge
from the beginning – it was her family home – and in a touching letter in
the book of comments, they say how privileged they were to hand over to
Michel and Pierre. When our inspector arrived only a month after the
reopening, and finishing touches were still being made, the Riperts had
come to tea and to see the changes. They were as enchanted as we were.

The new owners (Michel is also manager) had more experience of being
guests than hoteliers, but they knew what they liked and, with great style,
they have created a stunning hotel. They have now finished renovating all
14 bedrooms in soothing colours, with terracotta floors and smart fabrics.
They have thought of everything (a strip of carpet set into the stair tiles to
eliminate noise) and nothing is too much trouble: 'It's a three-star hotel,
but we like to give four-star service.' In the secluded gardens, they have
made a gorgeous pool, where they will give you a light lunch, and a *table
d'hôte* is provided five nights a week.

～

NEARBY Les Baux-de-Provence (7 km); Avignon (20 km).
LOCATION in quiet, residential lane on S edge of town; car parking
FOOD breakfast, light lunches (mid-Jun to mid-Sep), evening snacks (Mon, Wed,
Fri, Sat)
PRICE €€
ROOMS 14; 12 double, twin, triple and family, 2 suites, all with bath or shower; all
rooms have phone, TV, air conditioning, minibar
FACILITIES sitting room, dining room, terrace, garden, swimming pool
CREDIT CARDS MC, V **CHILDREN** accepted
DISABLED one specially adapted room
PETS accepted
CLOSED Jan to Apr
PROPRIETORS Michel Dimeux and Pierre Ticot

THE SOUTH

ST-RÉMY-DE-PROVENCE

DOMAINE DE VALMOURIANE

~ COUNTRY HOTEL ~

petite route des Baux, 13210 St-Rémy-de-Provence (Bouches-du-Rhône)
TEL 04 90 92 44 62 **FAX** 04 90 92 37 32
E-MAIL info@valmouriane.com **WEBSITE** www.valmouriane.com

IF YOU WANT TO KNOW what *herbes de Provence* smell like, then take a room at Philippe and Martina Capel's Domaine de Valmouriane and simply open your window. Tucked away in a peaceful fold in the rocky hills of the Alpilles, this beautifully converted farmhouse is surrounded by pines, cypresses, rosemary, juniper and lavender – scents and flavours you will come across again in its dining room. Beyond a wide lawn are a sheltered swimming pool and a tennis court and if you want to go further afield a ten-minute drive will take you to Les Baux – but as cars are kept out you might prefer to walk there along the marked woodland trail.

The house has tiled floors and is tastefully decorated with Provençal fabrics and fine antique furniture. The old kitchen, with a huge fireplace, is a cosy winter sitting room and in summer there is a canopied terrace for open-air dining: the cooking is contemporary Provençal and the traditional staples are given stylish twists with fresh herbs and spices. There is also a well-informed selection of local wines to choose from. Two of the smartly comfortable bedrooms have their own private terraces and several others on the ground floor have doors opening directly outside.

~

NEARBY Les Baux-de-Provence (5 km); Avignon (24 km).
LOCATION 4 km W of town on road to Baux; car parking
FOOD breakfast, lunch, dinner
PRICE €€€€-€€€€
ROOMS 12 double and twin with bath; all rooms have phone, air conditioning, minibar
FACILITIES sitting room, bar, dining rooms, terrace, garden, swimming pool, tennis
CREDIT CARDS AE, DC, MC, V
CHILDREN welcome
DISABLED one specially adapted room
PETS not accepted
CLOSED never
PROPRIETORS Philippe and Martina Capel

THE SOUTH

St-Tropez

LA PONCHE
～ TOWN HOTEL ～

3 rue des Remparts, 83990 St-Tropez (Var)
Tel 04 94 97 02 53 **Fax** 04 94 97 78 61
E-MAIL hotel@laponche.com **WEBSITE** www.laponche.com

YOU MIGHT NOT THINK that St-Tropez would be our kind of town, but La Ponche is our kind of hotel, at least when we're feeling like a treat, and recent positive reports indicate that readers seem to share our view. Tucked away in a tiny square overlooking the small fishing port and tiny beach of La Ponche (where Vadim's *And God Created Woman* was filmed, starring Brigitte Bardot), this cluster of 17thC houses offers a compelling combination of sophistication and warmth. What began as a simple fishermen's bar in 1937 has been steadily transformed over the years by Simone Duckstein into a stylish, arty four-star hotel, full of personal touches. Paintings by the artist Jacques Cordier cover the walls.

You can eat on a terrace, looking across a square to the sea, or in one of several areas indoors, including the main dining room – unpretentious but sophisticated. The food is memorable, particularly the seafood. Bedrooms are captivating and very comfortable. All have been smartly revamped, with stylish colour schemes and slick bathrooms. A couple of noisier bedrooms facing the street may persuade you to sleep with the double-glazing windows closed and the air conditioning on.

～

Nearby beaches: Les Graniers (100 m); La Bouillabaisse (1 km); Tahiti (4 km).
Location in heart of old town, overlooking Port des Pêcheurs; car parking and garage
Food breakfast, lunch, dinner
Price €€€€
Rooms 18; 11 double and twin, 2 family, 3 suites, 2 apartments, all with bath; all rooms have phone, TV, air conditioning, minibar, safe
Facilities sitting room, bar, dining room, lift
Credit cards AE, MC, V **Children** accepted
Disabled access difficult
Pets accepted
Closed mid-Nov to mid-Feb
Proprietor Simone Duckstein

THE SOUTH

St-Tropez

LE YACA

~ SEASIDE HOTEL ~

1 boulevard d'Aumale, 83994 St-Tropez (Var)
TEL 04 94 55 81 00 **FAX** 04 94 97 58 50
E-MAIL hotel-le-yaca@wanadoo.fr **WEBSITE** www.hotel-le-yaca.fr

JUST A HUNDRED METRES OR SO from the picturesque Port des Pêcheurs, Le Yaca occupies several old town houses (one was home to Colette in the 1920s), which have been knocked together in the most charming corner of old St-Tropez. The rather grand reception hall is in the middle, but once you leave this and find yourself in the warren of passageways and staircases, you get a real feel for the old buildings.

Le Yaca is the antithesis of St-Trop flash (apart, that is, from its prices). Discreet and casually chic, the only glitz here is to be found in beautiful woven Moroccan fabrics on the beds or Oriental lanterns lighting the dining terrace. Bedrooms are individually decorated with great taste and flair; cool white against old terracotta floors, antique furniture, wall hangings and the odd rug, exotic orchids. Bathrooms are impeccable with Hermès bath goodies and fluffy white robes. Rooms on the top floors enjoy a glimpse of the sea over sun-baked roof tiles, and there are three stunningly stylish suites. Excellent Italian food is served in the relaxed, sunny restaurant; in warm weather, you can eat in the delightful and peaceful garden beside a small pool.

The Hurets have opened another, smaller but equally classy hotel, Le Y, 50 metres down the road. It has 15 rooms, a garden and style to spare.

~

NEARBY beaches: Les Graniers (100 m); La Bouillabaisse (1 km); Tahiti (4 km).
LOCATION in centre of old town, 100 m from Port des Pêcheurs; valet car parking (public or private)
FOOD breakfast, light lunch on request, dinner
PRICE €€€€€-€€€€€€
ROOMS 28; 23 double and twin, 2 single, 3 suites, all with bath or shower; all rooms have phone, TV, air conditioning, minibar, safe, hairdrier
FACILITIES restaurant, bar, terraces, garden, swimming pool
CREDIT CARDS AE, DC, MC, V **DISABLED** not suitable **PETS** accepted
CLOSED mid-Oct to Apr
PROPRIETORS M and Mme Huret

THE SOUTH

LES STES-MARIES-DE-LA-MER

HOSTELLERIE DU MAS DE CACHAREL
~ COUNTRY HOTEL ~

route de Cacharel, 13460 Les Stes-Maries-de-la-Mer (Bouches-du-Rhône)
TEL 04 90 97 95 44 **FAX** 04 90 97 87 97
E-MAIL mail@hotel-cacharel.com**WEBSITE** www.hotel-cacharel.com

A KILOMETRE FROM THE ROAD and on a 70-hectare estate adjoining a nature reserve, this small hotel was built in the '60s by film director and photographer Denys Colomb de Daunant, who made the beautiful slow-motion film, *The Dream of the Wild Horses*. Now run by his son, Florian, a former shipbroker, it has remained very simple and unpretentious. There's no television (much frowned on) and the ground-floor rooms – looking into a courtyard and out to the marshes – are basic, and charming, with white walls and some contain huge grainy photographs of horses. There are also plenty of horses to ride; the family has about 60.

With no restaurant, there's a bar and tables in a huge beamed barn, decorated with mounted bulls' horns, cattle bells and farm implements. The centrepiece is a massive 18thC stone fireplace. An *assiette campagnarde* – of ham, goats' cheese and sausages – is served, with wine, from noon to 8 pm. The stables are close by, and can be visited any time. The bird life, all around, is a wonder; there's a constant parade of flamingos. The frenetic tourist activity in Les Stes-Marie-de-la-Mer, 5 km down the road, is in another world. The Colomb de Daunants are delightful hosts.

~

NEARBY Arles (39 km); Aigues-Mortes (31 km); Nîmes (54 km).
LOCATION in the marshes of the Camargue; car parking
FOOD breakfast, light meals (noon to 8 pm)
PRICE €€
ROOMS 15; 12 with bath, 3 with shower; all rooms have phone
FACILITIES bar, barn, garden, swimming pool, riding
CREDIT CARDS MC, V
CHILDREN welcome
DISABLED one suitable room
PETS accepted
CLOSED never
PROPRIETORS Colomb de Daunant family

THE SOUTH

LES STES-MARIES-DE-LA-MER

MAS DE LA FOUQUE
~ COUNTRY HOTEL ~

route du Petit-Rhône, 13460 Les Stes-Marie-de-la-Mer (Bouches-du-Rhône)
TEL 04 90 97 81 02 **FAX** 04 90 97 94 84
E-MAIL info@masdelafouque.com **WEBSITE** www.masdelafouque.com

OVER A CANDLELIT DINNER, a young woman was confiding to her companion how much she loved him. But his eyes were elsewhere: a large grey heron was wading through the pond. The evening floor show, as seen through the picture windows here, is extraordinary: white horses and the little black bulls of the Camargue wander through the reeds and grasses of the marshes and squadrons of pink flamingos fly overhead. This Spanish-style whitewashed hotel, on the water's edge is a four-star luxury ranch with a helicopter pad, exotic bathrooms, whirlpool baths and a starry clientele. Viviane, charming and glamorous, oversees everything, and reporters who stayed here in July 2004 couldn't fault it.

Many of the exotically redecorated rooms – carved headboards or driftwood beds, covered with white linen spreads and draped in mosquito netting – have private terraces built over the lagoon for sunbathing and bird watching. (Take binoculars.) There's a comfortable bar, smart *salon* and restaurant, where the food is excellent, with elegantly presented regional dishes (many vegetables and herbs are home grown). Recent innovations include gypsy Flamenco music on Saturday evenings and a private motor launch to take you to deserted beaches or to watch the wildlife.

~

NEARBY Arles (35 km); Aigues-Mortes (26 km); Nîmes (50 km).
LOCATION in the Camargue, 4 km NW of the town; car parking
FOOD breakfast, lunch, dinner
PRICE €€€€
ROOMS 13; 6 double, 4 twin, one family, 2 suites, all with bath; all rooms have phone, TV, air conditioning, minibar, hairdrier; 4 have whirlpool baths
FACILITIES 2 sitting rooms, bar, dining room, terraces, garden, swimming pool, fishing, putting, private motor launch, helipad
CREDIT CARDS AE, DC, MC, V **CHILDREN** accepted
DISABLED one specially-adapted room **PETS** accepted
CLOSED early Nov to late Mar, Christmas, New Year; restaurant Tue Sep to Jul
PROPRIETOR Didier Rivière

THE SOUTH

LE SAMBUC

MAS DE PEINT

~ COUNTRY HOTEL ~

Le Sambuc, 13200 Arles (Bouches-du-Rhône)
TEL 04 90 97 20 62 **FAX** 04 90 97 22 20
E-MAIL contact@masdepeint.net **WEBSITE** www.masdepeint.com

THIS IS CAMARGUE CHIC, achieved at lavish expense by the owners, the Bons, whose cattle-branding mark appears on the crisp, white linen in an exquisite little hotel created out of an 18thC stable attached to their own house. Mme Bon, an architect and interior designer, has considerably altered the building to make lovely, spacious rooms with wooden beamed ceilings, sandstone floors, paintwork the colour of sugared almonds and enviable antiques. The whole ensemble feels like a wing for private guests rather than a hotel, which is the way it's meant to be. Everyone eats – sometimes a little awkwardly – in the old-fashioned kitchen, from which emanate inviting smells before dinner; vegetables and herbs come from the garden. A harness hangs in the hall, shelves are filled with books, there's a quiet little reading room, and a newspaper for the breakfast table. Jacques Bon, who breeds bulls and horses, is often in and out, inviting visitors to come and see his stock and his farm, on which he grows rice. The bedrooms are in classic country-house style; some have cast-iron baths and little wooden staircases up to a galleried bathroom. There's a discreet swimming pool hidden from the house.

~

NEARBY Arles (20 km); Avignon (36 km); Nîmes (31 km).
LOCATION in open countryside; car parking
FOOD breakfast, lunch, dinner
PRICE €€€
ROOMS 11; 8 double and twin, 3 suites, all with bath; all rooms have phone, TV, air conditioning, minibar, safe
FACILITIES sitting rooms, dining room, garden, swimming pool, riding
CREDIT CARDS AE, DC, MC, V
CHILDREN welcome
DISABLED no special facilities
PETS accepted
CLOSED early Jan to mid-Mar
PROPRIETORS M and Mme Bon

THE SOUTH

SEILLANS

HOTEL DES DEUX ROCS

∼ VILLAGE HOTEL ∼

place Font d'Amont, 83440 Seillans (Var)
TEL 04 94 76 87 32 **FAX** 04 94 76 88 68
E-MAIL deux-rocs-seillans@wanadoo.fr **WEBSITE** www.hoteldeuxrocs.com

IT'S ALL CHANGE AT THIS CAPTIVATING blue-shuttered hotel in a charming medieval hill village, which has long been one of our favourites. Mme Hirsh has finally retired at the age of 81, and Bruno and Judy Germanaz have taken over. He is French and the *chef de cuisine*; she is Australian and responsible for everything else. True professionals, they have 25 years' experience of working together in the hotel and restaurant business. Judy tells us that they have redecorated all the bedrooms and bathrooms, bought brand new beds and laid fresh carpets. Despite the improvements, they are keen to keep 'the charm of the hotel as created by Mme Hirsch. Definitely, no TV in the rooms' and meals are still served by the fountain in the little cobbled square in front. What heartwarming news, as we've always felt the secret of the Deux Rocs' enduring appeal is that it conforms to what everyone *expects* of a small unspoiled hotel in Provence.

An American visitor named it his favourite hotel on a recent trip through Provence: 'Dinner was delicious ... we had a crispy duck that melted off the bone and fish served in butter paper. Though there was a beautifully decorated dining room, we opted to eat next to a fire Bruno made for us in the living room. The bedroom was light, airy, and decorated tastefully in simple *Côte d'Azur* style'. He also fell in love with the picturesque village, a former artists' colony, where Max Ernst lived at the end of his life.

∼

NEARBY Lac de St-Cassien (15 km); Grasse (32 km); St-Raphael (33 km); Cannes (47 km); Gorges du Verdon (40 km).
LOCATION at top of small village; limited car parking or car park above hotel
FOOD breakfast, lunch, dinner
PRICE ⓔ
ROOMS 14 double and twin, 6 with bath, 8 with shower; all rooms have phone
FACILITIES sitting room, bar, dining room, terrace **CREDIT CARDS** MC, V
CHILDREN accepted **DISABLED** access difficult **PETS** accepted
CLOSED Nov to mid-Mar
PROPRIETORS Bruno and Judy Germanaz

THE SOUTH

SERIGNAN-DU-COMTAT

LE PRE DU MOULIN

∼ VILLAGE HOTEL AND RESTAURANT ∼

route du Ste-Cécile-les-Vignes, 84830 Sérignan-du-Comtat (Vaucluse)
TEL 04 90 70 05 58 **FAX** 04 90 70 05 62
E-MAIL hvc@ifrance.com **WEBSITE** www.hostellerieduvieuxchateau.com

YOU MIGHT NOT RECOGNIZE the name, but this hotel is not new to the guide. It used to be the Hostellerie du Château, run by the delightful Truchots, and Le Pré du Moulin was the restaurant, which they also ran but had to give up when Madame became too arthritic. At this point, they handed over the restaurant to the Alonsos: Pascal, a talented young chef, and his Swiss wife, Caroline, an equally talented manager. On the Truchots' recent retirement from hotel-keeping, they took over the hotel as well and changed its name. It is a handsome 18thC farmhouse turned *logis* in a picturesque village with spacious, comfortable and reasonably priced rooms (the ones with attractive new timber-decked terraces are particularly good value). In an airy barn-like building next door, the restaurant is very highly regarded, popular with locals and visitors alike.

When we last visited, we found the hotel traditional and endearing with its old-fashioned bar, sitting and breakfast rooms and sunny terrace, but, as we go to press, the Alonsos have a major refurbishment in hand, and we would welcome new reports. At present they haven't updated the hotel website, but when they do, the web address is likely to change.

∼

NEARBY Orange (8 km); Avignon (40 km); Mont Ventoux.
LOCATION on edge of the village set back from the road to Ste-Cécile-les-Vignes; car parking
FOOD breakfast, lunch, dinner; half-board obligatory Apr to Oct
PRICE €€
ROOMS 8; 7 double and twin, one family, 7 with bath, one with shower; all rooms have phone, TV, minibar, hairdrier; some have air conditioning, safe
FACILITIES sitting room, bar, breakfast room, restaurant, terrace, garden, swimming pool
CREDIT CARDS AE, MC, V **CHILDREN** welcome
DISABLED one ground floor room **PETS** not accepted **CLOSED** 2 weeks Feb, one week Sep; restaurant Mon and Thu lunch Sep to Jul, Sun dinner
PROPRIETORS Pascal and Caroline Alonso

THE SOUTH

AUBERGE DE TOURRETTES

~ VILLAGE RESTAURANT-WITH-ROOMS ~

11 route de Grasse, 06140 Tourrettes-sur-Loup (Alpes-Maritimes)
TEL 04 93 59 30 05 **FAX** 04 93 59 28 66
E-MAIL info@aubergedetourrettes.fr **WEBSITE** www.aubergedetourrettes.fr

TALENTED CHEF CHRISTOPHE DUFAU and his Danish wife Katrine opened their restaurant-with-rooms in the shell of a typical village inn in July 2000. High in the Midi hills, Tourrettes is only a few kilometres from tourist-ridden St-Paul, but refreshingly quiet and unassuming. The hotel sits on the edge of the village, looking over unspoiled, wooded hillsides towards the coast below.

The focal point of the place is the airy, open-plan restaurant which occupies a glassed-in terrace and enjoys fabulous views. The decoration is simple, stylish and unstuffy; clean, contemporary lines, warm tiled floors, shades of white, natural linen tablecloths, much wood and an olive tree in a terracotta pot. There is a terrace for warmer weather. Our inspector was hugely impressed with the food and reasonable prices. Fresh, local ingredients (plenty of fresh herbs from the garden) are prepared with flair and real skill: lobster terrine *en gelée* flavoured with orange; asparagus served with parmesan chips and a delicately-flavoured *mousseline;* chicken stewed with pickled lemons. 'Excellent and sophisticated, with flavours that are subtle rather than robust', is how a recent reporter describes the food. He continues, 'It's good enough to drive an hour from the seaside for'. There is an 'interesting local wine list and expert advice' to accompany it. The simple bedrooms, which he considers merely 'adequate', reflect the colours of Provence, a contemporary take on a traditional theme.

~

NEARBY Vence (6 km); St-Paul-de-Vence (11 km); Nice (25 km).
LOCATION on main road on edge of village; car parking
FOOD breakfast, lunch, dinner
PRICE €€
ROOMS 6 double and twin, all with bath; all rooms have phone, TV, minibar
FACILITIES restaurant, bar, garden, terrace **CREDIT CARDS** AE, DC, MC, V
CHILDREN accepted **DISABLED** access difficult **PETS** accepted
CLOSED one week end Nov, mid-Jan to mid-Feb; restaurant Mon and Tue Oct to May
PROPRIETORS Christophe and Katrine Dufau

THE SOUTH

TRIGANCE

CHATEAU DE TRIGANCE

~ CONVERTED CASTLE ~

83840 Trigance (Var)
TEL 04 94 76 91 18 **FAX** 04 94 85 68 99
E-MAIL chateautrigance@wanadoo.fr **WEBSITE** www.chateau-de-trigance.fr

FOR MORE THAN 30 YEARS, Jean-Claude Thomas and his wife have run this characterful and comfortable hotel near the dramatic Gorges du Verdon. Nowadays their son, William, is involved. Trigance remains a welcome port of call in a region of rough terrain and few villages. On arrival, you might be taken aback. Is this fortress, perched high on a rocky peak, really your hotel? (Yes.) And if it is, how are you to penetrate its defences? (until recently you had to climb a steep flight of 100 steps – now, to the relief of most guests, you can reach the castle by car.) Once inside, you are in the Middle Ages. M. Thomas has painstakingly rebuilt his 11thC castle stone by stone (villagers had stolen many of them to build their own houses); if you ask, you can see photographs of the various stages of his amazing project. The impressive stone-vaulted, candlelit dining room (with a knight in armour at the entrance), and the sitting room below, are windowless and highly atmospheric, furnished in medieval style. Most of the bedrooms (cut into the hill) are similar, with canopied beds, antique furniture, tapestries and banners – and stunning views from their windows. You can have breakfast on the battlements. The cooking is surprisingly good, considering the remote location.

~

NEARBY Gorges du Verdon (10 km); Castellane (20 km).
LOCATION at 750 m, overlooking tiny village, 10 km NW of Comps-sur-Artuby; car parking
FOOD breakfast, lunch, dinner; room service
PRICE €€
ROOMS 10 double and twin, all with bath; all rooms have phone, TV, hairdrier
FACILITIES sitting room, dining room, terrace
CREDIT CARDS AE, DC, MC, V **CHILDREN** accepted
DISABLED not suitable **PETS** accepted
CLOSED Nov to mid-Mar
PROPRIETORS Thomas family

THE SOUTH

DOMAINE DE LA PONCHE
~ COUNTRY HOTEL ~

84190 Vacqueras (Vaucluse)
TEL 04 90 65 85 21 **FAX** 04 90 65 85 23
E-MAIL domaine.laponche@wanadoo.fr **WEBSITE** www.hotel-laponche.com

'WHAT A FIND', wrote the reader who told us about this new hotel in wine country near the jagged Dentelles de Montmirail. 'Admittedly we were tired, hungry and in need of a bed for the night when we called in here, but we couldn't believe our luck. Our room was enormous, with a fabulous bathroom, and dinner was excellent.'

Enormous is the word: lofty ceilings striped by vast beams and bedrooms which are like prairies compared to most hotel rooms. They are decorated *à la mode* with spartan good taste involving pastel colours for the walls, wrought-iron or wooden beds, one or two good pieces of country furniture; the more expensive have sitting areas, and the bathrooms are, as reported, huge and excellent. The public rooms are also large-scale; the laid-back sitting room made cosy by a huge open hearth.

The fine old blue-shuttered 17thC *bastide*, surrounded by its own vines, olive and cypress trees, was converted into a hotel four years ago by two Swiss sisters and the French husband of one of them. They are good cooks, making their own fresh pasta to add to their repertoire of tasty Provençal dishes. Light lunches are served around the lovely flowery pool.

~

NEARBY Côtes-du-Rhône vineyards; Vaison-la-Romaine (20 km).
LOCATION signposted 2 km N of Vacqueras, on D8 to Cairanne; car parking
FOOD breakfast, lunch, dinner
PRICE €€€
ROOMS 6; 4 double and twin, 2 suites, all with bath; all rooms have phone, hairdrier
FACILITIES sitting room, dining room, terrace, garden, swimming pool
CREDIT CARDS MC, V
CHILDREN accepted
DISABLED access difficult
PETS accepted
CLOSED never
PROPRIETORS Ruth Spahn, Madeleine Frauenknecht, Jean-Pierre Onimus

THE SOUTH

VAISON-LA-ROMAINE

HOSTELLERIE LE BEFFROI
∼ TOWN HOTEL ∼

rue de l'Évêché Haute Ville, 84110 Vaison-la-Romaine (Vaucluse)
TEL 04 90 36 04 71 **FAX** 04 90 36 24 78
E-MAIL lebeffroi@wanadoo.fr **WEBSITE** www.le-beffroi.com

THE HOTEL OCCUPIES two beautiful houses in the same street of this medieval hilltop town – one was built in the 16th century for the Comte de Saint Véran, the other, built in the 17th century, was the home of the Marquis de Taulignan. There are plenty of beams, old stone, and polished red-tiled floors in both, and views from the terraces look down to the new town below, which is built around two sites of Roman excavations. (Some of the houses in the old town were built of stone from the ruins.) The Beffroi is above it all – even in the hottest weather there's a fresh breeze.

The friendly, young and often very busy, proprietor, Yann Christiansen (the hotel has been in the family for three generations now) and his wife, Christine, constantly strive to come up with ways of making the hotel even more comfortable and convenient for their guests. Serving lunchtime salads on the terrace has proved a great success. At dinner, the cooking is traditional Provençal. A swimming pool with fine views of the rooftops below and an ingenious mini-golf course nearby are added attractions in summer. Recent readers disagree about the ease of parking, but are in accord on the subject of the 'helpful'...'young, friendly and enthusiastic staff'. One warns that the next-door bell chimes twice on the hour every hour; whilst the other enthuses that the hotel 'is a delight', 'dinner was delicious' and 'Our only regret was we could not stay longer'.

∼

NEARBY Orange (25 km); Avignon (40 km).
LOCATION in the old town, up a steep hill; car parking
FOOD breakfast, lunch, dinner
PRICE €€
ROOMS 22; 8 double, 13 twin, one single, 12 with bath, 10 with shower; all rooms have phone, TV, minibar, hairdrier
FACILITIES sitting room, dining room, terraces, garden, swimming pool, mini-golf (summer only) **CREDIT CARDS** AE, DC, MC, V **CHILDREN** welcome **DISABLED** not suitable
PETS accepted **CLOSED** Feb to late Mar; restaurant late Oct to Apr
PROPRIETORS M. and Mme Christiansen

THE SOUTH

MAISON PIC
~ TOWN HOTEL ~

285 avenue Victor Hugo, 26001 Valence (Drôme)
TEL 04 75 44 15 32 **FAX** 04 75 40 96 03
E-MAIL pic@relaischateaux.fr **WEBSITE** www.pic-valence.com

THE FOOD'S THE THING HERE, as it always has been. The first Pic restaurant was founded almost a century ago in Le Pin by Sophie Pic – the Valence restaurant was the project of her son André – and it seems perfectly fitting that things should have come full circle with another woman at the helm in Pic's celebrated kitchen. Anne-Sophie is a worthy heir to this dynasty of renowned chefs; she brings a feminine touch not only to her cuisine, but also to the hotel's decoration and atmosphere. Maybe the secret of her success is that she and her staff strive to make people feel like guests, rather than customers.

You don't have to face a drive after dinner if you'd rather not, since there are 15 smart, comfortable rooms: each one is different and named after a scent. They have a smart new Provençal look: wood floors, refined colour schemes – either fresh and pale or warm and rich – and white tiled bathrooms. Some have small balconies. All are very attractive and stylish. There is also a calm, flowered terrace, shaded by 100-year-old lime trees, and a lovely open-air swimming pool. The copious Pic breakfast served in your room is almost as delicious as dinner.

~

NEARBY Vercors mountains; the Rhône.
LOCATION in town centre; car parking
FOOD breakfast, lunch, dinner
PRICE €€€€-€€€€€
ROOMS 15 double with bath; all rooms have phone, TV, air conditioning, minibar, hairdrier, safe
FACILITIES sitting room, restaurant, terrace, swimming pool, French billiards
CREDIT CARDS AE, DC, MC, V
CHILDREN accepted
DISABLED one specially adapted room
PETS accepted
CLOSED never; restaurant Sun dinner, Mon and Tue Nov to Mar, 3 weeks Jan
PROPRIETOR Anne-Sophie Pic

THE SOUTH

VENCE

LA ROSERAIE
~ TOWN VILLA ~

avenue Henri Giraud, 06140 Vence (Alpes-Maritimes)
TEL 04 93 58 02 20 **FAX** 04 93 58 99 31

THE WHOLE FEELING of this pale pink *belle époque* villa is of a rambling family house – straw hats and little bunches of dried flowers hang on the walls and there are old photographs and prints. M Marteton has been busy updating the hotel since he took over some years ago: smart, wrought-iron garden furniture and wooden, colonial-style sunbeds have replaced white plastic, for example. The mature garden is full of exotic plants and trees – a banana palm, a 100-year-old giant magnolia, orange trees and oleander. The reception area/sitting room is immediately inviting, with low beamed ceiling, little stone fireplace, Provençal fabrics and pleasing objects. A smell of lavender lingers in the air.

The bedrooms have remained largely the same: bright and sunny. One particularly pretty room is in an attic under the eaves, with heavy beams, rough brick walls and arched window under the roof, with a beautiful carved wrought-iron bed. Another room has a clawfoot bath; others have handmade ceramic tiles from Salernes. All are spotless and well equipped. The hotel is not in a pretty part of Vence, though.

~

NEARBY Matisse chapel; Vence old town; Cannes (15 km).
LOCATION on outskirts of town; 10 km N of Cagnes-sur-Mer; car parking
FOOD breakfast
PRICE ⓔⓔ
ROOMS 13 double and twin, 11 with bath, 2 with shower; all rooms have phone, TV, minibar, hairdrier; some have safe, one has air conditioning
FACILITIES sitting room, breakfast room, terrace, garden, swimming pool
CREDIT CARDS AE, DC, MC, V
CHILDREN accepted
DISABLED 4 rooms on ground floor
PETS accepted
CLOSED mid-Nov to mid-Feb
PROPRIETOR M. Marteton

THE SOUTH

VENCE

AUBERGE DES SEIGNEURS ET DU LION D'OR
~ TOWN HOTEL ~

place du Frêne, 06140 Vence (Alpes-Maritimes)
TEL 04 93 58 04 24 **FAX** 04 93 24 08 01

FIND THE HUGE ASH TREE, and you will find this elegant town house, which has been a hotel since 1895 and in the family since 1936. The only thing that has changed over the years is the faces of the guests, who once numbered artists such as Renoir and Modigliani. Once inside, you'll find a large, rather gloomy reception hall with old tiled floors, lumbering country antiques, bits of olive press, a spinning wheel, a huge shaggy dog, nooks, crannies and curiosities. Off this is the restaurant, where Mme Rodi prepares delicious rack of lamb or chicken on the ancient spit over the open fire. There is also a fabulous *soupe de poissons* and *le tourton des patres*, a kind of cheese pie. Breakfast is simple, but particularly good, with stewed fruit, fromage frais, cheeses, breads and homemade jams. Bedrooms are quite spartan, but not without charm. There are some superb antique pieces, and many rooms have their original terracotta tiled floors, with bright Provençal fabrics and bowls of fresh fruit. They vary widely in shape and size; bathrooms have been renovated. But, nothing else modern here, and God forbid there should be any suggestion of televisions, a website, or even a brochure. Perhaps some modernity will creep in when Madame (a character) finally hands over to her daughter, but not too much, we hope.

Recent reports are excellent. Guests relish the *auberge*'s old-fashioned charm and the picturesque town.

~

NEARBY Matisse chapel; Vence old town; Cannes (5 km).
LOCATION on square near town centre; public car parking nearby
FOOD breakfast, lunch, dinner
PRICE €
ROOMS 10 double and twin, all with shower **FACILITIES** sitting room, restaurant, bar
CREDIT CARDS DC, MC, V **CHILDREN** accepted
DISABLED access difficult **PETS** accepted
CLOSED mid-Nov to mid-Mar; restaurant closed Mon, lunch Tue, Wed and Thu
PROPRIETOR Daniele Rodi

THE SOUTH

VILLENEUVE-LES-AVIGNON

HOTEL DE L'ATELIER
～ TOWN HOTEL ～

5 rue de la Foire, 30400 Villeneuve-les-Avignon (Gard)
TEL 04 90 25 01 84 **FAX** 04 90 25 80 06
E-MAIL hotel-latelier@libertysurf.fr **WEBSITE** www.hoteldelatelier.com

THIS BED-AND-BREAKFAST in a 16thC cardinal's house was rescued from fatigue and shabbiness four years ago by Agnès and Gui Lainé, who, fresh from the worlds of cinema and advertising, used their ingenuity and skill to create a hotel of great character and style without spending a fortune. They were lucky to inherit so many splendid features: the stone staircase, huge battered wooden doors, beamed ceilings and ancient fireplace, to which they added fresh decoration and fabrics, pretty lamps and wall-lights, a mixture of wooden and painted furniture and sisal flooring. The Lainés moved on in December 2003, handing over to Gérard and Annick Burret, whilst some of the very friendly and attentive members of staff remain. We haven't been able to visit since the Burrets took over, but they tell us that they have filled the hotel with striking modern art. Bedrooms are all different, simple yet elegant.

At the back of the house is a lovely courtyard, where you can eat breakfast under the shade of fig trees and a vine, and through a stone gateway beyond is a gloriously overgrown 'secret garden', a riot of oleander, geraniums and climbing roses in early summer. It's hard to believe that Avignon is only a 10-minute bus-ride across the Rhône.

～

NEARBY Avignon; Fort St-André; Chartreuse du Val de Bénédiction.
LOCATION in the town centre; limited car parking
MEALS breakfast
PRICE €
ROOMS 23 double and twin, all with bath or shower; all rooms have phone, TV, hairdrier
FACILITIES sitting room, breakfast room, garden
CREDIT CARDS AE, DC, MC, V
CHILDREN accepted
DISABLED not suitable **PETS** accepted
CLOSED early Jan to mid-Feb
PROPRIETORS Gérard and Annick Burret

THE SOUTH

LE COTTAGE

SEASIDE HOTEL

*21 rue Arthur-Rimbaud, 66703
Argèles-sur-Mer (Pyrénées-
Orientales)*
TEL 04 68 81 07 33
FAX 04 68 81 59 69
E-MAIL info@hotel-lecottage.com
FOOD breakfast, lunch, dinner
PRICE €-€€ **ROOMS** 34
CLOSED mid-Oct to Apr;
restaurant lunch Mon to Sat

THE CHAINE DES ALBERES is the last gasp of the Pyrenees before they reach the Mediterranean and Argèles-sur-Mer is virtually the last stop in France before the Spanish border. Le Cottage is a modern hotel in a residential area with splendid views. Painted cane and wrought-iron furniture helps to keep the rooms cheerful but the real secret of the place is L'Orangeraie, its restaurant, which has developed a name for the delicate touch it has brought to Mediterranean cooking and the strength of its regional wine list. Combined with candlelight on the linen-clad tables under the palms on a starry night, they make a heady mix.

LE VIEUX CASTILLON

HILLTOP VILLAGE HOTEL

*rue Turion Sabatier, 30210
Castillon-du-Gard (Gard)*
TEL 04 66 37 61 61 **FAX** 04 66 37 28 17
E-MAIL vieux.castillon@ wanadoo.fr
FOOD breakfast, lunch, dinner
PRICE €€€€ **ROOMS** 35
CLOSED early Jan to late Feb;
restaurant lunch Mon and Tue

THE OBVIOUS THING to do with a cluster of medieval houses above a breathtaking view of the vineyards of the Ventoux valley is to leave one or two charming ruins as conversation pieces and turn the rest into a luxurious hotel well defended outside against the mistral (by walls) and inside from the summer heat (by air conditioning). The flowery rooms vary somewhat in size and outlook but the quality of the cooking in their handsome beamed restaurant on the other side of the bridge is consistently excellent and backed up by an agreeably broad offering of Côtes du Rhône. Beautiful gardens and an attractive pool complete the package.

THE SOUTH

CAZILHAC

LA FERME DE LA SAUZETTE

CONVERTED FARMHOUSE
*route de Villefloure, 11570
Cazilhac (Aude)*
TEL 04 68 79 81 32 **FAX** 04 68 79 65
99 **E-MAIL** info@lasauzette.com
WEBSITE www.lasauzette.com
FOOD breakfast, dinner
PRICE €
ROOMS 5 **CLOSED** Nov, Jan

If YOU'RE NOT CERTAIN about wanting full Gallic immersion during your trip, then go and enjoy the warm welcome you'll get from Chris and Diana Gibson in their old stone farmhouse near Carcassonne. Surrounded by vineyards, its five well-decorated and comfortable (no smoking) bedrooms are above the old winery: they have all the beams you could wish for – and splendid bathrooms to go with them. Breakfast and dinner (both excellent) are taken club-style round a single large table. In winter there's a fire to sit by, and in summer you have the run of a veranda, a terrace and the garden.

LOURMARIN

AUBERGE LA FENIERE

RESTAURANT-WITH-ROOMS

*route de Cadenet, 84160
Lourmarin (Vaucluse)*
TEL 04 90 68 11 79 **FAX** 04 90 68 18
60 **E-MAIL** reine@wanadoo.fr
WEBSITE www.reinesammut.com
FOOD breakfast, lunch, dinner
PRICE €€€ **ROOMS** 9
CLOSED mid-Nov to Feb

If YOU FANCY A GOURMET DINNER and a bed on the premises in the Luberon we would recommend this Michelin-starred restaurant where the chef is a talented, self-taught and charming woman, Reine Sammut. It's certainly friendlier than the chi-chi Moulin de Lourmarin, and we thought the food every bit as good. The feminine touch is easy to detect in such dishes as *foie gras* sautéed in honey, a tart of sea bass topped with caramelized apples, or *pigeonneau fermier* eaten in the fingers, accompanied by Camargue rice. Bedrooms, with little terraces overlooking the inviting pool, are smart-modern if a little anodyne, and there are two kitsch gypsy caravans for romantic twosomes. Breakfast is a gourmet experience.

THE SOUTH

PEGOMAS

LE BOSQUET
COUNTRY HOTEL

74 chemin des Périssols, 06580
Pégomas (Alpes-Maritimes)
TEL 04 92 60 21 20
FAX 04 92 60 21 49 **E-MAIL**
hotel.lebosquet@wanadoo.fr
FOOD breakfast
PRICE €
ROOMS 23
CLOSED Feb

SET BETWEEN CANNES AND GRASSE in a plain 1960s building, with large shady grounds which include fruit trees, a pool, tennis court, children's play area and ping pong table, this is the sort of unpretentious yet beguiling family-run hotel beloved of this guide and a perfect spot for a holiday with the kids. As well as the 15 simple bedrooms, there are eight useful studios with kitchenettes and private terraces. Added attractions are a couple of golf courses and the sea, all within easy reach. You are also guaranteed a warm welcome and homemade jam for breakfast. 'We love it, and standards are just the same as ever', runs our latest report.

PLAN-DE-LA-TOUR

MAS DE BRUGASSIERES
COUNTRY GUESTHOUSE

Plan-de-la-Tour, 83120 Ste-
Maxime (Var)
TEL 04 94 55 50 55
FAX 04 94 55 50 51
E-MAIL mas.brugassieres@free.fr
FOOD breakfast **PRICE** €-€€
ROOMS 14 **CLOSED** mid-Oct to
mid-Mar

'VERY RELAXED – an excellent place to unwind,' is the verdict of one visitor to this modern 'farmhouse' set in lush gardens surrounded by vineyards. 'Yes, it's got a laid-back feel,' says our reporter. 'The tone is set by a huge wooden sofa from Sumatra piled with Indian cushions, with lots of pot plants dotted around, and a friendly, shaggy dog padding about.' Bedrooms are fairly basic but cheerful, with rustic tiled floors, functional furniture, Indian fabrics and Moroccan lamps; the Provençal tiled bathrooms are each in a different colour. Some lead directly on to the pretty, rambling garden and swimming pool. Breakfast is informal, served from 8 am until whenever you like, or you can rise late and have brunch by the swimming pool.

THE SOUTH

St-Laurent-du-Verdon

LE MOULIN DU CHATEAU

VILLAGE HOTEL

04500 St-Laurent-du-Verdon (Alpes-de-Haute-Provence) **TEL** 04 92 74 02 47 **FAX** 04 92 74 02 97 **E-MAIL** info@moulin-du-chateau.com **FOOD** breakfast, dinner **PRICE** €-€€ **ROOMS** 10 **CLOSED** mid-Nov to Mar

A DEVOTEE OF OUR GUIDES wrote to us with such enthusiasm about this hotel in a tiny village close to the Gorges du Verdon that we hurried to send our own inspector there, who warmly concurred. Swiss-French Nicolas Stämpfli and his Swiss-Italian wife Edith, both ex-teachers, took four years to convert their old mill into an utterly peaceful retreat with simple, colourful bedrooms and delicious 'Mediterranean' set-menu dinners, which are presented with the easy-going grace and good humour that imbues the whole hotel. The restaurant is only open to residents and there is no swimming pool – so that guests can enjoy total peace and quiet.

St-Mathieu

BASTIDE ST MATHIEU

COUNTRY HOTEL

35 chemin de Blumenthal, 06130 St-Mathieu, Grasse (Alpes-Maritimes) **TEL** 04 97 01 10 00 **FAX** 04 97 01 10 09 **E-MAIL** info@bastidestmathieu.com **FOOD** breakfast **PRICE** €€€€ **ROOMS** 5 **CLOSED** never

A GROWN-UP RETREAT IN FOOTHILLS outside Grasse, this 18thC *bastide* is the pet project of professional hoteliers, Inge and Arie van Osch. They have lavished love and care on its conversion, at pains to find just the right lamp, mirror, painted chest or cashmere blankets. The furniture is a happy mix of antique and contemporary. The result is a luxurious small hotel, well designed and strikingly decorated, with the feel of an exclusive private house. Of the original features, there's a sprinkling of beams, occasional stone walls and fireplaces, which contrast with some bold colour schemes. Even the smallest bedroom is the size of a junior suite in most other hotels. Also a lovely pool in gardens full of the scents of Provence.

THE SOUTH

LE ST-PAUL
VILLAGE HOTEL

86 rue Grande, 06570 St-Paul-de-Vence (Alpes-Maritimes)
TEL 04 93 32 65 25 **FAX** 04 93 32 52 94 **E-MAIL** le.st.paul@wanadoo.fr
WEBSITE www.lestpaul.com
FOOD breakfast, lunch, dinner; room service
PRICE €€€€ **ROOMS** 19
CLOSED 3 weeks Dec, 3 weeks Jan

IF YOU CAN AFFORD IT, here is another exceptionally captivating place to stay in pricey St-Paul-de-Vence, in a beautifully restored 16thC former private residence in the centre of the village. The interior has been done out with real panache; smallish bedrooms are beautifully decorated, many with *trompe l'oeil* murals of sea views framed by tropical plants. Some of the rooms have real views across hills and valley towards the sea, and these are the most desirable. The elegant restaurant is also decorated here and there with frescoes of flowers and fruit, and there is a little terrace for summer dining. The cooking of Frédéric Buzet is praised by Gault Millau and by recent guests alike. Solicitous, friendly service. A treat.

OSTALARIA CARDABELA
RESTAURANT-WITH-ROOMS

10 place Fontaine, 34725 St-Saturnin-de-Lucian (Hérault)
TEL 04 67 88 62 62 **FAX** 04 67 88 62 82
FOOD breakfast; lunch and dinner (at Mimosa) **PRICE** €·€€
ROOMS 7 **CLOSED** late Oct to mid-Mar; restaurant Mon, lunch Tue to Sat, Sun dinner Sep to Jun

THIS SMALL, ELEGANT HOTEL in a quiet village west of the Hérault is another string to the bow of the Mimosa, a superb restaurant down the road at St-Guiraud (tel 04 67 96 67 96; fax 04 67 96 61 15) where Bridget Pugh, a former prima ballerina, pursues her present career as a top-flight *cuisinière*. Her husband David, oh lucky man, devotes much of his time to stocking his cellar with wine good enough to match her cooking. The bedrooms in this old stone house named after a thistle are a fair size and stylishly decorated, and there is a kitchen for guests' use. As the Cardabela is run with a minimal staff, let them know when you plan to arrive so that someone is here to welcome you.

THE SOUTH

SÉGURET

LA TABLE DU COMTAT

VILLAGE HOTEL

Séguret, 84110 Vaison-la-Romaine (Vaucluse)
TEL 04 90 46 91 49
FAX 04 90 46 94 27
FOOD breakfast, lunch, dinner
PRICE €€
ROOMS 8 double and twin
CLOSED Feb

'**S**URELY THE MOST CHARMING small hotel in Provence', says one devotee of this eyrie at the top of one of the region's most captivating villages; 'a wonderful spot', says another. It's certainly a business getting here by car, winding up round steep, narrow streets, but once tucked into a parking space at the top you are rewarded by magnificent views of the plain below, and by the delights of a much modernized, but essentially old-fashioned *auberge*. The food is not cheap, but it is good, if eclectic, the public rooms light and airy and the bedrooms simple and comfortable, with attractive furnishings. The delightful terrace shares the view, and there is a pool.

LE THOR

LA BASTIDE ROSE

COUNTRY GUESTHOUSE

99 chemin des Croupières, 84250 Le Thor (Vaucluse)
TEL 04 90 02 14 33
FAX 04 90 02 19 38
E-MAIL poppynicole@yahoo.com
FOOD breakfast; lunch and dinner by arrangement **PRICE** €€€€
ROOMS 7 **CLOSED** never

ON A BANK OF THE SORGUE, this lovely old former paper mill, now the home of Poppy and Pierre Salinger (famous as JFK's press secretary) is protected from the world by trees and lawns. Poppy used to be an antiques dealer and her professional eye shows in the style she has brought to the house. Guests have the run of the downstairs – including an open kitchen and an honesty bar – and upstairs the bedrooms are washed in striking colours with some beautiful antiques and little pieces of Limoges: the suites have wonderful views. There are fridges on the upstairs landings for guests to use. Cold lunches are on offer and dinner as well if you book a day ahead.

THE SOUTH

TORNAC

DEMEURES DU RANQUET

RESTAURANT-WITH-ROOMS

route St-Hippolyte-du-Fort, Tornac, 30140 Anduze (Gard) **TEL** 04 66 77 51 63 **FAX** 04 66 77 55 62 **E-MAIL** le-ranquet@avignon-et-provence.com **FOOD** breakfast, lunch, dinner **PRICE** €€€ **ROOMS** 10 **CLOSED** mid-Nov to mid-Dec; check restaurant on booking

SET AMONGST PINES and scrub oak in the peaceful foothills of the Cévennes, the Demeures du Ranquet is the kind of place that lingers in the memory for all the right reasons. The main building, a long, low well-restored farmhouse, is principally devoted to the restaurant and the comfortable bedrooms are in chalets scattered amongst the trees on the slope above the swimming pool – some are air conditioned. In summer the restaurant's tables sally forth on to the terrace and out under the trees where hammocks also lie in wait to help you through those long hours between lunch and dinner. The cuisine is a real treat: inventive, original and fresh, and supported by an excellent wine list.

VALLON-PONT-D'ARC

LE MANOIR DU RAVEYRON

VILLAGE INN

rue Henri Barbusse 07150 Vallon-Pont-d'Arc (Ardèche) **TEL** 04 75 88 03 59 **FAX** 04 75 37 11 12 **E-MAIL** le.manoir.du.raveyron@wanadoo.fr **WEBSITE** www.manoir-du-raveyron.com **FOOD** breakfast, dinner **PRICE** € **ROOMS** 12 **CLOSED** Nov to Mar

IT SOUNDS GRAND, but is nothing of the sort: this is the sort of rustic village inn that is the bedrock of French hotelkeeping – a two-fireplace *logis* offering simple but satisfactory accommodation, modest prices, a warm welcome and excellent wholesome food (visit the place on a Sunday and you'll find it bursting at the seams with lunching families). The hotel faces an ugly modern building; but the surroundings do not intrude, because the old stone building is set well back from the street, behind gates and a large and leafy courtyard garden. '... super, a warm welcome, lovely room, offers of help with luggage etc, really good food and good rates', is the latest unequivocal endorsement we've received of this place.

CORSICA

HOTELS IN CORSICA

WE HAVE NEVER FOUND more than a handful of hotels in Corsica which fit our criteria and live up to our exacting standards; maybe we are missing some hidden gems – do let us know if there is a hotel, however simple, perhaps deep in the interior, or on a little cove, that you love, or at least that you would happily return to. We know of plenty of places which are 'perfectly okay', but only a few which stand out. It's a shame, because Corsica is a wonderful place. The rugged island, with a turbulent history to match, looks like a mountain thrust from the sea, pointing an accusatory and gnarled northern finger, Cap Corse, toward the Genoan Riviera. Its wild and often surprising scenery is its chief glory, ringed by a 960-km coastline of world-class sandy beaches, quiet coves, fishing villages, jagged headlands and tumbling rocks. The interior comprises an extraordinary variety of landscapes. There are snow-capped mountains, rocky peaks and clear pools and streams, forests of chestnut and *laricio* pine (used by the Romans for masts), vineyards, olive and orange groves, tropical palms, even a region of arid desert. Almost two-thirds is covered with the thick tangle of scented shrubs and wild flowers known as *maquis*.

As well as the recommendations which follow, we would like to give honourable mention to **La Giraglia**, at Barcaggio (tel 04 95 35 60 54), a simple, creeper-covered stone building in a superb position overlooking the sea in a lovely wild part of Corsica, well off the beaten track; and to **Sole e Monti** (tel 04 95 78 62 53), another simple, peaceful *auberge* at Quenza, a hill village in the centre of Corse-du-Sud near the beauty spot, Col de Bavella.

CORSICA

CALVI

LA SIGNORIA

COUNTRY HOTEL

*route de la Fôret de
Bonifato,20260 Calvi (Corse)*
TEL 04 95 65 93 00
FAX 04 95 65 38 77
E-MAIL info@hotel-la-signoria.com
WEBSITE www.hotel-la-
signoria.com
FOOD breakfast, dinner
PRICE €€€€ **ROOMS** 10
CLOSED Nov to Apr

SINCE LA SIGNORIA made its first appearance in our guide a few years back, we have had positive feedback from two readers, both extolling its virtues of peace and quiet, its calm atmosphere, stylish simplicity and its eclectic, rustic-chic Mediterranean decoration – paint effects on plaster walls and on doors, uncluttered rooms and so on. The hotel is a 17thC country house set in lush grounds which are filled with trees – eucalyptus, olives, palms and pines. Inventive and delicious food is served in a beamed, ochre-washed dining room, or, in warmer weather, on the covered terrace at prettily painted wrought-iron tables and chairs overlooking the smart and inviting swimming pool. There is also tennis and a *hammam* (steam room).

ERBALUNGA

CASTEL' BRANDO

VILLAGE GUESTHOUSE

*Erbalunga, 202222 Brando
(Corse)*
TEL 04 95 30 10 30
FAX 04 95 33 98 18
E-MAIL info@castelbrando.com
WEBSITE www.castelbrando.com
FOOD breakfast
PRICE €€€ **ROOMS** 42
CLOSED mid-Nov to mid-Mar

WE WERE ALERTED to this 'absolutely delightful' hotel by a reader. 'It's just one of those things' he comments. 'The owners have an innate understanding of how to create an attractive, welcoming atmosphere.' Erbalunga is a postcard-pretty fishing village and artists' colony and the hotel is a 19thC mansion, restored with care and flair by local couple Joëlle and Jean-Paul Piéri. The grounds are full of magnificent palm trees, there are shady places to sit and take breakfast or tea, and a heated pool. The air conditioned apartments, with kitchenettes and satellite TV, make an excellent base, and the charming hosts will tell guests about the best places to dine, and sights off the beaten track. (There are two specially adapted rooms for disabled guests.) More reports welcome.

CORSICA

MONTICELLO

A PASTURELLA
VILLAGE INN

Monticello, 20220 l'Ile-Rousse
(Haute-Corse)
TEL 04 95 60 05 65
FAX 04 95 60 21 78
E-MAIL info@a-pasturella.com
WEBSITE www.a-pasturella.com
FOOD breakfast, lunch, dinner
PRICE € **ROOMS** 12
CLOSED early-Nov to mid-Dec

W E HAVE ALWAYS BEEN fond of this modest little 'gem', set in a peaceful
hill village in the lovely Balagne region, with views which sweep
down to L'Ile-Rousse and its bay, noted for its fine sandy beaches. The
inn stands on the village square, its bar at the very heart of local life,
and its restaurant much appreciated for wholesome and generous food,
with specialities such as *fricassée de sardines à la Nepita, piatu
casanu, terrine de cabri, soupe de poissons, tianu de calamars*.
Bedrooms are simple and functional but thoughtfully done out, with a
dash of colour in the curtains and bedspreads. The four rooms in the
annexe are the best bet, because they have balconies which, like the
other rooms, have fine views over the valley.

PORTICCIO

LE MAQUIS
SEASIDE HOTEL

20166 Porticcio (Corse-du-Sud)
TEL 04 95 25 05 55
FAX 04 95 25 11 70
E-MAIL info@lemaquis.com
WEBSITE www.lemaquis.com
FOOD breakfast, lunch, dinner;
room service
PRICE €€€€€
ROOMS 25
CLOSED early Jan to mid-Feb

L E MAQUIS IS SET in a breathtakingly pretty spot, perhaps the prettiest
of any hotel in Corsica, on a little inlet in the Gulf of Ajaccio, overlooking verdant gardens and a beautiful stretch of sandy beach.
Proprietress Mme Salini is very much in charge, and her hotel, opened in
1972, is carefully decorated, with comfortable bedrooms. Ask for a room
overlooking the sea, with a terrace. In L'Arbousier, the hotel's restaurant, excellent meals are served by the pool in warm weather – mostly
seafood and traditional Corsican dishes. A quiet, sophisticated hotel on
an otherwise crowded coast; for nature lovers the wild beauty of inland
Corsica is close at hand. Reports please.

HOTEL NAMES

In this index, hotels are arranged in order of the most distinctive part of their name; very common prefixes such as 'Auberge', 'Hôtel', 'Hostellerie' and 'Le/La/Les' are omitted, but more significant elements such as 'Château' are retained.

Hotel Names

Hotel Names

HOTEL NAMES

HOTEL LOCATIONS

In this index, hotels are arranged by the name of the city, town or village they are in or near. Hotels located in a very small village may be indexed under the name of a larger place nearby.

HOTEL LOCATIONS

HOTEL LOCATIONS

Hotel Locations